A HISTORY OF SETTLEMENT IN IRELAND

A HISTORY OF
SETTLEMENT IN
IRELAND

Edited by Terry Barry

London and New York

First published 2000
by Routledge
11 New Fetter Lane, London EC4P 4EE

Simultaneously published in the USA and Canada
by Routledge
29 West 35th Street, New York, NY 10001

Routledge is an imprint of the Taylor & Francis Group

Typeset in Goudy by Taylor & Francis Books Ltd
Printed and bound in Great Britain by TJ International Ltd, Padstow, Cornwall

British Library Cataloguing in Publication Data
A catalogue record for this book is available from the British Library.

Library of Congress Cataloguing in Publication Data
A history of settlement in Ireland/edited by Terry Barry
Includes bibliographical references and index
1. Human settlements–Ireland–History. 2. Ireland–History geography. 3. Human
geography–Ireland. 4. Landscape changes–Ireland–History. I. Barry, Terry.
HN400.3.A8H57   1999
307.1'4'09415–dc21   99-31496

ISBN 0–415–18208–5

CONTENTS

LIST OF ILLUSTRATIONS

Plates

Figures

CONTRIBUTORS

John Andrews, member of the Royal Irish Academy, was Associate Professor of Geography in Trinity College Dublin. His main academic interest is in the history of cartography, with especial reference to Ireland. His latest book, *Shapes of Ireland*, was published in 1997.

Terry Barry is Senior Lecturer in the Department of Medieval History in Trinity College Dublin. He is the author of *The Archaeology of Medieval Ireland* (1994), published by Routledge.

Gabriel Cooney is Associate Professor of Archaeology in University College Dublin. He is the author of *Landscapes of Neolithic Ireland*, published by Routledge in 1999.

Charles Doherty lectures in the Department of Early Irish History in University College Dublin. He has written on Irish hagiography, settlement history, relics, trade and exchange and a variety of other topics.

Patrick J. Duffy is Associate Professor of Geography in the National University, Maynooth. His main academic interests are rural and historical geography. He is author of *Landscapes of South Ulster: A parish atlas of the diocese of Clogher* (1993).

Robin Glasscock lectures in historical geography in the University of Cambridge, and is a Fellow of St John's College. He has written extensively on the historical geography of medieval Britain and Ireland, and was the founder of the Group for the Study of Irish Historic Settlement.

Brian Graham is Professor of Human Geography, School of Environmental Studies, University of Ulster at Coleraine. He has published widely on research topics concerned with the cultural and historical geography of Europe. He edited *In Search of Ireland: A cultural geography* for Routledge in 1997.

Anngret Simms, member of the Royal Irish Academy, is Associate Professor of Geography in University College Dublin. She is a joint editor of the *Irish Historic Towns Atlas*, and has published on aspects of the settlement history of Ireland and Central Europe.

William J. Smyth is Professor of Geography in University College Cork. He is the author of books and articles on Irish historical geography, especially of the sixteenth and seventeenth centuries.

Matthew Stout is a an independent scholar. He was one of the editors of the *Atlas of the Irish Rural Landscape* (1997), and he has written *The Irish Ringfort* (1997).

Kevin Whelan is Michael J. Smurfit Director of the University of Notre Dame's Keough Centre at Newman House, Dublin. He has published many books and articles, including *Fellowship of Freedom: The United Irishmen and the 1798 Rebellion*, Cork University Press, 1998.

FOREWORD

Robin Glasscock

This book sets out to be an overview of the settlement history of Ireland interpreted by contributors who are experts in the periods about which they write; as such it will surely be a welcome addition to the literature. It results from a meeting in Dublin to mark a 'coming of age' of the Group for the Study of Irish Historic Settlement (GSIHS). In writing this Foreword I have faith that they will cover a lot of ground, in all senses, raise many interesting issues and highlight the problems that await new work; of course it will be up to readers and reviewers to decide whether they have.

Settlement changes, whether they be in form (e.g. of houses, clachans, crossroads settlements, estate villages, market towns) or in distribution are brought about by human decision-making in the context of environment, demography and culture. I am as guilty as anyone of saying that a settlement has 'migrated'; it is, of course, the people who have moved to somewhere else. As conditions have changed over time, be they climatic, demographic or social, so human responses have been different and have generally become more complex (and therefore more difficult to unravel) in recent times with technical progress and influences from a wider world. Whereas continuity of settlements used to be a dominant theme, recent studies, helped along by an array of scientific advances for studying changing vegetation, dating and detection of features below ground, have shown that settlement over time has been in a continual state of flux. In some periods there was widespread abandonment of land, houses and farms whereas in others, particularly at times of population and economic growth, there was a significant increase in the number of settlements, rural and urban. In all periods there were regional variations which on the one hand make generalisation more difficult but on the other underpin the value of local studies in elucidating what was happening and why from one place to another. It was with a view to encouraging the interplay of general views and local studies that the GSIHS was first conceived.

In the 1960s and early 1970s I had the good fortune to be working alongside many who were involved in furthering our understanding of landscape and settlement history. The emphasis was still on prehistory. Building on the pioneer work of earlier scholars – and I am thinking here of men such as Wood-Martin,

Macalister, Ó Ríordáin and Oliver Davies – archaeologists were still mainly concerned with matters prehistoric. De Valera, O'Kelly and Eogan were at work in the south, Collins and Evans (although he was no longer excavating) in the north. While there was increasing interest in the problems of the ringforts within Early Christian Ireland (Proudfoot's paper on 'The economy of the Irish rath' appeared in 1961, the same year as the De Paors published their *Early Christian Ireland*) the study of later medieval settlement still lagged far behind. In Dublin the historian Jocelyn Otway-Ruthven was doing marvellous work from documentary sources on medieval agriculture and manors but although she had visited one or two places about which she was writing, mainly near Dublin, her work seldom took her into the field. On a personal note she was immensely helpful to me when I first got interested in medieval sites in Tipperary but I vividly recall her look of astonishment when I suggested that we might go and look at some of them on the ground. 'You won't find anything there', she said. In many cases she was of course right, but the potential of deserted sites as reservoirs of future medieval archaeology had not yet made its impact, despite earlier work, for example that by Ó Ríordáin and Hunt at Caherguillamore, Co. Limerick. In the north medieval archaeology was being encouraged academically by Martyn Jope and, in the field, by Dudley Waterman who, in my view, deserves special mention. Very much 'his own man' he brought his exceptional talents for excavation, interpretation and draughtsmanship to bear on sites of all periods including many medieval ones (which might almost get forgotten after his great achievements at Emain Macha). Along with Jope and Pat Collins he was directly responsible for *An Archaeological Survey of County Down* (1966) which stood out for many years, as in some ways it still does, as the exemplar of the detailed recording of sites and monuments in a particular county. Meanwhile the contributions of folklore and folklife were being advanced in north and south by the work of Danaher (Ó Danachair), Thompson and Gailey and by the foundation of the Ulster Folk Museum at Cultra in 1958.

Alongside the professionals there were then, as there still are, a huge number of interested and very well-informed amateurs involved, often through their local societies, in history, archaeology, geography and folklife, indeed in all aspects of settlement history from beehives to booleys, kilns to kitchens and spades to souterrains. There is surely no corner of the country without a local society and their importance has in no way diminished with the increasing professionalisation of the last fifty years. When working on medieval settlements I was given invaluable help by many who knew their local areas better than the backs of their hands and I cannot miss the opportunity to pay tribute to them and to their work. Some will read this and know they are among them; they will forgive me for singling out by name four who have since died, George Hadden in Wexford, Billy English in Athlone, Tom Hoyne in Kilkenny/Castlecomer and Bob Davidson in Down. Their local knowledge was enthusiastically and willingly shared. I have no doubt that all the academics who have contributed to this book could supply their own list of those who have helped them in unravelling the history of settlement in different parts of the country. Long may the local societies flourish to focus local interest and to publish the work of their enthusiasts.

In the 1960s there was no obvious forum where locals and professionals could meet to share their knowledge. True there were the larger societies in Dublin and Belfast (the Royal Society of Antiquaries and the Ulster Archaeological Society) but except for their field excursions they didn't then promote 'get-togethers' and they weren't all that accessible if you happened to live and work in say Limerick, Roscommon or Fermanagh. Moreover, there was only limited contact, usually at a personal level, between north and south, east and west. An opportunity existed to form some sort of 'umbrella' body to focus debate about settlement history and especially about the problems of the medieval and post-medieval periods. After a great deal of letter-writing and personal contact the GSIHS was founded in 1969 and the first weekend conference took place in Limerick in 1970. (Did Cruise's Hotel really charge us as much as £1.17.6 for bed and breakfast?) The spring conference became the annual event which it continues to be; in the early years Limerick was followed by Kilkenny (1971), Athlone (1972), Mallow (1973), Enniskillen (1974) and Wexford (1975). Like St Patrick we roamed the country converting to the cause! By 1972 there were members from twenty-seven counties: are all thirty-two represented now?

Like all societies the GSIHS has had its ups and downs; there have been some years of relative inactivity but these have been outweighed by a general sense that the Group was doing useful work, at first largely through personal contact and shared knowledge but, more recently, through publications. It certainly seems to have lived up to one of its stated aims namely … 'to encourage, co-ordinate and publish the study of Irish historic settlement'; the long series of peripatetic annual meetings and field visits has brought the sites, monuments and problems of particular areas to the attention of others working elsewhere both in Ireland and abroad. Not unimportantly, contacts and shared interests have led to lasting friendships. On the publication side the early type-written Bulletins and lists of articles in journals have been replaced by more substantial Newsletters containing articles and reviews and, beginning in 1985 with Brian Graham's *Anglo-Norman settlement in Ireland*, it has produced six valuable monographs on various aspects of historic settlement including tower houses, English colonisation, eighteenth-century urban improvement and, most recently, ringforts. It is to be hoped that this monograph series, recently supported by the Four Courts Press, will continue to enhance the reputation of the Group. In one sense these publications 'advise' (if they are read!) but there is still much scope for the Group to be a more forceful and influential voice in matters of policy relating to research, survey, conservation and excavation – another of its stated aims. Individuals can do so much; their case is often strengthened if supported by a collective view which reflects a wide range of experience and expertise.

The study of historic settlement in Ireland has made huge advances since 1969. More use has been made of aerial photography, geophysical survey, the detailed examination of standing buildings and the excavation of those that have now gone. There have been many major publications, among them F.H.A. Aalen, *Man and the Landscape in Ireland*, (1978); J.H. Andrews, *Plantation Acres*, (1985); T.B. Barry *The Archaeology of Medieval Ireland*, (1987); John Bradley (ed.) *Settlement and Society in Medieval Ireland. Studies presented to F.X. Martin O.S.A.*, (1988); B.J. Graham and L.J. Proudfoot (eds) *An Historical Geography of Ireland*, (1993). Much of this work has been drawn upon by Aalen, Whelan and Stout in their magnificent *Atlas of the Irish Rural Landscape*, (1997) which has deservedly found such a wide readership throughout the country. There is enormous interest in the historic past; it is to be hoped that the GSIHS will continue to foster it through its activities and its publications and thereby move the subject onwards into the new millennium.

ACKNOWLEDGEMENTS

This book developed out of the twentieth anniversary conference of the Group for the Study of Irish Historic Settlement held in Dublin in 1989, at which it was decided that the papers should also be published. I would like to thank all the contributors for both their perseverance and their patience which has meant that this book has finally come to see the light of day.

I would like to thank especially Dr Ruth Johnson, Curator of DVBLINIA, without whom this book would not have been produced. She spent many hours editing the contributions and she also produced the very successful bibliography which you will find at the end of the volume. Professor Anngret Simms was also very helpful both in reading the draft copy of the book and in the whole editing process. I would also like to thank the library staff in the Royal Irish Academy and Trinity College Dublin, for all their assistance.

The staff of Routledge, Taylor and Francis Books Ltd are also owed a debt of deep gratitude by the editor and authors for their efficiency and support in ensuring that this book saw the light of day: especially Victoria Peters, the Archaeology Editor, her Assistant Editor, Nadia Jacobson; and Barbara Duke, Senior Production Editor. Finally, I must also thank the external copy editor, Sophie Richmond, for all her extremely useful observations and corrections.

Financial support has come from the Department of Medieval History, Trinity College Dublin, the Group for the Study of Irish Historic Settlement, the Institute of Irish Studies, Queen's University, Belfast and from the School of Irish Studies, Dublin, for which I am very grateful.

Terry Barry

1

READING A LANDSCAPE
MANUSCRIPT

A review of progress in prehistoric settlement
studies in Ireland

Gabriel Cooney

Introduction

Looking back from the end of the millennium to commemorate the foundation
of the Group for the Study of Irish Historic Settlement in 1969, it is appropriate
to review Irish prehistoric settlement studies using that year as a baseline. In
many ways 1969 was a watershed which marked the beginning of a major phase
of activity in Irish prehistoric studies which still continues. That year saw the
publication in the *Ulster Journal of Archaeology* of review articles on the
Neolithic[1] and the Earlier Bronze Age[2] in the north of Ireland, followed by
Harbison's[3] review of the Earlier Bronze Age in Ireland and Woodman's[4] discussion of settlement in the Irish Mesolithic. The following decades have seen
major advances in prehistoric studies, both in terms of the understanding of the
pattern of settlement within major periods during Irish prehistory and the
diachronic changes in settlement in particular regions.

During the period under review five major texts dealing with Irish
prehistory[5] have been published. Mallory and McNeill's[6] consideration of the
prehistory of Ulster as part of a wider treatment of the archaeology of the
northern part of the island is also an important general discussion. Important
period-based reviews have appeared covering the Mesolithic;[7] the Bronze Age[8]
and the Iron Age.[9] Comparing all these texts it is clear that the interpretation
of prehistoric settlement is influenced by both changes in our interpretative
approaches and the accumulation of new material. Excavation, fieldwork and
chance discovery have continued to increase the database with which archaeologists work. One indicator of the increase in archaeological work is that the
number of excavations has jumped from 36 carried out in 1971 to more than
330 in 1995[10] with the probability that this trend will continue (but it should
be noted that a major component of this increase is due to the excavation of
historic sites). An important trend in the last thirty years has been the systema-
tisation of data collection. In this context the gathering pace of archaeological
heritage inventory work has been of fundamental importance. At the time of

writing thirteen county inventories have been produced by the Archaeological Survey of Ireland, the Heritage Service (for Carlow, Cavan, Cork – three volumes, Galway (West), Laois, Louth, Meath, Monaghan, Offaly, Wicklow and Wexford). In addition a number of detailed county or area archaeological surveys have appeared.[11]

A feature of these inventory and survey volumes has been the utilisation of the aerial photographic record to bring into the archaeological record many additional low-visibility sites.[12] The broader recognition of the importance of low-visibility archaeology has been an important development. This can be seen for example in the results of pipeline[13] and field-walking surveys.[14] The need to deploy a range of dedicated techniques to identify low-visibility archaeology has meant, for example, that geophysical survey has become a standard part of archaeological practice. Alongside the increasing impact of rescue archaeology there have been a number of important research initiatives, most notably the Discovery Programme, set up in 1991 and in 1996 established as a company funded by the state through the Heritage Council to carry out archaeological research. The Discovery Programme chose the problems of later prehistoric settlement as the focus of the first set of research programmes.[15] The Discovery Programme has also been to the forefront in the development of new approaches such as the interpretation of geophysical survey data[16] and the use of geographical information systems as part of a regional research framework.[17] Looking at these trends collectively one major effect has been to redress the emphasis on standing, monumental archaeology with a focus on the need also to recover low-visibility archaeology. This has direct implications for settlement studies specifically because so many prehistoric domestic structures were constructed of perishable materials and, more broadly, because it lessens the bias in the archaeological record.

In a broad sense then there have been major advances in Irish prehistoric settlement studies since the 1960s, as by definition all of the work outlined above increases our knowledge of settlement in Ireland during prehistory. The chronological basis of Irish prehistory has been greatly improved through radiocarbon dating and dendrochronology, particularly the dedicated programmes of dating site types.[18] These dating techniques make it possible to sub-divide periods such as the Neolithic[19] and the Bronze Age[20] on the basis of radiocarbon dates. This is a important advance in that we are no longer reliant on the archaeological data itself as a source of dating and it has provided an independent dating framework within which to look at social and cultural developments. However, it would have to be said that comparatively less attention has been paid to understanding the nature and extent of prehistoric settlement or to the dynamic processes underlying the ways in which settlement patterns developed over time. It would appear that the ability to identify environmental marker dates in the dendrochronological record has led to the assumption that these would automatically evoke a human response[21] and to the seductive mirage that we can see social changes as simple one-off events

2

rather than processes taking place through time. There has been much concern with documenting the archaeological record as opposed to considering how effectively this record can be used to reconstruct settlement patterns.[22] This attitude may be traced to a number of factors such as a concern with documenting a threatened record, the traditional cultural-historical viewpoint that archaeological theory and data can be separated and the view that archaeological evidence may have limited potential for the analysis of settlement in any detailed way. Of course we must be critically aware of the limitations of the archaeological record, but that record has in many instances been treated at face value without any detailed consideration of the formative and the post-depositional factors that may have influenced and distorted its present form.[23] For example, there has been little discussion of the direct link between the extent and nature of archaeological fieldwork and the quality and form of archaeological data that it creates. Also, with few exceptions, there has been little regard for the theoretical debates and advances that have taken place in the field of prehistoric studies since the late 1960s.[24] In overview, the 'New' or processual archaeology of the 1970s and 1980s has had an influence primarily through the application of new techniques and the post-processual archaeology that developed in the 1980s with its many strands is only now beginning to have a wider influence in Ireland. In terms of the reluctance of archaeologists to engage in theoretical debate it should be remembered that this is also an international phenomenon,[25] and that in the case of Ireland it has also become entangled in the vexed question of how an island with a distinct archaeological tradition and a complex history reacts to international trends.[26]

It is also relevant to remember that the number of archaeologists who are synthesising settlement data in Irish prehistory is still quite small. The result is that their work has been very influential. Thus, for example, our understanding of the pattern of Mesolithic settlement is indebted to Woodman's analyses, [27] much of our framework and approach to the Late Bronze Age is the result of Eogan's work[28] and the problems of Iron Age settlement have been very well articulated by Raftery.[29] While we have the major advantage of these overviews of particular periods, in the light of the reluctance to engage in theoretical debate there is a danger that these may become the firm guidelines for future research rather than being themselves further tested. Perhaps more critically, researchers have tended to stay within the confines of particular periods. The result has been to negate one of the major assets of the prehistoric evidence, the diachronic perspective, which has the potential to give insights into broader questions about the evolution of settlement patterns. After all, as Estyn Evans put it, the prehistoric period 'witnessed the taming of the land, the establishment of rural settlements, of local attachments to distinctive sub-regions, of enduring modes of life and attitudes'.[30] The emphasis however has been on describing the features of different periods and their background rather than on the wider questions of possible regularities, repetitions and discontinuities of pattern when the evidence is viewed over the long term. It was precisely these questions that were deliberately placed at the centre of the approach taken to Irish prehistory by Cooney and Grogan.[31] As one example, the settlement data over 7,000 years of Irish prehistory would appear to have significant potential for analysis using the *Annales* approach, [32] where we could examine the impact of processes operating at different wavelengths of time (from short-term events to long-term influences) on society and settlement.[33] This approach works best at the regional level and one of the encouraging signs in prehistoric studies in Ireland is the growing realisation of the importance of regional studies and the diversity in social, cultural and economic developments that they give witness to. Here the major advances in our understanding of settlement are discussed in terms of the major prehistoric periods with reference to regional case studies where appropriate.

The Mesolithic, 7500–4000 BC

It is still the case that Ireland appears to be one of the areas of Europe last occupied by *Homo sapiens sapiens*. There is no definite evidence for Palaeolithic settlement.[34] Ireland became an island early in the early post-glacial period and this has had a fundamental, long-term impact on the character of the fauna and flora and of course on human settlement.[35] Our earliest definite evidence for settlement is during the Mesolithic period, over 9,000 years ago. In the interpretation of this period when people were living a gathering, fishing and hunting lifestyle, dramatic changes have taken place over the last thirty years. The vast bulk of the evidence dating to this period consists of lithic tools and debitage. As recently as the early 1970s Woodman[36] was still using the chronological scheme put forward by Movius[37] and modified by Mitchell.[38] This saw the Mesolithic (Middle Stone Age) or Larnian as characterised by a large flake industry beginning c. 6000 BC and overlapping with the Neolithic (the Late Stone Age, characterised by a series of cultural changes including the introduction of agriculture) in the form of a so-called 'Ultimate Larnian' which either stratigraphically or by the occurrence of products associated with farming clearly interdigitated with the activities of early farmers.

In the early 1970s, however, Woodman[39] was also trying to accommodate the recognition of a separate type of lithic industry producing microliths. Subsequently radiocarbon dates have made clear that this microlithic industry predates the Larnian one. This microlithic industry is the basis for the recognition of an Early Mesolithic starting before 7000 BC and seen at sites like Mount Sandel, Co. Derry[40] and Lough Boora, Co. Offaly[41] which contrasts with a Later Mesolithic dominated by large flake production and use as at sites like Newferry[42] and Ferriter's Cove, Co. Kerry.[43] Notable features of the archaeological evidence are the lack of very definite evidence for an overlap between the Early and Later Mesolithic industrial traditions, the striking insularity of the Later Mesolithic and its overlap with the Neolithic. Looking first at the question of the initial human settlement of Ireland it seems probable that the

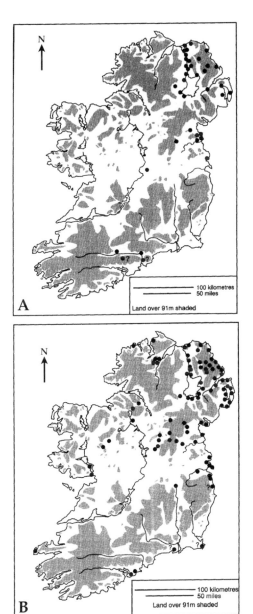

Figure 1.1 Distribution of Early Mesolithic (A) and Later Mesolithic (B) sites in
Ireland

Source: Cooney and Grogan (1994), after Woodman (1989).

background to settlement is the western coast of Britain, where, after all, Irish mountain peaks would have been visible and the early post-glacial sea level would have been lower, making the Irish Sea crossing narrower than later in prehistory.[44]

Taking the gazetteer of over 170 Mesolithic sites compiled by Woodman[45] and recognising that this twenty-year-old database has been augmented by significant additions, particularly outside the then-known concentration in north-east of Ireland, it is clear that the bulk of the Mesolithic finds occur in low-lying locations, at less than 30 m. More specifically, they are concentrated in 'close to water' situations, either coastal, lakeside or riverside (Figure 1.1). The same trends occur in the location of sites discovered since the publication of the gazetteer. Most notably, the number of sites in the Munster area has increased since Woodman shifted his research focus to there[46] and as a result of other work, including the Ballylough Project[47] and Anderson's field-walking and excavation at Kilcummer in the Blackwater valley, Co. Cork.[48] There are some exceptions to the general trend of lowland siting. For example, in Co. Antrim there are some finds from the uplands[49] and in Co. Meath there are a number of microliths and typical Later Mesolithic implements from the Crossakeel area, close to Loughcrew, which are above 122 m OD.[50]

The preference for settlement location close to water appears to be linked with the subsistence activities evidenced on excavated sites, in particular a reliance on fish, especially salmonids, with lesser emphasis on a range of resources including plant foods such as hazel nuts, shellfish and wild animals such as pig. The site locations are in areas which would have given easy access to a rich and varied range of food resources. In contrast to the perceived subsistence strategies in Britain and the Continent,[51] red deer appears to have had a very limited importance as a food resource for Mesolithic people in Ireland, to such an extent that it has been suggested that this species may only have been introduced into Ireland by people at a late stage in the Mesolithic or in the Neolithic.[52] Related to the question of red deer exploitation is the problem of the extent to which Mesolithic people in Ireland manipulated the forest environment. Evidence for forest clearance has elsewhere been linked to the use of open, cleared areas as attractive browse for animals so that they could be hunted more easily. The evidence for forest clearance in the Irish Mesolithic is very restricted and equivocal.[53] It is perhaps best interpreted as showing clearance in the vicinity of occupation sites.

It seems clear that food resources would have been exploited in a complex demographic and settlement arrangement to ensure supply throughout the year. Two different types of hunter-gatherer settlement systems have been proposed by Binford[54] involving a number of different kinds of settlement site; in a logistic strategy people operated out of base camps located in areas of varied resource availability necessitating only one or two shifts in a yearly cycle while in a foraging system people moved more frequently, mapping on to seasonally available resources in different areas. There is a debate about the nature and degree of mobility in the Mesolithic settlement pattern, how this might have developed or changed over time and how it corresponds or differs to the wider west European pattern.[55] Woodman[56] has put forward a specific annual resource exploitation model for the Early Mesolithic site at Mount Sandel based on the excavated evidence there and, as it stands, Mount Sandel is the only example known of a Mesolithic base camp (Figure 1.2), occupied for a significant part of the year. Most of the identifiable sites would appear to be either specialised function sites or transitory camps. This is particularly a problem for the Later Mesolithic where the lithic evidence comes from locations where specialised

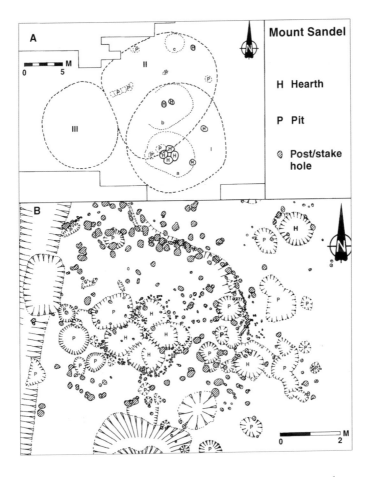

Figure 1.2　The Early Mesolithic base camp at Mount Sandel, Co. Derry, showing features of central house area (B) and activity zones (A); III the flint-working zone, both I) and II) with evidence of occupation

Source:　After Woodman (1985a).

tasks were carried out over restricted periods, and where residential bases may be thus difficult to define or detect.[57] It has been suggested that in the vicinity of the known specialised sites there were more permanent camps which would have served as the bases for a variety of specialised activities.[58] At Lough Derravaragh, Co. Westmeath, for example, there are specialised function sites[59] along the shore of what would have been a dry island in a wetland landscape during the Later Mesolithic (Figure 1.3) and it seems plausible and testable to suggest that this island was a more significant focus of activity.

So there are some important comparisons and contrasts to be drawn between the two periods. Woodman[60] suggested that because of the lack of clear evidence for base camps in the Later Mesolithic, there may have been a shift from a more sedentary lifestyle in the Early Mesolithic to a more mobile pattern in the Later.[61] It should be stressed, however, that there is in fact only one base camp known from the Irish Mesolithic; that, superficially at least, the amount of material at some of the Later Mesolithic sites suggests prolonged activity; and that on environmental grounds one could equally argue that there would have been greater clustering of resources and higher productivity in the Later Mesolithic period. This also ties in with the wider west European pattern of

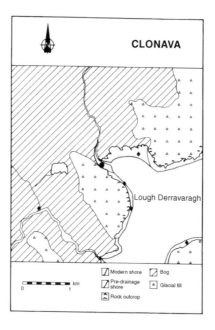

Figure 1.3 Later Mesolithic material at Clonava, Lough Derravaragh, Co. Westmeath (main concentration shown with dot, locations of other material shown with lozenge symbol)

Source: Based on Mitchell (1972).

evidence for a greater degree of sedentism in the later stages of the Mesolithic.[62] On the other hand, as outlined above, there are many aspects of the Irish Mesolithic that are different to elsewhere and if the model suggested by Woodman is correct then it would be further confirmation of the contrast between Mesolithic society in Ireland and other regions of western Europe.

One important point to bear in mind in looking at the Mesolithic period is the issue of environmental changes. It is clear that there were significant changes in sea level and the character of the forest cover during the Mesolithic which would have had a direct impact on people and settlement. Continued environmental change since the Mesolithic has made interpretation of the archaeological data more difficult. For example, Woodman[63] points out that in river valleys the Later Mesolithic sites appear to be more low-lying than the Early ones. This may relate to the fact that Early Mesolithic material may now be covered by alluvial material and it is one demonstration that environmental changes going on since early in the Mesolithic have coloured our view of the period. The environmental areas in which most Mesolithic material occurs are those most vulnerable to erosion and to coverage by peat or alluvial deposits. Furthermore, it is clear that a lot of this material has turned up as the result of deliberate search policies and this must raise again the question as to whether we as yet have a representative distribution pattern of Mesolithic settlement. For example, radiocarbon dates indicating Mesolithic activity have come from the excavation of later sites such as Curraghatoor, Co. Tipperary (enclosure)[64] or from previously unknown locations, as on Valencia Island, Co. Kerry (timber platform).[65] So there are a whole series of research questions arising from progress over the last thirty years. These include further work on: the distribution of settlement, the changes that characterised the transition from the Early to the Later Mesolithic, the extent to which the higher zones of the landscape were exploited and the value of identifying wetland sites with preservation of a range of materials that would give more insights into settlement and subsistence strategies.

The Neolithic, 4000–2500 BC

Compared to the Mesolithic, recent study of the Neolithic has not resulted in the same dramatic change in the archaeological framework used to understand the period, but there has been a quantitative explosion in our knowledge of different aspects of this period, particularly in relation to settlement. An ongoing debate has developed about the beginnings, character and pattern of settlement of the Neolithic. When Case[66] wrote about this at the end of the 1960s it was taken as a truism that farming was introduced to Ireland and Britain as the result of demic diffusion. In relation to settlement patterns, the concept of shifting cultivation, with farmers moving on after a period of time to cultivate new land and gradually establishing a territorial base, was dominant. This view, which had a major influence on the interpretation of Neolithic settlement, was largely derived from interpretation of the pollen record with its evidence of landnam clearances followed by forest regeneration[67] which seemed to fit well with the model of shifting cultivation utilised by Boserup[68] to interpret patterns of subsistence farming strategies. A number of significant changes in interpretation have taken place since then.

Looking at the question of the beginnings of the Neolithic, there has been a major reassessment of the elm decline and its relationship to the beginning of farming. The elm decline was in the past viewed as representing the first major farming impact on the predominantly forested environment, around 4000 BC. Most authorities would now view the elm decline as a result of disease rather than as being directly caused by human activity.[69] Furthermore it was suggested on palynological grounds that the beginning of farming in Ireland may substantially predate the elm decline[70] with what has been identified as cereal-type pollen present from before 4500 BC, although this is a subject of considerable debate.[71] This debate is clearly of major import as it may mean extending the Neolithic by several hundred years and has implications for understanding the background and development of the Neolithic and the role of the indigenous hunter-gatherers in the introduction of food production. If the period of overlap between the Mesolithic and Neolithic was lengthy then it allows for the gradual replacement of foraging by farming.[72] If, on the other hand, there was little overlap then it suggests a process and a time at which the Neolithic package became attractive to indigenous foragers,[73] or the movement of people from adjacent Europe to the offshore islands of Ireland and Britain.[74] At the moment the role of indigenous hunter-gatherers is seen as the principal dynamic in this process in Britain,[75] while in Ireland the likelihood of some population movement being involved is still strongly suggested.[76] This argument for some element of demic diffusion is based on the stable, strongly insular character of the Irish Late Mesolithic and the reality of the introduction of new plant and animal species and agricultural skills onto an island.[77] At the moment there is relatively little archaeological evidence to support a date for the beginning of the Irish Neolithic much before 4000 BC. (The dating evidence from the excavations at the megalithic cemetery at Carrowmore, Co. Sligo is best interpreted as in line with the dating of other megalithic tombs and there is no diagnostic Mesolithic material from the excavations.)[78] The most definite evidence in this regard is the domesticated cattle bone from the Late Mesolithic site at Ferriter's Cove, dating to before 4300 BC.[79] But this takes us no further in terms of recognising who was responsible for introducing farming. As Aidan O'Sullivan[80] has shown, a whole series of complex interactions of foraging and farming activities could have taken place once farming was introduced, adding as it did a number of plant and animal species which would have significantly diversified the nature and character of the exploitable environment.

Our understanding of how people perceived and organised the landscape has also changed dramatically over the last thirty years. Radiocarbon dates indicate that while some of the clearances were short term[81] they often lasted several hundred years, and in some cases the landscape may have remained open right through the Neolithic.[82] It has been argued that the shifting cultivation model is inappropriate for prehistoric temperate European conditions where the prevalent wide spectrum, mixed farming strategy could have provided the basis for secure long-term occupation of farmed areas.[83] The most important archaeological back-up of this has been the discovery of Neolithic field systems, particularly in north-west Mayo as the result of the work of Caulfield.[84] While Céide Fields (Figure 1.4) is the largest, most regular and best-known example, smaller-scale systems and stretches of field boundaries are known from other areas as far apart as Antrim,[85] Donegal[86] and Kerry, as for example from Valencia Island.[87] In all cases these consist of boundaries protected from removal by the fossilisation of the landscape under blanket bog. This raises the issue of whether field boundaries were utilised in areas that have continued on in agricultural use and the author has argued elsewhere[88] that we should assume this would frequently have been the case. By contrast, in Britain the emphasis in interpretation over the last ten years has shifted to regarding Neolithic settlement as based on mobility, with the continuing importance of the use of wild resources and bounding of the land seen as more a feature of the Bronze Age.[89] There are a number of reasons for this stance but important factors are the

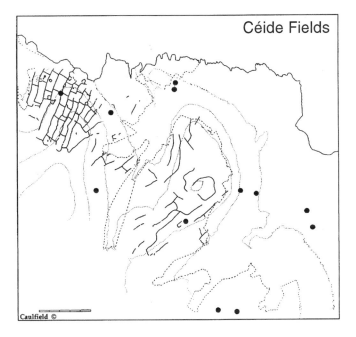

Figure 1.4　Layout and extent of Céide Fields, Co. Mayo as of the end of the 1995 survey season (megalithic tombs indicated by dot symbol)

Source:　Courtesy Séamas Caulfield.

suggestions of a considerable degree of continuity from the Mesolithic and the paucity of recognisable domestic structures from southern Britain. By contrast, one of the striking features of Neolithic archaeology in Ireland has been the regular discoveries of further Neolithic houses[90] (Figure 1.5; Plate 1.1). Particularly significant discoveries in recent years have been the two houses at

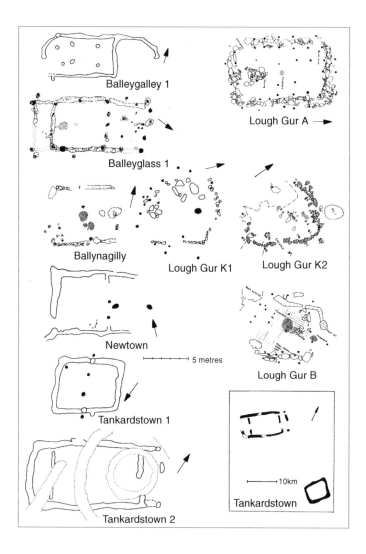

Figure 1.5   Plans of rectangular Neolithic houses with inset of the Tankardstown, Co.
Limerick site plan

Source: From Grogan (1996)

12

Tankardstown, Co. Limerick,[91] the house at Newtown, Co. Meath, [92] the two houses at Ballyharry, Co. Antrim[93] and the excavation of the Neolithic settlement, including two houses, at Ballygalley, Co. Antrim.[94] While the model of single, rectangular houses is still predominant, these and other sites show that a range of arrangements were in use, including the possibility of two or more houses, circular as well as rectangular houses and the provision of enclosures around some houses as at Lough Gur. The limited extent of excavation at some of these sites has also to be borne in mind, alongside the extensive character of the settlement on Knockadoon, Lough Gur revealed through a long-term research project.[95] Work at the Knowth passage tomb complex has demonstrated that the character of individual settlements was dynamic, with changing foci, phases of enclosure and changes in house design.[96] Landscape projects such as those at Carnlough[97] (see Figure 1.6) and Ballylough[98] demonstrate that these settlements stood in a cultural landscape within which not only were

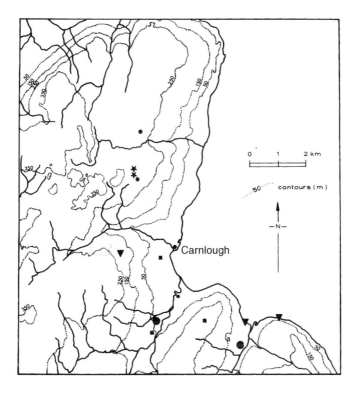

Figure 1.6   Distribution of known Neolithic groups of material in the Carnlough area, Co. Antrim (large dots indicate possible main settlements; stars – hollow-scraper dominated sites; squares – end-scraper dominated sites; triangles – industrial sites; small dots – miscellaneous)

Source: From Woodman (1985b).

13

Plate 1.1   Aerial view from the west of the excavation of the rectangular house and the overlying court tomb at Ballyglass, Co. Mayo (see Ó Nualláin 1972)

Source: Photo L. Swan.

there bounded areas, but also there would have been specialised activity sites as signified by the occurrence of a restricted range or specific set of artifact types.[99] It would seem that people deliberately placed the permanent sites in specific locations: sheltered, southerly-facing and with access to a water supply and a range of land types.[100] The use of substantial houses was established early in the Neolithic[101] and over time the pattern of settlement appears to have become regionalised and more diverse. At Lough Gur in the later stages of the Neolithic there is evidence of social differentiation within the settlement, reflected in the enclosure of some of the house sites and the concentration of prestige items on these enclosed sites.[102] Some evidence of settlement hierarchy and concern with defence comes from the north-east with the recognition of Donegore Hill, Co. Antrim as a large, enclosed hilltop settlement[103] and the probability that the settlement at Lyles Hill nearby[104] was of a similar nature. One notable feature of the Neolithic with wider implications for Irish prehistory is that while rectangular and circular houses appear to have been in use contemporaneously, over time the circular house form became dominant.[105] Circular houses would remain the dominant element in domestic architecture until the eighth/ninth centuries AD and we should be giving attention to the social context of the

14

beginning of this long tradition as Lynn[106] has given to its end. Indeed, the evidence for Neolithic settlement has significant potential for the analysis of the use and organisation of social space within and around houses.

Work has continued on the most visible aspect of the Neolithic, namely megalithic tombs and other burial and ceremonial sites.[107] In terms of understanding contemporary settlement, what is relevant is the specific relationship between tombs and houses and broader patterns of distribution of different kinds of tombs as a guide to the pattern of settlement. Looking at the association between houses and megalithic tombs we may be talking here again simply about differential preservation of settlement evidence in protected situations under the mounds of these tombs, but it is clear that there was also an association between the idea of the houses for the living and the dead (Plate 1.1).[108] More broadly, the quantity of the tombs, now over 1,560,[109] compared to the relatively small number of known settlement sites, means that in terms of looking at regional or national settlement trends the tombs have been discussed in the context of their relationship with contemporary settlement.[110] That relationship would seem to be very varied, both over time and space. Most importantly in this regard has been a recognition of the need to break away from the traditional, cultural-historical model of different types of tombs representing different, successive societies or people with different ethnic identities.[111] Radiocarbon dates indicate that there was a substantial overlap in the construction and use of court, portal and passage tombs. Added to this, in distributional terms there are areas where different types occur in close proximity, as in the case of the Cooley Peninsula, Co. Louth (Figure 1.7). So we have to face the probability that in some areas different tombs were used by the same people, perhaps with different roles in mind. Looking at the complex interlocking distribution patterns, it is clear that any simple dichotomy between a society based on local territories exemplified in the building of a court tomb, and a more complex and regionally based social organisation based on the construction of passage tombs[112] is an inadequate explanation, perhaps owing more to the framework of explanation current in the 1970s than to any Neolithic reality. It is clear, for example, that groupings of tombs – 'cemeteries' – are not just a feature of passage tombs, an assumption that had been at the core of the analytic convention of seeing the passage tombs as different from other megalithic tombs, but that groupings of other tombs also occur.[113] In detailed regional studies it is clear that the position of tombs in the landscape may in some cases have been central to potential settlement zones whereas in other cases they may have been peripheral or even occurred in a distinct cemetery.[114] Over time there may have been a change in the character and role of the tombs in Neolithic society, as local foci were complemented by tombs with a wider role, perhaps reflecting the increasing scale of social interaction.[115] A notable feature has been the recognition of a distinctive form of burial monument, the so-called Linkardstown cists, with an emphasis on single burial.[116] These are concentrated in the southern part of the island and are again contemporary with megalithic tombs. This may indicate a regional trend in south

15

Leinster and adjoining areas of Munster where individuals rather than the ancestors were the focus of celebration and social cohesion. It can also be taken as an
example of the regionalisation that occurred alongside greater inter-regional
contacts. The latter is illustrated by the widespread movement of porcellanite
axes from the production sites at Tievebulliagh and Rathlin Island, Co. Antrim,
the occurrence of substantial numbers of British axes in Ireland[117] and the popularity of international styles of pottery (Grooved Ware and Beaker) at the end of
Neolithic. All of these portable artifacts are also a reminder that people in
different regions was in contact and how social change and innovation were
articulated. The similarities and differences in regional sequences of activity can
be seen, for example, in the evidence from Lough Gur,[118] the Boyne Valley (see
below) and Ballynahatty in the Lagan valley, Co. Down.[119]

It is the combination of artifact and site studies that offers the best opportunities to build on advances in our knowledge of this period. As with the
Mesolithic, systematic field-walking in key areas offers us great potential to utilise
the most common material surviving from Stone Age societies, lithics, to gain a
better understanding of the distribution of settlement across the landscape.
Sourcing studies afford the chance to weigh up the importance of local versus
regional or more exotic resources. We need more regional studies of Neolithic
sites and artifacts and at the level of excavation it is salutary to remember that
Lough Gur still represents the most extensive excavation of a settlement site.

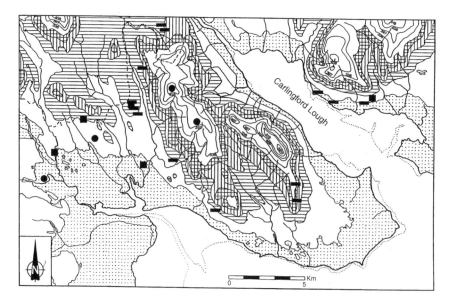

Figure 1.7   Location of known Neolithic types of megalithic tombs on the Cooley
Peninsula, Co. Louth and adjoining areas (dots – passage tombs; rectangles –
court tombs; squares – portal tombs)

The Bronze Age, 2500–600 BC

For studies of Bronze Age settlement, the problem is not so much that there is any shortage of archaeological material but that this is fragmented and its character and range changes over time. In terms of sub-divisions of this period there are two schemes currently in usage; the first rests on dividing the period into an Earlier (2500–1200 BC) and Later Bronze Age (1200–600 BC), the second on a recognition of an Early (2500–1700 BC), a Middle (1700–1200 BC) and a Late (1200–600 BC) Bronze Age. For the purposes of this overview the broader division of the period is utilised. There is a very good range of burial evidence, particularly for the earlier part of the period, a large number of ceremonial sites, again particularly for the earlier part of the Bronze Age, and a plentiful supply of metal artifacts. By contrast with the first two of these sets of data the range of the artifactual evidence increases through time. Bronze objects were the most widespread metal artifacts in use and there have been major advances in our understanding of the mining and associated processes involved in the extraction of copper through O'Brien's work at the Beaker period mining site at Ross Island, Killarney, Co. Kerry[120] and the mines on Mount Gabriel, near Schull, Co. Cork where the main period of use seems to have been 1700–1500 BC.[121]

One of the important developments in recent years has been a major advance in our understanding of settlement, particularly for the later part of the period.[122] Traditionally the recognition of Bronze Age settlement sites has been difficult[123] but there have been a range of important discoveries through a combination of pipeline survey, radiocarbon and dendrochronological dating and the research strategy of the Discovery Programme which in its first tranche of projects focused on the later prehistoric period.[124] What has increasingly come to the fore also is the need to see the fragmentation of the evidence as the result of distinct patterns reflecting deliberate and complex human action in the Bronze Age. We need to look at the range of evidence in combination to understand settlement in the landscape.[125] One of the exciting aspects of Bronze Age studies in particular has been the recognition of the complementarity of evidence in different zones in the landscape, thus we are beginning to link activity in upland and lowland, dryland and wetland areas. One important research initiative has been the recognition of the importance of coastal wetlands, preserved, for example, in the modern mud flats of the Shannon estuary.[126] Looking at a more traditional aspect of the evidence it is clear that many of the metal artifacts appear to have been deliberately deposited and not accidentally lost or discarded. This complex use and role of material culture has also to be borne in mind in the broader interpretation of the archaeological record.

There are a number of settlement sites dating from the end of the Neolithic and the start of the Bronze Age, indicated both by radiocarbon dates and the use of Beaker and other contemporary ceramic styles. Interestingly, many of these are in places already occupied in the Neolithic, as at Knowth, Newgrange (see discussion below) and Lough Gur.[127] The old view of the users of Beaker pottery as intrusive pastoralists with a mobile settlement pattern has largely given way to a recognition of the probability that we are looking at the presence of new artifact styles introduced through contact and exchange rather than any large population movement,[128] although there has been a recent revival of the debate about 'Beaker people'.[129] The actual evidence for the economic and settlement pattern is very thin.[130] The large faunal assemblage from Newgrange has assumed importance in this light and van Wijngaarden-Bakker[131] has interpreted it as showing an economy based on the exploitation of cattle and pigs with transhumance to the coastal areas to avail of pasture. This is based on a view that the soil resources in the Boyne Valley had been very adversely affected by the activities of the passage tomb builders, a view that can be strongly contested.[132] Mount[133] has argued convincingly that the Newgrange assemblage has to be seen in the context of the particular ceremonial activities going on on the site as well as the evidence for people living there. The evidence from Newgrange, Knowth and other sites indicates intensive activity during the Beaker period in the Boyne Valley, which suggests that it continued as a focus for settlement and ceremony.[134]

Despite the paucity of known settlement sites for much of the rest of the Earlier Bronze Age, the extensive character of the distribution of the main sources of evidence, such as burials and metal artifacts, makes it clear that much of the landscape was utilised at one stage or other during the Earlier Bronze Age.[135] Several trends can be detected behind this evidence. Regional studies have shown that the areas of exploitation may have changed somewhat from the Neolithic[136] (see Figures 1.7 and 1.8), representing both continuity and actual expansion of the areas settled, including the utilisation of areas that appear not to have been previously considered as important. At least in part these changes can probably be related to advances and diversification in prehistoric agricultural practices.[137] It is worth commenting that this trend appears to post-date the Beaker 'phase'. In general terms there appears to be an increasing use of more low-lying areas along river valleys. It is plausible to view this as the beginning of a different cycle of settlement activity, involving significant expansion into new areas. However it coincides with, and in some cases may directly relate to, evidence for the acceleration of blanket bog growth in upland areas.[138] Ironically, the increasing evidence for field systems and associated settlement in the middle and later parts of the Bronze Age, as at Carrownaglogh,[139] Belderg,[140] Cashelkeelty[141] and Valencia Island,[142] comes from areas that were close to and would come to be covered by bog, so they were by definition at the margins of the contemporary agricultural landscape. However, there is the possibility of picking up prehistoric field boundaries in the modern farmed landscape, using aerial photography, in areas like Kilkenny which may have been core areas of settlement.[143]

Interestingly, it seems that in landscape terms the burials, settlements and metal artifacts may have been placed in different niches or zones, indicating in

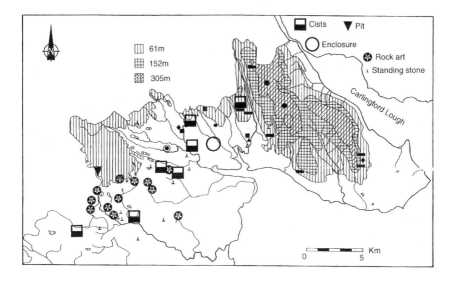

Figure 1.8 Distribution of megalithic tombs and known Early Bronze Age monuments and sites on the Cooley Peninsula and adjoining area of Co. Louth (only) (megalithic tomb symbols as in Figure 1.7 with the addition of small triangles – wedge tombs; lozenges – unclassified tombs)

a different sense a very structured/bounded landscape. Thus in the Lough Gur area the burial evidence suggests a shift away from Lough Gur itself to the south, while the metal artifacts continue to cluster around Lough Gur. From the location of the burials in valley bottoms it would seem likely that the settlement sites themselves were at slightly higher levels in these valleys.[144] Thus, by combining different sets of evidence, we can begin to see more of the organisation of settlement and also to understand the nature of the individual aspects of the evidence. Looking at evidence of actual settlement sites in the earlier part of the Bronze Age, such as the Beaker sites in the Boyne Valley and later sites such as those at Cullyhanna, Co. Armagh,[145] Meadowlands, Downpatrick, Co. Down,[146] Carrigdirty, Co. Limerick[147] and Chancellorsland, Co. Tipperary,[148] it seems appropriate to think of settlements largely consisting of small clusters of circular houses and other structures, some possibly enclosed.[149] Social organisation would seem to have been predominantly at a local scale, as indicated by the replication and distribution of cemeteries and ceremonial monuments of similar size.[150] Reading the complex range of evidence from the burials is difficult, but at the very least it is clear that there was ascribed social ranking, probably based on family or kin groups, and horizontal differentiation on a gender basis.[151] It is clear that in this locally based world there was a very complex view of the landscape involving domestic and ceremonial elements,

19

'natural' and built features, which were combined in a variety of ways to serve as the local perceptual basis of people's lives, as illustrated in Moore's[152] analysis of the Bronze Age landscape in the Araglin and Monavar valleys in the Monavullagh mountains, Co. Waterford.

A settlement type of a temporary nature that increasingly appears to form part of the Bronze Age landscape from about 1500 BC on is the *fulacht fiadh*, or burnt mound, resulting primarily from cooking using heated stones in a trough. Radiocarbon dates indicate that these are concentrated in the later part of the second millennium BC.[153] While in the past seen as indicative of a mobile settlement pattern, it seems more reasonable to interpret them as bringing into use wet zones of the landscape that are unlikely to have been part of the permanently farmed landscape.[154] The sheer number of these sites, over 4500, the fact that this represents only a proportion of the original distribution, and the density of sites in counties such as Cork, Waterford, Kilkenny and Tipperary make them a vitally important component in any reconstruction of regional settlement patterns[155] (see Figure 1.9). This wide use of the landscape, incorporating the core agricultural areas and those used on a seasonal basis or in more

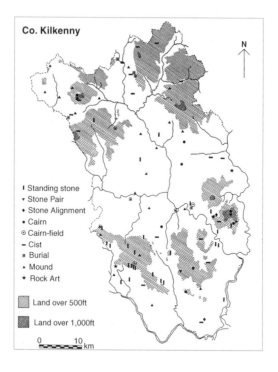

Figure 1.9   Different categories of Bronze Age sites in Co. Kilkenny
Source: From Condit (1990).

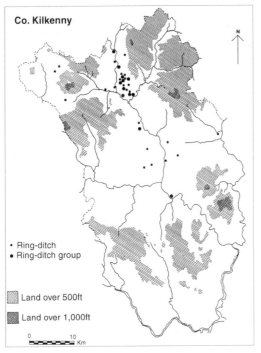

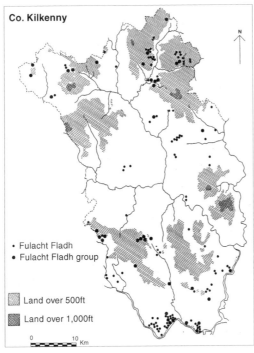

extensive way, or to exploit resources such as the forest or wetlands, is also suggested by the first major phase of the construction of trackways across narrow parts of raised bogs, as in the Mountdillon complex, Co. Longford.[156] Here and elsewhere the removal through milling of the upper level of bogs has to be borne in mind, but it does appear that the Bronze Age was the first major period of trackway construction, although a small number of Neolithic trackways are known. In the first instance this may relate to increased human activity in the Irish midlands during the Bronze Age. As a specific example, the large-scale clearance seen in the pollen record round 1000 BC is matched by a peak in trackway construction. It would appear that the construction of trackways reflects periods of agricultural and settlement expansion rather than a reaction to 'events' of climatic deterioration.[157]

Evidence for the Later Bronze Age (1200–500 BC) is still dominated by metal artifacts but very significant changes in the archaeological record have taken place in recent years. The most significant is the recognition of a range of settlement sites falling into a number of categories. The dating of the trivallate hillforts at Haughey's Fort in the Navan complex[158] and at Mooghaun, Co. Clare[159] to between 1200–1000 BC establishes clearly that hillforts have to be regarded as a feature of this period. Further support for this comes from the Later Bronze Age settlement activity, including a large circular house, within the multivallate hillfort at Rathgall, Co. Wicklow.[160] There was Later Bronze Age activity within Navan Fort itself, in the form of a ditched enclosure with an internal structure underlying the complex sequence of Iron Age activity.[161] Excavation at the multivallate cliff-edge fort at Dún Aonghasa (Plate 1.2) revealed a complex Later Bronze Age occupation with circular houses and evidence for metalworking. The occupation spans the period between 1300–800 BC.[162] Both the location of these Later Bronze Age settlements and their character, for example the evidence from Haughey's Fort for the storage of grain, perhaps gathered from a hinterland, the access to large breeds of animals and gold production,[163] suggest that they are at the top of a settlement, social and economic hierarchy. In this context it seems very probable that there would have been a ceremonial or ritual aspect to activity on such sites.[164] Other elements in this structure are represented by sites like that at Clonfinlough, Co. Offaly, a wetland, lakeside enclosed site defined by a timber palisade within which there were at least three circular houses with central hearths and plank floors.[165] The site is dated dendrochronologically to around 900 BC. It can be compared to other sites such as Lough Eskragh, Co. Tyrone,[166] Knocknalappa, Co. Clare and Rathinaun, Co. Sligo.[167] Another category of wetland site can be recognised from the evidence at Moynagh Lough, Co. Meath[168] and Killymoon, Co. Tyrone[169] where the material seems to suggest not so much a standard residential site as a location for activities such as metal production, cereal processing and deliberate deposition that might be associated with a high-status site. Representing sites that are enclosed but not heavily protected in this settlement structure is the settlement at Curraghatoor, Co. Tipperary where there was

Plate 1.2 Aerial view from the south of the cliff-edge fort at Dún Aonghasa, Aran
Islands, Co. Galway; excavation of the interior (Cotter 1966) revealed Later
Bronze Age occupation

Source: Photo Dúchas.

a cluster of buildings, including a circular house, apparently within a palisade[170]
(Figure 1.10). Similar open or unenclosed sites occur, for example, the Later
Bronze Age settlement at Lough Gur.[171]

The work of the North Munster project in trying to assess the character
of Later Bronze Age settlement through an integrated assessment of all the
archaeological data on a regional basis has led to the formulation of an important model of Later Bronze Age settlement[172] within which it is possible to see
the role of the different site types outlined above (Figure 1.11). It should be
remembered of course that it is a regional model and that patterns of settlement
are likely to have differed somewhat from region to region. At the top of the
structure and social scale are hillforts, whose location and size suggest a regional
concern. Substantially defended hilltop enclosures are seen to represent a lower
and more locally based social stratum. Into this category might also fit enclosed
lakeside sites and at the lowest and most local level are the enclosed, but not
heavily protected, and the open house clusters. In the case of the latter particularly it is clear that what is represented are residential units consisting of a
main house and ancillary structures.[173] The presence of social ranking is clearly

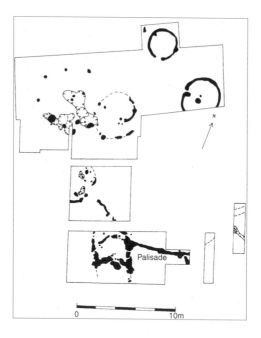

Figure 1.10 Plan of the Later Bronze Age settlement at Curraghatoor, Co. Tipperary
Soure: From Doody (1997)

represented in the patronage that can be presumed to have been required to support the specialist craftworkers producing high-quality metalwork and in the display and deliberate deposition of such material.[174] It should not occasion any surprise, then, that there is a strong element of ceremonial and ritual activity reflected in the evidence from sites like Moynagh and Killymoon and even more clearly in the deposition of material in the King's Stables[175] close to Haughey's Fort.

There is a continued popularity of the view that this complex social and settlement network, elements of which seem to date right across the Late Bronze Age, is the result of a short-term climatic downturn associated with the impact of a volcanic eruption, Hekla 3, in Iceland between 1159–1141 BC.[176] Again it seems there is a difficulty here in attempting to use a single environmental event to explain a social process which developed over perhaps hundreds of years. A much more important set of environmental data relevant to the character and economic success of Later Bronze Age settlement may be the evidence for the apparent increase in arable farming from 1400–1300 BC, [177] with a distinct farming expansion around 1000 BC,[178] and the gradual climatic deterioration that apparently set in from 800 BC. In the case of Mooghaun, it would appear that the first substantial human impact on the local

24

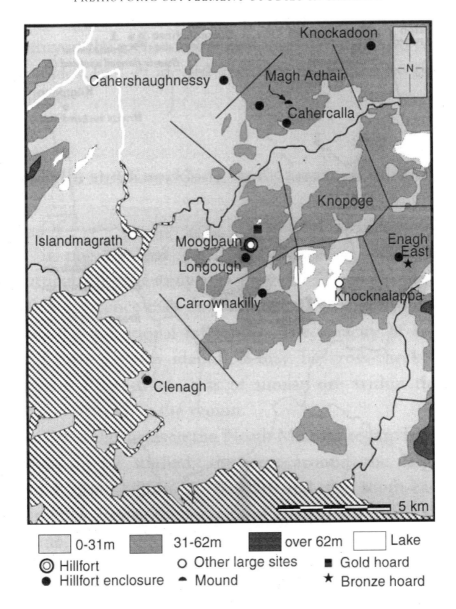

Figure 1.11 Model of Later Bronze Age settlement organisation in south-east Clare showing possible territorial divisions

Source: From Grogan *et al.* (1996).

environment took place in the Bronze Age, and that a phase of high-intensity land use correlates with the construction and use of the hillfort to be followed by an apparent reduction in farming activity.[179]

While it is clear that the recognition of different forms and scales of settlement probably reflects a society with increasing social stratification, one interesting contrast with the Neolithic and Earlier Bronze Age is that the character of the mortuary record changes and becomes less conspicuous. On the other hand the deliberate deposition of metalwork, often in hoards,[180] becomes more apparent. The separation of gold and bronze objects, ornaments and more 'utilitarian' items may indicate deliberate dualities of action.[181] The metalwork also suggests distinct regional differences[182] and indeed differences within regions, such as North Munster,[183] and in this, as in other aspects of the Later Bronze Age, there is a continuity into the Iron Age. It is clear that site complexes that were to take on a central role in early medieval archaeology, history and mythology were already important at this time. These complexes are a reminder of the spatial complementarity of different types of sites and the complexity of human activity that they suggest. If we take on board the hierarchy of settlement suggested on the basis of the North Munster evidence, there is a very strong indication of a framework of regional entities that are perhaps more often sought in the prehistoric Iron Age as the precursor to the early historic pattern.[184]

Recent work on this period has provided a wide ranging agenda for future research, including a better understanding of Earlier Bronze Age settlement, a critical discussion of the environmental background to the human history of the period and, in the case of the Later Bronze Age, an assessment of the implications of the results of a number of on-going projects. What we can recognise now is that the Later Bronze Age is a critical period in Irish prehistory and that in many ways it is the Later Bronze Age rather than the Iron Age that best fits the tag of a heroic, Celtic society.[185]

The Iron Age, 600 BC–AD 500

The problems in trying to reconstruct settlement patterns for this period are probably greater than for any of the other preceding periods in Irish prehistory. In his comprehensive review Raftery[186] entitled one of his chapters 'the invisible people' and in this and a series of relevant publications he has commented on the virtual absence of significant associations, the paucity of burials and clearly recognisable settlements, and the selective nature of the surviving remains. What has happened in recent years is that there has been a lot of work on the known archaeological data belonging to this period.[187] But the perceived inadequacy of this evidence in being composed almost entirely of unassociated metal and other objects and the problem of whether some hillfort and related sites date to this period is still a dominant feature of the Irish Iron Age. In the light of the recent detailed discussion of this period[188] and in recognition of the difficulties of interpreting the data from a settlement perspective, the discussion here is somewhat briefer than for earlier periods.

One aspect of the thorny question of the introduction of iron into Ireland, which is important in the settlement sphere, is that the character of the new material does not suggest any large-scale immigration and indeed indicates a great degree of continuity from the Later Bronze Age. While this may be set against the linguistic and mythological view of the introduction of the Iron Age,[189] it does have important implications. It now seems likely that the organisation of settlement in the Iron Age was along lines that became established in the Later Bronze Age. There is a striking continuity of activity at high-status sites such as Emain Macha[190] which suggests that this transition occurred without any great social upheaval. Indeed there is wider evidence of continuity of events and symbolic activity in the Navan complex.[191] This continuity can be seen in other aspects of the archaeological evidence, for example in burial practice.[192] Bearing in mind what has already been said, it is perhaps appropriate to see developments in the Later Bronze Age as paving the way for the introduction of the Iron Age, for example as seen in the appearance of novel high quality metalwork which could have fulfilled a demand for new prestige items. This might also at least in part explain why the earliest phase of the Iron Age has such a limited character.[193] There is a distinct regionalisation seen in the Iron Age after 300 BC between a La Tène north and a non-La Tène south.[194] This can be seen for example in the concentration of hillforts in the south and south-west of Ireland and the absence of La Tène material on these sites.[195] This and the other evidence discussed above suggests that this regionalisation should perhaps been seen more in the light of Later Bronze trends and less as being later reflected in the archaeology of early medieval Ireland.

As we have seen, hillforts were built in the Later Bronze Age and some of these sites were used in the early centuries AD. However there is very limited evidence for their construction and use in the final centuries BC. On the other hand, hillforts and related sites are still regarded as a key aspect of the Irish Iron Age.[196] Resolving this problem is obviously central to our interpretation of the Iron Age and the relationship between the Bronze Age and Iron Age. The application of aerial photography has led to significant additions to the number of hillfort sites known and perhaps the most important discovery has been Condit's[197] documentation of the complexity of the pairs and groups of hillforts overlooking the Slaney Valley near Baltinglass in Co. Wicklow. These seem to occur in two groups, on either side and above the river valley, and can be read as part of a pattern of hillforts in strategic and commanding locations extending from Wicklow to Clare.[198] Again this pattern seems likely to have its origins in the Late Bronze Age.

The Iron Age features of Emain Macha,[199] Tara[200] and Dún Ailinne[201] fit with the description of these sites as special/royal in the early Irish literature and they continued to be used well into the first millennium AD. These royal and related sites clearly stand at the apex of the settlement hierarchy, as

Plate 1.3   The oak trackway at Corlea, Co. Longford dated to 148 BC (Raftery 1996)
Source: Photo B. Raftery

indicated by their size and form, their spacing in the landscape, irregular as it may be, and the associated artifactual assemblage. In the case of Emain Macha, the construction of the large ceremonial timber structure correlates in date, *c*. 100 BC, with the building of the Dorsey earthwork,[202] which is traditionally seen as part of the southern frontier of a proto-historic polity (a kingdom?) based on Emain Macha. Further west in Monaghan a 'continuation' of the Dorsey – the Black Pig's Dyke linear earthwork – has been dated to between 500–25 BC.[203] An earthwork controlling the crossing of the Shannon at Drumsna, Co. Roscommon dates to the fourth century BC.[204] Work on the Claidh Dubh linear earthwork, which crosses the Blackwater Valley from the Ballyhoura Hills to the Nagle Mountains in Co. Cork indicates that it may date to the early centuries of the first millennium AD.[205] The massive oak trackway at Corlea, Co. Longford (Plate 1.3) has been dated to 148 BC.[206] The large-scale use of oak timbers at some of the sites mentioned here has made it possible to date these structures by dendrochron-ology, but it also reflects the scale of harnessing and organisation of human effort that was involved in the construc-tion of these features in the landscape. It is clear that there is an increased visibility of territorial definition, reflecting the emergence of regional as well as local polities.

Lower down the settlement hierarchy our evidence is very scattered. On Scrabo Hill in Co. Down there is an enclosed hilltop settlement (Figure 1.12) with a Iron Age date[207] that might reflect a lower-order settlement, as does the evidence of small circular structures within a ringfort enclosure at Lislackagh, Co. Mayo.[208] This is indicative of the limited evidence of Iron Age settlement,

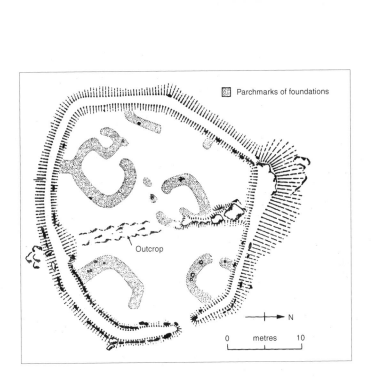

Figure 1.12 Hut enclosure on Scrabo Hill, Co. Down with an Iron Age date
Source: From the Archaeological Survey of Co. Down, E.M. Jope (1966)

but broadly speaking it again suggests continuity from the Later Bronze Age. Small numbers of ringfort sites may date to the period from the beginning of the Iron Age to the fourth century AD.[209] But our knowledge of economic and social organisation is limited and much of it depends on the extent to which the character of early medieval Ireland can be projected back into the Iron Age. Lynn[210] has suggested that the ringfort complex specifically developed in the fifth and sixth centuries AD in the context of improved iron technology and agricultural developments that were introduced through increased contact with late and sub-Roman Britain.[211] These innovations brought about agricultural expansion and social change resulting in pressure on land and the adoption of ringforts (and crannogs) as defended farmsteads.

One aspect of the evidence that is worth commenting on is the interpretation of the organisation of farming through the pre-Christian Iron Age. On the one hand there is increasing evidence for cereal production in the last few centuries BC, particularly in the form of querns, including the introduction of rotary, specifically beehive querns.[212] This contrasts with the picture suggested in the early historic literature with its emphasis on cattle production. It also runs counter to the pollen evidence which suggests a fall-back in activity in the landscape and a decrease, sometimes termed a collapse or a crisis, in farming

29

associated with worsening climatic conditions, followed by an expansion in arable farming at the end of the second century AD.[213] It should also be remembered that ideas about collapse or crisis in Iron Age farming are very much based on the evidence for woodland regeneration but that this woodland itself would have been an important resource and that it may well have formed an integral part of what was perceived as the social landscape in late prehistoric times rather than being in any sense marginal.[214]

It can be concluded, then, that there are still major unresolved problems in Iron Age settlement. Much of the basic settlement data for the period still has to be recognised.[215] As well as reflecting the difficulties of recognising domestic material of this period, at least some of the problems involve our understanding of the degree of continuity between the Iron Age and Late Bronze Age, and indeed between the Iron Age and what emerges in the early medieval period. It might be useful also to examine more critically the correlation that is made between the recognition of this period as a problematic one in terms of the nature of the archaeological data and an environmental scenario of long-term deterioration allied to periods of more acute problems followed by a recovery in the early centuries AD. For example, the difficulty of recognising archaeological material as dating to the Iron Age appears to be directly related to problems such as the poor preservation of ferrous artifacts rather than to any argument that such material is not present.[216] As with earlier periods we should be aware of the need to explicitly identify the basis for our interpretative approaches before using them to reconstruct the conditions of life during the Iron Age.[217]

Looking at current views on the Iron Age it is perhaps ironic that a time traditionally seen as marking the emergence of Irish Celtic society and as bringing a major phase of Irish settlement (the pre-Celtic period) to an end, should now increasingly be seen to continue trends in settlement form and location developed earlier in prehistory. There is good evidence from the first century AD onwards that there was significant contact across the Irish Sea with Roman Britain. This comes in the form of Roman and Romano-British material culture,[218] including burials.[219] It was arising from these contacts that the framework of changes that brought about the end to Irish prehistory emerged.[220]

Conclusion

It will be clear that while there has been a lot of progress in recent years, in many ways this has also just provided us with better questions and data to improve our interpretation of Irish prehistoric settlement. On the other hand, the detail of settlement discussed above should make it clear that prehistory cannot be written off as unamenable to settlement analysis or irrelevant to long-term perspectives on the course of Irish settlement. In recent discussions by historical geographers there still seems to be the view that this 7000-year period can be summarised as a series of events, or as simply a static and undecipherable background to the dynamics of the course of settlement in the historic period.[221] There is a danger in this tendency to hive off Irish prehistory as a unit and as a 'foreshortening of time' to use MacDonagh's[222] phrase, that it will contribute to the concept of this very long period of time as witnessing a kind of vague settlement continuity which Graham and Proudfoot[223] have quite rightly criticised for the historic period as offering an inadequate and mythic view of the Irish past.

Looking in general terms at some of the themes discussed above, it is clear that we must get away from simple models of settlement that emphasise mobility and utilisation of different zones at different periods and where mono-causal explanations, such as climatic change, technological innovation or population movement are seen as adequate to describe social change. During prehistory, settlement was distributed in a complex way across the landscape. From the Neolithic period on, settlement appears to have been based on a mixed agricultural system which would have encouraged and required the use of different ecological zones. Settlement activity over much of the landscape is likely from Mesolithic times and, without implying an evolutionary model of continuous population growth, it seems likely that the general trend was towards increasing population. Some areas of the landscape show re-use through the greater part of prehistory and, not surprisingly, these are often areas of economic significance which became loaded with overtones of ritual, religious or political significance. The three of course may have been interwoven, as in the case of Tara.[224] Again prehistory has something to offer in the wider field of Irish historic settlement studies in that the evidence suggests that we need to consider all aspects of the data as offering insights into the social landscape rather than separating it into series of data sets to be analysed, as seems to be a popular approach to settlement analysis in later periods. It is also clear that we have to set prehistoric people in a historical context and see them as having a past which had a major role in their lives and societies.

The layers of significance referred to above are one of the indications of long-term continuity that we see in the prehistoric settlement record which should not be lightly dismissed. This is not to suggest that there were not also major discontinuities, but long-term continuity is one of the wavelengths of time, place and process that should be considered in trying to understand the dynamics of prehistoric settlement. Developments in the cultural record can be fitted alongside long-term trends to explain shorter-term cycles of social and cultural changes. For example, ideas and innovations arising from the patterns of migration, exchange, trade and contacts abroad would have been the hall-mark of social elites in particular.[225] At the same time social changes and developments may have deliberately linked to and used the past as a way of legitimising the place and power of the current elite.[226] Individual events of commemoration or celebration at ceremonial sites could be dismissed as insignificant but they provided a mechanism to maintain day-to-day stability in society and to articulate social change.

Aalen[227] commented on the interesting dichotomy between prehistoric and historic events from the end of the early medieval period. Prehistoric continuity was contrasted with the historic evidence for invasions. This dichotomy may not necessarily be a contradiction, however, but rather a reflection of a changing European perspective and world view in which Ireland became identified as a peripheral region rich for conquest and/or colonisation. In prehistoric times the situation was very different in that the influences from outside would not have had the same cohesion or aim, and may indeed have been dominated and directed by events within Ireland. So we need to remember the specific context of Irish prehistory and not to dismiss it as either a marginal prologue to Irish history or as a period that can be viewed through the lens of Irish history. After all, Irish history had not yet happened.

Acknowledgements

I would like to thank Eoin Grogan, Finola O'Carroll and Aidan O'Sullivan for their comments on an earlier draft of this chapter which has benefited greatly from their input. My thanks to Seamus Caulfield for Figure 1.4. The title of the chapter owes its inspiration to John Montague's poem 'A Lost Tradition' but it is argued that archaeology offers us a skill to interpret the prehistoric landscape. The views expressed are solely those of the author.

Notes

1 Case (1969a).
2 ApSimon (1969).
3 Harbison (1973).
4 Woodman (1973/4).
5 Herity and Eogan (1977); Harbison (1988); O'Kelly (1989); Cooney and Grogan (1994); Waddle (1998).
6 Mallory and McNeill (1991).
7 Woodman (1978).
8 Waddell and Shee Twohig (1995).
9 Raftery (1994).
10 Compare Delaney (1972); Bennett (1996).
11 For example, Co. Donegal, Lacy (1983); the barony of Ikerrin, Stout, G. (1984); the Dingle Peninsula, Cuppage (1986); Co. Louth, Buckley and Sweetman (1991); North Kerry, Toal (1995); the Iveragh Peninsula, O'Sullivan, Ann and Sheehan (1996).
12 For example Condit and Gibbons (1990); Condit (1997).
13 Cleary et al. (1987); Gowen (1988).
14 Cooney (1990a); Green and Zvelebil (1990); Zvelebil et al. (1996).
15 Anon. (1992); Eogan (1997); Waddell (1997).
16 For example Newman (1997).
17 Synnott (1996).
18 For example Brindley and Lanting (1989/90); Brindley et al. (1989/90).
19 Sheridan (1995).
20 O'Brien, W. (1993); Brindley (1995).
21 For example Baillie (1995a, 1995b).

22 See discussion in Woodman (1992a, 1992b); Cooney (1993, 1995).
23 But see discussion in Briggs (1981); Mount (1997) as important exceptions.
24 For example Binford (1983); Hodder (1987); Shanks and Tilley (1987a, 1987b); Whittle (1988); Hodder (1992); Preucel and Hodder (1996).
25 For example Champion (1991).
26 See Cooney (1995, 1996); Woodman (1995).
27 For example Woodman (1978, 1985a).
28 For example Eogan (1964, 1983).
29 For example Raftery (1983, 1984, 1994).
30 Evans (1981, 16).
31 Cooney and Grogan (1994).
32 For example Braudel (1972).
33 For archaeological approaches see Bintcliff (1991); Knapp (1992).
34 Mitchell and Ryan (1997, 79–80).
35 For example Woodman (1986).
36 Woodman (1973/4).
37 Movius (1942).
38 For example Mitchell (1970).
39 Woodman (1973/4).
40 Woodman (1985a).
41 Ryan (1980).
42 Woodman (1977).
43 Woodman and O'Brien, M. (1993).
44 Woodman (1981, 1986).
45 Woodman (1978).
46 For example Woodman (1984, 1989).
47 Green and Zvelebil (1990).
48 Anderson (1993).
49 Woodman and Johnson (1996).
50 Dillon (1990).
51 See Price (1987); Smith, C. (1992).
52 Van Wijngaarden-Bakker (1989).
53 Edwards, K.J. (1985); Mitchell and Ryan (1997); Preece et al. (1986).
54 Binford (1980).
55 See Woodman (1985c, 1986, 1987); Cooney and Grogan (1994); Mallory and Hartwell (1997).
56 Woodman (1985a).
57 Woodman and Anderson (1990, 381, 386).
58 Cooney and Grogan (1994).
59 Mitchell (1972).
60 Woodman (1986).
61 Woodman (1985c).
62 Price (1987); Whittle (1996).
63 Woodman (1986).
64 Doody (1997, 102).
65 Mitchell (1989).
66 Case (1969a, 1969b).
67 For example Pilcher et al. (1971).
68 Boserup (1965).
69 For example Mitchell and Ryan (1997, 157–8).
70 Lynch (1981); Groenman-van Waateringe (1983); Edwards and Hirons (1984).
71 See O'Connell (1987).

72 For example see Zvelebil and Rowley-Conwy (1984, 1986); Williams, E. (1989); Whittle (1990); Monk (1993); Zvelebil (1994).
73 For example Thomas (1988).
74 For example Baillie (1995a, 145–7).
75 For example Thomas (1991, 1996).
76 For example Mallory and McNeill (1991); Cooney and Grogan (1994).
77 See relevant discussion on patterns on Mediterranean islands in Patton (1996).
78 Burenhult (1984); Bergh (1995); Caulfield (1983).
79 Woodman and O'Brien, M. (1997, 1993).
80 O'Sullivan (1997).
81 For example Molloy and O'Connell (1987).
82 Edwards (1985).
83 Rowley-Conwy (1981); Barker (1985).
84 Caulfield (1978, 1983, 1988); Molloy and O'Connell (1995).
85 Woodman (1983).
86 Lacy (1983).
87 Mitchell (1989); O'Sullivan, Ann and Sheehan (1996).
88 Cooney (1991, 1997).
89 Thomas (1991); Barrett (1994); Edmonds (1995).
90 See discussion in Grogan (1996).
91 Gowen (1988); Gowen and Tarbett (1988).
92 Halpin (1995).
93 Crothers (1996).
94 Simpson (1995, 1996).
95 O'Ríordáin (1954); Grogan and Eogan (1987).
96 Eogan (1991); Eogan and Roche (1997).
97 Woodman (1983).
98 Zvelebil *et al.* (1987); Green and Zvelebil (1990).
99 See discussion in Woodman (1983); Woodman *et al.* (1991/2); Mallory (1991/2).
100 Cooney and Grogan (1994).
101 See Sheridan (1995).
102 Grogan and Eogan (1987).
103 Mallory and Hartwell (1984).
104 Gibson and Simpson (1987).
105 See Grogan (1996).
106 Lynn (1978, 1994).
107 See discussion in Bergh (1995); Cooney (1990b); Cooney and Grogan (1994); Condit and Cooney (1997); O'Kelly (1982); Eogan (1986); Ó Nualláin (1989); Shee Twohig (1990).
108 For example Hodder (1990).
109 Walsh, P. (1997).
110 For example Cooney (1983).
111 As in Eogan (1991); Herity (1991).
112 For example Herity and Eogan (1977); Darvill (1979).
113 Cooney (1990b).
114 Cooney (1990b); McMann (1994); Bergh (1995); Mount (1996).
115 For example Sharples (1985, 1992); Sheridan (1985/6).
116 Ryan (1981); Manning (1985); Brindley and Lanting (1989/90).
117 Cooney and Mandal (1995); Sheridan (1986); Sheridan *et al.* (1992).
118 Grogan and Eogan (1987); Grogan (1988).
119 Hartwell (1991, 1994); Mallory and Hartwell (1997).
120 O'Brien, W. (1995a, 1995b).

121 O'Brien, W. (1990, 1994).
122 For example Doody (1987a, 1987b, 1997).
123 For example see discussion in Doody (1993).
124 Eogan (1997); Waddell (1997).
125 Cooney and Grogan (1994).
126 O'Sullivan, Aidan (1996a, 1996b).
127 Grogan and Eogan (1987).
128 Burgess and Shennan (1976); Harrison (1980).
129 See Brodie (1994); O'Brien, W. (1995a); Taylor (1994).
130 See Woodman (1985b); Monk (1985/6).
131 Van Wijngaarden-Bakker (1974, 1986).
132 See Cooney (1991).
133 Mount (1994).
134 For example O'Kelly et al. (1983); Eogan (1984); Eogan and Roche (1997); Sweetman (1976, 1985, 1987); Stout, G. (1991).
135 Harbison (1973); Cooney and Grogan (1994).
136 For example Mallory and Hartwell (1997, 23); Moore and Woodman (1992, 13–15).
137 Sherratt (1981).
138 Smith, A.G. (1975); Edwards (1985); Mitchell and Ryan (1997, 202–9).
139 Herity (1981); O'Connell (1986).
140 Caulfield (1978).
141 Lynch (1981).
142 Mitchell (1989).
143 See Condit (1990).
144 Grogan (1988); Cooney and Grogan (1994).
145 Hodges (1958); Mallory and McNeill (1991).
146 Pollock and Waterman (1964).
147 O'Sullivan, Aidan (1996b).
148 Doody (1997).
149 Cooney and Grogan (1994, 99).
150 Mount (1997); Walsh, P. (1993); Gibbons and Higgins (1988).
151 See Mount (1995, 1997).
152 Moore (1995).
153 Brindley et al. (1989/90).
154 See discussion in Buckley (1990); O'Sullivan and Condit (1995).
155 Condit (1990).
156 Raftery (1996, 411–14).
157 See discussion in Baillie and Brown (1996); Raftery (1996, 411–17).
158 Mallory (1991, 1994); Warner (1994).
159 Grogan and Condit (1994).
160 Raftery (1976).
161 Waterman (1997).
162 Cotter (1996).
163 Mallory (1995).
164 For example Mallory (1995, 84–5).
165 Moloney et al. (1993).
166 Williams, B. (1978).
167 Herity and Eogan (1977); Mitchell and Ryan (1997, 230–1).
168 Bradley, J. (1991, 1996).
169 Hurl (1995).
170 Doody (1997).

171 Cleary (1995).
172 Grogan *et al.* (1996).
173 See discussion in Cleary (1995); Doody (1997).
174 Cooney and Grogan (1994).
175 Lynn (1977).
176 For example Woodman (1992a); Baillie (1995b); Mitchell and Ryan (1997).
177 Mitchell and Ryan (1997, 233).
178 For example Weir (1994, 1995).
179 Molloy (1997).
180 Eogan (1983).
181 For example Waddell (1992).
182 Eogan (1974); Cooney and Grogan (1994).
183 Grogan *et al.* (1996).
184 Cooney and Grogan (1994); Mitchell and Ryan (1997, 225).
185 Koch (1991); Mallory and McNeill (1991); Waddell (1995).
186 Raftery (1994).
187 For example Raftery (1983, 1984).
188 Raftery (1994).
189 For example see discussion in Harbison (1988, 168–72); Cooney and Grogan (1991); Raftery (1994); Waddell (1995).
190 Waterman (1997).
191 Cooney and Grogan (1991); Mallory (1994).
192 Raftery (1981); O'Brien, E. (1990).
193 See discussion in Cooney and Grogan (1994); Raftery (1994).
194 See discussion in Caulfield (1981); Raftery (1994).
195 Raftery (1994, 59–60).
196 Raftery (1994, Chapter 3).
197 Condit (1992, 1997).
198 Grogan *et al.* (1996, Figure 19).
199 Waterman (1997).
200 Newman (1997).
201 Wailes (1976, 1990).
202 Lynn (1991/2); Baillie (1988); Waterman (1997).
203 Walsh, A. (1987).
204 Condit and Buckley (1989).
205 Doody and Masterson (1996).
206 Raftery (1996).
207 Mallory and Hartwell (1997, 27–8).
208 Walsh, G. (1995).
209 See discussion in Caulfield (1981); Lynn (1983); Edwards, N. (1990); Stout, M. (1997).
210 Lynn (1983).
211 See also discussion in Mytum (1991).
212 Caulfield (1977, 1981); for macroscopic plant remains see Monk (1985/6).
213 Raftery (1994, 121–7); Mitchell and Ryan (1997, 246).
214 O'Sullivan, Aidan (1996c, 15).
215 See site list in Warner *et al.* (1990).
216 See discussion in Cooney and Grogan (1994).
217 For example see Cooney (1993).
218 Bateson (1973, 1976).
219 Raftery (1981, 1994); Bourke (1989); O'Brien, E. (1990).
220 Mytum (1991); Raftery (1994).

221 Smyth (1993); Whelan (1994); but see Aalen *et al.* (1997) for a more detailed treatment.
222 MacDonagh (1980, 2).
223 Graham and Proudfoot (1993, 5).
224 See Bhreathnach (1995); Newman (1997).
225 For example Bradley, R. and Chapman (1984).
226 For example see Clarke *et al.* (1985).
227 Aalen (1983).

References

Aalen, F.H.A. (1983) 'Perspectives on the Irish landscape in prehistory and history', in T. Reeves-Smith and F. Hamond (eds) *Landscape Archaeology in Ireland*, Oxford: BAR Brit. Ser.116, 357–77.

Aalen, F.H.A., Whelan, K. and Stout, M. (1997) *Atlas of the Irish Rural Landscape*, Cork: Cork University Press.

Anderson, E. (1993) 'The Mesolithic: fishing for answers', in E. Shee Twohig and M. Ronayne (eds), *Past Perceptions: The Prehistoric Archaeology of South-West Ireland*, Cork: Cork University Press, 16–24.

Anon. (1992) *The Discovery Programme: Strategies and Questions*, Dublin: The Discovery Programme.

ApSimon, A.M. (1969) 'The Earlier Bronze Age in the North of Ireland', *Ulster Journal of Archaeology* 3rd Ser. 32: 28–72.

Baillie, M.G.L. (1988) 'Dating of the timbers from Navan Fort and Dorsey, Co. Armagh', *Emania* 4: 37–42.

Baillie, M.G.L. (1995a) *A Slice Through Time: Dendrochronology and Precision Dating*, London: Batsford.

Baillie, M.G.L. (1995b) 'Dendrochronology and the chronology of the Irish Bronze Age', in J. Waddell and E. Shee Twohig (eds), *Ireland in the Bronze Age*, Dublin: The Stationery Office, 30–7.

Baillie, M.G.L. and Brown, D.M. (1996) 'Dendrochronology of Irish bog trackways', in B. Raftery (ed.), *Trackway Excavations in the Mountdillon Bogs, Co. Longford 1985–1991*, Dublin: Irish Archaeological Wetland Unit Transactions 3, 395–402.

Barker, G. (1985) *Prehistoric Farming in Europe*, Cambridge: Cambridge University Press.

Barrett, J. (1994) *Fragments from Antiquity*, Oxford: Blackwell.

Bateson, J.D. (1973) 'Roman material from Ireland: a re-consideration', *Proceedings of the Royal Irish Academy* 73C: 21–97.

Bateson, J.D. (1976) 'Further finds of Roman material from Ireland', *Proceedings of the Royal Irish Academy* 76C:171–80.

Bennett, I. (ed.) (1996) *Excavations 1995*, Dublin: Wordwell.

Bergh, S. (1995) *Landscape of the Monuments: A Study of the Passage Tombs in the Cúil Irra Region, Co. Sligo, Ireland*, Stockholm: Riksantikvarieämbetet Arkeoloeiska under Sökninar.

Bhreathnach, E. (1995) *Tara: A Select Bibliography*, Dublin: Discovery Programme/Royal Irish Academy, Discovery Programme Monographs 1.

Binford, L.R. (1980) 'Willow smoke and dog's tails: hunter-gatherer settlement systems and archaeological site form', *American Antiquity* 45: 4–20.

Binford, L.R. (1983) *In Pursuit of the Past*, London: Thames and Hudson.

Bintcliff, J. (ed.) (1991) *The Annales School and Archaeology*, Leicester: Leicester University Press.

Boserup, E. (1965) *The Conditions of Agricultural Growth*, London: Allen and Unwin.

Bourke, E. (1989) 'Stoneyford, a first-century Roman burial from Ireland', *Archaeology Ireland* 3, 2: 56–7.

Bradley, J. (1991) 'Excavations at Moynagh Lough, County Meath', *Journal of the Royal Society of Antiquaries of Ireland* 121: 5–26.

Bradley, J. (1996) 'Moynagh Lough in the Bronze Age', *Archaeology Ireland* 10, 1: 24–6.

Bradley, R.J. and Chapman, R.W. (1984) 'Passage graves in the European Neolithic: a theory of converging evolution', in G. Burenhult, *The Archaeology of Carrowmore: Environmental Archaeology and the Megalithic Tradition at Carrowmore, Co. Sligo, Ireland*, Stockholm: Institute of Archaeology, University of Stockholm, Theses and Papers in North-European Archaeology 14, 348–56.

Braudel, F. (1972) *The Mediterranean and the Mediterranean World in the age of Phillip II* (revised edition: trans: S. Reynolds), London: Collins.

Briggs, C.S. (1981) 'Some problems of survey and study in prehistoric Ireland: highland and lowland distributions in central Ulster, 3600–1800 BC', in D. Spratt and C. Burgess (eds) *Upland Settlement in Britain*, Oxford: BAR Brit. Ser. 143, 351–63.

Brindley, A.L. (1995) 'Radiocarbon chronology and the Bronze Age', in J. Waddell and E. Shee Twohig (eds) *Ireland in the Bronze Age*, Dublin: The Stationery Office, 4–13.

Brindley, A.L. and Lanting, J.N. (1989/90) 'Radiocarbon dates for Neolithic single burials', *Journal of Irish Archaeology* 5: 1–7.

Brindley, A.L., Lanting, J.N. and Mook, W.G. (1989/90) 'Radiocarbon dates from Irish fulachta fiadh and other burnt mounds', *Journal of Irish Archeology* 5: 25–33.

Brodie, N. (1994) *The Neolithic–Bronze Age Transition in Britain*, Oxford: Tempus Reparatum. BAR Brit. Ser. 238.

Buckley, V.M. (ed.) (1990) *Burnt Offerings: International Contributions to Burnt Mound Archaeology*, Dublin: Wordwell.

Buckley, V.M. and Sweetman P.D. (1991) *Archaeological Survey of County Louth*, Dublin: Stationery Office.

Burenhult, G. (1984) *The Archaeology of Carrowmore: Environmental Archaeology and the Megalithic Tradition at Carrowmore, Co. Sligo, Ireland*, Stockholm: Institute of Archaeology, University of Stockholm, Theses and Papers in North-European Archaeology 14.

Burgess, C.B. and Shennan, S. (1976) 'The Beaker phenomenon: some suggestions', in C. Burgess and R. Miket (eds), *Settlement and Economy in the Third and Second Millennia BC*, Oxford: BAR Brit. Ser. 33, 309–31.

Case, H.J. (1969a) 'Settlement patterns in the north Irish Neolithic', *Ulster Journal of Archaeology* 3rd Ser. 32: 3–27.

Case, H.J. (1969b) 'Neolithic explanations', *Antiquity* 43: 176–86.

Caulfield, S. (1977) 'The beehive quern in Ireland', *Journal of the Royal Society of Antiquaries of Ireland* 107: 104–38.

Caulfield, S. (1978) 'Neolithic fields: the Irish evidence', in H.C Bowen and P.J. Fowler (eds), *Early Land Allotment*, Oxford: BAR Brit. Ser. 48, 137–44.

Caulfield, S. (1981) 'Some Celtic problems in the Irish Iron Age', in D. Ó Corráin (ed.), *Irish Antiquity: Essays and Studies presented to Professor M J O'Kelly*, Cork: Tower Books, 205–15.

Caulfield, S. (1983) 'The Neolithic settlement of north Connaught', in T. Reeves-Smith and F. Hamond (eds), *Landscape Archaeology in Ireland*, Oxford: BAR Brit. Ser. 116, 195–215.

Caulfield, S. (1988) *Céide Fields and Belderrig Guide*, Killala: Morrigan.

Champion, T. C. (1991) 'Theoretical archaeology in Britain', in I. Hodder (ed.), *Archaeological Theory in Europe: The Last Three Decades*, London: Routledge, 129–60.

Clarke, D.V., Cowie, T.G. and Foxon, A. (1985) *Symbols of Power at the Time of Stonehenge*, Edinburgh: HMSO.

Cleary, R.M. (1995) 'Later Bronze Age settlement and prehistoric burials, Lough Gur, Co. Limerick', *Proceedings of the Royal Irish Academy* 95C: 1–92.

Cleary, R.M., Hurley, M.F. and Twohig, E.A. (eds) (1987) *Archaeological Excavations on the Cork-Dublin Gas Pipeline (1981–82)*, Cork: UCC, Archaeological Studies No 1.

Condit, T. (1990) 'Preliminary observations on the distribution of fulachta fiadh in County Kilkenny', in V.M. Buckley (ed.), *Burnt Offerings: International Contributions to Burnt Mound Archaeology*, Dublin: Wordwell, 18–23.

Condit, T. (1992) 'Ireland's hillfort capital', *Archaeology Ireland* 6, 3: 16–20.

Condit, T. (1997) *Ireland's Archaeology from the Air*, Dublin: Town House.

Condit, T. and Buckley, V.M. (1989) 'The "Doon" of Drumsna – gateways to Connacht', *Emania* 6: 12–14.

Condit, T. and Cooney, G. (eds) (1997) *Brú na Bóinne*, Dublin: Archaeology Ireland.

Condit, T. and Gibbons, M. (1990) 'A bird's eye view of our past', *Technology Ireland* 2, 5: 50–4.

Cooney, G. (1983) 'Megalithic tombs in their environmental setting, a settlement perspective', in T. Reeves-Smith and F. Hamond (eds), *Landscape Archaeology in Ireland*, Oxford: BAR Brit. Ser. 116, 179–94.

Cooney, G. (1990a) 'The Mount Oriel Project: an introduction', *County Louth Archaeological and Historical Journal* 22, 2: 125–33.

Cooney, G. (1990b) 'The place of megalithic tomb cemeteries in Ireland', *Antiquity* 64: 741–53.

Cooney, G. (1991) 'Irish Neolithic landscapes and landuse systems: the implications of field systems', *Rural History* 2, 2: 123–39.

Cooney, G. (1993) 'A sense of place in Irish prehistory', *Antiquity* 67: 632–41.

Cooney, G. (1995) 'Theory and practice in Irish archaeology', in P. Ucko (ed.), *Theory in Archaeology: A World Perspective*, London: Routledge, 263–77.

Cooney, G. (1996) 'Building the future on the past: archaeology and the construction of national identity in Ireland', in M. Díaz-Andreu and T. Champion (eds) *Nationalism and Archaeology in Europe*, London: UCL Press, 146–63.

Cooney, G. (1997b) 'Images of settlement and the landscape in the Neolithic', in P. Topping (ed.) *Neolithic Landscapes*, Oxford: Oxbow Monograph 86, 23–31.

Cooney, G. and Grogan, E. (1991) 'An archaeological solution to the "Irish" problem?', *Emania* 9: 33–43.

Cooney, G. and Grogan, E. (1994) *Irish Prehistory: A Social Perspective*, Dublin: Wordwell.

Cooney, G. and Mandal, S. (1995) 'Getting to the core of the problem: petrological results from the Irish Stone Axe Project', *Antiquity* 69: 969–80.

Cotter, C. (1996) 'Western Stone Fort Project: interim report', *Discovery Programme Reports* 4: 1–14.

Crothers, N. (1996) ' Ballyharry's Game…', *Archaeology Ireland* 10, 4: 12–14.

Cuppage, J. (1986) *Archaeological Survey of the Dingle Peninsula*, Ballyferriter: Oidreacht Chorca Dhuibhne.

Darvill, T. (1979) 'Court cairns, passage graves and social change in Ireland', *Man* 14: 311–27.

Delaney, T. (1972) *Excavations 1971*, Belfast: AYIA.

Dillon, F. (1990) 'An analysis of two lithic collections', unpublished MA thesis, University College Dublin.

Doody, M. (1987a) 'Ballyveelish, Co. Tipperary', in R.M. Cleary, M.F. Hurley and E.A. Twohig (eds), *Archaeological Excavations on the Cork–Dublin Gas Pipeline (1981–82)*, Cork: University College Cork, Archaeological Studies No. 1, 9–35.

Doody, M. (1987b) 'Late Bronze Age huts at Curraghatoor, Co.Tipperary', in R.M. Cleary, M.F. Hurley and E.A. Twohig (eds), *Archaeological Excavations on the Cork–Dublin Gas Pipeline (1981–82)*, Cork: University College Cork, Archaeological Studies No. 1, 36–42.

Doody, M. (1993) 'Bronze Age settlement', in E. Shee Twohig and M. Ronayne (eds), *Past Perceptions: The Prehistoric Archaeology of South-West Ireland*, Cork: Cork University Press, 93–100.

Doody, M. (1997) 'Bronze Age settlements in Co. Tipperary: fifteen years of research', *Tipperary Historical Journal* 1997: 94–106.

Doody, M. and Masterson, B. (1996) 'The Claidh Dubh: interim report', *Discovery Programme Reports* 4, 22–5.

Edmonds, M. (1995) *Stone Tools and Society*, London: Batsford.

Edwards, K. J. (1985) 'The anthropogenic factor in vegetational history', in K.J. Edwards and W.P. Warren (eds), *The Quaternary History of Ireland*, London: Academic Press, 187–220.

Edwards, K.J. and Hirons, K.R. (1984) 'Cereal pollen grains in pre-elm decline deposits: implications for the earliest agriculture in Britain and Ireland', *Journal of Archaeological Science* 11: 71–80.

Edwards, N. (1990) *The Archaeology of Early Medieval Ireland*, London: Batsford.

Eogan, G. (1964) 'The Later Bronze Age in Ireland in the light of recent research', *Proceedings of the Prehistoric Society* 14: 268–351.

Eogan, G. (1974) 'Regionale gruppierungen in der Spätbronzezeit Irlands', *Archaologisches Korrespondenzblatt* 4, 3: 19–27.

Eogan, G. (1983) *Hoards of the Irish Later Bronze Age*, Dublin: University College, Dublin.

Eogan, G. (1984) *Excavations at Knowth 1*, Dublin: Royal Irish Academy Monographs in Archaeology.

Eogan, G. (1986) *Knowth and the Passage Tombs of Ireland*, London: Thames and Hudson.

Eogan, G. (1991) 'Prehistoric and early historic culture change at Brugh na Bóinne', *Proceedings of the Royal Irish Academy* 91C: 105–32.

Eogan, G. (1997) *The Discovery Programme: Initiation, Consolidation and Development*, Amsterdam: Negentiende Kroon-Voordracht.

Eogan, G. and Roche, H. (1997) *Excavations at Knowth 2*, Dublin: Royal Irish Academy Monographs in Archaeology.

Evans, E.E. (1981) *The Personality of Ireland*, 2nd edition, Belfast: Blackstaff Press.

Gibbons, M. and Higgins, J. (1988) 'Connemara's emerging prehistory', *Archaeology Ireland* 2, 2: 63–6.

Gibson, A.M. and Simpson, D.D.A. (1987) 'Lyles Hill, Co. Antrim', *Archaeology Ireland* 1, 2: 72–5.

Gowen, M. (1988) *Three Irish Gas Pipelines: New Archaeological Evidence in Munster*, Dublin: Wordwell.

Gowen, M. and Tarbett, C. (1988) 'A third season at Tankardstown', *Archaeology Ireland* 2, 4: 156.

Graham, B.J. and Proudfoot, L.J. (eds) (1993) *An Historical Geography of Ireland*, London: Academic Press.

Green, S.W. and Zvelebil, M. (1990) 'The Mesolithic colonisation and agricultural transition of south-east Ireland', *Proceedings of the Prehistoric Society* 56: 57–88.

Groenman-van Waateringe, W. (1983) 'The early agricultural utilisation of the Irish landscape: the last word on the elm decline?', in T. Reeves-Smith and F. Hamond (eds), *Landscape Archaeology in Ireland*, 217–32, Oxford: BAR Brit. Ser. 116.

Grogan, E. (1988) 'The pipeline sites and the prehistory of the Limerick area', in M. Gowen (ed.), *Three Irish Gas Pipelines: New Archaeological Evidence in Munster*, 148–57. Dublin: Wordwell.

Grogan, E. (1996) 'Neolithic houses in Ireland', in T. Darvill and J. Thomas (eds), *Neolithic Houses in Northwest Europe and Beyond*, Oxford: Oxbow Monograph 57, 41–60.

Grogan, E. and Condit, T. (1994) 'New hillfort date gives clue to Late Bronze Age', *Archaeology Ireland* 8, 2: 7.

Grogan, E. and Eogan, G. (1987) 'Lough Gur excavations by Séan P. Ó Ríordáin: further Neolithic and Beaker habitations on Knockadoon', *Proceedings of the Royal Irish Academy* 87C: 299–506.

Grogan, E., Condit, T., O'Carroll, F., O'Sullivan, A. and Daly, A. (1996) 'Tracing the late prehistoric landscape in North Munster', *Discovery Programme Reports* 4: 26–46.

Halpin, E. (1995) 'Excavations at Newtown, Co. Meath', in E. Grogan and C. Mount (eds), *Annus Archaeologiae*, Dublin: OIA, 45–54.

Harbison, P. (1973) 'The Earlier Bronze Age in Ireland', *Journal of the Royal Society of Antiquaries in Ireland* 103: 93–153.

Harbison, P. (1988) *Pre-Christian Ireland*, London: Thames and Hudson.

Harrison, R.J. (1980) *The Beaker Folk*, London: Thames and Hudson.

Hartwell, B. (1991) 'Ballynahatty – a prehistoric ceremonial centre', *Archaeology Ireland* 5, 4: 12–15.

Hartwell, B. (1994) 'Late Neolithic ceremonies', *Archaeology Ireland* 8, 4: 10–13.

Herity, M. (1981) 'A Bronze Age farmstead at Glenree, Co. Mayo', *Popular Archaeology* 2, 9: 36–7.

Herity, M. (1991) 'Phases of the Irish Neolithic', *Journal of Indo-European Studies* 19: 29–47.

Herity, M. and Eogan, G. (1977) *Ireland in Prehistory*, London: Routledge and Kegan Paul.

Hodder, I. (1987) *Reading the Past*, Cambridge: Cambridge University Press.

Hodder, I. (1990) *The Domestication of Europe*, Oxford: Blackwell.

Hodder, I. (1992) *Theory and Practice in Archaeology*, London: Routledge.

Hodges, H.W.M. (1958) 'A hunting camp at Cullyhanna Lough, near Newtown Hamilton, County Armagh', *Ulster Journal of Archaeology* 3rd Ser. 21: 7–13.

Hurl, D. (1995) 'Killymoon – new light on the Late Bronze Age', *Archaeology Ireland* 9, 4: 24–7.

Knapp, A.B. (ed.) (1992) *Archaeology, Annales, and Ethnohistory*, Cambridge: Cambridge University Press.

Koch, J.T. (1991) 'Eriu, Alba and Letha: when was a language ancestral to Gaelic first spoken in Ireland?', *Emania* 9: 17–27.

Lacy, B. (1983) *Archaeological Survey of County Donegal*, Lifford: Donegal County Council.

Lynch, A. (1981) *Man and Environment in South-west Ireland, 4000 BC–AD 800*, Oxford: BAR Brit. Ser. 85.

Lynn, C. J. (1977) 'Trial excavations of the King's Stables, Tray Townland, County Armagh', *Ulster Journal of Archaeology* 3rd Ser. 40: 42–62.

Lynn, C.J. (1978) 'Early Christian period domestic structures: a change from round to rectangular', *Irish Archaeological Research Forum* 5: 29–45.

Lynn, C.J. (1983) 'Some "early" ring-forts and crannogs', *Journal of Irish Archaeology* 1: 47–58.

Lynn, C.J. (1991/92) 'Excavations at the Dorsey, County Armagh, 1977', *Ulster Journal of Archaeology* 3rd Ser. 54/55: 61–77.

Lynn, C.J. (1994) 'Houses in rural Ireland, AD 500–1000', *Ulster Journal of Archaeology* 3rd Ser. 57: 81–94.

MacDonagh, O. (1983) *States of Mind: A Study of Anglo-Irish Relations, 1780–1920*, London: Allen and Unwin.

McMann, J. (1994) 'Forms of power: dimensions of an Irish megalithic landscape', *Antiquity* 68: 525–44.

Mallory, J.P. (1991) 'Excavations at Haughey's Fort: 1989–1990', *Emania* 8: 10–26.

Mallory, J.P. (1991/2) 'A neolithic settlement at Bay Farm II, Carnlough, Co. Antrim', *Ulster Journal of Archaeology* 3rd Ser. 54/54: 3–12.

Mallory, J.P. (1994) 'The other twin: Haughey's Fort', in J.P. Mallory and G. Stockman (eds), *Ulidia*, Belfast: December Publications, 187–92.

Mallory, J.P. (1995) 'Haughey's Fort and the Navan complex in the Late Bronze Age', in J. Waddell and E. Shee Twohig (eds), *Ireland in the Bronze Age*, Dublin: Stationery Office, 73–86.

Mallory, J.P. and Hartwell, B. (1984) 'Donegore Hill', *Current Archaeology* 8, 9: 271–5.

Mallory, J.P. and Hartwell, B. (1997) 'Down in prehistory', in L. Proudfoot (ed.), *Down History and Society*, Dublin: Geography Publications, 1–32.

Mallory, J.P and McNeill, T.E. (1991) *The Archaeology of Ulster*, Belfast: Institute of Irish Studies, Queen's University Belfast.

Manning, C. (1985) 'A Neolithic burial mound at Ashleypark, Co. Tipperary', *Proceedings of the Royal Irish Academy* 85C: 61–100.

Mitchell, G.F. (1970) 'Some chronological implications of the Irish Mesolithic', *Ulster Journal of Archaeology* 3rd Ser. 33: 3–14.

Mitchell, G.F. (1972) 'Some ultimate Larnian sites at Lough Derravaragh, Co. Westmeath', *Journal of the Royal Society of Antiquaries in Ireland* 102: 160–73.

Mitchell, G.F. (1989) *Man And Environment in Valencia Island*, Dublin: Royal Irish Academy.

Mitchell, G.F. and Ryan, M. (1997) *Reading the Irish Landscape*, Dublin: Country House.

Molloy, K. (1997) 'Prehistoric farming at Mooghaun: a new pollen diagram from Mooghaun', *Archaeology Ireland* 11, 3: 22–6.

Molloy, K. and O'Connell, M. (1987) 'The nature of the vegetational changes at about 5000 BP with particular reference to the elm decline: fresh evidence from Connemara, Western Ireland', *New Phytologist* 106: 203–20.

Molloy, K. and O'Connell, M. (1995) 'Palaeoecological investigations towards the reconstruction of environment and land-use changes during prehistory at Céide Fields, western Ireland', *Probleme der Küstenforschung im südlichen Nordseegebiet* 23: 187–225.

Moloney, A., Jennings, D., Keane, M. and McDermott, C. (1993) *Excavations at Clonfinlough, County Offaly*, Dublin: Irish Archaeological Wetland Unit Transactions 2.

Monk, M.A. (1985/6) 'Evidence from macroscopic plant remains for crop husbandry in prehistoric and Early Historic Ireland: a review', *Journal of Irish Archaeology* 3: 31–6.

Monk, M.A. (1993) 'People and environment: in search of the farmers', in E. Shee Twohig and M. Ronayne (eds), *Past Perceptions: The Prehistoric Archaeology of South-West Ireland*, Cork: Cork University Press, 35–52.

Moore, M.A. (1995) 'A Bronze Age settlement and ritual centre in the Monavullagh Mountains, County Waterford, Ireland', *Proceedings of the Prehistoric Society* 61: 191–243.

Moore, M.A. and Woodman, P.C. (1992) 'The prehistory of Waterford', in W. Nolan and T.P. Power (eds), *Waterford History and Society*, Dublin: Geography Publications, 1–26.

Mount, C. (1994) 'Aspects of ritual deposition in the Late Neolithic and Beaker periods at Newgrange, Co. Meath', *Proceedings of the Prehistoric Society* 60: 433–43.

Mount, C. (1995) 'New research on Irish Early Bronze Age cemeteries', in J. Waddell and E. Shee Twohig (eds), *Ireland in the Bronze Age*, Dublin: The Stationery Office, 97–112.

Mount, C. (1996) 'The environmental siting of Neolithic and Bronze Age monuments in the Bricklieve and Moytirra Uplands, Co. Sligo', *Journal of Irish Archaeology* 7: 1–11.

Mount, C. (1997) 'Early Bronze Age burial in south-east Ireland in the light of recent research', *Proceedings of the Royal Irish Academy* 97C: 101–93.

Movius, H.L. (1942) *The Irish Stone Age: Its Chronology, Development and Relationships*, Cambridge: Cambridge University Press.

Mytum, H. (1992) *The Origins of Early Christian Ireland*, London: Routledge.

Newman, C. (1997) *Tara: An Archaeological Survey*, Dublin: Discovery Programme/Royal Irish Academy, Discovery Programme Monographs 2.

O'Brien, E. (1990) 'Iron Age burial practices in Leinster: continuity and change', *Emania* 7: 37–42.

O'Brien, W. (1990) 'Prehistoric copper mining in south-west Ireland: the Mount Gabriel-type mines', *Proceedings of the Prehistoric Society* 56: 269–90.

O'Brien, W. (1993) 'Aspects of wedge tomb chronology', in E. Shee Twohig and M. Ronayne (eds), *Past Perceptions: The Prehistoric Archaeology of South-West Ireland*, Cork: Cork University Press, 63–74.

O'Brien, W. (1994) *Mount Gabriel. Bronze Age Mining in Ireland*, Galway: Galway University Press.

O'Brien, W. (1995a) 'Ross Island and the origins of Irish-British metallurgy', in J. Waddell and E. Shee Twohig (eds) *Ireland in the Bronze Age*, Dublin: The Stationery Office, 38–48.

O'Brien, W. (1995b) 'Ross Island – the beginning', *Archaeology Ireland* 9, 1: 24–7.

O'Connell, M. (1986) 'Reconstruction of local landscape development in the post-Atlantic based on palaeoecological investigations at Carrownaglogh prehistoric field system, County Mayo, Ireland', *Review of Palaeobotany and Palynology* 49: 117–76.

O'Connell, M. (1987) 'Early cereal-type pollen records from Connemara, western Ireland and their possible significance', *Pollen et Spores* 29: 207–24.

O'Kelly, M.J. (1982) *Newgrange, Archaeology, Art and Legend*, London: Thames and Hudson.

O'Kelly, M. J. (1989) *Early Ireland: An Introduction*, Cambridge: Cambridge University Press.

O'Kelly, M.J., Cleary, R.M. and Lehane, D. (1983) *Newgrange, Co. Meath, Ireland: The Late Neolithic/Beaker Period Settlement*, Oxford: BAR, Int. Ser. 190.

Ó Nualláin, S. (1972) 'A Neolithic House at Ballyglass near Ballycastle, Co. Mayo' in *Journal of the Royal Society of Ireland* 102: 49–57.

Ó Nualláin, S. (1989) *Survey of the Megalithic Tombs of Ireland, 5, Co. Sligo*, Dublin: The Stationery Office.

Ó Ríordáin, S.P. (1954) 'Lough Gur excavations: Neolithic and Bronze Age houses on Knockadoon', *Proceedings of the Royal Irish Academy* 56 C: 297–459.

O'Sullivan, A. (1996a) 'Marshlanders', *Archaeology Ireland* 9, 1: 8–11.

O'Sullivan, A. (1996b) 'Late Bronze Age intertidal discoveries on North Munster estuaries', *Discovery Programme Reports* 4: 63–74.

O'Sullivan, A. (1996c) 'Exploring ancient woodlands', *Archaeology Ireland* 10, 2: 14–15.

O'Sullivan, A. (1997) 'Last foragers or first farmers?', *Archaeology Ireland* 11, 2: 14–16.

O'Sullivan, A. and Condit, T. (1995) 'Late Bronze Age settlement and agriculture by the marshlands of the upper Fergus estuary, Co. Clare', *The Other Clare* 19: 5–9.

O'Sullivan, A. and Sheehan, J. (1996) *The Iveragh Peninsula: An Archaeological Inventory of South Kerry*, Cork: Cork University Press.

Patton, M. (1996) *Islands in Time: Island sociogeography and Mediterranean Prehistory*, London: Routledge.

Pilcher, J.R., Smith, A.G., Pearson, G.W. and Crowder, A. (1971) 'Land clearance in the Irish Neolithic: new evidence and interpretation', *Science* 172: 560–2.

Pollock, A.J. and Waterman, D.M. (1964) 'A Bronze Age habitation site at Downpatrick', *Ulster Journal of Archaeology* 3rd Ser. 27: 31–58.

Preece, R.C., Coxon, P. and Robinson, J.E. (1986) 'New biostratigraphic evidence of the post-glacial colonization of Ireland and for Mesolithic forest disturbance', *Journal of Biogeography* 13: 487–509.

Preucel, R.W. and Hodder, I. (eds) (1996) *Contemporary Archaeology in Theory: A Reader*, Oxford: Blackwell.

Price, T.D. (1987) 'The Mesolithic of Western Europe', *Journal of World Prehistory* 1: 225–305.

Raftery, B. (1976) 'Rathgall and Irish hillfort problems', in D.W. Harding (ed.), *Hillforts – Later Prehistoric Earthworks in Britain and Ireland*, London: Academic Press, 339–57.

Raftery, B. (1981) 'Iron Age burials in Ireland', in D. Ó Corráin (ed.), *Irish Antiquity: Essays and Studies Presented to Professor M.J. O'Kelly*, Cork: Tower Books, 173–204.

Raftery, B. (1983) *A Catalogue of Irish Iron Age Antiquities*, Marburg: Veröffentlichung des Vorgeschichtlichen Seminars Marburg, Sonderband 1.

Raftery, B. (1984) *La Tène in Ireland: Problems of Origin and Chronology*, Marburg: Veröffentlichung des Vorgeschichtlichen Seminars Marburg, Sonderband 2.

Raftery, B. (1994) *Pagan Celtic Ireland: The Enigma of the Irish Iron Age*, London, Thames and Hudson.

Raftery, B. (1996) *Trackway Excavations in the Mountdillon Bogs, Co. Longford 1985–1991*, Dublin: Irish Archaeological Wetland Unit Transactions 3.

Rowley-Conwy, P. (1981) 'Slash and burn in the temperate European Neolithic', in R. Mercer (ed.), *Farming Practice in British Prehistory*, Edinburgh: Edinburgh University Press, 85–96

Ryan, M. (1980) 'An Early Mesolithic site in the Irish midlands', *Antiquity* 54: 46–7.

Ryan, M. (1981) 'Poulawack, Co. Clare: the affinities of the central burial structure', in D. Ó Corráin (ed.), *Irish Antiquity: Essays and Studies presented to Professor M.J. O'Kelly*, Cork: Tower Books, 135–46.

Shanks, M. and Tilley, C. (1987a) *Re-Constructing Archaeology: Theory and Practice*, Cambrige: Cambridge University Press.

Shanks, M. and Tilley, C. (1987b) *Social Theory and Archaeology*, London: Polity Press.

Sharples, N. (1985) 'Individual and community: the changing role of megaliths in the Orcadian Neolithic', *Proceedings of the Prehistoric Society* 51: 59–74.

Sharples, N. (1992) 'Aspects of regionalisation in the Scottish Neolithic' in N. Sharples and A. Sheridan (eds), *Vessels for the Ancestors*, Edinburgh: Edinburgh University Press, 322–31.

Shee Twohig, E. (1990) *Irish Megalithic Tombs*, Princes Risborough: Shire.

Sheridan, A. (1985/6) 'Megaliths and megalomania: an account, and interpretation, of the development of passage tombs in Ireland', *Journal of Irish Archaeology* 3: 17–30.

Sheridan, A. (1986) 'Porcellanite artifacts: a new survey', *Ulster Journal of Archaeology* 3rd Ser. 49: 19–32.

Sheridan, A. (1995) 'Irish Neolithic pottery, the story in 1995', in I. Kinnes and G. Varndell (eds) *Unbaked Urns of Rudely Shape*, Oxford: Oxbow Monograph 65, 5–21.

Sheridan, A., Cooney, G. and Grogan, E. (1992) 'Stone axe studies in Ireland', *Proceedings of the Prehistoric Society* 58: 389–416.

Sherratt, A. (1981) 'Plough and pastoralism: aspects of the secondary products revolution', in I. Hodder, G. Isaac and N. Hammond (eds), *Pattern of the Past: Studies in Honour of David Clarke*, Cambridge: Cambridge University Press, 261–305.

Simpson, D.D.A. (1995) 'The Neolithic settlement at Ballygalley, Co. Antrim', in E. Grogan and C. Mount (eds), *Annus Archaeologiae*, Dublin: OIA, 37–44.

Simpson, D.D.A. (1996) 'The Ballygalley houses, Co. Antrim, Ireland', in T. Darvill and J. Thomas (eds), *Neolithic Houses in Northwest Europe and Beyond*, Oxford: Oxbow Monograph 57: 123–32.

Smith, A.G. (1975) 'Neolithic and Bronze Age landscape changes in Northern Ireland', in J.G. Evans, S. Limbrey and H. Cleere (eds), *The Effects of Man on the Landscape: The Highland Zone*, London: Council for British Archaeology Research Report 11, 64–74.

Smith, C. (1992) *Late Stone Age Hunters of the British Isles*, London: Routledge.

Smyth, W.J. (1993) 'The making of Ireland: agendas and perspectives in cultural geography', in B.J Graham and L.J. Proudfoot (eds), *An Historical Geography of Ireland*, London: Academic Press, 399–438.

Stout, G. (1984) *Archaeological Survey of the Barony of Ikerrin*, Roscrea: Roscrea Heritage Society/AnCO.

Stout, G. (1991) 'Embanked enclosures of the Boyne region', *Proceedings of the Royal Irish Academy* 91C: 245–84.

Stout, M. (1997) *The Irish Ringfort*, Dublin: Four Courts Press/GSIHS.

Sweetman, P.D. (1976) 'An earthen enclosure at Monknewtown, Slane, Co. Meath', *Proceedings of the Royal Irish Academy* 76C: 25–72.

Sweetman, P.D. (1985) 'A Late Neolithic/Early Bronze Age pit circle at Newgrange, Co. Meath', *Proceedings of the Royal Irish Academy* 85C: 195–221.

Sweetman, P.D. (1987) 'Excavation of a Late Neolithic/Early Bronze Age site at Newgrange, Co. Meath', *Proceedings of the Royal Irish Academy* 87C: 283–98.

Synnott, P. (1996) 'Geographical Information Systems: an archaeological application', *Discovery Programme Reports* 4: 73–84.

Taylor, J.J. (1994) 'The First Golden Age of Europe was in Ireland and Britain', *Ulster Journal of Archaeology* 3rd Ser. 57: 37–60.

Thomas, J. (1988) 'Neolithic explanations revisited: the Mesolithic–Neolithic transition in Britain and south Scandinavia', *Proceedings of the Prehistoric Society* 54: 59–66.

Thomas, J. (1991) *Rethinking the Neolithic*, Cambridge: Cambridge University Press.

Thomas, J. (1996) *Time, Culture and Identity: An Interpretive Archaeology*, London: Routledge.

Toal, C. (1995) *North Kerry Archaeological Survey*, Dingle: Brandon/FAS.

Van Wijngaarden-Bakker, L.H. (1974) 'The animal remains from the Beaker settlement at Newgrange, Co. Meath: first report', *Proceedings of the Royal Irish Academy* 74C: 313–83.

Van Wijngaarden-Bakker, L.H. (1986) 'The animal remains from the Beaker settlement at Newgrange, Co. Meath: final report', *Proceedings of the Royal Irish Academy* 86C: 17–111.

Van Wijngaarden-Bakker, L.H. (1989) 'Faunal remains and the Irish Mesolithic', in C. Bonsall (ed.), *The Mesolithic in Europe*, Edinburgh: John Donald, 125–33.

Waddell, J. (1992) 'Women in ancient Europe', *UCG Women's Studies Centre Review* 1: 29–37.

Waddell, J. (1995) 'Celts, Celticisation and the Irish Bronze Age', in J. Waddell and E. Shee Twohig (eds), *Ireland in the Bronze Age*, Dublin: The Stationery Office, 158–69.

Waddell, J. (1997) 'Ireland's Discovery Programme: progress and prospect', *Antiquity* 71: 513–18.

Waddell, J. (1998) *The Archaeology of Prehistoric Ireland*, Galway: Galway University Press.

Waddell, J. and Shee Twohig, E. (eds) (1995) *Ireland in the Bronze Age*, Dublin: The Stationery Office.

Wailes, B. (1976) 'Dún Ailinne: an interim report', in D.W. Harding (ed.), *Hillforts – Later Prehistoric Earthworks in Britain and Ireland*, London: Academic Press, 319–38.

Wailes, B. (1990) 'Dún Ailinne: a summary excavation report', *Emania* 7: 10–21.

Walsh, A. (1987) 'Excavating the Black Pig's Dyke', *Emania* 3: 4–11.

Walsh, G. (1995) 'Iron Age settlement in Co. Mayo', *Archaeology Ireland* 9, 2: 7–8.

Walsh, P. (1993) 'In circle and row: Bronze Age ceremonial monuments', in E. Shee Twohig and M. Ronayne (eds), *Past Perceptions: The Prehistoric Archaeology of South-West Ireland*, Cork: Cork University Press, 101–13.

Walsh, P. (1997) 'In praise of field-workers: some recent megalithic discoveries in Cork and Kerry', *Archaeology Ireland* 11, 3: 8–12.

Warner, R. (1994) '*Emania* Varia 1', *Emania* 12: 66–72.

Warner, R., Mallory, J. and Baillie, M.G.L. (1990) 'Irish Early Iron Age sites: a provisional map of absolute dated sites', *Emania* 7: 46–50.

Waterman, D.W. (1997) *Excavations at Navan Fort 1961–71*, completed and edited by C.J. Lynn, Belfast: The Stationery Office.

Weir, D. (1994) 'The environment of Emain Macha', in J.P. Mallory and G. Stockman (eds), *Ulidia*, Belfast: December Publications, 171–9.

Weir, D. (1995) 'A palynological study of landscape and agricultural development in County Louth from the second millennium BC to the first millennium AD', *Discovery Programme Reports* 2, 77–126.

Whelan, K. (1994) 'Settlement patterns in the west of Ireland in the pre-Famine period', in T. Collins (ed.), *Decoding the Landscape*, Galway: Centre for Landscape Studies, UCG, 60–78.

Whittle, A. (1988) *Problems in Neolithic Archaeology*, Cambridge: Cambridge University Press.

Whittle, A. (1990) 'Prolegomena to the study of the Mesolithic–Neolithic transition in Britain and Ireland', in D. Cahen and M. Otte (eds), *Rubane et Cardial*, Liège, ERAUL 39: 209–27.

Whittle, A.W.R. (1996) *Europe in the Neolithic: The Creation of New Worlds*, Cambridge: Cambridge University Press.

Williams, B.B. (1978) 'Excavations at Lough Eskragh, Co. Tyrone', *Ulster Journal of Archaeology* 3rd Ser. 41:37–48.

Williams, E. (1989) 'Dating the introduction of food production into Britain and Ireland', *Antiquity* 63: 510–21.

Woodman, P.C. (1973/4) 'Settlement patterns of the Irish Mesolithic', *Ulster Journal of Archaeology* 3rd Ser. 37: 1–16.

Woodman, P.C. (1977) 'Recent excavations at Newferry, Co. Antrim', *Proceedings of the Prehistoric Society* 43: 155–200.

Woodman, P.C. (1978) *The Mesolithic in Ireland*, Oxford: BAR, Brit. Ser. 58.

Woodman, P.C. (1981) 'The post-glacial colonisation of Ireland: the human factors', in D. Ó Corráin (ed.), *Irish Antiquity: Essays and Studies Presented to Professor M.J. O'Kelly*, Cork: Tower Books, 93–100.

Woodman, P.C. (1983) 'The Glencloy Project in perspective', in T. Reeves-Smith and F. Hamond (eds), *Landscape Archaeology in Ireland*, Oxford: BAR, Brit. Ser. 116, 25–34.

Woodman, P.C. (1984) 'The early prehistory of Munster', *Journal of the Cork Historical and Archaeological Society* 89: 1–11.

Woodman, P.C. (1985a) *Excavations at Mount Sandel 1973–77*, Belfast: HMSO.

Woodman, P.C. (1985b) 'Prehistoric settlement and environment', in K.J. Edwards and W.P. Warren (eds), *The Quaternary History of Ireland*, London: Academic Press, 251–78.

Woodman, P.C. (1985c) 'Mobility in the Mesolithic of northwestern Europe: an alternative explanation', in T.D. Price and J.A. Brown (eds), *Prehistoric Hunter-Gatherers: The Emergence of Cultural Complexity*, London: Academic Press, 325–39.

Woodman, P.C. (1986) 'Problems in the colonisation of Ireland', *Ulster Journal of Archaeology* 3rd Ser. 49: 7–17.

Woodman, P.C. (1987) 'The impact of resource availability on lithic industrial traditions in prehistoric Ireland', in P. Rowley-Conwy, M. Zvelebil and H.P. Blankholm (eds), *Mesolithic Northwest Europe: Recent Trends*, Sheffield: Department of Archaeology and Prehistory, University of Sheffield, 138–46.

Woodman, P.C. (1989) 'The Mesolithic of Munster: a preliminary assessment,' in C. Bonsall (ed.), *The Mesolithic in Europe*, Edinburgh: John Donald, 116–24.

Woodman, P.C. (1992a) 'Filling in the spaces in Irish prehistory', *Antiquity* 66: 295–314.

Woodman, P.C. (1992b) 'Irish archaeology today: a poverty amongst riches', *The Irish Review* 12: 34–9.

Woodman, P.C. (1995) 'Who possesses Tara? Politics in archaeology in Ireland', in P. Ucko (ed.), *Theory in Archaeology: A World Perspective*, London: Routledge, 278–97.

Woodman, P.C. and Anderson, E. (1990) 'The Irish Later Mesolithic: a partial picture', in P.M. Vermeersch and P. Van Peer (eds), *Contributions to the Mesolithic in Europe*, Leuven: Leuven University Press, 377–87.

Woodman, P.C. and O'Brien, M. (1993) 'Excavations at Ferriter's Cove, Co. Kerry: an interim statement', in E. Shee Twohig and M. Ronayne (eds), *Past Perceptions: The Prehistoric Archaeology of South-West Ireland*, Cork: Cork University Press, 25–34.

Woodman, P.C. and Johnson, G. (1996) 'Excavations at Bay Farm I, Carnlough, Co. Antrim, and the study of the "Larnian" technology', *Proceedings of the Royal Irish Academy* 96C: 137–235.

Woodman P.C., Doggart, R. and Mallory, J.P. (1991/92) 'Excavations at Windy Ridge, Co. Antrim, 1981–2', *Ulster Journal of Archaeology* 3rd Ser. 54/55: 13–35.

Zvelebil, M. (1994) 'Plant use in the Mesolithic and its role in the transition to farming', *Proceedings of the Prehistoric Society* 60: 35–74.

Zvelebil, M. and Rowley-Conwy, P. (1984) 'Transition to farming in northern Europe: a hunter-gatherer's perspective', *Norwegian Archaeological Review* 17: 104–28.

Zvelebil, M. and Rowley-Conwy, P. (1986) 'Foragers and farmers in Atlantic Europe', in M. Zvelebil (ed.), *Hunters in Transition*, Cambridge: Cambridge University Press, 67–96.

Zvelebil, M., Moore, J., Green, S.W. and Henson, D. (1987) 'Regional survey and analysis of lithic scatters: a case study from south-east Ireland', in P. Rowley-Conwy, M. Zvelebil and H. P. Blankholm (eds), *Mesolithic Northwest Europe: Recent Trends*, Sheffield: Department of Archaeology and Prehistory, University of Sheffield, 9–32.

Zvelebil, M., Macklin, M.G., Passmore, D.G. and Ramsden, P. (1996) 'Alluvial archaeology in the Barrow Valley, southeast Ireland: the "Riverford Culture" revisited', *Journal of Irish Archaeology* 7: 13–40.

2

SETTLEMENT IN EARLY IRELAND

A review

Charles Doherty

§9. *Monachus et virgo unus abhinc et alia ab aliunde in uno hospitio non conmaneant nec in uno curru a uilla in uillam discurreant nec absidue inuicem confabulationem exerceant.*

A monk and a virgin, the one from one place, the other from another, shall not take lodging in the same inn, nor travel in the same carriage from village to village, nor carry on prolonged conversations together.

§17. ... *et postea non in una domo nec in una uilla habitent.*

... and afterwards they shall not live in the same house or in the same village.[1]

The above edition and translation was made by Ludwig Bieler in 1963. There is nothing wrong with the translation as such: but is it appropriate? More recently the text has been re-edited and translated by a working party of the Ulster Society for Medieval Latin Studies and was presented at a symposium in the Queen's University, Belfast. It was subsequently published with commentary in 1976.[2] In this translation the term village has now become *settlement* in both passages.[3] Indeed, the need for changes such as this lay at the heart of the new study of the text. As W.C. Kerr pointed out in the introduction:

> But there were many instances where we felt that previous translations assumed too readily that there was no doubt about both the general and the particular sense of the Latin. Rightly or wrongly, we came to the conclusion that many of the words and expressions of individual canons and whole canons themselves were not meaningful because the exact connotation of Latin words in successive periods of the history of early Christian Ireland had not been established: our view is that much further research in a number of related fields is needed before the

thirty-four canons of the *Synod* can be understood and placed in a social and historical context.[4]

Discussing the passages quoted above Dolley wrote of the attitude of the symposium: 'They travelled in a *currus* whatever that was, and they travelled from – and here we admittedly ducked – "settlement to settlement", we being reluctant to give too particular a sense to the Latin *villa*.'[5]

To be fair to the members of the symposium, it would be difficult to know just how to translate this word. Again, in their notes to this canon they say 'we find the word in later hagiographers meaning "settlement" or "farm" (e.g. Conchubranus, *Monenna*, §6; Anonymous, *Vita S. Carthagi*, §33)'. But here again these translations beg the question.[6] And, of course, as with many of the Latin texts, especially canons, the possibility of a borrowing, directly or indirectly, from a Continental source must always be considered.[7] Even when we can recognise a foreign borrowing, that, of itself, does not mean that the borrowing is inappropriate in an Irish context. Those seeking to translate texts frequently rely on the current interpretations of historians and archaeologists who themselves are influenced by previous interpretations of the texts. So the problems of settlement terminology and its interpretation become part of a great circular argument that is hard to break.

The problem of translation is difficult, particularly when our understanding of the structures on the ground is imperfect. If words are being used which express an idea or a concept, then we may find that material structures on the ground are a mere shadow of the sophistication that would normally be implied by the word. For example in the sixth-century Penitential of Finnian we find in canon §23:

> Si qui<s> clericus homicidium fec<er>it <et occiderit proximum suum et mortuus fuerit,> .x. annis exterrem fieri de patria sua oportet et agat penitentiam vii annorum in alia urbe ...

> If any cleric commits murder and strikes down his neighbour and he is dead, he must become an exile from his country for ten years and do penance seven years in another city ... [8]

The problem here is the use of the word *urbs*. What could such a term mean in sixth-century Ireland? Bieler's note to his translation indicates the complexity of the problem:

> 'City': *urbe* [manuscript] V. The variant *orbe* [manuscript] S would seem to be merely a vulgar Latin spelling. *Urbs* here probably is an equivalent of the commoner *civitas*, meaning an ecclesiastical, in particular a monastic, establishment. As an alternative, Prof. Binchy would consider

some influence of OI *orb(a)e* (neut.), lit. 'patrimony, hereditary estate', but often = 'territory, region'.[9]

Plainly we can have the concept of a 'town' or a 'city' long before the physical conditions are present. A further difficulty arises in the case of Ireland. Since the country was never Romanised we have no Roman settlements, no sites (even though deserted and in ruins) that people of the early Middle Ages recognised to have had a Roman origin. In areas of Romanisation the words used to describe early settlements can take on a particular range of meaning. The very sensitive study of 'Bede's Words for Places', by J. Campbell[10] shows just how delicate the handling of such material needs to be; but how it is also possible to discover subtle nuances of meaning when the material is treated gently. The fact of Romanisation provides a certain yardstick against which to judge the evidence. In Ireland no such yardstick exists. Also, as Campbell points out in relation to the treatment of these words in Anglo-Saxon England, modern scholars may be over-zealous in their attempt to provide neat classifications of the terminology: 'The early uses of *urbs* and *burg* may indicate not so much the undue inclusiveness of these terms as the undue divisiveness of ours: town, fortress, monastery.'[11]

When it becomes an established idea that a particular country or area has only achieved a certain 'stage of development' then scholars not infrequently (subconsciously) inhibit evidence that might run counter to the generally received opinion. For example in the early ninth-century document known as *The Monastery of Tallaght*[12] we have a reference to a *negotiator* from Munster. The text is a mixture of both Latin and Irish. It is a collection of anecdotes, stories and statements of moral instruction from the circle of reformers known as the Céli Dé. This information, then, is purely incidental. The *negotiator* appears in Irish sections of the text, as in, '*Arale cendaigi taithigit hi tír muman ...*' and this is translated as 'a certain itinerant pedlar in Munster ... '.[13] This man enters the story as someone who carries news or information from one monastery to another as he goes about his business. He carried greetings from St Samthann of the monastery of Cluain Brónaig (Clonbroney, barony of Granard, Co. Longford) to members of the Céli Dé in Munster. Clearly there was a nexus of exchange in which he played a part. Indeed, as we learn from the eighth-century 'life' of Samthann §xxiii, Clonbroney was not unaccustomed to visiting merchants. Goods could come from as far afield as Iona, sent by members of the community. They were brought by ship to the mouth of the Boyne and from there to Clonbroney.[14] If this text had been a Latin text of the Continent then the translation would almost certainly have been *merchant*. Since Ireland was a 'tribal' society without 'villages' or 'towns' then the translation of *negotiator*, still less *cennaige*, as *merchant* would have to be avoided. Surely our *negotiator* is not very far removed from the class discussed by L. Kuchenbuch in his study of the social structure of the monastery of Prüm.[15]

As long as a society is perceived to be in a certain state sources are translated appropriate to that state – and, as I have mentioned earlier, such an attitude can produce a circular argument. This problem is compounded when the vernacular language becomes the main vehicle of expression. While Latin remains the international language similar words representing similar material conditions can be compared across cultures; but when a vernacular language comes into use, unless there is extensive glossing or translation literature, it can be extremely difficult to interpret native words against an international background.

Historiography of problem

In a Thomas Davis Lecture broadcast in 1953[16] Professor Binchy painted a panorama of early Ireland that has provided a stock examination statement to be discussed by students ever since. It has stood as a statement descriptive of early Irish society for so long because it is a truism – it explains all and it explains nothing. He said:

> It was a pattern of life that differed in almost every essential point from Irish society as we know it to-day. If you asked me to define its main characteristics, I should say that it was tribal, rural, hierarchical, and familiar (using this word in its oldest sense, to mean a society in which the family, not the individual, is the unit) – a complete contrast to the unitary, urbanised, egalitarian and individualist society of our time.[17]

It is important to realise that Binchy's contrast is with *modern society*, not other early medieval societies – a distinction not always realised by many who have used his statement. Binchy's main source for the above picture was the Old Irish law tracts which he regarded as being valid, 'say, from the coming of the Goidels down to the Norse invasions'.[18]

In dealing with his second (rural) characteristic of early Irish society he says:

> The example of Wales as well as Ireland shows that the urban civilisation which was transmitted to Northern and Western Europe through Graeco-Roman influence remained quite foreign to the Celtic-speaking peoples of these islands until it was more or less imposed on them by foreign conquerors. It is a curious paradox of history that we should be indebted to the wild Northmen for the introduction of cities and walled towns into Ireland. With the doubtful exception of Cashel, none of the larger cities and towns is of native provenance; they have all been superinduced from outside upon a rural pattern of life. Even the village, which was the basis of Anglo-Saxon England, had no place here; indeed, down to the present day the isolated holding remains characteristic of the country districts in Ireland and Wales in contrast to the typical group of houses clustered round the parish church in

England. It is a contrast which lies at the root of many differences and has had far-reaching consequences in the history of all three countries.[19]

One cannot but have a profound sense of unease with this view of the past. There is a feeling running through this paragraph that any kind of nucleation was quite impossible among the native population of Ireland and Wales. The example of a possible instance of native urbanism is Cashel, perched on its rock with (presumably) a cluster at its feet. This verges on the perverse – what of Armagh? It would not be too difficult to argue for urbanism[20] in places such as Armagh itself, Kildare, Derry, Downpatrick, Kilkenny, Kells, Louth, Roscommon – to mention only a few that come randomly to mind. The Norse were not urban dwellers when they arrived in Ireland at the beginning of the ninth century. And as for walls, it is extremely likely that the great stone wall of Dublin was built, not by the Norse, but by Muirchertach Ua Briain in the opening years of the twelfth century.

Again the typical group of houses clustered round the parish church in England may owe more to the paintings of Constable than any reality in pre-Norman England.[21] On the Continent the 'classical village' does not make an appearance before the end of the eleventh century.[22] It must be remembered too that although scholars use the term 'village' to describe nucleation in the early Middle Ages they are using a more modern concept:[23] 'Un fait trés remar-quable est qu'il n'existe dans nos sources aucun terme pour désigner un habitat groupé, aucun équivalent de nos mots "village" ou "hameau" (villa, on l'a vu désigne un territoire).'[24] The two words that scholars focus upon are the villa and vicus. Bede used these words for less important places. As J. Campbell points out 'They are used in a fairly general sense to mean something like [my emphasis] "village" and synonymously.'[25] On the Continent settlements of the Merovingian period are difficult to find since they frequently lie under the modern village. During the last ten years excavations have begun to reveal a glimpse of this 'habitat pré-villageois'.[26] The excavations at the small village of Villiers-le-Sec, 24 km north of Paris has provided new insights into this problem.[27] It was out of such 'pre-village' nucleations that the village, as such, began to emerge between the fifth and the tenth centuries. It emerged as the result of a political, social and economic transformation of society. The church was a focal point that eventually provided the religious unit of the parish, and the 'village' was to become the focal point for the civil unit.[28]

What is quite clear is that in the early Middle Ages the 'village' in a modern sense has not yet emerged. The 'pre-village' was essentially a territory which sometimes produced nucleation; and the concept of territory and nucleation was not often distinguished. Professor Binchy's comparison, therefore, has little substance. Such a view of the past has caused scholars to see early Ireland as exotically different when we ought to see it in the context of general north-west European culture: where the exotic is the exception and not the rule.

Binchy subsequently reinforced these ideas in a lecture given at the first

International Congress of Celtic Studies held in Dublin in 1959.[29] The very title, 'The passing of the old order', encapsulates Professor Binchy's attitude to the impact of the Norse on early Ireland, which, as he said, was 'deliberately chosen to suggest that the old order of Goidelic society, as mirrored in the Irish law-tracts, was drastically altered by the events of the ninth and tenth centuries'.[30] The Norse, he wrote, 'had a profound – one might even say a shattering – effect upon native Irish institutions'.[31] His title is almost certainly drawn from the first line of Fear Flatha ó Gnímh's poem, *Mairg do-chuaidh re ceird ndúthchais* (translated as 'The passing of the old order', by Osborn Bergin in his edition of the poem in *Studies* in 1925),[32] in which the poet bemoans the loss of patronage with the collapse of the Gaelic order at the hands of the English at the end of the sixteenth century – a whole world was rapidly disappearing. In terms of settlement, although Binchy accepted that 'some of the larger monastic foundations, particularly those with a school attached, already formed a compact group of inhabitants ...'[33] there was no question of them having an urban function:

> But the idea of a town, with a corporate personality distinct from that of the ruler, was quite foreign to the Gaelic mind until the Scandinavians set up their 'cities' in Dublin, Limerick, Waterford and elsewhere. Slowly, indeed unwillingly, the Irish followed their example; but though a few monastic settlements eventually grew into towns, all the larger urban centres are of Norse provenance. It would be difficult to exaggerate the formidable impact of these prosperous trading stations, with their local and overseas markets, their cash and credit sales, upon the primitive economy of their Irish neighbours.[34]

For Binchy, the Norse also 'forced a primitive and pastoral society to adopt, very much against the grain, a more progressive economic technique'.[35] Because Professor Binchy's views have had a profound – one might even say a canonical – effect upon scholars, it may be necessary to examine his position in more detail. We are brought to the crux of the problem of settlement in his contradistinction between 'primitive pastoralism' and 'progressive economic technique'. Binchy would seem to belong, at least in this area, to an 'earlier and confident generation' of historians as discussed by Glanville R.J. Jones:

> Influenced, if only indirectly, by Darwinian theories of unilinear evolution, they assumed that pastoral farming invariably preceded cultivation, and Wales, regarded as a remote and backward upland fastness, was deemed to have remained the preserve of nomadic pastoralists. On the basis of an analysis of written records and an equally theoretical elaboration of legal concepts, early Wales was envisaged as an area where Welsh patriarchs and their tribes roamed at will with their flocks and herds. Given the modern rural landscape of Wales, with its great

expanses of rough pasture and enclosed grazings, but at present, only fugitive patches of cultivation, it was not difficult for pioneer investigators to believe that the traditional way of life was almost exclusively pastoral. Large expanses of upland with an unpleasant ecological temper marked by bleakness, heavy rainfall, and scant sunshine – all unfavourable to cultivation – re-inforced this impression. Nevertheless, closer examination should have generated second thoughts.[36]

Indeed, Jones himself was one of those who was having second thoughts in the early 1960s.[37] With Professor Binchy's unique knowledge of early Irish law it is unlikely that he would have gone all the way along the road of the primitive pastoralists but he certainly leaned heavily in that direction. Nor may we any longer accept Binchy's basic thesis about the role of the Norse in the transformation of early Irish society. His over-emphasis on the law tracts on the one hand, and his lack of attention to the details of contemporary events as recorded in the annals for the seventh and eighth centuries on the other, led him to assign changes in society to the ninth and tenth centuries. The society of the law tracts was already experiencing rapid change long before the Norse appeared on the scene.[38] Nor did the Norse, when they arrived, come with the cultural baggage of urban life, with coinage and markets as Binchy suggests. His view of the Norse towns would seem to be of isolated settlements hugging the coast surrounded by primitive pastoralists. It has since become clear that the Norse towns became powerful, not just because of their involvement in international trade, but because they had settled in an extremely rich environment.

The classical 'village' of the Continent, as we have seen, is, in general, not to be sought any earlier than the eleventh century. We may not, like Binchy, compare Ireland and Wales unfavourably with areas that were to develop the village, during periods when the village has yet to evolve in those areas of comparison. But we may justifiably ask if Ireland and Wales had nucleation of a 'pre-village' type. The idea that there was no nucleation in Wales can no longer stand.

> Thus the laws convey a clear impression of small co-operative groups of tenants housed in hamlets. Their scarcity in modern Wales is no argument that they were merely the constructs of a lawyer's imagination. As later records reveal, many hamlets disappeared when their bond inhabitants fled during the later medieval period, whereas the better sited examples which prospered have been buried by subsequent village growth, as at Aberffraw, or by urban development, as at Denbigh.[39]

While not every township in Wales had nucleation it was much more frequent than supposed. This is surely the stage of the 'pre-village'. The *tir corddlan* (nucleal land) was the equivalent of the 'cultivated infield as recorded centuries later in many an Irish or Scottish hamlet'.[40] Many of the churches, too, were nucleated settlements, such as Llanynys.[41] Royal courts were the focus of nucleation and could be elaborate, as at Aberffraw.[42] Most of these settlements had bond-'villages' supporting the upper classes with their food rents and labour services, frequently supervised by a steward or a *maerdref*. This system may, at an early period, have been more widespread than the area of Wales.[43] To date it cannot be shown that any Welsh church had developed urban characteristics like the monastic towns of Ireland.[44] It has been argued recently that there was less surplus wealth available in Wales to make such development possible – at least until the immediately pre-Norman period.[45]

There is sufficient evidence from Irish sources to suggest that there was a 'pre-village' stage in Ireland not unlike that in Wales.[46] And we may include Scotland in this as well.[47] Whereas the Welsh legal evidence is contained in manuscripts of the thirteenth century and later, the basis of some of the texts may be argued to go back to the tenth century and earlier. This legal evidence can be augmented by other sources of the twelfth century and later. The difficulty of Welsh history is the paucity of legal sources (however difficult of interpretation) for the seventh and eighth centuries, but almost no contemporary law tracts for subsequent periods. It may be that commentaries written on the early tracts contain information relevant to settlement but, so far, it is the early tracts themselves that have most attracted the attention of legal historians. Yet it is in the area of settlement that a comparison of Irish and Welsh material has most to offer the researcher.

The 'pre-village' in early medieval Ireland

Against the Welsh background we might now take a preliminary look at some Irish evidence for 'pre-village' settlement. I might say first of all that I am going forward on the basis that major churches and monasteries in Ireland were urban and functioning as towns from at least the tenth century if not earlier; and, in the case of Armagh, from as early as the seventh century. Also that some smaller churches formed the core of 'pre-village' or 'village' nucleations. I think that only excavation, with this thesis in mind, will throw light on the problem.

Leo Swan has already made the very important point that many of the small enclosed burial grounds that dot the landscape are hardly evidence of monasticism. He has suggested that some of these sites were secular settlements of small communities of the early medieval period. Many acted 'as focal points for small rural communities ... providing a place of worship and burial'.[48] He also suggested that some may have their origins in non-Christian or pre-Christian society.[49] This is an interesting idea.

One type of church site may very well have origins of this kind – that is the *domnach*. The *domnach* was already recognised in the seventh century to be a church of the missionary period.[50] It has been suggested that Dunmisk, Co. Tyrone, may be a corruption of *Domnach Mescáin*.[51] If this is the case then the study of this site assumes an even greater importance.[52]

Domnach churches are frequently sited in areas called *mag* a 'plain' or a 'long-inhabited' area. As such they would seem to have been located in areas of population – indeed, if scholars are looking for populated areas in fifth-century Ireland then this would be a good place to start. Since such churches may be associated with early missionary diocesan centres and as such the earliest centres of pastoral care, the emphasis on Dunmisk as a *monastery*[53] is, perhaps, to place an unfortunate burden on the interpretation of this site. Early churches of this kind may very well have generated an early nucleation. In the light of this discussion the burial of people of all sexes and ages at Dunmisk is particularly significant.[54] Excavation both within and, particularly, outside such enclosures would be essential to determine the complete nature of the site.

It is interesting to note that the period of activity at Dunmisk (although there may be no precise dating) lies between the sixth century and its abandonment in the tenth.[55] Another site with strong secular associations has recently been excavated by Conleth Manning at Millockstown, Co. Louth.[56] Here there were three phases, dating between, approximately, the fourth century and the eighth or ninth century. The earliest habitation area was enclosed by a narrow ditch and assigned to the immediately pre-Christian period. In phase 2 a ring-fort was built within the earlier enclosure dating rather vaguely to the mid-first millennium AD. At some point it was handed over to the church. The final phase saw the enlargement of the enclosed area. The new enclosure was ecclesiastical containing both habitations and a cemetery. Two souterrains were also found within this new settlement capable of sheltering a large number of people, so it would seem to be a population centre.[57] The entire site was abandoned by the twelfth century and possibly as early as the tenth. The cemetery here, too, was mixed, containing males, females and children buried in lintel graves – a type of burial in common with those mentioned above.[58] What was the nature of this church? What population did it serve? There was another church in the same townland, Kildemock, the famous 'Jumping Church'. It was this church that became the centre of the parish in the Middle Ages. This parish 'included the whole of the townland of Millockstown along with nine other townlands'.[59]

Already by the seventh century churches had been abandoned.[60] Such a situation would not have been uncommon throughout the Middle Ages. Many such places were dependent on major churches and were part of their properties.[61] As such they were centres of farming and craft activities and paid their rents and tributes to the mother church. Other minor church enclosures may have been 'private' churches on a lord's estate. There were others, too, like those that Bede denounced in his *Letter to Egbert* in 734, in Anglo-Saxon England, that established bogus monasteries in order to avoid secular obligations. No doubt there were similar 'bogus' monasteries in Ireland, probably counted among the folk of the old churches (*aosa i senchellaib*), who had not properly performed their duties, and who are mentioned in the Céli Dé document, *The Monastery of Tallaght*[62] in the ninth century. Such places would surely exhibit a mainly secular activity if excavated. It is becoming clear that a more sensitive approach to different church types, even though there may be superficial similarities, is essential.[63]

Swan has also pointed to the relationship between many of the early church enclosures and parish boundaries.[64] Such a study is extremely important in our understanding of the pastoral mission[65] of the early Irish Church, whatever the precise date and definition of parish boundaries in themselves.[66] From the sources it is clear that these churches, of whatever kind, had their dependent farmers and craftsmen – the *manaig* and *senchléithe* among others[67] – many of whom would have been living in and around their churches and, thus, would have formed a basis for nucleation. Churches are natural focal points, and, as such, attract settlement. It is those sites that were deserted, at whatever time in the Middle Ages, that appear so dramatically in the countryside, but it can hardly be sufficiently stressed that these were the settlements that *failed* at some point in time. As with villages on the Continent, in England and elsewhere, the successful nucleations are to be found beneath our contemporary villages and small towns. It is to be hoped that the current stress on 'urban' archaeology will not cause this other aspect of the settlement picture to be neglected.

The hunt for the clachan

However, I would first like to look at the possibility of secular 'village' nucleation in Ireland. In 1939 Estyn Evans identified a settlement form that he was subsequently to call the *clachan*; 'it is now clear that throughout western Britain and in many parts of western and south-western Europe some kind of communal cultivation is of great antiquity, and that Meitzen's well-known map of Dörfer and Einzelhöfer needs drastic revision'.[68] Evans was examining two farming clusters in the middle of the mountains; Meenacreevagh, in the townland of Beltany, to the north of Errigal in Co. Donegal and Glentornan, on the southern shore of Lough Nacung Upper, to the south of the mountain. Although the settlements were unlikely to be older than 200 years, he saw them as having 'the interest of archaeological fossils, preserving in an impoverished way many of the characters of ancient Irish society'.[69] The settlements would seem to have started life as summer grazing ground and were part of the system of transhumance. Beltany itself is probably named from *Bealtaine*, 'May' since May Day was traditionally the beginning of this season.[70] As 'fossils' these sites represented the less substantial aspect of perhaps more elaborate and permanent settlements that would have been found on better land. He also made a comparison with the openfield villages of lowland England:

> While the rundale communities never reached the size of the openfield villages of lowland England, clusters of 30–40 houses were common in Donegal a century ago, and groups of up to a dozen have survived the disintegrating tendencies which attack them with increasing force.

Although they possess no ordered plan, and normally lack both inn and church, they are, in a functional sense, villages rather than hamlets. Communal life and the exchange of services are still characteristic.[71]

For Evans, two habitation types existed side by side from early Celtic times, that is, the nucleated clachan and the single farmstead. These modern settlements contained echoes of the distant Celtic past: 'The periodic redistribution of the arable strips is no longer found, but the principle of scattered ownership has been tenaciously adhered to and is linked with the old "Celtic" practice of equal division of lands of differing qualities among male heirs.' 'Another feature of tribal heritage to be noticed is the blood relationship of all the inhabitants in each "town".'[72] This paper became a classic and introduced an important stimulus to those engaged in settlement studies. It is unfortunate, however, that his tribes and their clans continued to haunt the pages of some historical geographers for a long time to come – and this despite the clear statement to the contrary by Duignan, only a few years later, in his work (frequently quoted by historical geographers) on early Irish agriculture, in which he referred to the work of MacNeill and Richey.[73] It was probably the work of Evans, though, that caused Duignan to look at the roll of the unfree class in early Irish agriculture, and he saw in the recent excavation of Twomile Stone in south Donegal by Oliver Davies the 'first recorded group of crofts belonging to members of this class'.[74]

By the late 1950s the pupils of Evans, and others, had begun to build on the foundations that he had laid down.[75] In 1955, Seán Mac Airt, in a short article on 'County Armagh: toponymy and history' introduced a new element into the debate about the prehistoric or early historic clachan. This was the word *baile* which he assumed 'is an old plebian term for a settlement, as opposed to the *Goidelic* rath'.[76] He went on to conclude:

A broad conclusion from these considerations would be that among the early name-makers in the County [Armagh] were the *achadh*-cattlemen and possibly the lowland *baile*-folk. They must have grown some grain, but not very much. One might visualise them as a people loth to bend their backs to the soil, preferring like Conor MacNessa, to while away their time by story-telling, ale-drinking, or playing fidchell.[77]

Quite! If we can withdraw quietly from this idyllic scene and join the real world we find that this idea was taken up by the historical geographers. As a means of explaining the lack of rath distribution in the east of Co. Down, Proudfoot suggested that 'other forms of settlement co-existed with the raths and that these were open clusters of settlement which have left little if any trace – proto-clachans if you like'.[78] He suggested that 'perhaps these open clusters were those referred to individually as *baile* and translated by the Anglo-Normans as ton and villa'.[79] The *baile* element, more numerous in east Down than in the west, when considered alongside the distribution of raths made up a more complete settlement pattern in Down. Proudfoot pointed out the serious lack of evidence for clachans in the period between 1350 and 1600 and, in particular, if the clachan were a settlement form of great antiquity – a part of the cultural heritage of Atlantic Europe – then there were many problems with the nature of this settlement form, even within the period during which they could be studied on the ground or in maps. Clachans appeared and disappeared, were associated with rundale and yet outlived it; single farms expanded into clachan settlements and then reconsolidated into single farms in the course of time.[80]

In an effort to resolve the problem of clachan continuity a series of excavations took place between 1956 and 1958 at Murphystown, Co. Down. Despite the finding of a few sherds of 'souterrain ware', which might indicate an early historic or medieval date, most of the evidence related to the nineteenth century. The excavation proved disappointing and inconclusive.[81] For Proudfoot, 'the most important general point which has emerged from such studies is the flexible nature of Irish settlement forms'.[82] It was this very theme which was taken up by McCourt in his important survey of rural settlement in 1971.[83] This is a most useful survey because it encapsulates all of the ideas that had been discussed up to that time as well as putting McCourt's own stamp on the problem. He saw the word *baile* as referring to clachan settlements, but pointed out that it also referred to a unit of land – the townland – and that it need not necessarily mean a clustered settlement. Also that the English 'town' from 'ton' was the Old English equivalent for *baile*.[84]

> But though 'ton', meaning a village in the English sense, was equated with *baile* in medieval documents from the twelfth to the fourteenth century, it must have been recognised at the time that there was no more than a passing resemblance between the two settlement forms. The English agricultural village, cast in its manorial shell and within the territorial framework of the parish, belonged to a feudal-manorial order; the Irish clachan was an outgrowth of tribal society and functioned within a framework of minute territorial divisions and an agrarian-tenurial system different from that of contemporary England.[85]

Tribal society is still alive and well; and we see a repetition of the situation in which a society, believed to be at a certain state of development, cannot, therefore, be equated with another.[86] If it was recognised at the time that there was no more than a passing resemblance between the two settlement forms then the medieval English must have been rather silly to have made such an equation in the first place.

But when the term 'tribal' is used are we talking about the seventh century or the ninth or the twelfth? If it is the period between the twelfth and the fourteenth century that was intended for comparison, was Irish society tribal during that period? Again, for an explanation of 'common grazings, co-operative ploughing, the frequent redistributions of cultivated and meadow land, and other communal obligations, and also in the scattered pattern of land holding' we are asked to look at the seventh-century law tracts.[87] Admittedly the *rí* could still be found in Ireland until the twentieth century[88] and our modern parliament is called a *Dáil*, but no one would imagine that they have anything in common with the institutions as they were in the pre-Norman period.[89] Support for the role of the kin-group in putting a brake on the fragmentation of joint-family property is sought in the *derbfhine*, that is, those descended from a common great-grandfather, but this kin structure was giving way to the *gelfhine*, that is, those descended from a common grandfather, by the eighth century (although it is possible that the word derbfhine was also used of this narrower unit).[90]

However tenacious Irish custom and tradition may be, these attempts to span 1,000 years and more can hardly inspire confidence as a method of demonstrating continuity in the existence of the clachan as a settlement form. Despite this, it is clear that agricultural groups survived as units from the Middle Ages; groups such as the *scullogues* that McCourt mentions, 'the inferior rank of husbandmen, called *scullogues*, herded together in villages and cultivated the land everywhere'.[91]

It may be necessary to digress here since the origin of McCourt's quotation raises problems. The matter of the *scullogues* is sufficiently important to gather all the information at this point.

Scullogues

There is no evidence for a 1776 edition as cited by McCourt. He may be referring to the 1767 edition. It would seem that he transposed the digits 6 and 7 of the year 1767. The text relating to the *scullogues*, however, appears on p. 13 of all extant editions, not p. 12. But there is a further discrepancy. McCourt's quotation nowhere appears in Taaffe's description. Taaffe's description is in praise of the *scullogue* class:

> This sort of self-defence, in keeping the lands uncultivated, had the further consequence, of expelling that most useful body of people, called *Yeomanry* in England, and which we denominated *Sculoags* in Ireland. Communities of industrious house-keepers, who in my own time, herded together in large villages, and cultivated the lands every where, till as leases expired, some rich grazier, negotiating privately with a sum of ready money, took these lands over their heads. – This is a fact well known. The *Sculoag race*, that great nursery of labourers and manufacturers, has been broke and dispersed in every quarter; and we have nothing in lieu, but those most miserable wretches on earth, the

Cottagers; naked slaves, who labour without food, and live while they can, without houses or covering, under the lash of merciless and relentless task masters![92]

On p. 149 McCourt refers to a description of the *scullogues* by Sir Henry Piers in 1682 printed in C. Vallancey's *Collectanea de rebus Hibernicis* (Dublin, 1770, Vol. I, pp. 116–17). His quote does not match exactly that of Piers but is clearly inspired by it.

> As to the inferior rank of husbandmen called, Sculloges, which may be Englished, farmer or husbandman, or yet more properly, boor, they are generally very crafty and subtle in all manner of bargaining, full of equivocations and mental reservations, especially in their dealings in fairs and markets; whereas if lying and cheating were no sin, they make it their work to over reach any they deal with, and if by any flight or fetch they can hook in the least advantage, they are mighty tenacious thereof, and will not forget the same, unless over-powered by the landlord, who is the party addressed to for justice.[93]

In fact McCourt's quote would seem to be an amalgam of elements of both descriptions. This is unfortunate since Taaffe (an apologist for the Catholic cause) had a positive and sympathetic view of the *scullogues* as a class, whereas, by contrast, the attitude of Piers is that of an alien antipathetic to the native population. This is of crucial importance in assessing the status of the *scullogue* class.

It is only with the break-up of their way of life that Taaffe sees the emergence of the poverty-stricken *cottagers*. We can hardly imagine that the *cottagers*, described in rhetorical language by Taaffe, had no houses for shelter, but perhaps they lived in cabins such as we see sketched by nineteenth-century travellers. The contrast surely suggests that the *scullogues*, previous to their reduction in status, lived in proper houses. While the picture of the *scullogues* may not have been as optimistic as Taaffe paints, neither may they have been as inferior as the description by Piers.

There is a further piece of evidence that may be relevant. It was first brought to my attention by a friend, Mary Golden, when we were postgraduate students, some years ago. This was a reference to Scolers who brought linen cloth into the market in Waterford City.

> Itm my Lorde Ossery useith the same in this countrey, and also letts the resort of people comeing to the mket of this cytye w^t fleshe, vaytayles, and mchanndyseis.

[Ossery: EDS Piers, 1st Earl of Ossory and 8th Earl of Ormond]

[the same: CD Irish custom]

Itm he letteith the Scolers, and others comeing hyther wyth lynnyn clothe, and takyth them to fyne, and taskeid them by the Barron of Berron s^chorith, his fermar.

[Scolers: EDS wandering scholars were known to the last generation under the name of 'poor scholars'; but here the connection must be with trade.]

[Berron: EDS Fitz Gerald alias Barron, Baron of Burnchurch, in the county of Kilkenney][94]

I think that the editors have confused the Scolers with the masters of the hedge-schools of the eighteenth century. Dr Ciarán Parker, whom I would like to thank for very kindly tracking down the exact reference for me, suggested that 'The reference is to "scolers" who were involved in trade in cloth in Waterford city. However, the editor's transcription of such terms may be erroneous.' It is difficult to imagine what else the word could have read. I believe that it *does* give us a glimpse of the kind of activities that scullogues were engaged in at a time in the sixteenth century when their lifestyle was still in a better state than it was to become 200 years later.

It may be important to remember that this class, as their name implies, were church tenants in the pre-twelfth-century period. As I have already suggested, this class, not just in Ireland, but all over Europe may have been in a slightly better position than their secular counterparts. They may, then, have survived the coming of the Normans and the changes of the later Middle Ages as a slightly stronger corporate body of tenantry than those belonging to secular lords.

This group took its name from the Latin *schola* which gave *scolóc* in Old Irish. Originally it meant a scholar, but by the twelfth century the 'scholars' are a group of tenants farming on monastic property. A senior monastic official was their overseer or manager, the *toísech na scolóc*, as we can read in the early twelfth-century (1117 x ?1133) charter in the Book of Kells.[95] As a working population on the estates of a great monastic town of the twelfth century this group was part of a structure that was closer to the 'feudal-manorial order' than the 'tribalism' that McCourt saw as providing the great contrast with England. The way in which such groups were organised in the twelfth century can have had little to do with their structure as Taaffe found them in the eighteenth century. The structure of which they were a part had not existed for over 500 years. The same would hold true for the descendants of the *betaghs* or *nativi* that appear in the Norman documents. It is very likely, as McCourt suggests, that they served their new Norman masters in much the same way as they had served their defeated Irish lord: 'the equivalent probably of the cultivating villeins of the English village'. It is interesting that as soon as they are rescued from 'tribalism' to the new state they may be placed in a position of comparison.[96]

Indeed both groups have left their names in some of the townlands such as Betaghstowne in the barony of Navan in Co. Meath and Sculogstow in the parish of Burgidge in Co. Wicklow which are marked on seventeenth-century maps.[97] Other examples are Ballybetagh, Betaghstown, Bettystown[98] and Ballybetagh House (Nat. Grid O 201 209) and Ballybetagh Wood (Nat. Grid O 207 207) close by. These places are to the south of Kiltiernan in Co. Wicklow. There is a Hortland, otherwise Ballysculloge or Scullogestown found in Lewis's *Topographical Dictionary*.[99] To the east of the northern tip of the Blessington lakes there is Ballynascoulloge Upper (Nat. Grid O 03 13) and Ballynascoulloge Lower (Nat. Grid O 045 142) both approximately 4 km south of Kilbride.[100] In the vicinity is Scurlocksleap[101] (Nat. Grid O 060 151) approximately 3.5 km south-east of Kilbride, Co. Wicklow. These are marked on the Map of the Wicklow Way.

There is also Scullogue Gap across the Blackstairs Mountains in Co. Wexford (Nat. Grid S 82 48). Scholarstown in Co. Dublin is presumably from scollogue as well. In Strongbow's charter to Glendalough quoted by Colmán Etchingham there is found 'Ruba Scolaige', which may be the same as 'Rosculli' of the Llanthony records and has been identified with Grange near Killoughter, a few miles north of Wicklow town near the coast.[102] There is also Trián na sgológ in *Lethbhaile Locha Muighe Brón isna Baireadachaibh, Tír Amhalghaidh* (Hz. 75 [MS H. 4, 13, TCD]) in Co. Mayo.[103]

McCourt has made the interesting suggestion that the siting of early manors may have been influenced by the availability of such groups for their labour potential and:

> that some acculturation took place, however, is suggested by the preva-
> lence in these localities of courtyard farm-types and their grouping
> around a central place or road crossing with a hint of formality that is
> in contrast to the amorphous character of the Irish clachan.[104]

From what we read of the clachan it would seem to be very much a spontaneous outgrowth of particular social conditions over a particular period of time.[105] But if clusters are deliberately organised or fostered as part of the economy of an institution, that is, of either Church or secular lordship, should we expect a hint of formality? If so, do we require acculturation to produce this? The amorphous clachan, as it is described to us from the seventeenth century to the present, surely, is much more the result of cultural collapse than a unit of cultural cohesion. However McCourt's suggestion may very well be worth further investigation.

McCourt also repeats Mac Airt's view that the inhabitants of the *bailes* were the remnants of prehistoric peoples 'left undisturbed by the Goidelic expansion' and may have had their origins in the Neolithic.[106] While the early historic population must have inherited much of its genetic make-up from all the peoples that had colonised the island during the prehistoric period – and the early Irish themselves were aware of different ethnic strands in the tribal population – there is nothing in the linguistic or archaeological record that suggests that there was anything but a common shared cultural tradition at the opening of the historic period. Unsuccessful tribal groups became subject to others, and as time went on unsuccessful branches of dynastic houses also became subject. There was a constant downward pressure that reduced those once noble to the status of commoner and those commoners to the status of serfs. It did not take Neolithic survivors to fill bond settlements. But what of the elusive *baile* – the settlements of the 'lesser-folk'?

The *baile*

The first major analysis of *baile* place-names since the classic paper read before the members of the Royal Irish Academy on 22 April 1861 by William Reeves[107] was by T. Jones Hughes in 1970.[108] Although he says that 'the townland net is in fact the only surviving administrative framework in Ireland with a continuous history of development going back to medieval times if not earlier … '[109] he does not explore the ultimate origin of the system. He saw the coming of the Normans as providing a watershed for his analysis:

> A cursory examination of Irish name elements will however reveal that this exclusiveness [i.e. from external influence] was rudely challenged and greatly modified as a result of the Anglo-Norman invasion of the late twelfth and thirteenth centuries, especially as the invaders brought with them ideas concerning the organisation and management of area which were radically different from those of the native.[110]

In common with so many scholars he assumed that the structure of society was radically different in Ireland in the twelfth century, but no attempt was made to investigate the nature of that society. To be fair to Professor Jones Hughes, he was simply accepting the commonly held ideas of both Norman and Irish society at the time. This led him to:

> recognise three general areas of influence: a zone of durable Norman rural occupation, discontinuous peripheral regions which were out of the reach of the invading culture and, in the third place, a broad but fragmented division where the native way of life was in varying degrees influenced by the presence of the stranger.[111]

He saw the English derived *town* and the Irish *baile* as equivalent. The *town* zone stood out:

in terms of its distinctive territorial distribution [and] may thus represent that part of Ireland which experienced the most durable impact of Anglo-Norman colonisation and settlement and there is a close relationship between its location and extent and the Pale as this has been depicted by historians.[112]

At first sight this seems a very reasonable conclusion. His overall view is that:

> Townlands were created at various times and for a variety of purposes. In the east and south of the country the majority appear to have crystallised as territorial divisions in the Middle Ages, and over much of Leinster the network was designed for the reallocation of land among alien settlers mainly in the thirteenth and fourteenth centuries.[113]

In other words they originated among the Normans as they settled the land after the conquest in the twelfth century. The idea then spread in the marcher areas, particularly after the Irish re-conquest in the late thirteenth and fourteenth centuries, and thence among the Gaelic Irish in the remainder of the country in the course of the later Middle Ages where the use of the term *baile* indicates the spread of this influence. But this analysis, based solely on the distribution of names, can be placed on its head if the English *tun* replaced the Irish *baile*: in other words if the Irish *baile* was the normal administrative unit at the time of the Norman conquest and corresponded to the English *tun*.

Although Jones Hughes does not mention an article by Liam Price which appeared in *Celtica* in 1963 they both reached similar conclusions.[114] Price suggested 'that this extended use of the word in place-names was a result of the coming of the English settlers and their use of the word "town" (*tun*) in giving names to their lands'.[115] He further argued that if:

> 'town' was changed into *baile* in the names of a lot of the places taken from English settlers at the time of the Irish recovery, then it can be understood that the new Irish occupiers would be likely to copy this way of naming their holdings and that place-names in *baile* would thus become general.[116]

Reeves had already, in 1862, laid out the evidence that would have indicated that such a conclusion was wrong.[117]

The suggestion by various scholars, mentioned above, that the distribution of the *baile* was complementary to that of the *rath* was placed under scrutiny in 1980 by Christopher Toumey.[118] He applied the tools of statistical analysis to the area of Co. Down. He highlighted many of the difficulties associated with the place-name evidence and challenged many of the underlying assumptions of earlier scholars:

The most serious one concerns the evidence and logic for the antiquity of the clachan. The evidence is largely conjectural, and the logic depends upon inferences from comparisons of rath-clachan distributions. Re-examination of those distributions does not support inferences of rath-clachan contemporaneity. Ethno-linguistic, corporate, and histo-riographical considerations also indicate that late prehistoric and early historic Irish society would not have been dichotomized as previously suggested.

Independently of the work of Toumey, Gillian Barrett also addressed this problem.[119] Again using statistical analysis χ^2 she examined the relative distri-bution of *rath* and *baile* in southern Donegal and in the Dingle area. Her conclusions were broadly similar to those of Toumey:

> It would appear therefore that the hypothesis suggesting complemen-tarity between areas of high ring-fort density and of townlands incorporating the element *baile* is not of general applicability, a conclu-sion which is reinforced by the general pattern of the two distributions at a national scale.[120]

While she accepted Price's suggestion that 'in the use of *baile* before A.D. 1200 the primary meaning was "a piece of ground"; not until the fourteenth century was it applied to small house clusters', she hesitated to accept his idea that 'the *baile* place-name element could be associated particularly with areas settled by the Normans but subsequently re-occupied by the Irish'.[121]

As I will suggest below, both these ideas are not entirely correct. Barrett produced two further articles on settlement in Co. Louth but no further light was thrown on the problem of the *baile*.[122]

Just at the point when it seemed that the hunt for the prehistoric or early historic clachan might prove fruitless, an upland site in Co. Antrim was exca-vated and interpreted as a transhumance village dating to the mid-first millennium AD.[123] The settlement was at 900 ft above sea level. It contained three large enclosures with associated curvilinear fields. In the western enclo-sure 11 round house platforms were found while there were 10 in the eastern one. In the third enclosure to the north 2 round houses survived, but there may have been more. Three of the round houses were excavated giving dates in the early historic period and, if all houses were contemporary, then the population may have been upward of 100 people. A rath lay 1,400 m to the north-west. Its field enclosures were contemporary with the others on the site.[124] Other such sites have since been recognised in Co. Antrim.[125] The interpretation of the site as a summer transhumance village seems the most likely, but if it can be shown, eventually, that all elements, including the rath, are contemporary, then it may take on a more permanent and even more important character. If it was a summer transhumance village then it was very substantial, although that is to judge it by the modern survivals. In the Middle Ages when such an institution was integral to the farming activity of a substantial part of the population then the size may be proportional to the population that used it.[126] Where was the lowland settlement that was its permanent base? Was it secular or ecclesiastical? An institution such as the Church would probably be in a better position to organise a more structured transhumance village than any group or body in the secular world. Or should it be seen as a permanent village encroaching on marginal land as the result of population pressure? The density of raths in the immediate area in Co. Antrim is well known. However, the discovery of such sites has little to do with clachan continuity.

In her recent valuable survey of the archaeology of early medieval Ireland, Nancy Edwards takes a negative view of the continuity of clachans and the existence of nucleated settlement: 'However, there is as yet little to support these hypotheses in the archaeological record, where, though open and partially enclosed settlements may have housed the lower echelons of society, they do not appear to have been nucleated.'[127] She pointed to the evidence of isolated souterrains that have little or no above-ground features but 'from time to time buildings have been successfully located indicating open or only partially-enclosed settlements with one or more houses and outbuildings'.[128] Some of the souterrains are large and extensive and it has been suggested that they were the refuge centres for unenclosed nucleated settlements above ground. Caution is necessary since aerial photography has revealed crop-marks that show above-ground enclosures around souterrains that had appeared, previously, to have been unenclosed. Nevertheless it is interesting to note that 'of the 3,000 examples recorded nationally, only 40% are recorded in association with enclosures'.[129] The dating of souterrains is loose but it is generally felt that they fall in the second half of the first millennium AD. The debate concerning the relationship between souterrain distribution and 'tribal' areas is lacking in sophistication – even assuming that 'tribal' areas exist for the period in question.[130] Ultimately it will require archaeology to prove or disprove the theory that souterrains, in some locations, are the underground element of unenclosed settlements, and more precise dating will be necessary before discussing the relationship between distribution patterns and communities.

The outstanding detailed studies of Duffy in 1981[131] and the important survey by Thomas McErlean in 1983 has placed the study of the townland on a new plane.[132] This work clearly demonstrated that a uniform system of land division lies behind the townland unit and that it was well in place by the twelfth century. Indeed, McErlean has shown the direction in which future work on this area ought to go. Ingeborg Leister, in her penetrating study of Co. Tipperary in 1976[133] also saw that many of the territorial and land assessment units of the later Middle Ages went back to the pre-Norman period. Her knowledge of pre-Norman society and politics was too insecure when she attempted a 'Probing into the origins',[134] to allow her to take proper advantage of the many insights that she had gained as a result of her study. Indeed, on the question of the *baile* she wrote, 'When we come to baile and house, however, which in the present context, are the most important grievances, we have to admit defeat.'[135] This has been a continuing source of weakness for historical geographers who would use early Irish source material. Having said this, Leister's work is extremely valuable and historians have yet to take proper account of it.

This fresh way of looking at the organisation of the *baile* and townland has entered the thinking of another recent survey dealing with the archaeology of Ulster by Jim Mallory and Tom McNeill.[136] In this work the Ballybetagh, approximating in extent to the parish (the parish was not, as they claim, 'intro- duced from England'; although in many parts it was brought to completion only by the early fourteenth century), is now recognised to be a pre-twelfth-century unit and, thus, a reasonable basis on which to examine distributions. Their chapter on 'Kings, Christians and Vikings *c.* 400–1177 AD', does not shy away from interpretation and, although it may cause the historian, frequently, to sharply inhale, it is thought-provoking and stimulating. In particular, the attempt to make the *rath* tell us more about the social hierarchy is an important step forward. The possibility of bondmen groupings is acknowledged and possible parallels in Wales, England and Scotland highlighted.[137] The differ- ence between the late developed village and the earlier 'pre-village' is also viewed as important for development in Ireland and refreshingly they point out that:

> It is traditional to contrast the dispersed settlement patterns of the 'Celtic' world with the nucleated pattern of the 'Germanic' world; it may well be that there was not that much difference in the seventh or eighth centuries, any more than there was a great difference between their art styles.[138]

It is the inappropriateness of this contrast that I have been emphasising in the course of this review. There may not have been as much difference in the eleventh and twelfth centuries either. Indeed, even at the level of field systems we must begin to exercise caution – even at this basic level we are probably dealing with a difference of degree rather than with fundamentally contrasting systems, as Robert Dodgshon has pointed out:

> If one is seeking a simple organising principle beside which to place the differences that existed between sub-divided fields in the various parts of Britain, then perhaps it should be seen as this trend 'from the vague to the definite', rather than some basic evolutionary scheme which distinguishes between fundamentally different *types* of tenure and then attaches the more primitive to field systems of the Celtic

fringe and the more advanced to the field systems of lowland England.[139]

The reason why a stark contrast has been made between Celtic primitivism and 'modern' feudalism for so long in the past, lies in the influence of the Irish law tracts. They have been a convenient short-cut to provide a picture of Irish society as a prelude to the coming of the Normans – even though they refer to a period almost 500 years before. Very little work has been done on the social and economic structure of twelfth-century Ireland. Most scholarly activity has been devoted to an analysis of the political situation. What reinforced the primitive tribalism was the account of the twelfth-century Irish by Giraldus Cambrensis. As Anngret Simms pointed out:

> We should see these unflattering remarks in a European context. At the very time when Gerald of Wales wrote unfavourably about the Irish, German chroniclers made similar statements about the Scandinavians and the Slavs. The issue here is that, in the twelfth century, the heart of Western Europe was economically more developed then [sic] its peripheral region [sic], be they Celtic, Scandinavian or Slav. And the observers felt that these underdeveloped regions were ripe for development.[140]

It might be pointed out that it is a world-wide phenomenon that those who take over lands to which they have no rights accuse the natives of misuse or no use of the land as a means of justifying their activities. Natives everywhere tend to view this activity as *exploitation* not development.[141]

Matthew Stout's recent book on the ringfort is an important contribution to our understanding of the problems associated with this settlement type and will provide a basis for future discussion.[142] Most recent of all is the massive contribution of Fergus Kelly on early Irish farming.[143]

Conclusion

The foregoing discussion is part of work in progress on the problems of settlement in early Ireland. As is obvious from the historiography of the subject discussed above, the problem of settlement cannot be adequately dealt with by a single discipline. It should be clear, too, that what I have discussed is much more revealing of the attitudes and assumptions of scholars than of the world of early Ireland. When the early Irish speak directly to us themselves, through the surviving documents, however difficult of interpretation and fragmentary that message may be, any attempt to explain the past without due regard to that message must be considered inadequate.

There has been a considerable number of (more often partial) excavations of raths over the years. But what is the function of the rath in the landscape? Is it the same in AD 550 as it is in 750, as in 950 or in 1150? How can any analysis of the artifacts be meaningful unless it is related to the society that produced them? When a 'rath' or a 'ringfort' becomes a classic settlement type it can seem timeless and locationless. Comparisons can be made, for example with places called *baile*. Under these circumstances, perhaps it is not surprising that the results have been ambiguous and disappointing.

In scholarship it is always more comforting to examine the 'classic' site, text or monument that provides the model for everything else. However, since life is a constant process of change it is the non-'classic' that often provides the best evidence for change. 'Rath-like' structures, 'motte-like' structures are likely to be of greater importance in demonstrating change in the settlement record. If the raths cease (at whatever time) as a settlement type, what replaced them? If unenclosed settlement becomes the norm, leaving little trace in the archaeological record, there is a danger that its importance is lessened simply because it is less visible. Such a change presupposes a transformation of society itself. That such a transformation was increasing in momentum between the tenth and the twelfth centuries can be demonstrated from the historical evidence.

Notes

1 L. Bieler, *The Irish Penitentials*, Scriptores Latini Hiberniae, vol. v (Dublin, 1963), pp. 54, 56.
2 M.J. Faris (ed.), *The Bishops' Synod* (*'The First Synod of St. Patrick'*), a symposium with text translation and commentary (Francis Cairns, School of Classics, University of Liverpool, 1976).
3 Ibid. pp. 2, 4.
4 Ibid. p. 9.
5 Ibid. p. 29.
6 Ibid. p. 41.
7 As the members of the symposium recognised, cf. p. 41.
8 Bieler, *Penitentials*, pp. 80–1.
9 Ibid. p. 243.
10 J. Campbell, 'Bede's words for places', in P.H. Sawyer, (ed.), *Names, Words, and Graves: Early Medieval Settlement* (School of History, University of Leeds, 1979), pp. 34–54.
11 Ibid. p. 43.
12 E.J. Gwynn and W.J. Purton (eds), 'The monastery of Tallaght', *Proceedings of the Royal Irish Academy*, 29c (1911), pp. 115–79.
13 Ibid. pp. 149–50.
14 C. Plummer, *Vitae Sanctorum Hiberniae*, vol. 2 (Oxford, 1910), pp. 259–60.
15 L. Kuchenbuch, *Bäuerliche Gesellschaft und Klosterherrschaft im 9. Jahrhundert. Studien zur Sozialstruktur der Familia der Abtei Prüm* (Wiesbaden, 1978), cf. 'Verkehr und Handel', pp. 299–305.
16 D.A. Binchy, 'Secular institutions', in M. Dillon (ed.), *Early Irish Society* (Dublin, 1954), pp. 52–65.
17 Ibid. p. 54.
18 Ibid. p. 53.
19 Ibid. pp. 55–6.

20 As I have in C. Doherty, 'The monastic town in early medieval Ireland', in H.B. Clarke and A. Simms (eds), *The Comparative History of Urban Origins in Non-Roman Europe: Ireland, Wales, Denmark, Germany, Poland and Russia from the Ninth to the Thirteenth Century*, British Archaeological Reports: International Series 255, 2 vols (Oxford, 1985), vol. 1, pp. 45–75. The study of this type of town has been neglected in Anglo-Saxon England but now see the comments of J. Blair, 'Minster churches in the landscape', in D. Hooke (ed.), *Anglo-Saxon Settlements* (Oxford, 1988), pp. 35–58, at p. 48.

21 For views of the problem see: H.P.R. Finberg, *The Agrarian History of England and Wales*, vol. 1: ii (Cambridge, 1972), pp. 423–7, 483–7; H.P.R. Finberg, *The Formation of England 550–1042* (Paladin, Frogmore, St Albans, 1976), pp. 83–7; P.H. Sawyer, *From Roman Britain to Norman England* (London, 1978), pp. 164–7; E. Miller and J. Hatcher, *Medieval England: Rural Society and Economic Change 1086–1348* (London, 1978), pp. 84–7; T. Unwin, 'Towards a model of Anglo-Scandinavian rural settlement in England', in D. Hooke (ed.), *Anglo-Saxon Settlements* (Oxford, 1988), pp. 77–98.

22 F. Bange, 'L'ager et la villa: structures du paysage et du peuplement dans la région mâconnaise à la fin du Haut Moyen Age (ixe–xie siècles)', *Annales, Économies, Sociétés, Civilizations*, 39, no. 3 (1984), p. 534; P. Demolon, 'Villes et villages dans le nord-est de la Neustrie du VIe au IXe siècle', and C. Lorren, 'Le village de Saint-Martin de Trainecourt à Mondeville (Calvados), de l'antiquité au haut Moyen Âge', in H. Atsma (ed.), *La Neustrie: Les pays au nord de la Loire de 650 à 850* (Jan Thorbecke Verlag, Sigmaringen, 1989), vol. 2, pp. 435–7, 439–65; Although there would seem to be no general agreement on the origin of the medieval village in Denmark it has been argued that the 'historical villages were permanently occupied from between the late 10th and the early 12th century … and that settlements were earlier moved at irregular intervals'. This comment appears in U. Näsman, 'The Germanic Iron Age and Viking Age in Danish archaeology: a survey of the literature 1976–1986', *Journal of Danish Archaeology*, 8 (1989), pp. 159–87, at p. 174. For the interesting example of Åland in Sweden see B. Roeck Hansen, 'Settlement change and agricultural structure in the late Iron Age and Medieval Åland', in *Geografiska Annaler*, 70B (1988), pp. 87–93. The problem of continuity is also discussed by M. Riddersporre, 'Settlement site – village site: analysis of the toft-structure in some Medieval villages and its relation to Late Iron Age settlements. A preliminary report and some tentative ideas based on Scanian examples', in *Geografiska Annaler*, 70B (1988), pp. 75–85. Similarly see M. Müller-Wille, W. Dörfler, D. Meier and H. Kroll, 'The transformation of rural society, economy and landscape during the first millennium AD: archaeological and palaeobotanical contributions from Northern Germany and Southern Scandinavia', in *Geografiska Annaler*, 70B (1988), pp. 53–68. For Anglo-Saxon England see the important collection of essays edited by D. Hooke (ed.), *Anglo-Saxon Settlements* (Oxford, 1988).

23 But note just how complex is the concept 'village' even in modern times. The discussion by P. Flatrès makes for very sobering reading: 'Hamlet and village', in R.H. Buchanan, E. Jones and D. McCourt (eds), *Man and his Habitat. Essays Presented to Emyr Estyn Evans* (London, 1971), pp. 165–85. Cf. also B.K. Roberts, *The Making of the English Village* (Longman, Harlow, Essex, 1987), pp. 6, 8.

24 F. Bange, 'L'ager et la villa', p. 544.

25 J. Campbell, 'Bede's words for places', p. 43. Cf. pp. 43–9 for a general discussion of the problem.

26 J. Cuisenier et R. Guadagnin (eds), *Un village au temps de Charlemagne: moines et paysans de l'abbaye de Saint-Denis du VIIe siècle à l'an mil*, Éditions de la Réunion des Musées Nationaux (Paris, 1988), p. 116.

27 R. Guadagnin, 'Archéologie de l'habitat rural du haut Moyen Âge', in J. Cuisenier et R. Gaudagnin (eds), *Un village au temps de Charlemagne*, pp. 142–4.

28 Ibid. pp. 116–17.

29 D.A. Binchy, 'The passing of the old order', in B. Ó Cuív (ed.), *Proceedings of the International Congress of Celtic Studies Held in Dublin, 6–10 July, 1959* (Dublin, 1962), pp. 119–32.

30 Ibid. p. 119.

31 Ibid. p. 119.

32 Edited by O. Bergin in *Studies*, xiv (1925), pp. 403–7. It was reprinted in O. Bergin, *Irish Bardic Poetry: texts and translations together with an introductory lecture by Osborn Bergin*, with a foreword by D.A. Binchy, compiled and edited by D. Greene and F. Kelly (Dublin, 1970), pp. 120–3, trans., pp. 266–8.

33 D.A. Binchy, 'The passing of the old order', p. 122.

34 Ibid. p. 122.

35 Ibid. p. 131.

36 G.R.J. Jones, 'Post-Roman Wales', in H.P.R. Finberg (ed.), *The Agrarian History of England and Wales*, vol. 1: ii (Cambridge, 1972), pp. 281–2.

37 G.R.J. Jones, 'The tribal system in Wales: a re-assessment in the light of settlement studies', in *Welsh History Review*, 1 (1961), pp. 111–14 and 'Die Entwicklung der ländlichen Besiedlung in Wales', in *Zeitschrift für Agrargeschichte und Agrarsoziologie*, 10 (1962), pp. 174–6. See also the comments of D. Ó Corráin, 'Some legal references to fences and fencing in early historic Ireland', in T. Reeves-Smyth and F. Hamond (eds), *Landscape Archaeology in Ireland*, British Archaeological Reports, British Series no. 116 (Oxford, 1983), pp. 247–51, at p. 250.

38 See C. Doherty, 'The Vikings in Ireland: a review', in H.B. Clarke, M. Ní Mhaonaigh and R. Ó Floinn (eds), *Ireland and Scandinavia in the Early Viking Age* (Dublin, 1998), pp. 288–330. See also F.J. Byrne, 'Tribes and tribalism in early Ireland', in *Ériu*, xxii (1971), pp. 128–66; and D. Ó Corráin, 'Nationality and kingship in pre-Norman Ireland', in T.W. Moody (ed.), *Nationality and the Pursuit of National Independence* (Belfast: Appletree Press, 1978), pp. 1–35.

39 Jones, 'Post-Roman Wales', p. 339. Cf. also W. Davies, *Wales in the Early Middle Ages* (Leicester University Press, 1982), pp. 19–27, 41–47 and G.R.J. Jones, 'The Dark Ages', in D.H. Owen (ed.), *Settlement and Society in Wales* (University of Wales Press, Cardiff, 1989), pp. 177–97.

40 Jones, 'Post-Roman Wales', p. 341.

41 Jones, 'Post-Roman Wales', pp. 343–9.

42 Jones, 'The Dark Ages', pp. 183–5.

43 S. Applebaum, 'Roman Britain', in H.P.R. Finberg (ed.), *The Agrarian History of England and Wales*, vol. 1: ii (Cambridge, 1972), pp. 264–5.

44 But possibilities are beginning to be explored. Cf. L.A.S. Butler, 'The "monastic city" in Wales: myth or reality?', in *Bulletin of the Board of Celtic Studies*, 28 (1979), pp. 458–67 and T.A. James, 'Air photography of ecclesiastical sites in South Wales', in N. Edwards and A. Lane (eds), *The Early Church in Wales and the West: Recent work in Early Christian Archaeology History and Place-Names*, Oxbow Monograph 16 (Oxford, 1992), pp. 62–76 and see the interesting evidence for Cornwall in the same collection of essays: A. Preston-Jones, 'Decoding Cornish churchyards', pp. 105–24, at p. 124.

45 Cf. H. Pryce, 'Ecclesiastical wealth in early medieval Wales', in N. Edwards and A. Lane (eds), *The Early Church in Wales and the West: Recent work in Early Christian Archaeology History and Place-Names*, Oxbow Monograph 16 (Oxford, 1992), pp. 22–32 at pp. 30–1.

46 A point already made by F.J. Byrne, 'Tribes and tribalism in early Ireland', p. 140. The possibilities have also been indicated by T. McErlearn, 'The Irish townland

system of landscape organisation', in T. Reeves-Smyth and F. Hamond (eds), *Landscape Archaeology in Ireland*, British Archaeological Reports, British Series no. 116 (Oxford, 1983), pp. 315–39, at 333–4.

47 Cf. K. Jackson, *The Gaelic Notes in the Book of Deer* (Cambridge, 1972), pp. 114–16.

48 L. Swan, 'Enclosed ecclesiastical sites and their relevance to settlement patterns of the first millennium AD', in T. Reeves-Smyth and F. Hamond (eds), *Landscape Archaeology in Ireland*, in British Archaeological Reports, British Series no. 116 (Oxford, 1983), pp. 269–80, at 276–8.

49 Ibid. p. 277.

50 L. Bieler (ed.), *Patrician Texts in the Book of Armagh*, Scriptores Latini Hiberniae, 10 (Dublin, 1979), p. 158; C. Doherty, 'The cult of St Patrick and the politics of Armagh in the seventh century', in J.M. Picard (ed.), *Ireland and Northern France, AD 600–850* (Dublin, 1991), pp. 61–2, 65.

51 Cf. J. Henderson and R. Ivens, 'Dunmisk and glass making in Early Christian Ireland', *Antiquity*, 66 (1992), pp. 52–64, at p. 56.

52 R. Ivens, 'Excavations at Dunmisk Fort, Co. Tyrone, 1984–86', *Ulster Journal of Archaeology*, 52 (1989), pp. 17–110, at p. 61. See also the short notice by Ivens in A. Hamlin and C. Lynn (eds), *Pieces of the Past* (Belfast, 1988), pp. 27–9.

53 J. Henderson and R. Ivens, 'Dunmisk and glass making', *passim*.

54 Ibid. p. 56. J.P. Mallory and T.E. McNeill, *The Archaeology of Ulster: From Colonization to Plantation* (Belfast, 1991), p. 208, point out that similar mixed burials were found at Derry Church, Co. Down.

55 Henderson and Ivens, 'Dunmisk and glass making', p. 56.

56 C. Manning, 'Archaeological excavation of a succession of enclosures at Millockstown, Co. Louth', in *Proceedings of the Royal Irish Academy*, 86c (1986), pp. 134–81.

57 Ibid. p. 163.

58 Ibid. pp. 164–5.

59 Ibid. p. 164.

60 C. Doherty, 'The cult of St Patrick and the politics of Armagh', pp. 60–1.

61 Cf. D. Ó Corráin, 'Early Irish churches: some aspects of organisation', in D. Ó Corráin (ed.), *Irish antiquity: essays and studies presented to Professor M.J. O'Kelly* (Cork, 1981), pp. 327–41.

62 Gwynn and Purton (eds), 'The Monastery of Tallaght' §§2, 4, 26: pp. 127–8, 137.

63 See the important survey by A. Hamlin, 'The early Irish Church: problems of identification', in N. Edwards and A. Lane (eds), *The Early Church in Wales and the West: Recent work in Early Christian Archaeology History and Place-Names*, Oxbow Monograph 16 (Oxford, 1992), pp. 138–44.

64 L. Swan, 'The Early Christian ecclesiastical sites of County Westmeath', in J. Bradley (ed.), *Settlement and Society in Medieval Ireland: Studies Presented to F.X. Martin, o.s.a.* (Boethius Press, Kilkenny, 1988), pp. 3–31.

65 See the recent study of this problem by C. Etchingham, 'The early Irish Church: some observations on pastoral care and dues', in *Ériu*, xlii (1991), 99–118. For the role of the tithe in the formation of parochial boundaries see the interesting discussion of G.W.O. Addleshaw, *The development of the parochial system from Charlemagne (768–814) to Urban II (1088–1099)*, University of York, Borthwick Institute of Historical Research. St Anthony's Hall Publications no. 6 (St Anthony's Press, York, 1954, rpr. 1970), p. 4. Cf. also by Addleshaw, *The beginnings of the parochial system*, no. 3 in the same series, 1953, repr. 1970; and also by him: *The pastoral organisation of the modern dioceses of Durham and Newcastle in the time of Bede*, Jarrow Lecture, 1963 (Rector of Jarrow, Jarrow on Tyne, 1963). For a more recent discussion see J. Blair, 'Minster churches in the landscape', pp. 35–58. I should like to thank my colleague Dr E. Colman for the following references: C. Violante, 'Pievi e

parrocchie nell Italia settentrionale durante i secoli xi e xii', in *Le istituzioni ecclesi-astiche della "Societas Christiana" dei seculi xi–xii*, being *Atti della vi settimana internationale di studio a Mendola* (Milan, 1977) and C. Violante, 'Le strutture orga-nizzative della cura d'anime nella campagne dell'Italia centrosettentrionale (secoli v–x)', in *Settimana di Studio Spoleto*, xxviii (1980). See also C. Boyd, *Tithes and Parishes in Medieval Italy* (Ithaca, 1952).

66 On this point see T. McErlearn, 'The Irish townland system', p. 333.

67 Cf. C. Doherty, 'Some aspects of hagiography as a source for Irish economic history', *Peritia*, 1 (1982), pp. 300–28.

68 E. Estyn Evans, 'Some survivals of the Irish openfield system', in *Geography*, xxiv (1939), p. 28.

69 Ibid. p. 24.

70 Cf. J.M. Graham, 'Transhumance in Ireland', *The Advancement of Science*, x, no. 37 (1953), p. 75. I wish to thank Professor S. Ó Catháin for the following account of booleying by Niall Ó Dubhthaigh as recorded by S. Ó hEochaidh, 'Buailteachas i dTír Chonaill', in *Béaloideas*, 13 (1943 [1944]), pp. 130–58 at p. 141. Ó Dubhthaigh was a native of Baile na Bealtaine, Beltany.

71 Evans, 'Some survivals', p. 30.

72 Ibid. p. 27.

73 M. Duignan, 'Irish agriculture in early historic times', in *Journal of the Royal Society of Antiquaries of Ireland*, 74 (1944), p. 127.

74 Ibid. p. 128.

75 Cf. R.H. Buchanan, 'Rural change in an Irish townland, 1890–1955', in *The Advancement of Science*, xiv, no. 56 (1958), pp. 291–300; and in the same journal, V.B. Proudfoot, 'Ancient Irish field systems', xiv, no. 56 (1958), pp. 369–71; 'Ireland', xv (1958), pp. 336–38, and in a fuller form in 'Clachans in Ireland', in *Gwerin*, ii (1958–9), 110–22.

76 S. Mac Airt, 'County Armagh: toponymy and history', in *Proceedings of the Irish Catholic Historical Committee 1955* (Dublin, 1955), p. 3.

77 Ibid. p. 5.

78 Proudfoot, 'Ireland', p. 337. Flatrès has suggested that a clachan can be a cluster of as low as two houses (P. Flatrès, 'Hamlet and village', p. 170). Which wall of the house does a 'proto-clachan' represent? H. Clarke has recently suggested that such a philosophical concept existed at core of Áth Cliath (cf. 'The topographical development of early medieval Dublin', *Journal of the Royal Society of Antiquaries of Ireland*, 107 (1977), p. 36). Indeed since it has been noted (Proudfoot, 'Clachans', pp. 117–18) that clachans have emerged in areas from which medieval rundale had disappeared and had evolved from a single farm, logically it is the single farm in such a case that can, with some justification, be called a 'proto-clachan'.

79 Ibid. p. 337.

80 Ibid. p. 338. For the dynamics of Scottish townships see R.A. Dodgshon, 'Changes in Scottish township organisation during the medieval and early modern periods', in *Geografiska Annaler*, 59B (1977), pp. 51–65; and R.A. Dodgshon and E. Gunilla Olsson, 'Productivity and nutrient use in eighteenth-century Scottish Highland townships', in *Geografiska Annaler*, 70B (1988), 39–51.

81 R.H. Buchanan and B. Proudfoot, 'Excavations at Murphystown, Co. Down', in *Ulster Journal of Archaeology*, 21 (1958), 115–26; R.H. Buchanan, J.H. Johnson and B. Proudfoot, *Ulster Journal of Archaeology*, 22 (1959), 130–3.

82 Proudfoot, 'Ireland', p. 338.

83 D. McCourt, 'The dynamic quality of Irish rural settlement', in R.H. Buchanan, E. Jones and D. McCourt (eds), *Man and his Habitat. Essays Presented to Emyr Estyn Evans* (London, 1971), pp. 126–64.

84 Ibid. p. 129.

85 Ibid. p. 129.
86 The frequent and tiresome comparisons that are made between conservative Irish 'tribalism' and 'advanced' or 'modern' feudalism has served as a cloak for lack of proper historical investigation into eleventh and twelfth-century Irish history. For an enlightened critique of the uses and abuses of the term 'feudalism' see E.A.R. Brown, 'The tyranny of a construct: feudalism and historians of medieval Europe', in *American Historical Review*, 79 (1974), pp. 1063–88 at p. 1077.
87 McCourt, 'The dynamic quality of Irish rural settlement', p. 132.
88 Cf. C. Ó Danachair, 'An Rí' (The King): an example of traditional social organisation', in *Journal of the Royal Society of Antiquaries of Ireland*, 111 (1981), pp. 14–28.
89 This error of historical reasoning was discussed by Marc Bloch in *The Historian's Craft* (Manchester University Press, 1954 rpr.1969), 'Nomenclature', pp. 156–89.
90 McCourt, 'The dynamic quality of Irish rural settlement', p. 134. This is a complicated problem. There seems to have been a narrowing of the extended kin-group in the early period. Cf. D.A. Binchy, 'The linguistic and historical value of the Irish law tracts', in *Proceedings of the British Academy*, 29 (1943), 195–227, repr. Dafydd Jenkins (ed.), *Celtic Law Papers* (Brussels, 1973), pp. 102–3; cf. also F.J. Byrne, *Irish Kings and High-Kings* (London, 1973), p. 123. T. Charles-Edwards, 'Kinship, status and the origins of the hide', in *Past and Present*, 56 (1972), p. 17. For a detailed examination of a modern system of kin-community see the excellent work of Robin Fox, *The Tory Islanders: A People of the Celtic Fringe* (Cambridge University Press, 1978) especially chapters 4–6. Cf. also R. A. Dodgshon, 'Symbolic classification and the development of early Celtic landscape', in E. Lyle (ed.), *Duality*, vol. 1 of *Cosmos: The Yearbook of the Traditional Cosmology Society* (Edinburgh, 1985), pp. 61–83, at p. 76. For a comment on fragmentation, dispossession and reconsolidation in the late sixteenth–early seventeenth century see P.J. Duffy, 'The territorial organisation of Gaelic landownership and its transformation in County Monaghan, 1591–1640', in *Irish Geography*, xiv (1981), pp. 1–26, at p. 10.
91 McCourt, 'The dynamic quality of Irish rural settlement', p. 141, quoting N. Taaffe, *Observations on Affairs in Ireland* (Dublin, 1776), p. 12; and McCourt, p. 149, referring to Sir H. Piers, 'A chorographical description of the county of West Meath. 1682', in C. Vallency, *Collectanea de rebus Hibernicis*, vol. I (Dublin, 1770), pp. 116–17.
92 N. Taaffe, *Observations on Affairs in Ireland from the Settlement in 1691, to the Present Time* (Dublin, 1766), p. 13. This 1766 edition is the earliest I could find.
93 Sir H. Piers, Baronet, A *Chorographical Description of the County of West-Meath Written in AD 1682*, printed in Major C. Vallancey, *Collectanea de Rebus Hibernicis*, vol 1, second edition, 1786 (reprinted facsimile by Meath Archaeological and Historical Society, 1981, p. 115).
94 From 'The presentments of the juries of the County and City of Waterford, 1537', in H.J. Hore and Rev. J. Graves (eds), *The Social State of the Southern and Eastern Counties of Ireland in the Sixteenth Century being The Presentments of the Gentlemen, Commonalty, and Citizens of Carlow, Cork, Kilkenny, Tipperary, Waterford, and Wexford, made in the Reigns of Henry VIII and Elizabeth printed from the originals in the Public Record Office London* [The Annuary of the Royal Historical and Archaeological Association of Ireland for the Years 1855, 1858, 1868 and 1869] (Dublin, 1870) p. 192.
95 G. Mac Niocaill, *Notitiae as Leabhar Cheanannais 1033–1161* (Cló Morainn, Baile Átha Cliath, 1961), p. 22; cf. C. Doherty, 'Some aspects of hagiography as a source for Irish economic history', p. 314. I feel more certain now that the scolócs mentioned in the Kells charters are simply farmers by the twelfth century. Niall Ua Flannacáin, king of Tethba, who was killed by his own people in 1036 (cf. *Annals of Ulster*) was called Scolóc, probably a nickname. The activity of this family had

little to do with scholarship. The leader of the students may be seen in the same annals in 1042 where one was killed: *Mael Petair H. hAilecan, fer leighinn 7 toisech m. leighinn Aird Macha do marbad do feraibh Fernmhuighi* (Mael Petair ua hAilecáin, lector and master of the students of Ard Macha, was killed by the men of Fernmag). Cf. also at 1166 where there is a *toisech macleighind* in Derry. I find no reference to the *toísech na scolóc* in the annals which again suggests that this is the less important office. The office of *taísech na macc légind* also occurs on a number of occasions in the Kells Charters. Óengus Úa Gamna held both offices, but if one may go by the dates of the charters he may have been overseer of the scolócs earlier in his career.

96 McCourt, 'The dynamic quality of Irish rural settlement', p. 143.
97 Cf. Y.M. Goblet (ed.), *A Topographical Index of the Parishes and Townlands of Ireland*, Irish Manuscripts Commission (Dublin, 1932), pp. 109, 348.
98 *General Alphabetical Index to the Townlands, Towns, Parishes and Baronies of Ireland. Based on the Census of Ireland for the Year 1851* (Dublin, 1861 [rpr. Baltimore, Maryland, 1984]).
99 S. Lewis, *A Topographical Dictionary of Ireland*, 2 vols (London, 1837 [rpr. Baltimore, Maryland, 1984]), vol. 2, p. 10.
100 Listed by de hóir following Price in Éamonn De hÓir, 'Nóta faoi bhéim na Gaeilge i Logainmneacha Chontae Chill Mhantáin', *Dinnseanchas*, III, Uimh. 3 (1969), p. 70, deriving *sculloge* from *scológ*.
101 This may be a personal name however: cf. Richard Butler, *Dean Butler: Some Notices of the Castle and of the Ecclesiastical Buildings of Trim* [orig. Trim, 1854] with in addition a short life of Richard Butler by C.C. Ellison (Meath Archaeological and Historical Society 1978), p. 193. Scurlogstown = William Scorlagge's town, referring to a parish contiguous to that of Laracor and now united in the parish of Trim in Co. Meath. In County Wicklow, however, the name is more likely to derive from Thomas Scurlock, abbot of St Thomas in Dublin, who became deputy chancellor in 1366 and treasurer of Ireland in 1375. Cf. A.L. Elliott, 'The abbey of St. Thomas the Martyr, near Dublin', reprinted in H.B. Clarke (ed.), *Medieval Dublin: The Living City* (Irish Academic Press, 1990), p. 66.
102 Cf. C. Etchingham, 'Evidence of Scandinavian settlement in Wicklow', in K. Hanningan and W. Nolan (eds) *Wicklow History and Society* (Dublin 1994), p. 126.
103 E. Hogan, *Onomasticon Goedelicum* (Dublin, 1910), p. 646.
104 McCourt, 'The dynamic quality of Irish rural settlement', pp. 143–4. Cf. also Ingeborg Leister in her detailed study of Tipperary *Peasant Openfield Farming and its Territorial Organisation in County Tipperary* (Marburg/Lahn, 1976), pp. 35–7 and *passim*. See also p. 60 where she points out that place-name evidence in Lower Ormond suggests that the demesne farms of manors were the result of primary clearance.
105 I. Leister, *Peasant Openfield Farming*, p. 11, came to the conclusion that while there might be continuity of tradition there was unlikely to be continuity in situ. She also suggested, p. 12, that 'we seem well advised to treat the clachan as incidental to a "tradition" of self sufficiency farming'.
106 McCourt, 'The dynamic quality of Irish rural settlement', pp. 157, 153.
107 W. Reeves, 'On the townland distribution of Ireland', *Proceedings of the Royal Irish Academy*, 8 (1862), pp. 473–90. This paper has recently been reprinted as a pamphlet to commemorate the centenary of his death: William Reeves, *On the Townland Distribution of Ireland. A paper (1861) by William Reeves sometime Bishop of Down & Connor & Dromore*. Reprinted, by permission, 151 years after his succession to the Curacy of Kilconriola (Ballymena), to mark the centenary of his death (12 January 1892), while President of the Royal Irish Academy. Introduced by

E. Dunlop and E. McKendry. Ascona Series: 6 (Braid Books and Moyola Books, 1992).

108 T. Jones Hughes, 'Town and baile in Irish place-names', in N. Stephens and R.E. Glasscock (eds), *Irish Geographical Studies in honour of E. Estyn Evans* (The Queen's University of Belfast, 1970), pp. 244–58.

109 Ibid. p. 244.

110 Ibid. p. 246.

111 Ibid. p. 246.

112 Ibid. p. 274.

113 Ibid. p. 244.

114 L. Price, 'A note on *baile* in place-names', *Celtica*, 6 (1963), pp. 121–6.

115 Ibid. p. 124.

116 Ibid. p. 125.

117 Reeves, 'Townland distribution'. Cf. also P. Power (ed.), *Crichad an Chaoilli. Being the Topography of Ancient Fermoy* (Cork University Press, 1932), p. 4.

118 C. Toumey, 'Raths and clachans: the homogeneity of early Irish society', in *Éire-Ireland*, Winter (1980), pp. 86–105.

119 G. Barrett, 'Problems of spatial and temporal continuity of rural settlement in Ireland, AD 400 to 1169', in *Journal of Historical Geography*, 8, no. 3 (1982), pp. 245–60.

120 Ibid. p. 253.

121 Ibid. p. 253.

122 G.F. Barrett, 'Ring-fort settlement in County Louth: sources, pattern and landscapes', in *Journal of the County Louth Archaeological and Historical Society*, xx, no. 2 (1982), pp. 77–95; 'The reconstruction of proto-historic landscapes using aerial photographs: case studies in County Louth', in *Journal of the County Louth Archaeological and Historical Society*, xx, no. 3 (1983), pp. 215–36.

123 B.B. Williams, 'Excavations at Ballyutoag, County Antrim', in *Ulster Journal of Archaeology*, 47 (1984), pp. 37–49. For a more up-to-date account, including a map and reconstruction of site, see her report 'Reading the upland landscape: Ballyutoag, Co. Antrim', in A. Hamlin and C. Lynn (eds), *Pieces of the Past*, pp. 36–8.

124 B.B. Williams, 'Early Christian landscapes in County Antrim', in T. Reeves-Smyth and F. Hamond (eds), *Landscape Archaeology in Ireland*, p. 239.

125 Ibid. pp. 233–46.

126 Cf. the place-name in Leinster, *Buaile Mór*, mentioned in S. Ó hInnse (ed.), *Miscellaneous Irish Annals* (AD 1114–1437) (The Dublin Institute for Advanced Studies, Dublin, 1947), pp. 94–5, under the year 1228. Of course this may not have been a transhumance village but a large compound for cattle management. It has not been identified.

127 N. Edwards, *The Archaeology of Early Medieval Ireland* (London, 1990), p. 47.

128 Ibid. p. 46. For a useful discussion of souterrains see R. Warner, 'The Irish souterrains and their background', in H. Crawford (ed.), *Subterranean Britain: Aspects of Underground Archaeology* (New York, 1979), pp. 100–44. See also the comments of C. Manning, 'Archaeological excavation of a succession of enclosures at Millockstown, Co. Louth', in *Proceedings of the Royal Irish Academy*, 86c (1986), pp. 134–81, at 165–6. For the literary evidence see A.T. Lucas, 'Souterrains: the literary evidence', *Béaloideas*, 39–41 (1971–73), pp. 165–91.

129 V.M. Buckley, 'Meath souterrains: some thoughts on Early Christian distribution patterns', in *Ríocht na Mídhe*, viii, no. 2 (1988–9), p. 64; cf. also in County Meath, George Eogan, 'Ballynee souterrains, County Meath', in *Journal of the Royal Society of Antiquaries*, 120 (1990), pp. 41–64.

130 Cf. Buckley, 'Meath souterrains', p. 65; and his 'Ulster and Oriel souterrains – an indicator of tribal areas?', in *Ulster Journal of Archaeology*, 49 (1986), pp. 108–10, and the reply of R. Warner in the same issue, 'Comments on "Ulster and Oriel souterrains"', pp. 111–12.

131 P.J. Duffy, 'The territorial organisation of Gaelic landownership and its transformation in County Monaghan, 1591–1640', in *Irish Geography*, xiv (1981), pp. 1–26; and his 'Patterns of landownership in Gaelic Monaghan in the late sixteenth century', in *Clogher Record*, x (1981), pp. 304–22.

132 T. McErlean, 'The Irish townland system of landscape organisation', in T. Reeves-Smyth and F. Hamond (eds), *Landscape Archaeology in Ireland*, pp. 315–39.

133 I. Leister, *Peasant Openfield Farming and its Territorial Organisation in County Tipperary* (Marburg/Lahn, 1976).

134 Ibid. pp. 64–70.

135 Ibid. p. 67.

136 J.P. Mallory and T.E. McNeill, *The Archaeology of Ulster: From Colonization to Plantation* (Belfast, 1991).

137 Ibid. pp. 222–25.

138 Ibid. p. 225.

139 R. Dodgshon, 'The landholding foundations of the open-field system', in *Past and Present*, 67 (1975), pp. 3–29, at p. 29.

140 A. Simms, 'Continuity and change: settlement and society in Medieval Ireland c. 500–1500', in W. Nolan (ed.), *The Shaping of Ireland: The Geographical Perspective* (The Mercier Press, Dublin, 1986), pp. 44–5.

141 Recently C. Freeman has pointed out how similar attitudes of scholars to ancient Greece and Rome are changing: 'The old diffusionist approach, the view that "superior civilizations" somehow passed on their cultures to other more stagnant societies (an approach which had its ideological home in European imperialism), has been replaced by approaches which stress how local cultures have the power to absorb and adapt foreign cultures to their own use', in C. Freeman, *Egypt, Greece and Rome. Civilizations of the Ancient Mediterranean* (Oxford University Press, 1996), pp. 5–6. For a global view of this problem see the stimulating work of E.W. Said, *Culture and Imperialism* (London, 1993).

142 M. Stout, *The Irish Ringfort*, Irish Settlement Studies, no. 5 (Four Courts Press, Dublin, 1997).

143 F. Kelly, *Early Irish Farming. A study based mainly on the law-tracts of the 7th and 8th centuries AD* (School of Celtic Studies, Dublin Institute for Advanced Studies, 1997).

3

EARLY CHRISTIAN IRELAND

Settlement and environment

Matthew Stout

Introduction

The fragmentary nature of evidence for the Early Christian period makes an interdisciplinary approach essential for the reconstruction of past landscapes and settlement patterns.[1] Despite the efforts of the Group for the Study of Irish Historical Settlement to foster interdisciplinary links, much modern research remains unconcerned with the need to present an integrated understanding of the past.[2] Would-be practitioners of a multidisciplinary approach may have been discouraged by the hostile reception which greeted Smyth's innovative contributions to Early Christian studies.[3] Although one such critic professed 'unqualified admiration' for his multidisciplinary approach,[4] Smyth was attacked for his dependence on secondary sources, especially his reliance on *Ancient Laws of Ireland*, the flawed Victorian English-language translation of early Irish law. More importantly, Smyth was justifiably admonished for minimising the importance of early Irish law as a source for settlement history.[5] Would these attacks have been less virulent, and shorter, if the academic in question had not strayed beyond the boundaries of his core discipline? In another instance illustrating the pitfalls of interdisciplinary research, consider-able space has been given by an archaeologist to changes in the social hierarchy of the period based on an outdated theory from the field of Early Irish Law.[6] Thus, multidisciplinarians become uneasy consumers of a published product beyond their individual expertise, of works whose limitations are often known only to those at the core of individual disciplines. Despite these inherent dangers, this chapter reviews recent developments in a wide range of specialisms which have improved our understanding of Early Christian settlement.

Written sources

Early Christian Ireland is an historic period, but only just, and the correct use of available material, the most extensive and diverse vernacular literature in medieval Europe, is one of the most daunting tasks facing the settlement historian.[7] Archaeology and landscape studies reveal a great deal, but the use of contemporary and near contemporary sources is essential if we are to illuminate the history and society which shaped that material culture and geography. Especially difficult has been the interpretation of the two most commonly used sources for Early Christian settlement; legal tracts and the Lives of the Saints.[8]

Early Irish law tracts are now recognised as the richest source of information on Early Christian society. Until recently, published interpretations of the laws suggested that they related to an Iron Age society and had little relevance to the legal workings of the Early Christian period.[9] Modern scholarship highlights the Christian component in the laws[10] (most of which were compiled in the early eighth century),[11] and as a result, their relevance to contemporary society. The ecclesiastical basis of the laws can be overplayed, however, and some writers have thrown out the secular baby with the Iron Age bath water, seeing an ubiquitous clerical hand in the authorship and administration of the entire secular legal system; in Ó Corráin's words: 'a Christian law for a Christian people'.[12] Charles-Edwards rejects the view, expressed by Ó Corráin et al., that the compilers of the law tracts were churchmen.[13] What matters most to land-scape studies, however, is the widespread acceptance that these laws had a practical legal function in common use throughout Ireland, giving settlement historians the license to relate these legal texts to their findings. Kelly's *Guide to Early Irish Law* (published 1988) provides an indispensable introduction to the subject while settlement historians of this period have applauded his detailed study of Early Christian farming.[14]

There is some disagreement on how best to approach the various law tracts. Charles-Edwards views the differences between laws of different dates as reflecting changes within the legal system and society, and warns against presenting an analysis without chronological depth,[15] although he admits that 'legal texts are far from ideal sources if one is concerned to attach dates to economic and social changes'.[16] Charles-Edwards emphasises a shift from close kinship which extended to males to the level of second cousins (*derbfine*), to a narrower kinship limited to first cousins (*gelfine*). This transition, which reduced the number of persons eligible for a share of kin lands, is attributed to population pressure on the one hand and to downward social mobility caused by a static population on the other.[17] There is little evidence to support either of these contradictory claims. Patterson's view of differences in the legal texts has broader implications for settlement historians. The Munster tract Uraicecht Becc is thought to describe an 'agro-artisanal social system' in contrast to the Ulster/North Leinster tract *Crith Gablach* which has its origins in an 'agro-pastoral, clan-based social system'.[18] The possibility that Munster society afforded greater status to artisans, due to its remote position and the presence of copper, seems like an extravagant conclusion to draw from these sources as the different emphasis of the various law tracts does not necessarily indicate regional variation. For example, *Crith Gablach*, which concentrates on secular grades and makes no mention of clerical rank, cannot be used as evidence for claiming that the northern half of Ireland was pagan. One would require supporting evidence in the form of demonstrably different settlement patterns before Patterson's claims could be given any credence. The distribution of ogham stones, with their concentration in Munster, and the north-eastern concentrations of souterrains (underground places of refuge) and, more exclusively, of souterrain ware, may be evidence of the type of regionalisation to which Patterson is referring.[19] Regional variation in settlement patterns must be a primary consideration in future research. A third approach to the laws, that taken by McLeod,[20] is to ascribe contradictions between legal tracts to transcription errors and to view them as elaborations of one basic legal system which applied throughout Ireland. This simplifies (some would say oversimplifies)[21] matters by removing temporal and geographical considerations. However, McLeod's work is in harmony with the atemporal approach to distribution analysis described below.

The early Irish laws describe in minute detail many aspects of Early Christian settlement. They set out the amount of land each grade of society was expected to have; between 14 ha (35 acres) for the lowest free grade, up to 100 ha (245 acres) for the king of a *túath*.[22] They prescribe where the different grades and their land holdings should be located within a *túath*.[23] A precise value is ascribed to a six-part land classification system and locational attributes are quantified, for example proximity to roadways, bogs and seas.[24] Enclosure of the landscape is attested by the description of four varieties of fences.[25] The morphology and archaeology of ringforts (enclosed farmsteads) are detailed, and these closely correspond with results from distribution analysis and excavation.[26]

There are many references to kin-lands (lands held jointly by the *derbfine*), and references to cooperative farming enterprises. As these are legal texts and because cooperative land dealings are more litigious than independent farming enterprises, early Irish law might over-emphasise the extent and importance of land redistribution within the *túath*. Of paramount importance, however, is not to assume that cooperation is synonymous with nucleated settlement. Nowhere in the laws is there a description of such a settlement and it is not even 'approximately true', as Charles-Edwards has suggested, that nucleated settlement was the expression of servile status.[27] Patterson concludes sensibly that 'clustering of residences [implied by laws relating to cooperative farming] does not imply that houses lay side by side in compact villages, but only that residences … were near enough for people to interact together regularly'.[28]

Of recent studies, Patterson makes the most satisfactory attempt at integrating law and landscape in a holistic description of Early Christian settlement and society.[29] She uses the large corpus of early Irish law to reconstruct the complex hierarchical and familial relationships which constituted secular Irish society.[30] These relationships of dependence/protection linking people of different rank controlled an individual's social and economic behaviour, resulting in a well-ordered, dynamic and prosperous society. As regards settlement, however, Patterson over-emphasises the significance of *buailteachas* (booleying), and generally endorses a view of settlement and economy which is unduly influenced by studies of (allegedly 'survival') subsistence farming economies of the north and west, and by descriptions of late medieval Gaelic society.[31] Neither source bears much relationship to the workings of a thriving and autonomous Early Christian society. Closer interdisciplinary cooperation would have improved Patterson's discussion of the historic landscape.

Similarly Charles-Edwards should have taken greater heed of settlement historians in his section on *tellach*, laws relating to entry onto lands in pursuit of legal claims.[32] Claimants have first to enter land over the *fert*, translated elsewhere as boundary mound,[33] or more convincingly as boundary ditch,[34] but by Charles-Edwards as grave mound.[35] He believes that burials on boundaries were designed to defend inherited land from the claims of outsiders. If this interpretation is correct, one would expect to find widespread archaeological evidence for the use of Early Christian burial mounds, or burial mounds of any date, as boundary markers. Surely burial in graveyards within ecclesiastical centres was the norm during this period. All conclusions, whether they have their origins in literary sources or in the landscape, need to be assessed against other types of evidence.

Another rich source for the Early Christian landscape is contained within the Lives of the Saints. As in legal studies, the use of hagiography by the settlement historian was also retarded by early academic conclusions, in this instance, the view that the Lives were written no earlier than the twelfth century,[36] and that each life was a political statement made in the interests of a church or diocese.[37] In fact, Sharpe has shown that the earliest Latin lives were written by the end of the eighth century and that lives in Irish were composed from the early ninth century.[38] Few accounts concern saints living after 640[39] and Patrick's life, for example, was written only 200 years after his death.[40] In Sharpe's view, the author was essentially an antiquary who brought to his task of writing these early lives an interest in the past and a sense of Ireland's history, traditions and customs.[41] The lives are, therefore, a valid and contemporary source for the study of the Early Christian landscape.

Early in this century, Plummer drew our attention to the potential of this source for landscape studies. He noted that Ireland, especially as described in the Connaught lives, was extensively wooded[42] and that saints came from backgrounds where pastoral pursuits dominated over tillage-based activity.[43] Doherty highlighted the importance of hagiography and other early church records as a source for economic and settlement history.[44] The Lives describe monasteries as holy 'cities of refuge' but also make clear their importance to secular society. From the eighth century, monasteries became the site of fairs in response to the need for local exchange.[45] Indeed, monasteries jealously guarded their church lands and maintained vassals in a system which paralleled the secular world.[46] Bitel has also written at length on monastic settlement based on the Saints' Lives.[47] She demonstrates how church foundations, far from being isolated communities, chose riverine locations and sites near harbours to facilitate labourers and traders. Saint Crónán, who moved his early isolated church to a new location on the *Slighe Dála*,[48] chastised Saint Mochuda for his isolation; 'To a man who avoids guests and builds his church in a wild bog, away from the level road, I will not go; but let him have beasts of the wilderness for his guests.'[49] Physical *and* human geography dictated monastic locations.

The Lives of the Saints are particularly revealing about the tensions which arose between the early church and secular powers. In the life of Patrick from the *Book of Lismore*, it is clear that although the ecclesiastic wanted an upland location for his church, the secular powers originally insisted on a low-lying, less favourable site.[50] A brave face was put on this inferior status; in the Life of Ciarán of Clonmacnoise, the Saint says 'if it were here [at Clonmacnoise] that I were, though this stead were low as regards place, it would be high as regards honour and reverence'.[51] This accords well with the low-lying riverine distribution of monastic enclosures as described by Swan.[52] There is a strong association between the early church sites described in the Saints' lives and milling, perhaps accounting for their riverine distribution. Indeed, the chief economic activities of church sites, as described in the Lives, seem to be tillage-based.[53] In a vision which Bridget is said to have related to Patrick, there is a description of cross-ploughing (necessary before the introduction of the mould-board plough) and an explicit association between the church and tillage; 'the first four ploughs which thou beheldest, those are I and thou, who sow the four books of the Gospel with a sowing of faith, and belief, and piety'.[54]

There is a wide range of contemporary sources, other than the Saints' lives and law which are relevant to the landscape historian.[55] The *Annals* provide settlement information in an oblique way by referring to sites as belonging to particular territories, and they also provide an historic framework for the Early Christian period. The veracity of that record, like that of the laws, has been examined by Warner. While the annals were written as an actual contemporary record from as early as the mid-sixth century,[56] even pre-Christian events, as early as 2,345 BC if Warner's analysis can be accepted, are accurately dated.[57] A greater confidence, therefore, can be given to foundation dates of Early Christian monasteries. In a similar vein, Warner persists in the 'nativist' view that Irish myth must be regarded as pseudo-history. He argues that myths relating to *Tuathal Techtmar* (credited with the creation of the late Iron Age creation of the kingdom of *Mide*) are veiled accounts of a significant Romano-British invasion of Ireland and, in turn, the foundation of the innovations which led to the dynamism of the Early Christian period.[58] Settlement references also abound in the miscellany of Irish sources. The location of ringforts on upper slopes, noted in the distribution analysis, is attested to in 'The adventure of Cian's son Teigue' a story from the *Book of Lismore*:

Still they advance, and so to a wide smooth plain clad in flowering clover all bedewed with honey; a perfectly flat and even plain it was, without either rise or fall of surface except three prominent hills that it bore, each one of these having on its side an impregnable *dún*.[59]

There is the well-known reference to the ringfort constructed of food in *Aislinge Meic Conglinne*,[60] and the beautiful eighth-century poem which contrasts the ephemeral lives of men with the enduring occupation of ringforts; in this case the large platform ringfort outside Rathangan, Co. Kildare;

Ind ráith i comair in dairfedo,	The fort opposite the oakwood
ba Bruidgi, ba Cathail,	Once it was Bruidge's, it was Cathal's,
ba hÁedo, ba hÁilello,	It was Aed's, it was Ailill's,
ba Conaing, ba Cuilíni	It was Conaing's, it was Cuiline's
ocus ba Máele Dúin.	And it was Maelduin's.
Ind ráith d'éis cach ríg ar úair,	The fort remains after each in his turn,
ocus int shlúaig foait i n-úir.	And the kings asleep in the ground.[61]

Strict academic practice does not permit the use of sources dating from the twelfth century to be applied to earlier Irish society, as I have attempted in the previous paragraphs. Nonetheless, when late sources seem to describe earlier phenomena free of political implications, like the reference to cross-ploughing or locational preference, is there not some justification for thinking that these late sources may be based on earlier material or traditions and that they too should be utilised? Interdisciplinary discussions on the vast corpus of Irish sources should provide guidelines on the dating, origins and applicability of these texts to Early Christian settlement.

Surveys

A different type of written source, but of unequalled importance, is the large body of authoritative archaeological survey now available. Among the most significant recent breakthroughs in settlement studies are the Sites and Monuments Records (SMRs) and *Archaeological Inventories* for pre-1700 field-monuments in Ireland. Prior to the early 1980s, distribution analysis of all periods, but especially of the Early Christian where there are such large numbers of settlement sites, was hampered by a lack of hard data about Ireland's archaeological monuments. The lack of progress in recording our rapidly diminishing stock of field monuments was first addressed by An Foras Forbartha (now subsumed in the Department of the Environment). This was followed by the creation of county and regional archaeological surveys which were part of local development schemes. Some of these published important contributions to the study of early settlement.[62] The need to provide a uniform coverage was met by the foundation, in 1987, of the Sites and Monuments Record Office, under the overall supervision of David Sweetman of the Office of Public Works (OPW).

Co-directors Geraldine Stout and Michael Gibbons completed SMRs for counties in the Republic of Ireland. These are in the form of annotated maps accompanied by a database providing site type (if known) and precise location.[63] Sweetman also assumed overall control of the current publishing phase of the Archaeological Survey of Ireland – the compilation of *County Inventories*.[64] These give brief summaries of more extensive field reports of all county monuments classified by site type. One full volume, for County Louth, which provides detailed descriptions, plans and photographs of all known archaeological monuments, has been published.[65] Along with the dedication of human resources, the OPW, and now *Dúchas*, has spearheaded efforts to computerise and make accessible to the wider public their huge archaeological database through the medium of a sophisticated Geographical Information System. The archaeological survey of the six northern Irish counties is also well advanced, although the early promise of the *Archaeological Survey of County Down* has not been fulfilled.[66] Most sites in the six counties have been visited in the field, with publication promised shortly. These publications, databases and archives are the logical starting point for all future studies of human settlement in the Irish landscape.

Environmental history

As early as 1956, Mitchell highlighted the use of palynological research in interpreting the Early Christian environment.[67] This science, which reconstructs local vegetation on the basis of pollen evidence, has the advantage that it is unbiased either geographically or politically, unlike the Early Christian written record: nor is it shrouded in the uncertainties of contemporaneity and uneven destruction rates which contaminate the study of upstanding settlement remains. Throughout Ireland, the pollen cores tell a remarkably similar story of the environment which must form the backdrop to any study of the period. The results of thirteen pollen diagrams throughout Ireland have been summarised by O'Connell, who, more than any other modern palynologist, concentrates on more recent (geologically speaking) quaternary events (Figure 3.1).[68] In Ireland the late Iron Age (to *c.* AD 250) is characterised by a lull in human activity which permitted a regeneration of woodland and scrub. From AD 250, however, this 'Late Iron Age Lull' was followed by a period of intense and prolonged human activity which left most of the sampled sites clear of woodland. Closer examination of the pollen record shows the nature of this activity and the probable technological advances which brought it about. In the Burren, and elsewhere in Ireland (Figure 3.2),[69] the hazel decline is a key indication of the upsurge in farming activity. This is accompanied by a rise in *Plantago Lanceolata*, an indicator of pastoral-based farming. About the same time, *c.* AD 300, the introduction of cereal pollen in the profile indicates increased tillage activity, attributed by Mitchell to the introduction of the coulter plough.[70] Finally, *c.* AD 600 there is a rise in *Artimisia* pollen, which grows when competition from other weeds is reduced. Mitchell believes that this occurred with the introduction of the mouldboard plough.[71]

Related to woodland clearance, and linked to the expansion of population and increased numbers of ringforts, is the evidence for soil erosion. On the slopes of Forth Mountain in Co. Wexford, a drainage trench revealed thin layers of organic material under 1 m of soil. These deposits were dated to c. AD 500 and attributed to the construction of a ringfort and subsequent farming 600 m upslope.[72] A similar phenomenon was observed in a pollen cores from the Burren, Co. Clare, where a layer of silty clay in the peat deposits was dated to c. AD 480. This too was associated with the construction of a nearby ringfort and intensive grazing.[73]

The overall picture of an Early Christian upsurge in activity facilitated by advances in farming techniques is echoed in palaeozoological studies. This field has been dominated by animal bone analysis undertaken by McCormick. His work on the faunal remains from three important Early Christian excavations established the nature of animal husbandry in that period.[74] The inhabitants of Moynagh Lough, Knowth and Lagore, Co. Meath, practised a cattle-based, primarily dairy cattle economy, with sheep- and pig-rearing of minor importance. Of even greater significance than these findings, McCormick discovered that the composition of the dairy herd (71 per cent female) exactly mirrored the dairy herd as described in *Crith Gablach*, the eighth-century early Irish law tract

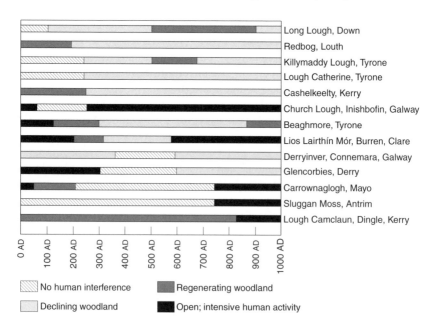

Figure 3.1   Summary of thirteen pollen diagrams
Source: After O'Connell (1991).

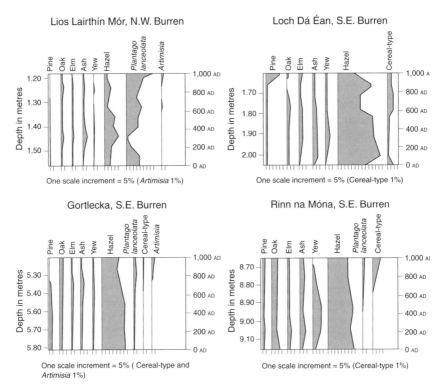

Figure 3.2 Pollen diagrams from the Burren, Co. Clare
Source: After Jelicic and O'Connell (1992).

on status.[75] More recently, McCormick has offered a bold hypothesis which, if true, further accentuates the marked discontinuity between the late Iron Age and Early Christian periods.[76] It has long been held that the slaughter of calves at an early age, noted in excavated sites as far back as the Middle Bronze Age, is an indication of dairying, as calves were considered to be in direct competition with the human population for milk. However, the Saint's lives and Laws draw attention to the need, in primitive breeds, for the calves to be present to stimulate the lactation reflex; therefore, the fact that calves were slaughtered in the first nine months is evidence *against* dairying in primitive herds. McCormick believes that this trait would have been bred out of the cattle if dairying had begun over a thousand years earlier. A prehistoric date was attributed to the introduction of dairying in Britain and Ireland at, for instance, the Middle Bronze Age site of Grimes Graves, Norfolk, where 47 per cent of cattle were slaughtered before they were 8 months old (Figure 3.3). In contrast, only 4 per cent of cattle from that age group were slaughtered at Moynagh Lough crannóg in Co. Meath. Liam Breatnach has highlighted facts which have implications for McCormick's conclusion.[77] The use of a *tulachan* or dummy calf was

89

recorded in nineteenth-century Scotland.[78] Thus it becomes possible that the need for calves to be present at milking was an enduring trait in cows or that the use of a *tulachan* was itself an enduring tradition which even in the Early Christian period had no bearing on the ability to give milk. Nonetheless, the possibility that dairying, and the resulting improvement in diet,[79] was introduced at the beginning of the Early Christian period could help to explain the upsurge in population which is implicit in the evidence for woodland clearance and the widespread construction of settlement sites. Further, it shows that in this period we have the origins of a diet in which milk products played a primary role; along with oats, also present in the Early Christian period,[80] these persisted as the primary diet of rural Irish people until the introduction of the potato.

Excavation

McCormick's work highlights the importance of archaeological discoveries for developing an understanding of Early Christian settlement. Excavations have established the date and function of the many forms of settlement in Ireland and recent excavations have shown the link between material culture and the written record. The dating of ringforts, Ireland's most numerous archaeological monument, has been particularly problematic. The uncertainty about the time span of occupation within these defended farmsteads has retarded efforts to analyse their distribution as an indicator of Early Christian settlement and society. The sheer number of sites, over 45,000, contrasts with the virtual absence of secular settlement for all prehistoric and historic periods prior to the

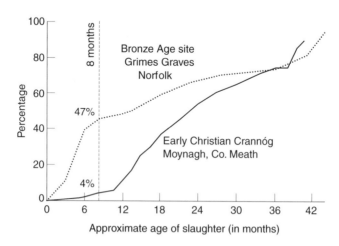

Figure 3.3   The slaughter of calves at an early age in the Middle Bronze Age site of Grimes Graves

Source: After McCormick (1992).

seventeenth century. Because of their large number, it seemed logical that some of these sites might fill the settlement void in other periods. Archaeological excavation, relying solely on stratigraphy as a dating device, seemed at first to support this approach. Ó Ríordáin argued that the ringfort at Cush and its associated souterrain pre-dated a bronze age burial.[81] It is more probable that the souterrain was later than the burial and was in fact cut through and then back-filled with the layer associated with the burial.[82] Further, no convincing evidence has been presented to firmly fix a half dozen *possibly* early sites into the pre-Christian Iron Age.[83] At the other end of the spectrum was Rynne's excavation of a double-banked ringfort near Shannon Airport.[84] He concluded that a seventeenth-century rectangular house was contemporary with the construction of the enclosing banks. Both Ó Ríordáin and Rynne based their conclusions solely on stratigraphic evidence, which can be problematic, especially in the case of structures set into wall foundations dug through earlier layers. Despite the extremes in dating produced from these excavations, it was still widely accepted that most ringforts dated from the Early Christian period. Finds from ringforts typically include a selection of items which date from the second half of the first millennium: wheel-made pottery, especially E ware;[85] a coarse pottery indigenous to Ireland known as souterrain ware;[86] glass beads; bone, bronze and iron pins; and artefacts of bone and metalwork dated to the period on art historical grounds.

The more widely accepted dating evidence is confirmed by the modern techniques of dendrochronology and the increasingly refined use of radiocarbon dating. Baillie, a leading world scholar in the development of dendrochronology, has constructed a detailed oak tree-ring chronology for Ireland reaching from the present day back to 5289 BC. This allows most oak samples from excavations to be dated to within a year. In turn, the dendrochronological record provides a basis on which to calibrate results and enhance the precision of radiocarbon dating.[87] Modern dating testifies to a much shorter span of years for the construction and occupation of ringforts and allied crannóg lake settlements than was indicated by the uncertain stratigraphical evidence. A cursory examination of the scientific dating evidence from 47 sites provides 114 dendro and radiocarbon dates spanning the years AD 236 (from a pre-ringfort occupation phase) to AD 1387. Over half the determinations date between AD 540 and AD 884, while nearly two-thirds of sites have the mid-point of their date range falling between AD 600 and AD 900. The firm conclusion is that the majority of Ireland's many ringforts and crannógs were occupied and probably constructed during a 300-year period from the seventh to the ninth centuries.[88] Further, the dating of different phases of occupation on some ringforts shows two-thirds of them to have been in use over a period spanning at least two centuries.[89] Although 71 per cent of these dates come from Ulster (45 per cent from Co. Antrim alone), there is no suggestion of any regional variation in the range of dates.[90] However, these dates do highlight how archaeological research in the Early Christian period has been dominated by Ulster archaeologists.

The function of various site types is a less vexed issue than that of dating. Proudfoot's summary of the economy of the Irish ringfort, based on excavations prior to 1960, provides us with a clear picture of the mixed tillage and livestock farming methods practised by ringfort dwellers.[91] Mytum dealt with essentially the same subject matter in his analysis of the farming economy, small-scale manufacturing and trade, albeit from a contentious processualist perspective.[92] The most outstanding individual excavation of recent years has been of the platform ringfort in Deer Park Farms, Co. Antrim. Here, Lynn found a tell-like accumulation of layers, in which, due to water-logging, the foundations of a large number of wooden structures and finds survived. The results from this site seriously challenged the notion that platform ringforts were medieval in date (the doorjambs of one house were felled in AD 648): more importantly, it showed the close link between the detailed morphological information contained in the law tracts and excavated finds. Thirty houses were found, only three or four of which were inhabited at any one time, indicating long occupation of the site. The houses had many of the features described in the law tracts for a farmer of the lowest independent (ócaire) grade, including houses conjoined in a figure of eight. The ócaire was also said to have a share in a mill and one of the wooden finds from Deer Park Farms, which would have perished on a dry site, was a paddle from a horizontal mill.[93]

In recent years, research excavations themselves have been infrequent, and Monk's programme concentrating on a group of ringforts at Lisleagh in Co. Cork is rare indeed. Two adjacent sites are being completely and meticulously excavated, ultimately revealing the function and status of these sites of various sizes and their relationship to one another.[94] Monk also wishes to place the excavated ringforts in the context of a detailed survey of other sites in the area. Without exception, past excavation results have given little indication of where a site figured in the local distribution. There is no indication if a site was typical, or the largest or smallest in an area; at the core or periphery of a meaningful territorial unit; in an upland or lowland position relative to other ringforts and ecclesiastical sites in an area. Monk's findings promise to address these shortcomings. In many cases, our knowledge of the excavation findings is based on short papers in a variety of popular books, journals, lectures and professional newsletters.[95] Final excavation reports are eagerly awaited.

During the twenty-five years that the GSIHS has been in existence, it has become commonplace to consider that church sites fulfilled a proto-urban function in Early Christian Ireland. The perceived certainty about their function, or perhaps the massive size of some of the early monastic centres, has meant that research excavations of this site type have been rare in Ireland. Amongst a few notable exceptions has been Swan's excavation of Kilpatrick, near Killucan, Co. Westmeath.[96] Only preliminary results are available, but these confirm perceptions gleaned from contemporary historical sources. Rare imported pottery from the Mediterranean confirms both the early date and international trading contacts which are characteristic of the early church in Ireland. Evidence was also uncovered for specialised manufacturing areas within the massive enclosure. Also significant was the massive proportions of the fosse enclosing the monastic site; up to 6 m wide at the top and 2.20 m deep. Evidence for an inner bank makes these defences even more impressive. A fosse of almost identical proportions enclosed the monastery at Tullylish, Co. Down.[97] While symbolically the enclosure might mirror the celestial city, it formed a large barrier here on earth, which both defined and defended the wide range of activities within the enclosure. Other important excavations of monastic sites were Lackenavorna, Co. Tipperary,[98] Reask, Co. Kerry[99] and Millockstown, Co. Louth.[100] The latter two show how monastic enclosures developed from small, possibly secular centres.

Horizontal mills are commonly found in association with early ecclesiastical centres, a juxtaposition confirmed at Williams' excavation of the ecclesiastical enclosure at Killylane, Co. Antrim.[101] Because these mills often survive in waterlogged conditions, it has been possible to recover a large number of precisely dateable timbers which have been of fundamental importance in the construction of Baillie's 7,000-year tree-ring chronology.[102] As a result, horizontal mills are the most accurately dated Irish field monument, and the largest corpus of first millennium watermill sites in the world.[103] They were mainly constructed within a 262-year period, between AD 581–843.[104] As these dates agree, in a general way, with the dating of ringforts and crannógs, the dynamism of the Early Christian period and the evidence for profound population growth becomes ever more apparent.

The excavations around the passage tomb at Knowth, Co. Meath have produced a great deal of evidence for Early Christian occupation, much of which is difficult to relate to settlement elsewhere in Ireland beyond the fact that it highlights the reoccupation of many prehistoric monuments in the Early Christian period. From the eighth century, the tomb at Knowth became the focus for an extensive, unprotected settlement consisting of thirteen houses and nine souterrains.[105] This is the only solid evidence for clustered, undefended secular settlement in the Early Christian period.[106] Souterrains, many leading from the floors of houses, others hidden at the back of satellite passage tombs, seem to have provided sufficient protection for the residents of this community. This is significant because it may mean that the many souterrains in Ireland unassociated with enclosing banks represent undefended, albeit dispersed, homesteads. Knowth was a royal site from about AD 800, but why such an unusual settlement form developed there is unknown. The souterrain within the Dowth passage tomb may suggest a similar type of settlement to that found at Knowth. Elsewhere, it is necessary to be cautious with regard to the undefended nature of souterrains. At Marshes Upper, near Dundalk in Co. Louth, recently published excavations of a large area surrounding two groups of souterrains produced evidence that most, if not all, the souterrains were associated with ringforts.[107] Gowen's excavation highlights the need to excavate outside known archaeological features as well as inside. It would be very valuable to learn, for example, the extent of settlement which took place outside ringforts and ecclesiastical enclosures.

Distribution

Much of the early analysis of ringfort distributions did not have the advantage of the clear chronological and functional backdrop which has emerged from modern excavation. As a result, the conclusions reached in earlier research need to be completely overhauled. Because of the belief that ringfort occupation spanned a 1,500-year period, a temporal dimension was projected into distributions which are, regardless of the time span of occupation, atemporal. Evans,[108] Davies[109] and Fahy[110] published works explaining distribution patterns which in their views developed over time. Davies, to take one example, published the result of decades of field work in south Ulster. He identified three types of ringfort: round drumlin top, long oval and waterside, and postulated that the native, or prehistoric people had occupied the round sites, while oval and waterside ringforts represented an intrusion from the south. These conclusions are entirely without foundation. Similarly without foundation was a more recent attempt to explain the distribution of ringforts in north-east Leinster. Graham and Barrett suggested that the continued construction of ringforts in the medieval period outside the area of Norman control accounted for the comparatively small number of ringforts in the Norman zone.[111] Statistics were used to support the valid hypothesis that ringforts in north Leinster are more numerous in the north-west but the obvious atemporal explanations for this were not explored, such as the attraction of settlement to the better drained slopes also in the north-west, and, in Louth, the possible alternative to ringfort occupation offered by unenclosed settlements associated with the numerous low-lying souterrains in the county. Mytum further complicates matters by suggesting that one-sixth of the c. 60,000 ringforts (his estimation) were occupied at any one time.[112] This begs the question as to which sixth and, if true, invalidates any effort to examine settlement and society on the basis of surviving distributions. Mytum's approach led him to conclude that ringforts were occupied only by the upper echelons of society; a conclusion incompatible with excavation results and less complex, but more compelling explanations of their distribution.[113]

The most convincing settlement models for this period are those which propose a relationship between sites in existing static distributions. These concentrate on the known domestic/farming pursuits of the ringfort occupants. Numerous studies have shown that ringforts are located on better agricultural land, demonstrating a marked preference for well-drained slopes. Since Fahy, these studies have used statistics to prove that distribution was dictated by environmental factors.[114] Accepting that predominantly pastoral-based communities chose the best farming locations, more complex settlement models seek to explain distribution patterns within environmentally favoured areas, with special reference to the inter-relationship between ringforts and their occupants (Figure 3.4).[115] That a relationship between ringforts did exist is implicit in the popular belief that each ringfort has a view of five neighbouring enclosures. Mitchell, whose *Irish Landscape* has the most impressive ideas about the period packed into the smallest amount of prose, describes this settlement model as 'defence in depth'.[116] Ringfort defences, although often intimidating, seem best designed to withstand lightning cattle raids as opposed to sieges designed to annex territories and populations. The tight distribution of sites allows for neighbours to come rapidly to the aid of the occupants of endangered ringforts or, alternatively, provides places where fleeing victims could find shelter and regroup for counter-attack.

Most ringforts are simple, single-banked enclosures (81 per cent in the south-west midlands) with internal diameters between 20 m and 44 m (84 per cent).[117] The existence of bivallate- and, more rarely, trivallate-ringforts having diameters in excess of 44 m suggests a hierarchy of enclosures which may have

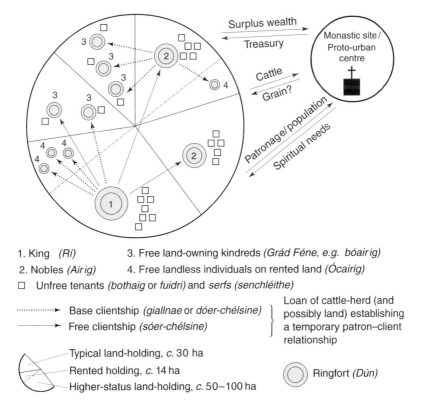

1. King *(Rí)*
2. Nobles *(Airig)*
3. Free land-owning kindreds *(Grád Féne, e.g. bóairig)*
4. Free landless individuals on rented land *(Ócairig)*
□ Unfree tenants *(bothaig* or *fuidri)* and *serfs (senchléithe)*

┈┈┈➤ Base clientship *(giallnae* or *dóer-chélsine)*
─────➤ Free clientship *(sóer-chélsine)*

} Loan of cattle-herd (and possibly land) establishing a temporary patron–client relationship

Typical land-holding, *c.* 30 ha
Rented holding, *c.* 14 ha
Higher-status land-holding, *c.* 50–100 ha

⊚ Ringfort *(Dún)*

Figure 3.4 Model of an Early Christian *túath* based on contemporary law tracts
Source: After Simms (1986) with additions by the author.

mirrored hierarchies in secular society. This concept was articulated as early as 1821 when a model of ringfort distribution fused both hierarchical and defensive concepts (Figure 3.5).[118] Warner's analysis of Clogher, Co. Tyrone, showed a documented royal site located in a central place position at the junction of two routeways in the midst of a grouping of less imposing ringforts.[119] In addition, the royal ringfort was adjacent to an ecclesiastical centre and a ritual site. While stressing that historical evidence alone can positively identify royal sites, Warner suggested indicators of high-status enclosures elsewhere in Ireland; adjacent ritual mounds, small but heavily defended probably multivallate sites, and excavation evidence for wealth, large houses and mixed industrial waste. Herity has published another detailed study of ringforts, this time near the royal site of Cruachain in Co. Roscommon.[120] In this densely populated region (1.34 sites per square km on average rising to nine sites per square km against an average for Ireland of 0.55 ringforts per square km) ringforts were located on elevated or gently sloping ground but are absent from the ridge tops and uplands dominated by ritual monuments.[121] This may not mean, as Herity has suggested, that the ring-barrows and ringforts are contemporary, as a preference for slopes, as opposed to hilltops, is a commonly observed phenomenon. In addition, ecclesiastical sites in the area *are* located near 'ritual foci'.[122] Nonetheless, Herity has highlighted an important consideration in distribution studies; non-economic issues can influence human decision making. Like Warner, he noted that the minority of sites with two or more banks did not have larger living areas, but displayed a greater need for defence and exhibition of prestige.[123] In fact, a large number of study areas reveal that multivallate sites constitute *c.* 18 per cent of

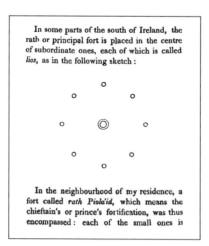

Figure 3.5 This 1821 description of Early Christian secular settlement is a precursor of recent hierarchical and defensive models

Source: Wood (1821).

the ringfort population.[124] This is evidence for a consistent and widespread settlement hierarchy which must mirror a similar social stratification.

These conclusions clarified the need to develop a classification which placed individual ringforts in the overall settlement hierarchy. I attempted to do this in work on the distribution of over 300 ringforts in two baronies in the south-west midlands (Ikerrin, Co. Tipperary and Clonlisk, Co. Offaly).[125] A multivariate classification method known as cluster analysis was used to define ringfort groupings. While credible in their own right (the groupings largely mirrored divisions observed in, for instance, Co. Down),[126] the distribution of the various ringfort groups was shown to exhibit explicable patterns throughout the study area. The real significance of the computer-derived classification was the way in which the conclusions based on ringfort morphology and distribution corresponded to the picture of a settlement hierarchy provided in the early Irish law tracts (Figure 3.6). One group (cluster 2 – shown in Figure 3.6 as the residence of an *aire forgill*) closely resembled Warner's description of royal compatible sites. The laws indicated a central location for high-status sites; cluster 2 ringforts were most centrally located within the modern townland network. Small enclosures (cluster 5) were located in close proximity to the high-status ringforts, corresponding to Wood's early hierarchy/defence model. These small ringforts were linked to the *ócaire* class who had no land in their own right but rented holdings from those with higher status. A group of large ringforts (cluster 4) was located in more isolated, strategically significant regions near barony and townland boundaries. The *aire déso*, equated by McLeod with the *aire échta* of similar status,[127] had an interterritorial military function which would fit in well with a multifunctional farmstead in a strategic location. Most numerous (38 per cent) were typical univallate ringforts with internal diameters averaging 30 m (cluster 3). Enclosures in this group were on good land, but in less strategic locations, and were rarely associated with high-status enclosures. These were ascribed to the independent *bóaire*, the lowest grade of freeman who held land in his own right. Low-lying platform ringforts (cluster 1), possibly farmsteads of less well-off *bóaire*, completed the classification. This model should now be tested in other areas of Ireland, especially where there are excavated ringforts.

A chronology of sites is impossible from archaeological survey alone and all ringforts are regarded as being contemporary in the above atemporal distribution analyses. Archaeological and written evidence supports this approach by providing evidence for ringfort locations which remained occupied over centuries. The implications for this in relation to population studies are profound. If it is assumed that 45,000 enclosures were occupied at the one time in Ireland during the seventh and eighth centuries, and each contained a single family and a couple of servants (ten persons?) then a secular population of *c.* 450,000 could be a reasonable estimate. Add to this the population of ecclesiastical enclosures and a population of *c.* 500,000 is suggested; this is close to the 'less than half a million' figure mooted by Byrne in the 1960s.[128] These figures

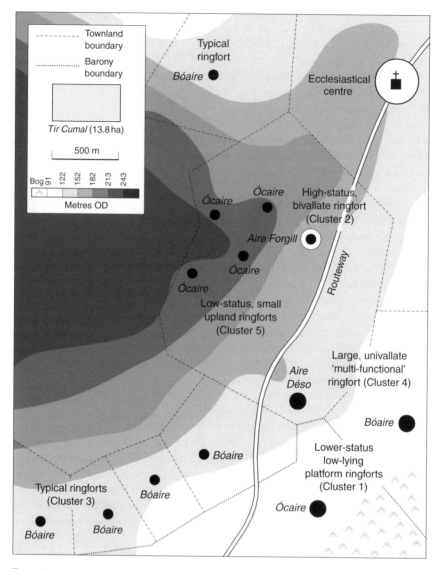

Figure 3.6   Model of Early Christian settlement based on the law tracts and the existing
distribution of ringforts, ecclesiastical sites, territorial boundaries and
topography in two baronies in the south-west midlands

Source: Adapted from Stout, 1997.

are merely enlightened guesswork, but they draw attention to the potential
for population studies contained in distribution analysis; and the need for
settlement historians to consider more carefully the problem of the pre-seven-
teenth-century population profile of Ireland.

As the *c.* 60,000 townland units have their origins in this period, many writers have examined the distribution of townland names for evidence of Early Christian settlement patterns. This branch of study has borne little tangible fruit. Proudfoot observed that *baile* townlands and ringforts had a complementary distribution in Co. Down, suggesting (respectively) nucleated and dispersed settlement forms. But on closer examination this dichotomy was less marked and not present at all in the Dingle peninsula, Co. Kerry and southern Co. Donegal.[129] Efforts to find a relationship between ringfort distribution and townland names in Co. Dublin also failed.[130] Recently published distribution maps of the *rath*, *lios* and *dún* townlands display patterns which may explain the lack of correlation between place names and settlement. *Dún* townlands are evenly distributed throughout Ireland reflecting the distribution of ringforts. *Lios* townlands, however, are rarely present in Leinster while *rath* townlands show a marked concentration in the south-east.[131] These complementary distribution patterns mimic areas of Anglo-Norman influence and suggest the imprecise naming (but not origins) of these territorial units after relic features in periods following the abandonment of ringforts as a widespread settlement form. Place names are of greater significance in relation to Early Christian ecclesiastical sites. *Domhnach* townlands reflect the distribution of the early Patrician church and may also indicate, in the south-west, church foundations independent of Patrick's mission.[132] Ecclesiastical sites and place names display a greater continuity than do their secular counterparts.

The Early Christian church, particularly the ecclesiastical enclosure, has been the subject of detailed, if less rigorous, settlement analysis. Swan has identified *c.* 600 large ecclesiastical enclosures, the proto-urban centres of Early Christian Ireland.[133] These are most densely distributed in the counties of the central plain; they are commonly found near rivers and, as a result are seldom located above the 120 m contour. In Westmeath half the existing parishes have one early church site which suggests that parish boundaries have their origins in the Early Christian period. There are as many as 120 early churches in that county alone.[134] The low-lying riverine distribution is at odds with the distribution of ringforts, but one study has, nonetheless, established a tentative link between the low-lying/religious and upland/secular populations.[135] There was a close statistical correlation between the number of ringforts and ecclesiastical sites in the eight Co. Dublin baronies. In Co. Offaly, the link between secular and ecclesiastical populations was not evident; however, the complementary distribution (upland ringforts and lowland churches) was confirmed. Ecclesiastical centres were located near arteries of communication. By contrast, ringforts, perhaps as a defensive policy, shunned probable routeways. In most cases, the high-status secular sites were at some remove from ecclesiastical centres, findings at odds with Warner's Clogher-based conclusions.[136]

The archaeology and distribution of ecclesiastical sites in Co. Offaly is the subject of a detailed study by FitzPatrick.[137] The worldly nature of Early Christian churches, hinted at by their location on arteries of communication, is confirmed in this analysis. The important monastic sites in Offaly played an integral role in the competition between rival political entities. Modern Co. Offaly is at the place in Ireland where the five Early Christian provinces met. As a result, church sites were patronised by rival kings and became active participants in territorial disputes. As the concept of sacral kingship developed in Europe, high cross iconography was used to support the coalition between secular and ecclesiastical power. FitzPatrick interprets the representation of King David as a symbol of Ui Néill claims to being the ordained high kings. Churches in boundary areas were used by rival territories in symbolic ways. Birr, an ecclesiastical site in Munster, just south of a provincial boundary, was chosen for the synod which accepted *Cáin Adomnáin* (the law which protected the rights of women, children, but more significantly clerics). By so doing, this law strengthened the hegemony of the Ui Néill/Iona parties, establishing a foothold in Munster. One problem which remains to be addressed, however, is how the saints' hermitages of the missionary church developed into centres of ecclesiastical and political power. It is possible that secular powers manipulated the distribution of ecclesiastical centres for their own political ends. Alternatively, there may have existed an even spread of early church sites, and that only those churches in strategic locations were patronised, thereby becoming important.[138] Analysing the relative locations of successful, well-documented ecclesiastical sites and obscure undocumented ones could clarify these questions.

Souterrains also seem to have distribution patterns dictated by political considerations. Though they are often found within ringforts and ecclesiastical enclosures, their distributions are not coextensive, and it is probable that a large number of souterrains were not associated with any enclosing bank. They must, therefore, be considered as a settlement form in their own right. Buckley has described the three main concentrations of northern Irish souterrains. These are north-east Co. Derry/Co. Antrim, south Co. Antrim north-east of Lough Neagh, and north Co. Louth. In Buckley's view, 'these concentrations reflect the heartlands of tribal groups, and moreover tribal groups under pressure'.[139] Clinton has come to a similar conclusion drawing from research in Meath and adjacent counties. A particular style of souterrain (with beehive chambers) has a distribution which, although extending beyond the limits of modern Co. Meath, is also coterminous with an Early Christian political unit.[140] The relationship between ecclesiastical and political boundaries (often one and the same) and archaeological distributions must be an important consideration in future settlement research.

The distribution and classification of crannógs has been examined by Buckley. Five types of crannóg have been identified dating from the Bronze Age to the seventeenth century. However, the true Early Christian artificial island dwellings are clearly identifiable within these island occupation sites. Predictably, these are most commonly sited in the shallow inter-drumlin lakes found in Ireland north of the central plain.[141] Many crannógs are known to have been royal sites and the greatly increased amount of labour involved in constructing a crannóg, as opposed to a ringfort, also points to a higher status occupant.[142] Large-scale analysis of crannógs and surviving (probably contemporary) ringforts and church distributions should highlight the interdependence of lower-status individuals and ecclesiastics with royal or high-status sites. Work on the dating of crannógs stands in sharp contrast to the limited amount of research published on their distribution. Because of their waterlogged state, crannógs, like horizontal mills, provided many of the timbers which made it possible for Baillie to construct his tree-ring chronology. As a result, there are a large number of precise dates for this site type (see Stout 1997, table 1, pp. 24–8). The dates point to crannógs originating in the fifth century with most sites constructed during two short and intense phases between AD 524–648 and AD 722–926. Baillie attributes a lull in construction, between AD 648–722, to the effects of plague.[143]

Destruction and construction

The wealth of information which can be obtained from surviving settlement evidence is manifest, as is the importance of preserving our Early Christian heritage. Vast sums are spent, and correctly so, on preserving the ecclesiastical component of that heritage. But this takes place against a background of the continued large-scale destruction of the all-important, but less spectacular, secular settlements. Ringforts have been destroyed in their thousands since being comprehensively mapped in the 1840s. Much of this destructive orgy took place in recent times when the EEC financed a short-sighted programme of farm development. Large grants and large machines created the large fields which annihilated the rich grassland archaeology in much of Ireland. A c. 37 per cent destruction rate of all earthworks mapped on the various OS editions is a preliminary estimate based on the many archaeological surveys now available.[144] More recently, ringforts located in marginal areas, especially uplands immediately below the 300 m contour, have been threatened by afforestation. It is hoped that the recent European trend, towards extensification rather than intensification in farming, will lessen the threat to these vulnerable sites. The Rural Environmental Protection Scheme (REPS) should be deployed to ensure the preservation of ringforts in the Irish countryside by encouraging farmers, through grant-aid, to preserve archaeological monuments on their land.

It is difficult to imagine how a ringfort originally looked or functioned by simply examining the upstanding remains. This may in part explain why so little controversy accompanied their mass destruction. Attempts at ringfort reconstructions have made it possible for the wider public to visualise these monuments. One project involved the excavation of a ringfort prior to the reconstruction of the exposed features *in situ*, including an earth-cut souterrain and houses which were constructed and thatched with local hazel and rush.[145] Other reconstructions have been based on an amalgam of excavation results, but favouring the handful of ringforts with evidence for elaborate defences and gateways. The end result is often more reminiscent of forts in the American west than Early Christian farms. Nonetheless, the size of the interiors and the number of buildings enclosed does give the modern traveller to the Early Christian past an inkling of how efficient and secure the Irish ringforts were. At Craggaunowen, Co. Clare, this appreciation is further enhanced with the re-enactment of common domestic activities like spinning, weaving and grinding within their reconstruction.

Conclusion

From the range of sources discussed here, it is obvious that an adequate depiction of Early Christian settlement is only possible through the cooperation of a wide range of disciplines. The skills required are similarly varied. Close examination of pollen grains and animal bones must be correlated with the analysis of landscape and precise statistical work on distribution. The skilled work of the linguist dates, transcribes and ultimately translates the contemporary Irish descriptions of settlement and society of a thousand years ago. Closer cooperation will make our total appreciation of the past greater than the sum of its parts. An alliance between geographer and archaeologist, for instance, would provide background distribution analysis to enhance the findings of past and future excavations. All of those working outside the core of early Irish legal studies would greatly profit from an authoritative translation of *Corpus Iuris Hibernici*. Many non-specialists, especially those without Latin, would also welcome a translation of the Latin Lives of the Saints. But, as Doherty recommends in the preceding chapter, the translators must be alert to the most up-to-date research on historic settlement and landscape. The Group for the Study of Irish Historic Settlement provides an ideal forum for these essential multidisciplinary encounters of the future.

Acknowledgements

I wish to record my thanks to the following persons for their assistance in preparing this paper: Professor F.H.A. Aalen, Department of Geography, Trinity College Dublin; Professor John Andrews, Department of Geography, Trinity College Dublin; Dr Terry Barry, Department of Medieval History, Trinity College Dublin; Professor Liam Breatnach, Department of Irish and Celtic Languages, Trinity College Dublin; Mr Victor Buckley, *Dúchas*; Dr Finbar McCormick, Department of Archaeology and Palaeoecology, the Queen's University of Belfast; Professor Angrett Simms, Department of Geography, University College Dublin; Ms Geraldine Stout, Archaeological Survey of Ireland, *Dúchas*; Professor Kevin Whelan, Keough-Notre Dame Study Centre.

Notes

1 Although the term 'Early Christian' might be confusing in a European context, it most accurately describes the period in Irish history which spans the historic (or Late) Iron Age and Early Medieval periods. And, although the High Medieval

begins in Ireland with the Anglo-Norman invasion of 1169, this discussion, for reasons which are explained in the following chapter, is concerned with the years AD 400 to 900.

2 N. Patterson, 'Archaeology and the historical sociology of Gaelic Ireland' in *Antiquity*, 65 (1991), pp. 734–8.

3 D. Binchy, 'Irish history and Irish law 1' in *Studia Hibernica*, xv (1975), pp. 7–36, addressed reviews by Smyth; K. Nicholls, 'The land of the Leinstermen' in *Peritia*, iii (1984), pp. 535–58, a review of A. Smyth, *Celtic Leinster* (Dublin, 1982).

4 Nicholls, 'Land of the Leinstermen', p. 535.

5 Binchy, 'Irish history and Irish law', p. 20; W. Hancock, T. O'Mahoney, A. Richey and R. Atkinson (eds and trans.), *Ancient Laws of Ireland*, 6 vols (Dublin, 1865–1901).

6 H. Mytum, *The Origins of Early Christian Ireland* (London, 1992); see pp. 133–34, Fig. 4:18. D. Binchy (ed.), *Crith Gablach* (Dublin, 1941), pp. 101–2; K. McCone, *Pagan Past and Christian Present* (Maynooth, 1990), p. 64 and T. Charles-Edwards, *Early Irish and Welsh Kinship* (Oxford, 1993), pp. 6–7 believe that there is no foundation for Binchy's contention that the *ócaire* was more recently developed than other grades.

7 McCone, *Pagan Past*, p. 1.

8 For a recent review of these sources see M. Herbert, 'Hagiography' in K. McCone and K. Simms (ed.), *Progress in Medieval Irish Studies* (Maynooth, 1996), pp. 79–90 and L. Breatnach, 'Law' in McCone and Simms (ed.), *Progress*, pp. 107–22.

9 Binchy, 'Irish history and Irish law', p. 21.

10 D. Ó Corráin, L. Breatnach and A. Breen, 'The laws of the Irish' in *Peritia*, iii (1984), pp. 382–438; McCone, *Pagan Past*.

11 Charles-Edwards, *Irish Kinship*, pp. 6–7.

12 D. Ó Corráin, 'Early Ireland: direction and re-direction' in *Bullán*, i (1994), pp. 1–15; quotation on p. 4.

13 Charles-Edwards, *Irish Kinship*, p. 11; Ó Corráin, *et al.* 'Laws of the Irish'.

14 F. Kelly, *A Guide to Early Irish Law* (Dublin, 1988); F. Kelly, *Early Irish Farming* (Dublin, 1997).

15 Charles-Edwards, *Irish Kinship*, p. 12.

16 Ibid., p. 476.

17 Ibid., pp. 476, 60.

18 N. Patterson, *Cattle Lords and Clansmen: The Social Structures of Early Ireland*, 2nd edn (Notre Dame, 1994), pp. 40–53.

19 For the distribution of ogham, see Mytum, *Origins*, Fig. 2:3. Souterrain ware is discussed in M. Ryan, 'Native pottery in early historic Ireland' in *Proceedings of the Royal Irish Academy*, lxxiii C (1973), pp. 619–45; see Fig. 4.

20 N. McLeod, 'Interpreting early Irish law: status and currency (part 1)' in *Zeitschrift für Celtische Philologie*, xli (1986), pp. 46–65; N. McLeod, 'Interpreting early Irish law: status and currency (part 2)' in *Zeitschrift für Celtische Philologie*, xlii (1987), pp. 41–115.

21 Patterson, *Cattle Lords*, p. 15.

22 M. Stout, 'Ringforts in the south-west midlands of Ireland' in *Proceedings of the Royal Irish Academy*, xci C (1991), pp. 201–43; see p. 231, Table 7.

23 Ibid., pp. 231–32, Fig. 17. For the size of a *tír cumal*, the basic unit of early Irish land measurement, and holdings relating to each noble grade, see E. MacNeill, 'Ancient Irish law: law of status and franchise' in *Proceedings of the Royal Irish Academy*, xxxvi (1923), pp. 265–316, see pp. 286–7

24 M. Stout, 'Ringforts', p. 236, Table 8.

25 Kelly, *Guide*, p. 142; D. Ó Corráin, 'Some legal references to fences and fencing in Early Historic Ireland' in T. Reeves-Smyth and F. Hamond (ed.), *Landscape Archaeology in Ireland* (Oxford, 1983), pp. 247–52.
26 M. Stout, 'Ringforts', p. 232, Fig. 15.
27 T. Charles-Edwards, 'The Church and settlement' in P. Ní Chatháin and M. Richter (eds), *Ireland and Europe: The Early Church* (Stuttgart, 1984), pp. 160–75. See pp. 170–1.
28 Patterson, *Cattle Lords*, p. 109.
29 Ibid.
30 D. Binchy (ed.), *Corpus Iuris Hibernici i–vi* (Dublin, 1978).
31 Patterson, *Cattle Lords*.
32 Charles-Edwards, *Irish Kinship*, pp. 259–73.
33 Kelly, *Guide*, p. 186.
34 C. Watkins, 'Indo-European metrics and archaic Irish verse' in *Celtica*, vi (1963), pp. 194–249. See Binchy's translation, p. 221.
35 Charles-Edwards, *Irish Kinship*, p. 262.
36 R. Sharpe, *Medieval Irish Saints' Lives* (Oxford, 1991), p. 88.
37 Ibid., p. 363.
38 Ibid., p. 34.
39 Ibid., pp. 9–10.
40 Ibid., p. 14.
41 Ibid., pp. 364–6.
42 C. Plummer (ed.), *Vitae Sanctorum Hiberniae* (Oxford, 1910), p. clv.
43 Ibid., p. xcv.
44 C. Doherty, 'Some aspects of hagiography as a source for Irish economic history' in *Peritia*, i (1982), pp. 300–28.
45 Ibid., p. 302.
46 Ibid., pp. 317–18.
47 L. Bitel, *Isle of the Saints: Monastic Settlement and Christian Community in Early Ireland*, 2nd edn (Cork, 1994).
48 From the Latin life of St Cronan, see D. Gleeson, *Roscrea: Town and Parish* (Dublin, 1947), p. 7.
49 Bitel, *Isle of the Saints*, p. 38.
50 W. Stokes (ed. and trans.), *Lives of the Saints from the Book of Lismore* (Oxford, 1890), p. 165:

> Thereafter Patrick, at the angel's word, went to the Macha, to the place wherein Raith Dáire stands today. There was a certain wealthy and venerable man, named Dáire, at that time in Orior. Patrick asked this Dáire to give him a site for his church on Druim Sailech, the stead whereon Armagh stands today. Dáire said that he would not give him the hill, but that he would give him a site in the valley, where the Ferta stands today. … Dáire and his wife afterwards went wholly in accordance with Patrick's will, and they offered him the cauldron, and the hill for which he had previously asked, which is named Armagh today.

51 Ibid., p. 274.
52 L. Swan, 'Enclosed ecclesiastical sites and their relevance to settlement patterns of the first millennium A D', in Reeves-Smyth and Hamond, *Landscape Archaeology*, pp. 269–94. See p. 273.
53 M. Stout, 'Early Christian Settlement and Society in Ireland with Particular Reference to Ringforts', Unpublished PhD thesis (Trinity College Dublin, 1996), see pp. 277–84.

54 Stokes, *Saints from the Book of Lismore*, pp. 192–3:

> 'Declare the vision', saith Patrick. 'I beheld', saith Brigit, 'four ploughs in
> the south-east, which ploughed the whole island; and before the sowing
> was finished, the harvest was ripened, and clear well-springs and shining
> streams came out of the furrows. White garments were on the sowers and
> ploughmen. I beheld four other ploughs in the north, which ploughed the
> island athwart, and turned the harvest again, and the oats which they had
> sown grew up at once, and was ripe, and black streams came out of the
> furrows, and there were black garments on the sowers and the ploughmen.'
> 'That is not difficult', saith Patrick. 'The first four ploughs which thou
> beheldest, those are I and thou, who sow the four books of the Gospel with
> a sowing of faith, and belief, and piety. The harvest which thou beheldest
> are they who come unto that faith and belief through our teaching. The
> four ploughs which thou beheldest in the north are the false teachers and
> the liars who will overturn the teaching which we are sowing.'

J.H. Andrews has pointed out that, according to this passage, cross-ploughing was
abnormal and deplorable. Perhaps the tale dates from a period soon after the introduction of the new technology.

55 McCone, *Pagan Past*.
56 A. Smyth, 'The earliest Irish annals: their first contemporary entries, and the
earliest centres of recording' in *Proceedings of the Royal Irish Academy*, lxxii C
(1972), pp. 1–48.
57 R. Warner, 'The "prehistoric" Irish annals: fable or history?' in *Archaeology Ireland*,
iv (1990), pp. 30–3.
58 R. Warner, 'Tuathal Techtmar: a myth or ancient literary evidence for a Roman
invasion?' in *Emania*, xiii (1995), pp. 23–32.
59 S. O'Grady (ed. and trans.), 'The adventure of Cian's son Teigue' in *Silva
Gadelica: A collection of tales in Irish with extracts illustrating persons and places*
(London, 1892), p. i–xxxi.
60 K. Meyer (ed. and trans.), *Aislinge Meic Conglinne, The Vision of Mac Conglinne*
(London, 1892).
61 G. Murphy (ed. and trans.), *Early Irish Lyrics: Eighth to Twelfth Century* (Oxford,
1956), p. xvi. Also quoted in M. de Paor and L. de Paor, *Early Christian Ireland*
(London, 1961), p. 80, which remains one of the best introductions to the period.
62 B. Lacy, *Archaeological Survey of County Donegal* (Lifford, 1983); G. Stout,
Archaeological Survey of the Barony of Ikerrin (Roscrea, 1984); J. Cuppage *et al.*,
Archaeological Survey of the Dingle Peninsula (Ballyferriter, 1986). C. Toal, North
Kerry Archaeological Survey (Dingle, 1995); A. O'Sullivan and J. Sheehan, *The
Iveragh Peninsula: an Archaeological Survey of South Kerry* (Cork, 1996).
63 G. Stout, 'The Sites and Monuments Record for County Wexford; an introduction'
in *Journal of the Wexford Historical Society*, xi (1986–7), pp. 4–13. SMRs were given
legal status in recent legislation. They are now known as Records of Monuments
and Places (RMP).
64 *Dúchas* has published the following Archaeological Inventories: V. Buckley, *Louth*
(1986), A. Brindley, *Monaghan* (1986); M. Moore, *Meath* (1987); D. Power
(comp.), *Cork 1 (West Cork)* (1992); A. Brindley and A. Kilfeather (comp.),
Carlow (1993); P. Gosling (comp.), *Galway 1 (West Galway)* (1993); D. Power
(comp.), *Cork 2 (East and South Cork)* (1994); P. O'Donovan (comp.), *Cavan*
(1995); D. Sweetman, O. Alcock and B. Moran (comp.), *Laois* (1995); M. Moore
(comp.), *Wexford* (1996); C. O'Brien and D. Sweetman (comp.) *Offaly* (1997).

65 V. Buckley and P. Sweetman, *Archaeological Survey of County Louth* (Dublin, 1991). It is hoped that further complete volumes will follow the publication of the county inventory series.

66 E. Jope (ed.), *An Archaeological Survey of County Down* (Belfast, 1966).

67 G. F. Mitchell, 'Post-boreal pollen-diagrams from Irish raised-bogs (studies in Irish Quaternary deposits: No. 11)' in *Proceedings of the Royal Irish Academy*, lvii B (1956), pp. 14–251; see also G. Mitchell, 'Littleton Bog, Tipperary: an Irish agricultural record' in *Journal of the Royal Society of Antiquaries of Ireland*, xcv (1965), pp. 121–32.

68 M. O'Connell, 'Vegetational and environmental changes in Ireland during the later Holocene' in M. O'Connell (comp.), *The Post-Glacial Period (10,000–0 BP): Fresh Perspectives (Extended Summaries of Lectures)* (Galway, 1991), pp. 21–5.

69 L. Jelicic and M. O'Connell, 'History of vegetation and land use from 3,200 BP to the present in the north-west Burren, a karstic region of western Ireland' in *Vegetation History and Archaeobotany*, i (1992), pp. 119–40.

70 G.F. Mitchell, *The Shell Guide to Reading the Irish Landscape* (Dublin, 1986), p. 153; G.F. Mitchell amd M. Ryan, *Reading the Irish Landscape* (Dublin, 1997), provides an up-to-date summary of Early Christian landscape studies, see pp. 250–96.

71 Ibid., p. 162.

72 E. Culleton and G.F. Mitchell, 'Soil erosion following deforestation in the Early Christian period in south Wexford' in *Journal of the Royal Society of Antiquaries of Ireland*, cvi (1976), pp. 120–3.

73 Jelicic and O'Connell, 'History of vegetation', p. 134, Fig. 8.

74 F. McCormick, 'Dairying and beef production in Early Christian Ireland, the faunal evidence', in Reeves-Smyth and Hamond, *Landscape Archaeology*, pp. 253–67.

75 Ibid., pp. 256, 259.

76 F. McCormick, 'Early faunal evidence for dairying' in *Oxford Journal of Archaeology*, xi (1992), pp. 201–9. F. McCormick, 'Cows, ringforts and the origins of Early Christian Ireland' in *Emania*, xiii (1995), pp. 33–7.

77 Pers. comm.

78 A. Lucas, *Cattle in Ancient Ireland* (Kilkenny, 1989), see p. 54.

79 Dairy cattle produce three times the calories and four times the protein per unit of land than do cattle raised for meat only, see McCormick, 'Cows, ringforts and the origins of Early Christian Ireland', p. 35.

80 Mitchell, *Irish Landscape*, p. 168.

81 S. Ó Ríordáin, 'Excavations at Cush, County Limerick' in *Proceedings of the Royal Irish Academy*, xlv C (1940), pp. 83–181.

82 Ibid., p. 99.

83 S. Caulfield, 'Celtic problems in the Irish Iron Age' in D. Ó Corráin (ed.), *Irish Antiquity* (Cork, 1981), pp. 205–15

84 E. Rynne, 'Ringforts at Shannon airport' in *Proceedings of the Royal Irish Academy*, lxiii C (1964), pp. 245–77

85 C. Thomas, 'Imported pottery in Dark-Age western Britain' in *Medieval Archaeology*, iii (1959), pp. 89–111.

86 Ryan, 'Native pottery'.

87 M. Baillie, 'Dating the past' in M. Ryan (ed.), *The Illustrated Archaeology of Ireland* (Dublin, 1991), pp. 15–19.

88 M. Stout, *The Irish Ringfort* (Dublin, 1997), see pp. 24–9, Fig. 2, Table 1.

89 Ibid., p. 30.

90 D. Lambert, 'Irish ringforts: a review of their origins' in *Archaeological Journal*, cliii (1996), pp. 243–89.

91 V. Proudfoot, 'The economy of the Irish rath' in *Medieval Archaeology*, v (1961), pp. 94–122.

92 Mytum, *Origins*.

93 E. MacNeill, 'Ancient Irish law', p. 287. Lynn, 'Deer Park Farms, Glenarm, County Antrim' in *Archaeology Ireland*, i (1987), pp. 11–15.

94 M. Monk, 'Excavations at Lisleagh ringfort, north County Cork' in *Archaeology Ireland*, ii (1988), pp. 57–60; M. Monk, 'A tale of two ringforts: Lisleagh I and II' in *Journal of the Cork Historical and Archaeological Society*, c (1995), pp. 105–16; M. Monk, 'Early Medieval and Ecclesiastical Settlement in Munster' in M. Monk and J. Sheehan (eds), *Early Medieval Munster: Archaeology, History and Society* (Cork, 1998), pp. 33–52.

95 In the absence of complete excavation reports, three sources are particularly valuable for publishing interim results; *Archaeology Ireland*, *Excavations* and *Irish Association of Professional Archaeologists Newsletter*. A sister association of GSIHS, the *Dublin Group for Historical Settlement*, has a programme of lectures which are essential for keeping abreast of current research.

96 L. Swan, 'Excavations at Kilpatrick churchyard, Killucan, County Westmeath; July/August 1973 and 1975' in *Ríocht na Midhe*, vi (1976), pp. 89–96.

97 R. Ivens, 'The Early Christian monastic enclosure at Tullylish, County Down' in *Ulster Journal of Archaeology*, l (1987), pp. 55–121.

98 C. Manning, 'The excavation of the Early Christian enclosure of Killederdadrum in Lackenavorna, County Tipperary' in *Proceedings of the Royal Irish Academy*, lxxxiv C (1984), pp. 237–68.

99 T. Fanning, 'Excavation of an Early Christian cemetery and settlement at Reask, County Kerry' in *Proceedings of the Royal Irish Academy*, lxxxi C (1981), pp. 3–172.

100 C. Manning, 'Archaeological excavation of a succession of enclosures at Millockstown, County Louth' in *Proceedings of the Royal Irish Academy*, lxxxvi C (1986), pp. 135–81; The implications of excavations at Millockstown are explored in the following chapter.

101 B. Williams and M. Yates, 'Excavations at Killylane, County Antrim' in *Ulster Journal of Archaeology*, xlvii (1984), pp. 63–70.

102 M. Baillie, 'An interim statement on dendrochronology at Belfast', in *Ulster Journal of Archaeology*, xlii (1979), pp. 72–84

103 C. Rynne, 'Archaeology and the early Irish watermill', in *Archaeology Ireland*, iii (1989), pp. 110–14.

104 M. Baillie, 'Marker dates – Turning prehistory into history' in *Archaeology Ireland*, ii (1988), pp. 154–5.

105 G. Eogan, 'Prehistoric and early historic culture change at Brugh na Bóinne' in *Proceedings of the Royal Irish Academy*, xci C (1991), pp. 105–32. See pp. 120–21, Fig. 2, H2.

106 Another cluster of undefended house sites from the Early Christian period, at Ballyutoag, County Antrim, is in an upland position, and the excavator believed this to be a buaile (booly) settlement. B. Williams, 'Early Christian landscapes in County Antrim', in Reeves-Smyth and Hamond, *Landscape Archaeology*, pp. 233–46.

107 M. Gowan, 'Excavation of two souterrain complexes at Marshes Upper, Dundalk, County Louth' in *Proceedings of the Royal Irish Academy*, xcii C (1992), pp. 55–121.

108 E. Evans and M. Gaffikin, 'Belfast Naturalist's Field Club survey of antiquities: megaliths and raths' in *Irish Naturalist's Journal*, v (1935), pp. 242–52.

109 O. Davies, 'Types of rath in southern Ulster' in *Ulster Journal of Archaeology*, x (1947), pp. 1–14.

110 E. Fahy, 'Early settlement in the Skibbereen area' in *Journal of the Cork Archaeological and Historical Society*, lxxiv (1969), pp. 147–56.

111 G. Barrett and B. Graham, 'Some consideration concerning the dating and distribution of ringforts in Ireland' in *Ulster Journal of Archaeology*, xxxix (1975), pp. 33–45; G. Barrett, 'Problems of spatial and temporal continuity of rural settle-

ment in Ireland, AD 400 to 1169' in *Journal of Historical Geography*, viii (1982), pp. 245–60.

112 Mytum, *Origins*, pp. 131–2. The figure of one-sixth is based on the assumption that each ringfort was occupied for a 100-year period and that occupation within ring-forts spanned a 600-year period. The best estimate for the number of ringforts in Ireland is *c*. 45,000.

113 Ibid., pp. 152–5. His opinion is founded on the small number of sites occupied at any one time (10,000 by his calculations) and the lack of archaeological evidence for grain stores which is in turn evidence for the receipt of grain as tribute from the lower orders of society.

114 For example; G. Barrett, 'The ring-fort: a study in settlement geography with special reference to southern County Donegal and the Dingle area, County Kerry', Unpublished PhD thesis (Queen's University Belfast, 1972); B. O'Flaherty, 'A loca-tional analysis of the ringfort settlement of north County Kerry', Unpublished MA thesis (University College Cork, 1982); G. Stout, *Ikerrin*; I. Bennett, 'The settle-ment pattern of ringforts in County Wexford' in *Journal of the Royal Society of Antiquaries of Ireland*, cxix (1989), pp. 50–61; J. Farrelly, 'A sample study of ring-forts in County Leitrim', Unpublished MA thesis (University College Dublin, 1989).

115 A. Simms, 'Continuity and change: settlement and society in medieval Ireland *c*. 500–1500' in W. Nolan (ed.), *The Shaping of Ireland: The Geographical Perspective* (Cork, 1986), pp. 44–65.

116 Mitchell, *Irish Landscape*, p. 156.

117 M. Stout, 'Ringforts', see Figs 4a and 4b.

118 T. Wood, *An Inquiry Concerning the Primitive Inhabitants of Ireland* (Cork, 1821), p. 269. My thanks to Rolf Loeber for bringing this early reference to my attention.

119 R. Warner, 'The archaeology of early historic Irish kingship', in S. Driscoll and M. Nieke (ed.), *Power and Politics in Early Medieval Britain and Ireland* (Edinburgh, 1988), pp. 47–68.

120 M. Herity, 'A survey of the royal site of Cruachain in Connacht III: ringforts and ecclesiastical sites' in *Journal of the Royal Society of Antiquaries of Ireland*, cxvii (1987), pp. 125–41.

121 Ibid., pp. 134–7, Fig. 31. The mean density for all of Ireland is 0.55 ringforts per square km.

122 Ibid., p. 141.

123 Ibid., p. 132.

124 18 per cent (n = 119) of sites were multivallate at Cruachain, County Roscommon; ibid., p. 128; 18 per cent (n = 120) in parts of Leitrim, Farrelly, *A sample study of ringforts*, p. 27; 13 per cent (n = 39) in north Kerry, O'Flaherty, *Locational analysis of the ringfort*, p. 106; 18 per cent (n = 163) in Louth, Buckley and Sweetman, *Survey of County Louth*, p. 152; 18 per cent (n = 132) of the total number of ringforts sampled in Dingle, Kerry and in Donegal, Barrett, 'The ring-fort', pp. 56, 60; 19 per cent (n = 201) in the south-west midlands, M. Stout, *Ringforts*, p. 207.

125 M. Stout, *Ringforts*.

126 Jope (ed.), *Survey of County Down*.

127 McLeod, 'Interpreting early Irish law: (part 2)', pp. 50, 54.

128 F. Byrne, 'Early Irish society (1st–9th century)' in T. Moody and F. Martin (eds), *The Course of Irish History* (Cork, 1967), pp. 43–60; see p. 45.

129 Barrett, 'The ring-fort', pp. 304–12. In Down, *baile* townlands comprised 28 per cent of the area and contained 25 per cent of ringforts. A statistical analysis of rath/clachan relationships is also attempted in C. Tuomey, 'Raths and clachans: the homogeneity of Early Irish society' in *Éire/Ireland*, xv (1980), pp. 86–105. This study is invalidated by the use of half-inch maps as a source for *baile* townlands and

the inclusion of less than 7 per cent of the county's ringforts in the analysis.

130 G. Stout and M. Stout, 'Patterns in the past: County Dublin 5000 BC–1000 AD' in F. Aalen and K. Whelan (eds), *Dublin from Prehistory to Present. Studies in Honour of J.H. Andrews* (Dublin, 1992), pp. 5–25. See p. 19.

131 D. Flanagan and L. Flanagan, *Irish Place Names* (Dublin, 1994), pp. 75–9, 111–115, 132–5.

132 Ibid., pp. 70–4.

133 L. Swan, 'Enclosed ecclesiastical sites'.

134 L. Swan, 'The Early Christian ecclesiastical sites of County Westmeath' in J. Bradley (ed.), *Settlement and Society in Medieval Ireland: Studies Presented to F.X. Martin* (Kilkenny, 1988), pp. 3–32.

135 G. Stout and M. Stout, 'Patterns in the past', pp. 5–25.

136 M. Clinton, 'Structural aspects of souterrains in Ireland', unpublished PhD thesis (National University of Ireland, Galway, 1988).

137 E. Fitzpatrick, 'The early church in Offaly' (Dublin, 1998) in W. Nolan and T. O'Neill (eds) *Offaly: History and Society*, pp. 93–130. See also E. Fitzpatrick and C. O'Brien, *The Medieval Churches of County Offaly* (Dublin, 1998).

138 Mytum, *Origins*, see pp. 60–79 which describes the development of the early church and its changing relationship to the secular community.

139 V. Buckley, 'Ulster and Oriel souterrains – an indicator of tribal areas?' in *Ulster Journal of Archaeology*, xlix (1986), pp. 108–10; Warner cast doubt on the dating implications of the political evidence, but does not entirely refute the relationship between tribal heartlands and souterrain concentrations. The tone of his rebuttal does not take note of the question mark in the title of Buckley's valuable contribution and, critically, Warner offers no other explanation of these distributions. See R. Warner, 'Comments on "Ulster and Oriel souterrains" in *Ulster Journal of Archaeology*, xlix (1986), pp. 111–12.

140 M. Clinton, pers. comm.

141 V. Buckley, pers. comm.

142 N. Edwards, *The Archaeology of Early Medieval Ireland* (London, 1990), see p. 41.

143 Baillie, 'Marker dates', pp. 154–5.

144 This crude measure is derived by comparing the number of positively identified ringforts with enclosures (in most cases destroyed ringforts) in those counties where preliminary field inspections have been completed. Longford had a destruction rate of 3 per cent, Westmeath 3 per cent, Cavan 4 per cent, Monaghan 12 per cent, Fermanagh 18 per cent, Galway 27 per cent, Meath 29 per cent, Donegal 39 per cent, Cork 39 per cent, Louth 45 per cent, Tyrone 52 per cent, Carlow 61 per cent, Antrim 66 per cent, Kildare 66 per cent, Down 79 per cent, Derry 80 per cent. More detailed analysis of destruction rates yielded the following results: 38 per cent in Ikerrin, Tipperary, see G. Stout, *Ikerrin*, p. 5; 44 per cent in Dingle, Kerry, see Barrett, 'The ring-fort'; 11 per cent in sampled areas of Leitrim, see Farrelly, *Sample study*, p. 23.

145 J. O'Sullivan, 'The Lisnagun project' in *Archaeology Ireland*, iv (1990), pp. 23–5.

4

RURAL SETTLEMENT IN
MEDIEVAL IRELAND

Terry Barry

Over the past twenty-five years there has been an increase in research on this aspect of our past landscape although there has only been a limited amount of archaeological excavation in comparison to the level of work within medieval urban settlements. Before the 1960s there had been only a few excavations on medieval rural settlements, such as the work by Hunt and Ó Ríordáin in Lough Gur, Co. Limerick,[1] but apart from these individual excavations there was no systematic study of the pattern of that settlement within the contemporary historical landscape. Nevertheless, from the 1970s onwards this has been balanced out somewhat by significant levels of fieldwork, especially of the earthwork remains of now deserted settlements, which has been accompanied by extensive research into the surviving manorial and taxation documents of the medieval Lordship. Both these lines of enquiry, which really need to be pursued in tandem, have produced a much better understanding of both the chronology and the processes behind the pattern of settlement in the period under discussion than was the situation during the first half of this century.

This chapter will first of all review the major lines of enquiry in medieval rural settlement suggested by Glasscock in his two classic articles on the subject,[2] and then see how much progress has been made over the period since they were published. Glasscock himself came from a long and distinguished tradition of English researchers, which included archaeologists, historians and geographers, who were determined to integrate all their particular research tools together in order to elucidate the rural settlement pattern of medieval England. They first concentrated upon the study of that quintessential English settlement form, the lowland village, many of which had their origins in the Middle Ages. Thus in 1952 John Hurst, the archaeologist, and Maurice Beresford, the economic historian, founded the Deserted Medieval Village Research Group in order to better co-ordinate all this research upon Britain's medieval rural settlement pattern. Some years later, in 1971, they decided that this concentration on desertion was much too limiting for the organisation, and so they dropped the word 'Deserted' in the title. The final phase of the Group's evolution was the growing realisation that villages could not be studied in isolation from the other forms of settlement such as the moated manor house sites, so it merged with the Moated Sites Research Group to become the Medieval Rural Settlement Group. In parallel to this development Beresford and Hurst were also excavating the Yorkshire village of Wharram Percy each summer from 1952 onwards. The Irish connection with the Group was established in the early 1960s when Robin Glasscock, an historical geographer, who had worked at Wharram Percy was appointed a lecturer in geography in Queen's University Belfast. Both by his fieldwork and by his familiarity with the manorial records, as well as his excavations of the nucleated settlement of Liathmore, County Tipperary, and the moated site at Kilmagoura, County Cork he pioneered this new integrated approach to medieval rural settlement studies in Ireland. In 1969 he also set up the Group for the Study of Irish Historic Settlement using the then Deserted Medieval Village Research Group as a model, to co-ordinate research on past settlement patterns, and especially those of the Middle Ages, by archaeologists, geographers and historians. It is a tribute to his vision that after thirty years of existence the Group is still thriving, holding an annual conference in different parts of the island which attracts many people to it, both amateur and professional, as well as publishing an impressive monograph series entitled 'Irish Settlement Studies'. In parallel with the foundation of the Group the historical research interests of historians such as Professor Otway-Ruthven of Trinity College Dublin also helped to focus attention on the Anglo-Norman settlement pattern in Ireland.[3]

Currently the Discovery Programme, Ireland's only archaeological research company, has commissioned a research feasibility study on medieval rural settlement as one of the two subject areas for future research. This is quite a departure for the organisation as in the past it has concentrated its research upon the prehistoric period. It also possibly marks a recognition among archaeologists in general that this important phase of our settlement pattern has often been under-researched in the past. This is despite the fact that the vast majority of known archaeological monuments in Ireland probably date back to the medieval period. Indeed, the research by O'Conor to date has revealed that while there have been many fieldwork studies and surveys of different medieval settlement forms, very few medieval rural sites have been excavated over the last decade or so.[4]

There has also been an increasing academic interest in recent years in the study of those other elements in the rural settlement pattern apart from the villages, such as the castles, moated sites, field systems and, to a lesser extent, rural industrial sites. This has meant that we now possess a much fuller picture of the pattern of this settlement than was the case in the past. There is also the dawning realisation among scholars, and especially among archaeologists, that sites need to be examined within their broader landscape context. It is no longer good research practice, for instance, to treat castles merely as high-status sites and not also to investigate the settlement clusters that often are to be found situated around them. This point was well illustrated by Cleary's excavation in the early 1980s of the remains of two of the late thirteenth- and fourteenth-century houses around Bourchier's Castle in Lough Gur, County Limerick.[5]

At the present time there seem to be two major areas where further research really needs to be focused more precisely. The first is to make an examination of the extent of dispersed settlement within the Anglo-Norman Lordship. Allied to this is an investigation of the form and extent of Gaelic rural settlement and how it was interrelated with Anglo-Norman settlement, which also needs much greater study. But, as O'Conor has recently stated, there have been very few archaeological excavations even of the most visible of Anglo-Norman rural settlement forms. Thus our current level of knowledge of the medieval rural settlement pattern in Ireland is still very rudimentary, and perhaps too dependent on utilising lowland England as a paradigm for what also happened here. Although there are obvious parallels between the two countries in the Middle Ages there are significant differences as well. Some of these differences are obvious, such as the relative under-population of Ireland especially in comparison to lowland England. But other differences are less easy to see, such as the effects of the established pre-Norman land holdings upon the later Anglo-Norman settlement pattern. Also, given the climatic differences between Ireland and lowland England the agricultural 'mix' to be found on many of the manors was also probably different.

Anglo-Norman settlement

One of the most studied areas of medieval rural settlement in Ireland has been the castles that the Anglo-Normans established both during their initial military phase of settlement as well as later. In the past they have often been studied in isolation from the settlement pattern around them, but now they are viewed more correctly as just one part of that pattern, albeit an important component. There is annalistic evidence to indicate that castles of some type were probably being constructed in pre-Norman Ireland, but there is still no archaeological evidence for them.[6] Nevertheless, it was undoubtedly the Anglo-Normans who introduced a complete network of earthwork castles on a large scale to Ireland. Classically these were always thought to have been the motte and bailey class of earthwork castle but more recent research has shown that these castles existed alongside another major type, the ringwork castle. The motte was an earthen mound, usually with a Christmas Pudding-type profile, with a fosse surrounding it. Sometimes it was accompanied by a bailey, often a sub-rectangular earthwork with a bank and fosse delineating its extent, which in Ireland is quite rare. It would seem that in reality both these types of early earthwork castle existed together, although scholars such as McNeill have suggested that the ringwork castle with our present state of knowledge cannot really be identified.[7] There is also increasing evidence to suggest that the mottes were probably occupied for a much longer period than Leask originally envisaged.[8] These earthwork castles were constructed at strategic locations to overawe the indigenous population, and in the main this was successfully achieved. There were some military reverses for the Anglo-Normans, however, at places such as Trim where the original ringwork castle was slighted by the Gaelic Irish and had to be rebuilt.[9] It is difficult to know how common this was as most early earthwork castles do not, of course, feature in the historical sources. Nevertheless, despite their initial difficulties the Anglo-Normans successfully established earthwork castles all over their Lordship which overawed the indigenous population for about a century or so. All together about 350 motte castles were constructed along with probably 100 or so ringwork castles, of which about 50 have been identified at present. New dendrochronological evidence from the keep at Trim has also indicated that the Anglo-Normans started constructing in stone very soon after their initial invasion, possibly even as early as the late 1170s.[10] By the beginning of the fourteenth century these stone castles had been built at most major population concentrations, such as Dublin, Kilkenny and Limerick, as well as at strategic locations including Athlone on the Connacht side of the River Shannon or indeed, at Trim itself on the River Boyne. The last great stone castles built by the Anglo-Normans were those, including Roscommon, which were constructed in the late thirteenth century as strategic fortifications in the troublesome province of Connacht. By the second half of the fourteenth century it would appear that no new large seigniorial castles were being built in Ireland which was hardly surprising given the socio-economic problems of that century. What seems to have happened was that alongside the general breakdown in the central authority of the Dublin government local lords now began to construct their own small stone defensive towers, the tower house, all over the island.[11]

As was discussed in an earlier chapter, the rural settlement pattern of pre-Norman Ireland was dominated by dispersed forms of settlement such as the ringfort. Apart from the Viking ports and the larger monasteries there were no settlement nucleations to speak of. But after the conquest of 1169–70 the Anglo-Normans set about establishing a hierarchical network of nucleated settlements within their Lordship. As well as establishing major towns inland such as Kilkenny, they also set up villages in the more prosperous areas of the eastern half of the country. Many of these villages were granted borough status to attract settlers from Britain to them, and they have been given the name 'rural borough' by Glasscock to differentiate them from true urban boroughs. The only part of the Lordship that did not appear to have had these village settlements was Ulster, where McNeill has suggested that the mottes or other castle types were just centres of local administration without any significant population accretion around them. This is not surprising when one considers the fact that there are also very few moated sites in Ulster as well. As I have argued elsewhere, this is probably because the Anglo-Norman colonists there did not feel secure enough to be protected solely by the defensive perimeter of low-lying moated sites, but required the additional protection afforded by either stone castles such as Carrickfergus or Dundrum, or by the numerous motte castles also found throughout Ulster. There is also some debate about the full extent of nucleated settlements even in the heartland of the Anglo-Norman colony close to Dublin, after the research by Simms and others around the present village of Newcastle Lyons in Co. Dublin. This involved the extensive use of phosphate analysis and showed that there was little evidence of extensive medieval settlement between the church and castle there. She argued that Ireland's townland system, which pre-dated the Anglo-Norman conquest, worked against the creation of sizeable nucleated settlements within the Lordship, and that the Anglo-Norman free tenants held land in dispersed locations within particular townlands.[12] If this pattern were repeated elsewhere in the Lordship it would mean that the villages or the 'rural boroughs' that are described in the contemporary manorial documents were really only manorial centres with the population living elsewhere. However, in much of the Lordship, and especially in the east, there are classic complexes of rectangular earthworks covering several hectares in area which would indicate that sizeable nucleated settlements were, in fact, also set up in Ireland.

Some good examples of these would include, of course, Newtown Jerpoint in Co. Kilkenny where there are at least twenty-two identifiable house platforms shown on the first edition of the Six-Inch Ordnance Survey map in 1839. These earthworks are shown so clearly by the cartographers that all the indications are that they date from the end of the settlement here, arguably in the seventeenth century, when it was going into sharp decline. Thus they represent the town at its low point rather than from its expansionary phase in the thirteenth century, when it was probably much larger.[13] And even places which were not granted borough status such as Kiltinan in County Tipperary have very extensive earthworks which indicate that at its *floruit* it must have had a sizeable population as well. It is a pity that since the aerial photograph by St Joseph was taken in the 1970s that the whole site has been deep ploughed so that the earthworks are no longer so visible (Plate 4.1). Nevertheless, despite all the damage that must have occurred to the archaeological strata, it would still be very much worthwhile to excavate here, especially as the original earthworks were so sharply defined. It is just possible that the earliest strata of the village occupation have remained intact so that a careful excavation of them may be able to tell the archaeologist much about the origins of this particular settlement. Other examples would include Baptistgrange in County Tipperary which is marked on the First Edition Six-Inch Ordnance Survey map as 'site of old village'. Although the earthworks here are neither as clear nor as extensive as those of Kiltinan there is also a ruined castle and church nearby, and excavations here too might assist in elucidating the general chronology of the entire settlement.

Most of Glasscock's original list of comparable sites were in Counties Kilkenny, Tipperary and Wexford but further research by Graham and others in the 1970s has revealed other likely examples elsewhere within the Lordship.[14] In 1987 there was a limited excavation of the sole identified deserted medieval

Plate 4.1   Kiltinan deserted medieval nucleated settlement, Co. Tipperary
Source: Cambridge University Collection of Air Photographs

village site in County Louth, that of Piperstown located some 8 km to the north of Drogheda. In some ways this is also a problematic village site as the low degraded motte was only identified as such by the Archaeological Survey of Ireland in the early 1970s, while there is no identifiable church site within the earthwork pattern of the village (Figure 4.1). Nevertheless, there are the remains of a medieval church around 1 km to the south-west of the village, which could also have acted as the parish church of the small nucleated settlement. The excavation uncovered a simple one-storied medieval dwelling house, some 8 m in length by 5.6 m wide externally. The western end, which was the living area, was separated from the animals in the eastern half by an internal partition, and a dry-stone flagged drain ran in an east–west direction through

115

its centre. Although the majority of finds recovered from this house were post-medieval in date there were also over fifty sherds of medieval cooking pottery of the late thirteenth or early fourteenth century in date, as well as a medieval hunting arrow head. These finds all indicate a medieval origin to this settlement, especially as there were no finds of prehistoric date. What is particularly interesting about this site is its probable late desertion date, sometime in the early eighteenth century, and increasingly it is becoming clear that most desertions of villages in Ireland took place in the post-medieval period, in marked contrast to the situation in the Midlands of England where the main period of desertion seems to have been in the later Middle Ages.[15]

When the question of dispersed settlement within the Anglo-Norman Lordship is examined it soon becomes apparent that the moated sites, often the defended farmsteads of the lesser Anglo-Norman aristocracy, were a major component. This is different to the contemporary situation in medieval England where many of the moated sites were located either within or very close to medieval nucleated settlements. The great majority of Irish sites are located more than 3 km away from the nearest known medieval nucleated

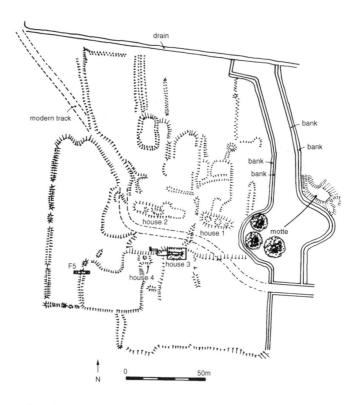

Figure 4.1   Plan of Piperstown deserted medieval village, Co. Louth

116

settlement, and are also found concentrated along the periphery of the Lordship, where the Anglo-Norman settlers obviously felt the need for additional security against the Gaelic Irish, especially in the period of their resurgence from the early fourteenth century onwards. All the admittedly limited archaeological evidence suggests that these moated sites mainly date from the late thirteenth to the early fourteenth century, and that the excavated examples on the periphery of the lordship only had very limited site occupation before they were over-run by the Gaelic Irish. More recently there is some interesting fieldwork evidence to indicate that the Gaelic Irish were also building some moated sites as well because some possible examples of the site type have been found in areas that were always under the control of Gaelic lords in the Middle Ages.[16] O'Conor has completed some useful research on one such moated site with a large oval enclosure attached to its north-eastern side which is located on Inishatirra Island in Drumharlow Lough, County Roscommon.[17]

Nevertheless, it has been estimated by Glasscock that there are at least 750 examples of these moated sites to be found on the landscape so they represent a major class of Anglo-Norman rural settlement site. Indeed, they still far outnumber the identified examples of nucleated settlements within the Lordship, which has been put at about 350 by Graham. And if you remove the large numbers of so called 'rural boroughs' from the equation it only leaves us with a small number of villages, with the Archaeological Survey of Ireland's total running currently at *c.* 102 examples.[18] Of course this may not be an entirely fair comparison because it is easier to identify moated sites on the landscape than the low-lying and often degraded rectilinear earthworks of an Anglo-Norman nucleated settlement. It is also possible to argue that there was greater continuity of site occupation with these nucleated settlements than for the more isolated moated sites, and thus many of the earlier medieval villages are probably hidden beneath their more modern successors.

Also, if we examine more closely the Anglo-Norman rural settlement pattern in areas that straddled the borders of the Lordship, as Meenan did for the Deserted Medieval Villages of County Westmeath, we find that it was probably more dispersed than would originally have been anticipated.[19] She was only able to locate possible house remains at 13 of the 150 possible DMV sites in that county, and she also found that their layouts were much more irregular than those found in either County Kilkenny or Tipperary. Her explanation for this apparent difference was that the major Anglo-Norman landholders located their manorial centres at pre-existing population concentrations, and that, especially on the borders of the Lordship, the pattern of settlement was particularly dispersed. These conclusions would fit in well with those of Simms and others, who wrote that the pre-existing townland system was 'most likely the reason why the medieval settlement pattern of Ireland was more dispersed than its contemporary counterparts in England and on the continent'.[20] Therefore, in the future it may be useful to examine closely the pattern of settlement along the peripheries of the Lordship to see whether there is a greater predominance of dispersal in these areas, as well as in some locations within the heartland of the colony, such as Newcastle Lyons in County Dublin.

Gaelic-Irish rural settlement

In the pre-Norman period the rural landscape was dominated by the dispersed ringfort, the defended farmsteads of the wealthier section of the population, which the present weight of scientific dating confirms were constructed in the early medieval period, and especially from AD 600–900.[21] Nevertheless, there are also several examples which indicate that they were still being occupied throughout the Middle Ages and beyond. One such site is the double-banked ringfort near Shannon Airport where R ynne excavated a seventeenth-century rectangular house in its interior.[22] In other, more easterly locations, some ringforts were re-utilised by the incoming Anglo-Normans, such as the example at Rathmullan, County Down which was continuously occupied from the eighth to the twelfth century, when it was then converted into a motte.[23]

Apart from these dispersed forms of settlement we still have not fully come to grips with the whole question of rural nucleated settlements within Gaelic-Irish dominated areas. Again, the limited and difficult nature of the contemporary documentary evidence is a problem in this regard, although later sources do hint at the existence of this type of settlement. The post-medieval sources also indicate that the Gaelic Irish generally lived in transient settlements such as those described by Bishop Lyon of Cork and Ross in Munster, where he wrote that 'the tenants continue not past three years in a place, but run roving about the country like wild men fleeing from one place to another'.[24] Even if we remove the probable element of hyperbole from this description of the 'wild Irish' by this distinguished cleric it still would suggest that these 'impermanent agglomerations', as they have been described by Nicholls[25] were a significant element in the settlement pattern of rural Ireland in the Middle Ages. The houses and associated structures of these settlements would have been constructed of flimsy materials such as wood, which could have been quickly taken up and re-erected elsewhere when the inhabitants moved from summer to winter pasture and vice versa. With such limited occupation it is hardly surprising that these settlements have yet to be recognised archaeologically, although they may be identified more readily by a comprehensive programme of remote sensing in areas where it is likely that such settlements were located. One has only to look at the recent research programme of remote sensing by the Discovery Programme on the Hill of Tara, County Meath to realise the great potential of this new method in interpreting the historic landscape. This non-destructive scientific-based archaeological research obviously has much potential for growth in the future.[26]

Some areas where this type of research might prove invaluable would include parts of the northern half of County Tipperary where Smyth has identified 'kin clusters' which may be the post-medieval successors of earlier medieval Gaelic-

Irish nucleated settlements. These are places such as Castlegrace, Newcastle and Knocklofty where the late sixteenth-century Elizabethan fiants reveal that these clustered settlements included not only the farming community but also craftspeople including carpenters, butchers and tailors among others.[27] It is obviously at such places that remote sensing, or indeed archaeological excavation, may reveal some evidence of earlier nucleated settlement.

Another important settlement type in medieval Ireland that has often been over-looked is that of the ecclesiastical foundations, especially those of the Continental religious orders such as the Cistercians and the Augustinians, as they often profoundly affected the rural settlement pattern of their immediate locality. Then, by the middle of the thirteenth century there came about a second wave of ecclesiastical colonisation, by the friars, which mainly affected the urban areas. However, later on in the Middle Ages there was another burst of activity associated with the resurgence of Gaelic-Irish lords in the north and the west. It has been estimated by Watt that during the fifteenth century more than fifty new friaries were set up in Ireland, especially by the Franciscan Third Order that established forty houses for both sexes mainly in Ulster and Connacht.[28] Some were located within nucleated settlements, such as Askeaton, County Limerick, but others were set up in the countryside, such as Ross, County Galway and Moyne, County Mayo which were both located at some distance away from any town.

In the later Middle Ages most parts of Ireland, both Anglo-Irish and Gaelic-Irish were dominated by the phenomenon of the dispersed tower house, the most widely distributed historic stone monument in the country (Figure 4.2). Cairns has described them as usually consisting of a single tower sometimes with the remains of a defended courtyard or bawn, and ancillary buildings.[29] The large majority of these were rectangular in plan but there are also a few examples of circular towers surviving, especially in areas such as north Tipperary. Also, given their architectural similarity with Scottish peel towers it is surprising that so few tower houses survive in the Province of Ulster, especially as the Antrim coast is only some 17 miles away from the Mull of Kintyre in Scotland. It has been estimated that there could have been up to 7,000 examples of these towers in total, constructed from the fourteenth to the seventeenth century.[30] Their great numbers vividly illustrate the importance of dispersed settlement within the late medieval settlement pattern, but we still have a problem here relating to the continuity of settlement at these locations because it has been very difficult for researchers such as Cairns in County Tipperary to establish any link between the inhabitants of the moated sites, which tend to be deserted by the first half of the fourteenth century, and those people who occupied the tower houses, most of which date to the fifteenth century or later, with only a small number of examples dating to the previous century. Obviously some of those families who left the moated sites during the Gaelic resurgence of the fourteenth century would have moved into the safer and more comfortable tower houses of the region, but this transitional period is almost impossible to establish satisfactorily

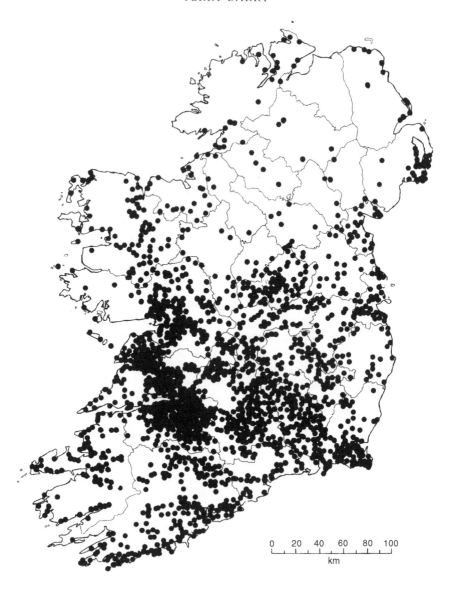

Figure 4.2   Distribution map of tower houses in Ireland

Source: Reproduced by kind permission of the Department of Irish Folklore, University College, Dublin.

in either the documentary or the archaeological record because of the general paucity of information surviving for this time. This is surely an area of research that needs to be developed further in order to fully elucidate the process of settlement continuity or otherwise in the later Middle Ages.

Again, not all tower houses were in dispersed locations, as Smyth has shown for County Tipperary, where several examples provided nodal points for nucleated settlements to grow up around, many of which survived until the seventeenth century. Indeed, he has shown that over half the known nucleated settlements in the county had a tower house or some other type of castle at their centre. This can also be shown in other areas of the country such as in Counties Limerick and Wexford where the same phenomenon is observable. In the latter county one such settlement is the deserted medieval port of Clonmines where there are at least two surviving tower houses as well as other stone structures surviving of this once thriving settlement. There are other tower houses surviving within existing urban areas, at Carlingford, County Louth and Dalkey in County Dublin, to give just two examples of this phenomenon.

While the origins of tower houses are somewhat problematic, it is easier to be sure about their demise, as it was the coming of more efficient siege warfare that spelt their end by the middle of the seventeenth century. Indeed, it is the seventeenth century which arguably witnessed the end of the medieval period in settlement terms at least. It is likely that many of the villages and towns created by the Anglo-Normans were finally deserted in this century as well, such as Newtown Jerpoint in County Kilkenny.[31] Undoubtedly the Cromwellian wars and the large-scale land resettlements that followed on all severely dislocated this original settlement pattern throughout the island.

Conclusion

This review of the research into medieval rural settlement in Ireland over the past twenty-five years or so indicates that, despite all the advances in our knowledge of the period, this is still an area which has been under-researched, and one which still has much untapped potential. Hopefully the initiative taken by the Discovery Programme initiating a new research project on the subject will bear fruit with possibly one or more properly targeted research excavations of either an Anglo-Irish or Gaelic-Irish site. This also has as a major part of its brief an investigation into how the site interfaced with its surrounding land-scape. It should also be preceded by an intensive programme of research into both the historical sources and into the secondary works relating to the site, as well as a full field survey utilising all the main remote sensing devices currently available on the market.

We are really still at the stage of identifying different types of medieval rural settlement on the landscape, but we need to move forward and start examining the socio-economic aspects of these settlements, as well. We also need to study their impact on the landscape more generally, and also to examine both the boundaries of these settlements and their internal layouts more closely. In his valuable analysis of the medieval rural settlement pattern for the Discovery Programme, O'Conor has suggested several critical avenues for future research, such as the question of whether the existence of small nucleated villages with many Anglo-Norman free tenants living in dispersed settlements in the surrounding townlands was a major feature of the initial period of Anglo-Norman settlement, or whether it was a secondary development. He has also indicated that for Gaelic-Irish rural settlement our understanding is largely based upon historical evidence from the later sixteenth and seventeenth century. Thus, he concluded that excavation of specifically targeted Gaelic-Irish settlement sites would be extremely valuable in informing us about the economy, the houses and other ancillary buildings, as well as the material culture of that part of Ireland that was still dominated by them.[32] All of those who are working in the same broad area of research would also probably support these research objectives. So the future looks bright for the development of medieval rural settlement studies in Ireland over the next few decades, with the active involvement of the Group for the Study of Irish Historic Settlement.[33]

Notes

1 S.P. Ó Ríordáin and J. Hunt, 'Medieval dwellings at Caherguillamore, County Limerick', *Journal of the Royal Society of Antiquaries of Ireland*, 72 (1942), 37–63.

2 R.E. Glasscock, 'Moated sites and deserted boroughs and villages: two neglected aspects of Anglo-Norman settlement in Ireland', in N. Stephens and R. E. Glasscock (eds), *Irish Geographical Studies* (Belfast, 1970), 162–77; 'The study of deserted medieval settlements in Ireland (to 1969)', in M.W. Beresford and J.G. Hurst (eds), *Deserted Medieval Villages* (London, 1971), 279–301.

3 A.J. Otway-Ruthven, 'The character of Norman settlement in Ireland', *Historical Studies*, 5 (1965), 75–84.

4 K. O'Conor, *The Archaeology of Medieval Rural Settlement in Ireland* (Dublin, 1998), 12–15.

5 R.M. Cleary, 'Excavations at Lough Gur, Co. Limerick: part III', *Journal of the Cork Historical and Archaeological Society*, 88 (1983), 51–80.

6 T. Barry, *The Archaeology of Medieval Ireland* (London, 1994), 54.

7 T.E. McNeill, *Castles in Ireland* (London, 1997), 63.

8 K. O'Conor, 'The later construction and use of motte and bailey castles in Ireland: new evidence from Leinster', *Journal of the Kildare Archaeological Society*, 17 (1991), 13–29.

9 *The Song of Dermot and the Earl*, trans. and ed. by G.H. Orpen (Oxford, 1892), lines 3223–339.

10 T. Condit, 'Rings of truth at Trim Castle, Co. Meath', *Archaeology Ireland* 10(3) (1996), 30–3.

11 See pp. 119–21.

12 K.J. Edwards, F.W. Hamond, A. Simms, 'The medieval settlement of Newcastle Lyons, Co. Dublin: an interdisciplinary approach', *Proceedings of the Royal Irish Academy*, 83C (1983), 351–76.

13 T.B. Barry, *The Archaeology of Medieval Ireland* (London, 1994), 75–81.

14. B.J. Graham, 'Anglo-Norman settlement in County Meath', *Proceedings of the Royal Irish Academy*, 75C (1975), 223–48.

15 C. Lewis, P. Mitchell-Fox and C. Dyer, *Village, Hamlet and Field* (Manchester, 1997), 152.

16 B.J. Graham, 'Medieval settlement in Co. Roscommon', *Proceedings of the Royal Irish Academy*, 88C (1988), 30–1.

17 K. O'Conor, 'The Moated Site on Inishatirra Island, Drumharlow Lough, Co. Roscommon', *County Roscommon Historical and Archaeological Society Journal*, 7 (1998), 1–3.

18 Archaeological Survey of Ireland, running total of 102 for the Republic of Ireland, 24 June 1997.

19 R. Meenan, *Deserted medieval villages of Co. Westmeath*, Unpublished M. Litt. thesis (Trinity College Dublin, 1985).

20 Edwards, Hamond and Simms, 'The medieval settlement of Newcastle Lyons', 364.

21 M. Stout, *The Irish Ringfort* (Dublin, 1977), 24, and see Chapter 3, 91–2.

22 E. Rynne, 'Some destroyed sites at Shannon airport, County Clare', *Proceedings of the Royal Irish Academy*, 63C (1964), 247–77.

23 C. Lynn, 'The excavation of Rathmullan, a raised rath and motte in County Down', *Ulster Journal of Archaeology*, 44–5 (1981–2), 65–171.

24 *Calendar of State Papers, Ireland*, 1596–7, p. 19.

25 K.W. Nicholls, *Land, Law and Society in Sixteenth-Century Ireland*, O'Donnell Lecture (Cork, 1976), 9.

26 C. Newman, *Tara: an archaeological survey* (Dublin, 1997), 6–18.

27 W. Smyth, 'Property, patronage and population: reconstructing the human geography of mid-seventeenth century County Tipperary', in W. Nolan (ed.), *Tipperary, History and Society* (1985), 125–6.

28 J.A. Watt, *The Church in Medieval Ireland* (Dublin, 1972), 193–4.

29 C.T. Cairns, *Irish Tower Houses* (Athlone, 1987), 3.

30 T.B. Barry, 'Late Medieval Ireland: the debate on social and economic transformation, 1350–1550', in B.J. Graham and L.J. Proudfoot (eds), *An Historical Geography of Ireland* (London, 1993), 108.

31 See p. 116.

32 K. O'Conor, pers. comm., 1997.

33 One tangible sign of this was the Group's organisation of two seminars on Gaelic-Irish medieval settlement.

5

URBANISATION IN IRELAND DURING THE HIGH MIDDLE AGES, c.1100 TO c.1350

Brian Graham

Introduction

Several themes are apparent in the rapidly growing body of research dealing with the development of urbanisation in Ireland during the High Middle Ages. Much of the work of the last two decades is methodologically diverse, drawing pragmatically from geography, history and archaeology. The result is a fusion of documentary interpretation and field observation. Second, a growing conviction has emerged that the Anglo-Norman military colonisation of Ireland, which began in 1169, did not constitute as abrupt a breakpoint in the evolution of Irish society as once was assumed. While the sudden and substantial increase in documentation after the onset of Anglo-Norman colonisation is one of the most important factors differentiating the urbanisation of the High Middle Ages from that of the earlier medieval period, it is important not to attribute social change to this factor alone. Finally, research into medieval Irish urbanisation has increasingly been informed by analogical parallels drawn from elsewhere in the British Isles and Europe, largely because the Anglo-Norman colonisation of the island was part of a much more extensive movement of peoples occurring throughout Europe during the twelfth and thirteenth centuries.

Continuity and medieval urbanisation

The argument for an indigenous pre-Anglo-Norman urbanisation in Ireland has been examined in Chapter 2. Despite the many difficulties of the evidence, it is clear that the actual number of early medieval towns must have been very small and, further, there is nothing to suggest that the elaboration of a hierarchical urban network was anything other than an achievement of the Anglo-Normans.[1] Nevertheless, it is apparent that particular early medieval towns provided some sort of basis for the development of urbanisation subsequent to 1169. This has long been assumed, albeit on the basis of quite flimsy evidence, in the case of the Hiberno-Norse towns – Dublin, Cork, Waterford, Wexford and Limerick – although it is only comparatively recently that large-scale archaeology in Dublin attested to an incontrovertibly well-developed pre-Anglo-Norman urbanism. It is now accepted that Hiberno-Norse Dublin was an organised, planned town with property plots, houses and defences, very much part of the wider Anglo-Norman world prior to the invasion. Moreover, excavation demonstrated the striking continuity of house plots and property boundaries from the tenth to thirteenth centuries, the Anglo-Normans not making any major effort to develop, improve or enlarge the city for at least 30 years after they gained control of it.[2] In contrast, excavations in Cork, which fell to the Anglo-Normans in 1177, indicate that the Anglo-Norman town was laid out on a virgin site and it is possible that its real precursor was not the Hiberno-Norse 'town' at all but the settlement around the Mac Carthaig castle.[3]

The sharp break in continuity and the subsequent shift in the centre of gravity of the settlement found at Cork is replicated at some of the pre-Anglo-Norman ecclesiastical or secular sites, which arguably generated urbanism in the several centuries prior to the Anglo-Norman invasion. A few Anglo-Norman towns were established around, or to one side of, these settlements, usually strengthened militarily by the addition of a motte. One major element of continuity comprised the single or double circular or elliptical enclosures, that surrounded the ecclesiastical cores of a number of pre-Anglo-Norman towns and which may have had a defensive role. The lines of these *enceintes* can still be traced in the morphology of a number of Irish towns including Kildare and Kells, Co. Meath (Figure 5.1). Another source of continuity – perhaps the single most important – was the market place, often found to the east or south-east of the ecclesiastical enclosure in the pre-Anglo-Norman town.[4] But in contrast to the continuity of plots which characterised twelfth-century Dublin, virtually no evidence survives as to the morphological organisation of early medieval towns of Irish origin. Again, the processes which juxtaposed the regularity of Anglo-Norman burgages with the existing settlements in the twelfth century have yet to be identified. The relatively simple plan of more or less straight streets, with rows of house plots running perpendicular to them, clearly differentiated the Anglo-Norman town from its predecessor, whatever form that took.

Finally, the concern with continuity should not obscure its converse. Only a very few early medieval ecclesiastical sites developed into reasonably substantial Anglo-Norman towns. Others such as Armagh, Derry and Tuam remained beyond the Anglo-Norman ambit and our understanding of their high medieval urban role is frustratingly sketchy. But other important potential early medieval sites – among them Glendalough, Clonmacnoise and Clonard – are major discontinuities, disappearing from the documentary record, apparently because they sank into decline soon after the invasion. It could be that they were poorly located to the colonists' scheme of settlement; conversely, they may have been neglected deliberately as part of a conscious attempt on the part of the Anglo-Normans to consolidate their political control by undermining existing

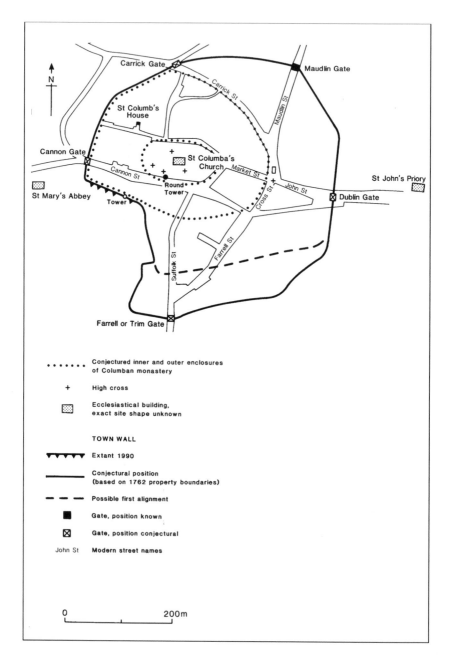

Figure 5.1 The morphology of Kells, Co. Meath, showing the projected lines of the early medieval enclosures and their relationship to the later medieval wall. Note the location of the market place in relation to the inner enclosure.

Source: After A. Simms, 'Kells', in *Irish Historic Towns Atlas*, 4 (Dublin, 1990), p. 3.

mechanisms and seats of power. The inference might also be made that these settlements possessed only the most limited urban economic and morphological structures if they could be abandoned so readily. Thus, the point is that while continuity played an important role – by no means yet fully understood – in the initial development of Anglo-Norman urbanisation, it was not an axiomatic process.

Medieval Irish urbanisation and its European context

The high medieval urbanisation of Ireland was part of a much more extensive development of European towns during the twelfth and thirteenth centuries. Throughout the continent, the town in its various guises fulfilled specific roles in the functioning of medieval society and thus the ways in which medieval Irish urbanisation evolved are replicated elsewhere. The Anglo-Normans brought with them to Ireland all the many methods which had evolved in Normandy, England and Wales, to put into practice the set of economic and social obligations which we have come to call feudalism. Although a much-debated concept, some agreement exists that the social structure now designated as such had two fundamental features. First, it was a decentralised, hierarchical political order that evolved in the early medieval period because of the weakness of central authority and its inability to prevent the rise of local warrior aristocracies. Accordingly, the system was characterised by fragmented and often weak sovereignty and political power. Dodgshon refers to 'the fissiparous tendencies of feudalism', reflecting the way in which power was devolved downwards rather than to the centre – as in the sovereign territorial state.[5] Although this mechanism was the only way in which a king's will could reach all his subjects, feudalism as a mode of economic organisation and social integration was inherently contradictory. The centre was forced to concede power to govern at all, but once secure in their geographical niches, feudal lords sought to maintain the effective independence of their territories from that locus of power.

Second, feudalism was an economic order involving estate or peasant family production and the appropriation by the warrior class (and Church) of the agricultural surpluses produced by the unfree peasantry (serfs or vassals). To achieve this, the élite had to impose political and economic control over resources (such as land, forest and game) and monopolies (including mills and small town markets). These processes enabled nobles at each level in a hierarchical chain, that descended from monarchs and the Church to dukes, barons and lesser nobles, to grant fiefs (which involved property rights and revenues) to their immediate dependants in return for homage and fealty (involving payments, advice and military service). Further, feudal – or seigneurial – lords were constantly thinking 'in terms of ensuring new sources of profit for themselves',[6] one of the most ubiquitous methods being the clearing of wastelands and the creation of new villages and small towns. Although northern France was the heartland of the feudal system, the processes of medieval internal colonisation ensured that the system was carried to the more remote corners of Europe, particularly as medieval population growth ensured an ever-increasing demand for land.

The significance of small town foundation, which occurred all over Europe, particularly in the twelfth and thirteenth centuries, also lies in the intensely unequal nature of medieval society. While people owed obedience and loyalty to their immediate superiors in a hierarchy of authority at the head of which was a king, many members of society – in particular the inhabitants of chartered boroughs or small towns – were personally free, a characteristic often used as an incentive to attract colonists to the new lands being cleared throughout medieval Europe. In addition, the major cities maintained an ambiguous relationship with feudalism. Their mercantile élites serviced the feudal economy but – to some extent – stood apart from it.[7] In visualising this more complex medieval world, Reynolds (in a notable critique of the feudal model) depicts a society with three essential strata.[8] At the top were the nobles and gentry (including the higher clergy) and, at the bottom, the 'plough pushers', the unfree peasants or manual labourers who owed work and rent services to the top stratum. But in between were the 'not noble but free', primarily the inhabitants of the small town and mercantile city worlds. Their freedoms were incorporated in the charters granted to settlements by kings or important feudal lords.

The chartered borough was one of the 'standard' methods of economic development employed throughout medieval Europe. Many such settlements were established in Normandy, England and Wales by feudal lords from the eleventh century onwards, the pace of foundation accelerating rapidly after 1100. The seigneur used a charter to give tenants a plot of land – the burgage – within a borough on which to build a house, and usually a small acreage outside the settlement with access for example to woodland (for building timber and firewood), peat bog and grazing. The inhabitants of a borough were also granted – at least in theory – a range of economic privileges and monopolies. In Anglo-Norman Ireland, where the most common package of borough rights was that modelled on the charter of the small Normandy town of Breteuil-sur-Iton, the legal status thus granted acted as an important motivation to encourage the migration of prospective tenants, who could expect to be freed from all but the most minimal of labour services.[9]

But the analogical context for the medieval Irish town extends beyond the heartland of European feudalism. As Simms has argued, the inception of the chartered borough helped to bring Ireland into the mainstream of European urban development.[10] The Anglo-Norman colonisation of the island was but a minor part of a widespread migration of people moving into the wastelands and peripheral regions of medieval Europe. Although large numbers of peasants emigrated to Ireland, there is no evidence of the nobility employing middlemen – such as the *locatores* who organised the medieval Germanic colonisations east of the Elbe – to co-ordinate this movement. Consequently, Empey regards

Wales as being a better exemplar for Ireland, the Anglo-Norman colonisation of the former being shaped too by the requirements of a military aristocracy rather than the broad-based peasant movement of central and eastern Europe.[11] Nevertheless, the colonisation of Ireland was more systematically organised than that of Wales, in that the position of the crown was more sharply defined and the feudal hierarchy better controlled.[12] But irrespective of the regional differences which inevitably occurred, by the late twelfth century, the chartered borough was a well established method through which the feudal élite could attract settlers and organise commerce and, eventually, seek to replace its initial motivation of conquest with that of profit.

The processes of Anglo-Norman urbanisation in Ireland

The crucial mechanisms of feudal spatial integration were the complementary concepts of lordship and urbanisation. Lordship in Ireland has been defined less as an area than a set of elaborate personal ties which bound lord and vassal. It was, however, synonymous with territory within which the lord exercised his prerogatives.[13] As Frame notes, Anglo-Norman Ireland has to be seen not as a single polity but as a *patchwork* of lordships.[14] The town was the crucial element in the geographical landscape of lordship, being the nexus of seigneurial military and economic control. But it was also through towns that feudal kings reached out to control their barons and strove to exert centralised control.

Therefore, as elsewhere in medieval Europe, the medieval Irish town can be understood only by its relationship to feudalism. There is considerable agreement as to the general factors which motivated the involvement of the feudal élite in town foundation throughout Europe. It must be remembered that the élite was itself hierarchically organised, a point highly significant to the elaboration of the developing urban network in post-conquest Ireland, both between and within lordships. Inevitably, the centres of the most important and powerful lords were the first Anglo-Norman towns to be founded. Their sites – frequently dominated by motte and, later, by stone castles – were chosen with regard to strategic factors such as control of territories and communications.

But just as the boundaries of Anglo-Norman lordships display a strong continuity with those of the earlier Irish political units, a number of these settlements had pre-Anglo-Norman antecedents. Thus in the Liberty of Meath, while Walter de Lacy gave a charter to the new town of Drogheda in 1194, he later incorporated his military *caput* at Trim and Kells, both – particularly the latter – important pre-Anglo-Norman settlements. That Trim was preferred to Kells as the military and administrative centre was probably a reflection of its centrality to the lordship as a whole.[15] Again, the first action of Theobald Walter in north Tipperary – where the patterning of subinfeudation was rather different to Meath and Leinster – was to fortify his *caput* of Thurles; only then did he set about the task of creating a network of dependent fiefs.[16] Thus it is not surprising that the most significant urban foundations in any particular lordship were likely to be the centres of the great lords' capital manors, replicating the experience of medieval England, where 'an early arrival' was the most significant contribution to eventual urban prosperity.[17] In Ireland, too, the towns which subsequently proved to be most successful, tended to be those associated with the most powerful lords.

Such towns, however, were relatively few in number – as were great lords. Colonisation of the lordships and seigneurial manors was the responsibility of the 'immediate lords of the soil'.[18] Thus the majority of medieval Irish boroughs were founded by Anglo-Norman fiefholders of comparatively minor significance. The same pattern occurred elsewhere in Europe; for example, by the end of the thirteenth century, up to two-thirds of all English boroughs were seigneurial in origin. The remainder comprised what Hilton has termed mercantile towns, places characterised by an urban division of labour in which the surplus was expended after its realisation in the small borough markets. These towns were the centres of trade, industry, administration and, increasingly, banking, and contrasted with the seigneurial boroughs, which functioned as the places where peasant surplus production was converted into cash; for the most part, the peasants sold their produce in order to buy other products for consumption. Increasingly, as labour services were commuted, the demand of the peasantry for cash expanded in order to pay money rent, fines and taxes, not only to the seigneurs but also to the state as the levies of centralised taxation proliferated. For its feudal lord, the borough provided profit from market tolls, fines, rents and taxes which could be spent on military equipment and the other necessities of a noble life.[19] It formed part of the mechanism by which the maximum profit could be abstracted from the feudal fiefdom. Therefore both seigneur and peasant *required* a market and, consequently, the borough was critical to the mutual dependence of peasantry and aristocracy.

In Ireland too, the chartered settlement fulfilled this role. Consequently the borough of the fiefholder – the 'knight of the soil' – was the principal settlement form through which that economy operated. So far, however, the discussion has been circumspect concerning the equation of borough with town, a problematical distinction which must now be addressed. First, a legal grant is insufficient evidence of urban foundation; as Reynolds succinctly states of the English context, the offer of urban life contained in a charter singularly fails as evidence that it developed.[20] Again, and perhaps more significant, there is the question of the division of labour. Musset used the expression, *bourgs ruraux*, to refer to the chartered settlements which proliferated in Normandy between 1050 and 1300. While these places possessed the legal attributes of a town, they were characterised by a division of labour in which agriculture remained dominant, and by the survival of feudal obligations on the part of *les bourgeois* who still regularly owed labour services.[21] This is very similar to Glasscock's concept of the Irish 'rural-borough'. As he observes, the custom of Breteuil was granted 'apparently freely and without royal authority' in medieval Ireland, resulting in manorial villages – although essentially agricultural in function – being given the inflated status of boroughs, perhaps in order to attract settlers.[22]

It is the case, however, that the market function – with its potential for linking the peasantry to a cash economy – also served to distinguish boroughs from rural settlements while, further, every community of burgesses contained within it the possibility of growth conferred by the charter. In turn, however, boroughs do need to be distinguished from towns because it is readily apparent that many were not characterised by an urban division of labour, their inhabitants remaining primarily agriculturalists. In part, these difficulties reflect no more than the constraints of the English language, which lacks a term to interpose between 'town' and 'village'. In this respect, French is rather more flexible with its intervening category of *bourg*, still used today to describe the settlement in the commune where the market is held and around which the agriculturalists' villages are organised.

In excess of 330 settlements in Anglo-Norman Ireland were distinguished by some form of urban constitution *c.* 1300 (Figure 5.2).[23] There may well have been more, as only a very few can be distinguished from extant charters, the remainder being identified from stray references to the occurrence of burgages and burgesses.[24] These settlements can best be classified by their roles in the feudal economy. No more than twenty-five can be categorised as mercantile towns, but a further eighty settlements can be identified as having possessed sufficient evidence of urban criteria to be classified as small towns, operating as the principal market centres within which peasant exchange occurred. Testimony to their seigneurial origin, almost 70 per cent developed around a castle core, undoubtedly the most potent symbol in the landscape of the feudal mode of production. Although a small number of the remaining settlements were market villages with no further evidence of borough status, the majority appear to have been rural-boroughs, this category accounting for almost 50 per cent of the settlements identified, a very similar percentage to Normandy where about half the places listed by Musset were classified as *bourgs ruraux*. In Ireland, the most prolific sub-category again comprised nucleations around castles. It is assumed that all rural-boroughs were local marketing centres, for the primary motivation of a knight was to ensure that others were excluded from reaping the direct profits of trading with his tenants. There may have been some specialisation of labour – as shown by the occasional evidence of bakers and brewers – but almost all rural-borough populations were agriculturalists. Nevertheless, rural-boroughs cannot be dismissed as mere agricultural manorial villages because they were differentiated from these, both economically and jurisdictionally during the Middle Ages. Rural-boroughs fulfilled a specific role, not only in the feudal society of Anglo-Norman Ireland, but in that of Europe generally.

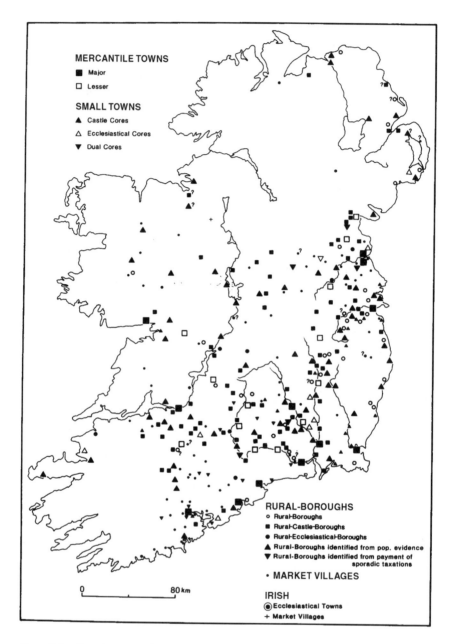

MERCANTILE TOWNS
■ Major
□ Lesser

SMALL TOWNS
▲ Castle Cores
△ Ecclesiastical Cores
▼ Dual Cores

RURAL-BOROUGHS
○ Rural-Boroughs
■ Rural-Castle-Boroughs
● Rural-Ecclesiastical-Boroughs
▲ Rural-Boroughs identified from pop. evidence
▼ Rural-Boroughs identified from payment of
    sporadic taxations

• MARKET VILLAGES

IRISH
◉ Ecclesiastical Towns
+ Market Villages

0   80 km

Figure 5.2   Distribution and classification of Anglo-Norman boroughs

The morphology, function and social geography of medieval Irish towns and boroughs

Apart from surviving monuments – particularly castles and churches – three diagnostic physical elements of the medieval Irish town – plan, plot pattern and walls – can be identified. Wherever the medieval urban layout can be reconstructed, it was predominantly linear. The houses often had their gable ends to the street with burgages behind. The market place – occasionally marked by a market cross – was either the main street of a linear town or sometimes a triangular extension at one end. A few town plans were more elaborate, the most common such form – as at Clonmel and Carrick-on-Suir, Co. Tipperary, or Drogheda, Co. Louth – being an irregular chequer (Figure 5.3). Uniquely, Kells, Co. Meath, developed on a concentric plan, presumably dictated by its pre-Anglo-Norman morphology (see Figure 5.1). Castles were normally located either on the edge of, or outside, the town.[25]

Second, numerous extant Anglo-Norman charters and many rentals refer to burgesses paying a rent, generally set at 12d per annum, included in which was a burgage, a plot of borough land varying between 25 and 30 feet wide, and usually having a length-width ratio of about 5:1.[26] While these long thin plots were an important diagnostic physical feature of the medieval town, not only in Anglo-Norman Ireland but also elsewhere in Europe, some caution needs to be expressed about their interpretation, particularly as it relates to continuity. Recent work in England, where the documentation is very much better than its Irish counterpart, suggests that complex patterns of continuity and piecemeal change of burgage patterns were characteristic, reflecting centuries of property development. Therefore, what might appear ostensibly to be typical medieval property patterns can prove to date only from the fourteenth and fifteenth centuries.[27]

The town wall formed the third characteristic element of medieval urban morphology. Thomas has identified around fifty Irish towns which were certainly walled during the High Middle Ages, the most intensive period of construction occurring between 1250 and 1320. Not all walls were of stone, a number being of suitably reinforced earth, while the larger towns had between four and six gates. The most extensive walled areas were at Drogheda and Kilkenny, which were both twin boroughs; the largest unitary walled town was New Ross, Co. Wexford, with an enclosed area of 39 ha.[28]

Partly because of the morphological orientation of much of this research, but also as a by-product of documentary deficiencies, rather more is known about the physical structure of Anglo-Norman towns in Ireland than of their economic and social functions, which, indeed, often have to be assumed. As discussed above, the evolution of a hierarchical urban system took place at the scale of 'robust, territorially concentrated private lordship', rather than that of Anglo-Norman Ireland as a whole. Thus, within any particular lordship, one might expect to find the network of towns and boroughs acting as the

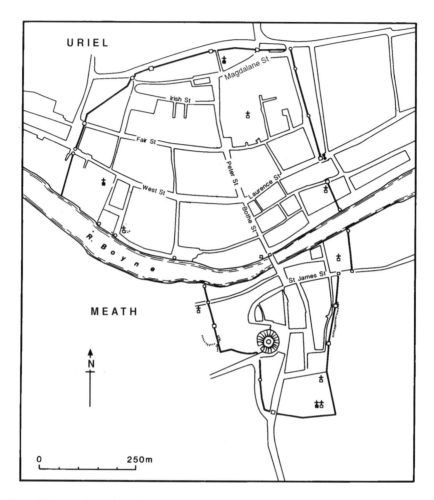

Figure 5.3   A planned Anglo-Norman town: Drogheda

Source: After J. Bradley, 'Planned Anglo-Norman towns in Ireland', in H.B. Clarke and A. Simms (eds), *The Comparative History of Urban Origins in Non-Roman Europe* (Oxford, 1985), p. 437.

framework for the sort of marketing circuits which have been identified in medieval England. Lords were granted markets on different days in their various boroughs so that middlemen – who collected the tolls – and itinerant traders could travel around from place to place. Although the evidence is extremely poor, some indications survive to support the contention that such a pattern occurred within particular lordships in Anglo-Norman Ireland. But nowhere can the precise hierarchical relationships of settlements be worked out. Again, little evidence survives of the division of labour. It can be assumed that the populations of rural boroughs were essentially agriculturalists, but even in the small market towns and larger mercantile centres, the degree of non-agricultural employment is unclear. Presumably, most industry took the form of food processing. There must also have been craftsmen of various sorts in the towns but rarely is any evidence found of them.

Despite the enduring importance of lordship, even the greatest of barons was not unconstrained by the demands of the crown. In addition to their economic roles, towns and boroughs fulfilled a jurisdictional role in the attempt by the latter – increasingly frustrated – to administer the Anglo-Norman colony as a whole. For example, the Town Subsidy of 1300 shows urban settlements and rural-boroughs being used as a framework for the collection of the sort of sporadic taxation characteristic of the Middle Ages, in this case to help support the crown's campaigns in Wales, Scotland and France. Towns and rural-boroughs also acted as the geographical basis for the activities of royal officials such as the escheator and justiciar, and as locations for the eyries of justices.

Undoubtedly the best-documented settlements are the twenty-five mercantile towns involved in Ireland's external trade. These were probably characterised by a burgher class – organised in guilds – comprised of artisans, traders and merchants. They were either directly in the hands of the crown or, conversely, held by baronial families who ranked at the peak of the feudal hierarchy. In the case of the latter, they were real economic assets. Youghal, Co. Cork, for example, provided over 60 per cent of the income of the estates of the lords of Inchiquin in the late thirteenth century.[29] All were walled and were most commonly located on the various navigable rivers; about half were ports. The latter – places like Dublin, Drogheda, Waterford, New Ross, Youghal and Cork – controlled Ireland's overseas trade, not only with Britain but also directly with continental Europe. They were also the largest towns. The most important inland centre seems to have been Kilkenny, *caput* of one of the greatest of the private lordships.

In terms of social geography, urban populations – and those of the rural-boroughs too – seem to have been primarily colonial. But that is not to say that the Gaelic Irish were excluded, for people with Gaelic names were always present in towns. There must have been some form of segregation because 'Irishtowns' survive in a number of medieval towns – Ardee, Co. Louth, Athlone, Clonmel, Drogheda, Dublin, Enniscorthy, Co. Wexford, and New Ross – while those at Kilkenny and Limerick were both separately walled. Indeed, Irishtown at Kilkenny possessed its own borough constitution. Again, there may have been separate suburbs at Dublin, Waterford, Wexford, Cork and Limerick for the descendants of the Hiberno-Norse – the Ostmen.

Some attention has been given to urban population, although again, the data available is poor and the calculations controversial. When the number of burgesses is known – usually from some form of rental – an estimate can be made of population size by using a household multiplier of five. It is apparent, however, that the population of a town or rural-borough was not necessarily composed entirely of burgesses and their families. Again, in many cases, it is possible that some burgesses were agriculturalists living outside the actual borough. Nor can population be estimated if a burgage rent alone is recorded in the documents. Although each burgess theoretically paid 12*d* for a plot, total burgage rents for a borough often included the burgesses' share in the common fields. Further, there is some evidence that burgage rents could vary while one individual often held several burgages. Given these various problems, estimates are very difficult. It is probable that very few towns had populations in excess of 2,000 inhabitants, and that indeed the majority had well under 1,000, and frequently fewer than 500 inhabitants.

The town in Gaelic Ireland during the High Middle Ages

So far, 'Anglo-Norman' has had to be used as a qualification in describing medieval Irish towns. Parts of the island, especially in the north and west but also in the midlands, remained beyond both direct control of the English crown and the subinfeudation process of lordship. It is difficult to conceive that the Gaelic leaders in these regions had no contacts with the Anglo-Normans, not just through war but also intermarriage. Indeed, there is a reasonable amount of evidence that many Anglo-Norman lords became wholly or partially assimilated into Gaelic society. Accepting this proposition of a considerable frequency of physical and cultural contact, we are faced with what remains the major enigma of medieval Irish urbanisation. Why, apparently, did Gaelic lords not adopt the concept of towns as a means of developing a territory when in eastern Europe, for example, Slavic princes were enthusiastic sponsors of towns?[30] Furthermore, this apparent disdain for the town during the High Middle Ages presents a significant problem – not yet addressed – to the entire theory of an early medieval indigenous urbanisation in Ireland. The problem is exacerbated by a lack of evidence, for, as Nicholls notes, there are virtually no documentary records for Gaelic Ireland for the first 150 years after the invasion. To put this deficiency in perspective, the major part of our knowledge of Anglo-Norman towns during the same period – often indeed the very evidence for their existence – comes from the documents – fiscal and legal – of the administration in Ireland. No comparable sources exist for Gaelic Ireland.

Thus it is just possible that the lack of evidence of high medieval urban settlements outside the Anglo-Norman colony reflects the absence of documentation. The few sources that do exist, however, stress the pastoral nature of the economy. Consequently, Nicholls believes that agglomerations of buildings were rare, the only examples being at ecclesiastical centres such as Armagh, Clogher, Clonfert and Rosscarbery. These places – and others like them – may have been towns; Rosscarbery for example, was described as a walled town with two gates and almost 200 houses in 1519.[31] One interesting possibility may be Killaloe where the borough may have been incorporated prior to the Anglo-Norman settlement of the kingdom of Limerick.[32] But the only other evidence of Gaelic lords founding chartered settlements, either immediately before or after the invasion, relates to a solitary attempt – probably abortive – by Cormac MacTomaltach to establish a market at Port-na-Cairge (Rockingham, Co. Roscommon) in 1231. Nor – with the possible exception of Sligo – does there appear to be any record of an Anglo-Norman borough continuing to exist under a Gaelic secular lord during the fifteenth and sixteenth centuries.[33] In contrast, ample evidence survives to show that Gaelic lords were enthusiastic castle builders and these may have provided nuclei for settlement agglomerations and exchange. Nevertheless, virtually nothing is known of the organisation of marketing in Gaelic Ireland, any evidence being very late. Towards the end of the fifteenth century, for example, English merchants in the ancient market towns of Meath were complaining about Irish markets at Cavan, Longford and Granard, which suggests that these may have been a recent development. But in terms of the evidence, it is not until the sixteenth century that a 'real town' of Gaelic provenance grew up under the protection of the O'Reillys at Cavan.[34]

Conclusion

As a result of the research briefly summarised here, we are part way towards an understanding of medieval Irish urbanisation. Substantial work has been completed on the most accessible topics but it is important that this is placed within the much wider context of the changing economic, social and political structures of medieval Ireland, supported by careful analogical analysis. In particular, the issues of urban continuity, both in the twelfth century and between the fourteenth and late sixteenth centuries, remain to be fully addressed. Again, given the ubiquity of medieval urbanisation throughout Europe during the Middle Ages, the apparent absence of the town in medieval Gaelic Ireland requires very careful thought. Perhaps, above all, it should be emphasised that because Anglo-Norman society in Ireland was organised from towns, the processes of urbanisation during the High Middle Ages constitute one of the most potent indicators of the ever shifting balance of continuities and changes which characterised the society and economy of medieval Ireland.

Notes

1 B. J. Graham, 'Urban genesis in early medieval Ireland', in *Journal of Historical Geography* 13 (1987), pp. 3–16; B. J. Graham, 'Early medieval Ireland: settlement as an indicator of economic and social transformation, c.500–1100', in B. J. Graham and L. J. Proudfoot (eds), *An Historical Geography of Ireland* (London, 1993), pp. 19–57.
2 An accessible summary of the Dublin excavations is contained in T. B. Barry, *The Archaeology of Medieval Ireland* (London, 1987), chapter 2.
3 J. Bradley and A. Halpin, 'The topographical development of Scandinavian and Anglo-Norman Cork', in P. O'Flanagan and C. G. Buttimer (eds), *Cork: History and Society* (Dublin, 1994), pp. 15–44.
4 J. H. Andrews, 'Kildare', in *Irish Historic Towns Atlas*, 1 (Dublin, 1986); A. Simms, 'Kells', in *Irish Historic Towns Atlas*, 4 (Dublin, 1990); J. Bradley, 'The early develop-

ment of the town of Kilkenny', in W. Nolan and K. Whelan (eds), *Kilkenny: History and Society* (Dublin, 1990), pp. 63–73.

5 R. A. Dodgshon, *The European Past: Social Evolution and Spatial Order* (London, 1987), p. 173.

6 G. Duby, *The Early Growth of the European Economy* (London, 1974), p. 187.

7 R. H. Hilton, *English and French Towns in Feudal Society: A Comparative Study* (Cambridge, 1992).

8 S. Reynolds, *Fiefs and Vassals: The Medieval Evidence Reinterpreted* (Oxford, 1994).

9 See, for example: J. Bradley, 'The medieval towns of Tipperary', in W. Nolan (ed.), *Tipperary: History and Society* (Dublin, 1985), pp. 34–59; B. Graham, 'Economy and town in Anglo-Norman Ireland', in J. Bradley (ed.), *Settlement and Society in Medieval Ireland: Studies Presented to F. X. Martin, o.s.a.* (Kilkenny, 1988), pp. 241–60; B. Graham, 'The town in the Norman colonisations of the British Isles', in D. Denecke and G. Shaw (eds), *Urban Historical Geography: Recent Progress in Britain and Germany* (Cambridge, 1988), pp. 37–52; H. B. Clarke and A. Simms, 'Towards a comparative history of urban origins', in H. B. Clarke and A. Simms (eds), *The Comparative History of Urban Origins in Non-Roman Europe* (Oxford, 1985), pp. 669–714.

10 A. Simms, 'Core and periphery in medieval Europe: The Irish experience in a wider context', in W. J. Smyth and K. Whelan (eds), *Common Ground: Essays on the Historical Geography of Ireland* (Cork, 1988), pp. 22–40.

11 C. A. Empey, 'Conquest and settlement patterns of Anglo-Norman settlement in North Munster and South Leinster', in *Irish Economic and Social History* 13 (1986), pp. 5–31.

12 R. R. Davies, *Domination and Conquest* (Cambridge, 1990).

13 See as one example: C. A. Empey, 'The Anglo-Norman settlement in the cantred of Eliogarty', in Bradley (ed.), *Settlement and Society*, pp. 207–28.

14 Robin Frame, 'Power and society in the Lordship of Ireland, 1272–1377', in *Past and Present* no. 76 (1977), pp. 3–33.

15 B. J. Graham, 'The high middle ages: *c.* 1100 to *c.* 1350', in Graham and Proudfoot (eds), *An Historical Geography of Ireland*, pp. 58–98.

16 C.A. Empey, 'Cantred of Eliogarty', in Bradley (ed.), *Settlement and Society*, pp. 207–28.

17 M. W. Beresford, *New Towns of the Middle Ages* (London, 1967), pp. 55–70; B. J. Graham, 'The evolution of urbanisation in medieval Ireland', in *Journal of Historical Geography* 5 (1979), pp. 111–25.

18 C.A. Empey, 'Conquest and settlement patterns of Anglo-Norman settlement in North Munster and South Leinster', p. 27.

19 See for example, R. H. Hilton, 'Towns in English feudal society', in *Review* III (1979), pp. 3–20; 'Small town society in England before the Black Death', in *Past and Present* no. 105 (Nov. 1984), pp. 53–78; 'Medieval market towns and simple commodity production', in *Past and Present* no. 109 (Nov. 1985), pp. 3–23.

20 S. Reynolds, *An Introduction to the History of English Medieval Towns* (London, 1977), p. 52.

21 L. Musset, 'Peuplement en bourgage et bourgs ruraux en Normandie', in *Cahiers de Civilisation Medievale* 9 (1966), pp. 177–208.

22 R. E. Glasscock, 'Moated sites and deserted villages and boroughs: Two neglected aspects of Anglo-Norman settlement in Ireland', in N. Stephens and R. E. Glasscock (eds), *Irish Geographical Studies in Honour of E. Estyn Evans* (Belfast, 1970), pp. 162–77; R. E. Glasscock, 'Land and people, *c.* 1300', in A. Cosgrove (ed.), *A New History of Ireland: II: Medieval Ireland, 1169–1534* (Oxford, 1987), pp. 205–39.

23 B. J. Graham, 'The definition and classification of medieval Irish towns', in *Irish Geography* 21 (1988), pp. 20–32.

24 Extant charters are contained in G. Mac Niocaill, *Na Buirgeisi*, 2 vols (Dublin, 1964).
25 J. Bradley, 'Planned Anglo-Norman towns in Ireland', in Clarke and Simms (eds), *Comparative Urban Origins*, pp. 411–67; J. Bradley, 'The role of town-plan analysis in the study of the medieval Irish town', in T. R. Slater (ed.), *The Built Form of Western Cities* (Leicester, 1990), pp. 39–59.
26 Bradley 'Towns of Tipperary', p. 38.
27 T. R. Slater, 'English medieval town planning', in Denecke and Shaw (eds), *Urban Historical Geography*, pp. 93–108; A. J. Scrase, 'Development and change in burgage plots: The example of Wells', in *Journal of Historical Geography* 15 (1989), pp. 349–65.
28 A. Thomas, *The Walled Towns of Ireland*, 2 vols (Dublin, 1992).
29 A. F. O'Brien, 'Medieval Youghal: The development of an Irish seaport trading town, *c.* 1200 to *c.* 1500', in *Peritia* 5 (1986), pp. 346–78.
30 A. Simms, 'Core and periphery', in Clarke and Simms (eds) *Comparative Urban Origins*, p. 33.
31 K. W. Nicholls, *Gaelic and Gaelicised Ireland in the Middle Ages* (Dublin, 1972); K W. Nicholls, 'Gaelic society and economy in the high middle ages', in A. Cosgrove (ed.), *New History of Ireland: II* (Oxford, 1987), pp. 397–438.
32 J. Bradley, 'The interpretation of Scandinavian settlement in Ireland', in Bradley (ed.), *Settlement and Society*, pp. 49–78; see p. 64.
33 Nicholls, *Gaelic and Gaelicised Ireland*, p. 122.
34 Nicholls, 'Gaelic society and economy', p. 404.

6

PLANTATION IRELAND

A review of settlement history

John Andrews

Plantation in Irish history means the assignment of crown or commonwealth land to head-tenants chosen for their political qualifications, in practice generally for their English nationality. These tenants paid very low rents but were bound by unusually specific conditions imposed by the government of the day with a view to the future maintenance of law and order. One such condition was that the land should be peopled by under-tenants who were also subject to political screening. Another was that defensible buildings should be erected on the new estates. Similar agreements may have existed among the lords and tenants of medieval Ireland: what distinguished the so-called plantation period is not so much the fact of plantation as the evidence relating to it. From the early years of Henry VIII onwards there was an apparently unprecedented wealth of Anglo-Irish official correspondence, memoranda, statistics, surveys and maps referring to this subject, without any diminution in the flow of purely legal and fiscal documentation relating to landed property initiated by the Anglo-Normans. Schemes for settling Englishmen in Ireland are recorded as early as 1515, but the first spatially detailed proposal was the plantation of Leix and Offaly in 1556. The last was the plantation of Ormond in 1630. These are the limits of the plantation period for the purposes of the present chapter.

No Irish political historian needs reminding that the plantations were almost totally unsuccessful. To the settlement historian their failure is less obvious. For instance the lack of present-day buildings surviving from the late sixteenth and early seventeenth centuries is not itself a sign of ineffectiveness: it may just reflect the ability of planters to get their way without wasting money on unnecessarily thick and durable walls like those considered indispensable by the Anglo-Normans. On this view it is not the substance but the form of settlement that one generation may expect to inherit from another. Unfortunately the differentiation of period settlement forms is still a matter of uncertainty in Ireland, as can be seen from the difficulty of proving that the triangular village green is a typical feature of plantation settlement.[1]

Perhaps the clearest proof of failure in official plantation settlement policies is that they were abandoned so completely and so soon, for by the terms of this chapter the Cromwellian, restoration and Williamite land transfers must all be

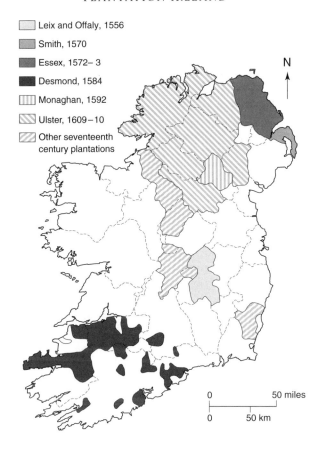

Leix and Offaly, 1556

Smith, 1570

Essex, 1572–3

Desmond, 1584

Monaghan, 1592

Ulster, 1609–10

Other seventeenth century plantations

N

0   50 miles

0   50 km

Figure 6.1   Sixteenth- and seventeenth-century plantation schemes

Source: Based, by permission, on Figures 2 and 6 in T.W. Moody *et al.*, *A New History of Ireland, iii* (Oxford, 1976).

disqualified for not imposing demographic or architectural specifications on the incoming landowners. The apparent indifference of the Cromwellians to the physical process of settlement is especially notable, considering their radicalism in matters of political and administrative geography. William Petty, for instance, made many maps of the contemporary scene, but his only attempt at mapping the future related to North America.[2] His generation had learned that for governments to re-plan the Irish landscape was a waste of time.

Yet the plantation period as here defined, short and unhappy as it was, offers one almost unique attraction, the attraction of settlement theory, in so far as Englishmen are willing to be theoretical about anything. In this chapter the main emphasis will be on this aspect of settlement history, though reference will also be made to some major conflicts between theory and practice. The documents embodying the ideas behind plantation policy have never been brought

together and properly edited. Those from the sixteenth century have however
been extensively reviewed by modern historians,[3] and those from the seventeenth century are well represented in print. For this later period, the ideas
behind the settlement process may be partly inferred, at some risk of arguing in
a circle, from the buildings that were actually constructed and recorded on
contemporary maps. With very few exceptions these ideas were not inspired by
classical precedent, or by the recent experience of Europeans outside Europe.[4]
Their sources lay nearer home. One was the life and landscape of post-medieval
England, itself admittedly changing fast but even in its most unsatisfactory state
generally accepted as something for Irishmen to envy. Hence the interminable
repetition of the words 'English' and 'in the English manner' in so many plans
for the reform of Irish architecture and Irish agriculture. The second model for
the new Ireland was, perhaps unexpectedly, the old Ireland, and particularly the
area still referred to as the Pale. Sixteenth-century administrators admired the
achievements of their early-medieval predecessors in Ireland and were anxious
to learn from late-medieval mistakes.[5]

The disadvantage here for the present-day historian is that both English and
Anglo-Irish precedents were too familiar and therefore too much taken for
granted to be fully described in plantation literature. It seems clear, however,
that in what is often seen as a revolutionary age, most theories were notably
unadventurous and backward-looking; and, if anything, the planners grew more
modest in suiting their intentions to available resources, especially in the
amount of land that they were prepared to give each English settler in Ireland.

Against this background of increasing realism, certain problems and precon-
ceptions remained constant. Given that there were too few Englishmen to fill
the whole of Ireland, where should the planters be planted? The view that the
plantation authorities deliberately kept the best land for the new settlers is one
of the most deep-rooted fallacies in popular Irish historiography. In fact the
dangers of such a policy were well known, and had been clearly summarised by
Edmund Spenser, a pioneer historical geographer, in his account of the Middle
Ages: by ignoring Ireland's bogs, mountains and forests, Spenser pointed out,
the medieval invaders had allowed these unattractive areas to harbour a native
Irish population which later emerged to destroy the English colony.[6] By the
early seventeenth century, the weight of theoretical opinion favoured placing as
many English colonists as possible in the most 'remote, barren and invaluable'
country, with the natives occupying more exposed and vulnerable positions
nearer the larger rivers and the coasts.[7] Of course this was never done, but in
the Ulster plantation of 1609 the government did at least defy medieval precedents by using a lottery to determine the distribution of more productive and
less productive baronies among the undertakers, servitors and natives.[8]

Everywhere in Ireland, throughout the period under review, the model for
British plantation was the shire and the shire town. Every shire was to be
divided into smaller territories comparable with the Anglo-Irish barony, often
introduced by some reassuringly archaic English term like hundred, wapentake

or bailiwick, each of which would have its own urban or proto-urban centre. The next division was the seignory, manor, 'proportion' or estate, generally expected to coincide with the ecclesiastical parish and to possess its own centrally placed village. Market functions would be shared between towns and villages according to local circumstances. Finally, there were the individual farms and farmhouses. The nearest approach to a complete description of such a system was an anonymous plan for a block of nine 12,000-acre seignories in Munster in 1586, hereafter referred to for brevity as 'the Munster model'.[9]

Not surprisingly, most plantation theorists give more detail for the higher than for the lower ranks of the settlement hierarchy. Towns had been the one undoubted success of the Anglo-Norman conquest, as well as the one undoubted

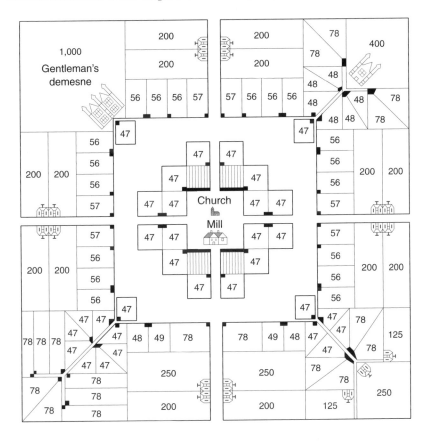

Figure 6.2   Proposed layout of a Munster seignory, 1586, with farm sizes in acres; in a square block of nine such seignories the central settlement would be a market town instead of a village

Source: Reproduced by permission from J.H. Andrews, 'Geography and government in Elizabethan Ireland', in N. Stephens and R.E. Glasscock (eds) *Irish Geographical Studies in Honour of E. Estyn Evans* (Belfast, 1970).

failure of the Celtic resurgence.[10] Most plantation schemes included at least one urban centre – in the programme for the six escheated counties of Ulster there were twenty-five towns[11] – and some projects consisted of nothing else, the rural hinterlands being left to take care of themselves (Table 6.1).

Very few new towns were proposed at greenfield sites. To define a suggested location as 'in' such and such a territory, or 'between' such and such other towns, was evidently too vague to be an acceptable formula. Sticking pins in empty spaces on a regional map, as attempted in 1598 by Francis Jobson when proposing new military garrisons in Ulster, would have been even less satisfactory.[12] Contemporary map makers and map readers, even Jobson in his more reflective moments, knew that their product was too inaccurate to yield meaningful bearings and distances. Lacking numerical co-ordinates, the authorities were forced to think in terms of familiar place names. There were other and more purely political reasons for preferring sites that were already well known, as Lord Deputy Arthur Chichester acknowledged when choosing a future administrative capital for Ulster. 'Armagh is now commodious', he wrote in 1607, 'but Dungannon is held in higher name by the people of the country.'[13] For Chichester and his colleagues, places held in high name by potential rebels would benefit from a stiff dose of Englishness locally administered. Another deciding factor was the presence of medieval castles or monastic churches that could be adapted to modern governmental or military requirements, for advocates of plantation had curiously little confidence in the state's ability to get anything built. It was the availability of buildings that led Derry rather than Lifford to be chosen for development in 1604, notwithstanding the alleged superior geographical advantages of Lifford.[14] Geographical advantages naturally played their part as well, for instance when Limavady was recommended by its proprietor in 1627 as a more central position than Derry for the local government of County Londonderry;[15] and reference was often made to navigations, bridges, fords or passes when justifying the locations of new towns. Ordinary road convergences were evidently too much taken for granted to be worth mentioning in this context: in fertile lowland country, as Fynes Moryson pointed out, the ways were 'most plain and generally good'.[16]

There were three urban show-places in plantation Ireland: Londonderry with 500 intended houses, Coleraine with 300, and Bandonbridge with about 460.[17] Otherwise all the proposed new towns were very small. In 1536, Robert Cowley had considered eighty households a realistic figure.[18] The Munster model allowed ninety-six households at the centre of a wapentake. Even more modestly, the Ulster plan of 1609 accepted forty households as a basis for municipal incorporation, a threshold later reduced to thirty and then to twenty, occasionally less than that.[19] These places might indeed be called 'rural boroughs' in intention as well as in reality. Borough status in fact had little significance in the everyday life of the ordinary town-dweller at this period, its main role being to pack the early seventeenth-century Irish parliament with Protestants. Local priorities were set out in order of preference in a charter of

Table 6.1 Some proposals for new towns in Ireland

1536	Ardglas, Armagh, Carlingford, Carrickfergus, Clare, Ferns, Leighlin, Nenagh, Sligo, Timolin, Wicklow, 2 towns in O'Brien's country
1551	Baltimore
1559	Arklow, Enniscorthy, Ferns, Roscrea, Wicklow
1562	Armagh, Lough Foyle
1566	Maryborough, Philipstown
1567	R. Bann, Lough Foyle, Strangford
1568	Armagh, Baltimore, Berehaven
1571	Elizabetha', Co. Down
1574	Donemayne
1574	Belfast, Blackwater, Coleraine, Lough Foyle, Glens-Route
1577	Sligo, Wicklow
1579	1 town per county in Connacht
1580	Burrishoole
1581	Roscommon
1582	Meelick
1584	Arklow, Coleraine, Lifford, Mayo, Newry, Sligo
1597	Belturbet
1600	Ballyshannon, Tralee or Castlemaine
1609–11	25 towns in Ulster
1619	Durrow
1619	Gorey
1622	Jamestown
1627	St Johnstown (Co. Longford)
1628	Banagher
1630	3 towns in Co. Tipperary

Sources: British Library, *Lansdowne MS 159* (1559); PRO, London: M.P.F. 95 (1581); S.P. 62/3/14, 23 (1551); S.P. 63: 6/34 (1562); 19/51–4 (1566); 21/56 (1567); 27/22 (1568); 45/78 (1574); 57/13 (1577), 17 (1574); 59/43 (1577); 66/45 (1579); 71/64 (1580); 88/59, 60 (1582); 112/23 (1584); *Calendar of Carew MSS, 1600*, 505 (1600); *Calendar of Patent Rolls, Ireland, Charles 1*, 250 (1627); *Calendar of State Papers, Ireland, 1597*, 208 (1597); 1615–25, 266 (1619); 448–9 (1622); 1647–60, 151 (1630); *Municipal Corporations, Ireland: First Report of Commissioners of Inquiry, H.C., 1835*, 511 (1619); *State Papers Henry VIII*, 3, ii, 326–7 (1536); R.J. Hunter, 'Towns in the Ulster plantation', in *Studia Hibernica*, xi (1971), 79 (1609–11); R.Loeber, 'Civilisation through plantation: the projects of Mathew De Renzi', in H. Murtagh (ed.), *Irish Midland Studies in Commemoration of N.W. English* (Athlone, 1980), 133 (1628); D.B. Quinn, 'Sir Thomas Smith (1513–77) and the beginnings of English colonial theory', in *Proceedings of the American Philosophical Society*, lxxix (1945), 543–60 (1571).

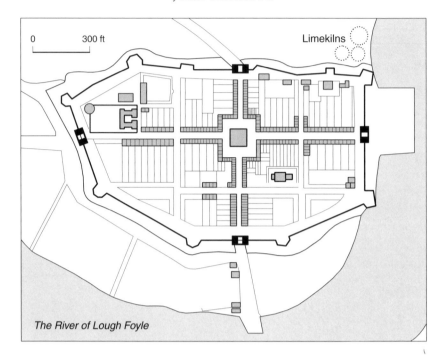

Figure 6.3   Thomas Raven's plan of Londonderry, 1622; in the original, the houses are drawn in profile

1604 providing that Derry should be 'not only walled, intrenched and inhabited but also incorporated' and defining the new settlement there as 'both a town of war and a town of merchandise'.[20] This preoccupation with security obscured the distinction between town and fort. As Spenser pointed out, citing Maryborough as one of his examples, forts would probably grow into towns.[21] Similarly, towns could be expected to double as forts. At the end of the period under consideration, in 1630, it was said of the medieval Anglo-Irish that 'wheresoever they had walled towns the country about them was kept by those towns and the English families were encouraged to keep up their lands, having so sure a retreat'.[22] The same writer's proposal for the plantation of Ormond was couched in appropriately defensive terms, and at Portarlington, in 1666, the practice of fortifying urban perimeters outlasted the plantation period altogether.[23]

The first planned urban enclosures were square or rectangular, as at Maryborough and Roscommon. Some later examples were irregular polygons, reflecting the increased tactical importance of the angle bastion and perhaps a sharper eye for the contours of the land. But in general the morphology of plantation towns attracted disappointingly little theoretical comment. Enniskillen does best with a directive to its proprietor that the new buildings should be arranged 'in streets and squares'.[24] Both terms deserve comment. Streets were not necessarily in themselves a badge of Englishness, for the pre-plantation Gaelic town of Cavan is known to have had a T-shaped street pattern in the 1590s.[25] But some Irish nucleated settlements do seem to have been totally without streets (an example was Pilltown in Co. Waterford, as mapped in *c.* 1602)[26] and at the ancient site of Donegal the founder of the new town was instructed in 1612 to provide a highway 'if there be no highway there'.[27] 'Square' in 1612 did not necessarily mean a public open space; the word may just as well have referred to gardens or to crofts.[28] But it does imply geometrical regularity, and such regularity was an almost universal feature of plantation theorising. It seems implicit for instance in the stipulation at Donegal and, three years later, at Killybegs that streets should be laid out 'as well for decency as for defence'.[29] Straight streets were more defensible because they gave longer views. 'Decency' involved rather more abstract concepts of order, authority and un-Irishness which could be symbolised by drawing out a new landscape with that simple but appropriately named appliance, the ruler. Certainly all new streets known to have been laid out in advance were straight, and by medieval standards wide – though no Irish settlement historian seems to have measured any of them.

It is possible, though not demonstrable, that Irish plantation town plans were inspired by the English and Welsh street grids inherited from the thirteenth century.[30] At neither period was there any standard layout for a new town. In typical compromising fashion, the English preference was for 'such manner and form as shall best suit with the site and situation of the place'.[31] The five parallel streets without cross links proposed for Roscommon in 1581 were some-what reminiscent of Flint in north Wales.[32] The checkerboard 'pattern to make the town by' mapped at Derry in about 1600 was similar to Caernarvon or Salisbury.[33] The quadrilaterals at Coleraine[34] and parts of Bandonbridge[35] were a combination of these two models, with Coleraine pushed out of its rectangular shape by a non-professional surveyor working for an individual planter, Sir Thomas Phillips, before the arrival of the London companies. The cruciform plan of Londonderry's main streets,[36] later echoed rather faintly at Jamestown, Co. Leitrim,[37] and much more clearly at Portarlington, Co. Leix,[38] has been interpreted as a copy of Vitry le François on the Marne, founded in 1545, or of a design for a sixteenth-century barracks.[39] However, this is a form which, like the simple checkerboard, may well have been invented more than once: it is essentially a grid in which the tactical need to minimise the number of open-ings in the town perimeter has given prominence to one main street in each direction. Even in a small town, the cross had its own symbolic force. What might be called the urbanity quotient was doubled at the point of intersection, and could be further enhanced by the construction of an eye-catching monu-ment, probably itself in the form of a cross. But if a borough had only thirteen burgesses, like St Johnstown, Co. Donegal, in 1618, there was no plausible alternative to the simplicity of the single street.[40]

In St Johnstown's only street all the plots were to measure 20 feet in frontage and 96 feet in depth. With more than one street there was a problem of matching plot-lengths with street junctions, but no theoretical attention seems to have been given to this subject. Thomas Raven's plan of Londonderry, in 1622, the first to show plot boundaries, makes one doubt whether such a skilled surveyor as Raven could possibly have been the designer of this town.[41] In their book *City Fathers* Colin and Rose Bell characterise Derry as 'a straightforward grid',[42] but in fact the plot lengths, far from being straightforward in the sense presumably intended, are confusingly unequal, and some of the future houses envisaged by the designer would have had no space behind them at all. As in other periods, decency had more appeal at the fronts of buildings than at the backs.

Most plantation town maps show the main streets as continuously built up. Houses were surprisingly small, at Coleraine as little as 12 feet wide,[43] and at Londonderry less than two-thirds the width of the average nineteenth-century street frontage at the town centre. Such houses were apparently built in the 'uniform' manner expressly prescribed in several government grants,[44] in marked contrast with contemporary attitudes to rural housing and also in opposition to the modern historical opinion that a true town must by necessity consist of socially heterogeneous individuals.[45] In Ireland the early seventeenth-century view was rather more like that of Shakespeare's historical plays: the townsman was typecast as tradesman or artificer, ranking well below the occupier of a late-medieval urban tower house for instance, though some new towns like Belfast did soon acquire their own complement of gentlefolk.[46]

Most pre-twentieth-century ideal urban landscapes have been dominated by public places and spaces – at Derry and Coleraine imposing citadels (never constructed), in Irish shire towns a sessions house and gaol, and in other boroughs a common hall, tolsel or market house, or at least an open-air market. Even proto-urban forts, like Benburb in 1588[47] and Dunnalong in 1600,[48] had land set aside for a market. The centrally placed market square, however, may have been a less obvious choice than Colin and Rose Bell imply. After all, the word 'diamond' used for this feature in post-plantation times is hardly suggestive of something commonplace,[49] and there had been no sign of a central square in plans for Maryborough in *c.* 1571, Roscommon in 1581 or Derry itself in 1600.

As an instrument of British control, the typical plantation blueprint made only slight and locationally unspecific provision for the natives.[50] 'Irish Street', 'Irish Quarter' and 'Irishtown' were later to emerge as local names,[51] but there are no Irish ghettos on the earliest town maps, except perhaps at Newry in 1568, where a separately enclosed 'base town' included a large green for cattle and numerous dwelling houses but no public buildings.[52] No map actually predicted extra-mural suburban growth for either nationality. On the contrary, expansion was often discouraged by common grazing lands and individually tenanted 'burgage acres' located immediately outside the town wall.[53] But many places outgrew their founders' expectations, and at such places the checkerboard and cruciform plans proved hard to maintain unless they harmonised with the pre-existing rural road system. Once the extra-mural commons had given way to enclosed farms, the natural result of unchecked growth was the ribbon suburb. Houses were already extending outside the fortifications at Newry in 1568 and the Blackwater fort in 1587,[54] and the confinement of other provincial towns like Galway within their medieval walls may be an observational illusion, produced by most early town maps having been drawn during or just after a native uprising.[55] In the more settled conditions of the late seventeenth century the cabin suburb was remarkably well developed in both plantation and medieval Irish towns, averaging more than 40 per cent of the total street frontage in a sample of seven plans drawn by Thomas Phillips in 1685.[56] It was the private landlords of post-medieval Ireland who reasserted the ideal of urban compactness. Their views may have been indirectly derived from plantation theory, but no documentary evidence on this point has been adduced, and in the earliest true estate settlements, like those mapped by Raven in east Down in 1625, the direction of influence between public and private thinking is uncertain. [57]

The difference between plantation towns and plantation villages is hard to define, especially as for much of this period the word 'town' was still acceptable in an avowedly rural sense. As in medieval times the distinction in men's minds was not only social but legal. New or old the ideal town was burghal while the ideal village remained manorial, with courts leet and baron, a manorial mill, a seneschal and of course a manorial lord. The ideal village was also parochial, but whereas only part of medieval Ireland had been manorialised, almost the whole country had been divided into parishes, most of which retain their pre-plantation names, and in practice it was not always thought urgently necessary for each new village to stand beside its own parish church. The main feature of a village was that its houses should be close together without having a common wall round them maintained at public expense. This eventually became the only sense in which the word 'village' is used in Ireland, whereas in England there remained an important secondary meaning in which the houses of a village could be widely scattered.

Villages in the Irish sense were proposed in Leix and Offaly in 1557,[58] in Ulster in 1567,[59] and in Munster in 1586, but without being made a formal obligation in any of these cases. That had to wait for the revised articles of the Ulster plantation in 1610, when undertakers were required to 'draw their tenants to build houses not scattered but together'.[60] In the Wexford scheme of 1614 each undertaker was to live with his tenants in a townreed,[61] an order repeated in the Longford plantation five years later.[62] As with plantation boroughs, the number of houses per settlement was small by non-Irish standards: thirty-two in the Munster village model, ten or twenty in the Ulster articles depending on the size of the estate. Actual sizes were often even smaller, at least in the early post-plantation period. In 1616 one Co. Londonderry resident suggested a quota of six houses, adding (with a touch of sarcasm) 'which is a great town in this country'.[63] In Raven's village plans for the same county the average number of dwellings already built was fifteen.[64] In all six escheated counties, as surveyed by Nicholas Pynner in 1618–19, the average for what Pynner called villages was eleven.[65]

In the Munster model the people of the village were labourers, craftsmen or tradesmen and only part-time farmers, but they all had shares in one common field as well as their individual holdings. This seems to be the only clear reference to an open field system in the whole of Irish plantation literature, farm layout being the one sphere in which the planners preferred to look forwards rather than backwards. Like contemporary English agricultural reformers, they believed in enclosures. More specifically, one writer of 1601 wanted new tenants 'to divide their arable land into fields, pastures or closes, each of them not more than twelve English acres' – a good example, incidentally, of the word 'arable' being used to mean ploughable rather than ploughed.[66] The tenants of enclosed and separate farms were nevertheless expected to live in villages, the logistical objections to this arrangement being recognised, and dismissed, in Francis Bacon's well-known reference to villagers in England walking two miles to get from their houses to their lands.[67] Some large farmers in Ulster did indeed begin by obeying this instruction. That is clear from Pynner's statistics and from the substantial stone and timber buildings shown on Raven's maps of 1622. But some of Raven's villages had already become miniature service centres, and henceforth it was the butchers, broguemakers, carders, smiths and ale sellers of Co. Londonderry who were being urged to concentrate in towns, townreeds and villages, rather than the full-time farmers.[68]

For the inhabitants of a British village in Ireland, without benefit of a town wall, safety lay not only in numbers but in the landlord's castle, house or bawn. This was another recurring theme. The villages planned for Leix and Offaly were mostly located near older fortified sites. The same was true in Munster, where the importance of defensible stone buildings was emphasised by prominently noting them near the beginning of each grant to a new planter at Askeaton, Castletown, Mallow, Newcastle, Tralee and elsewhere,[69] though the only early cartographic evidence for the association of castle and houses in this plantation is at Mogeely, Co. Cork, in 1598.[70] In Ulster physical proximity to the big house was an explicit principle of village planning, and among a total of fourteen London companies' villages in 1622, nine had new castles fronting on to or looking down the main street. Luckily it was not yet fashionable for large country houses to be hidden among extensive empty parklands: the main function of a park at this period was to accommodate animals and not to provide seclusion or aesthetic pleasure.[71]

Most of the Londonderry villages were either linear or cruciform, the houses widely spaced with their long axes parallel to broad straight streets. They have usually changed too much for their outlines to be traced on a modern base map – at any rate nobody appears to have published such a reconstruction – but Raven's unscaled impressions of Ulster villages are confirmed by the one accurate plan available from rural Co. Londonderry at this period, depicting the

Merchant Taylors' village of Macosquin in c. 1615 .[72] Here the street is 50 feet wide, the plots are 64 feet wide and 200 feet deep, and, as in some of the Raven maps, there are frontages amounting to half the village street-length which are without buildings. The houses measure 32 feet by 17 feet, about the size of a typical husbandman's house in contemporary England. This is one of the few plantation village layouts still clearly recognisable on the ground. The decline of other first-generation villages, and the rise of their numerous post-plantation rivals, are familiar themes in standard works on the historical geography of Ulster.

The lowest level of the plantation hierarchy was the individual farm. Most projects involved a graded series of rural households very different from the uniformity of the theoretical town. Freeholders, farmers, copyholders and cottagers were all carefully distinguished, some classes being further subdivided according to the number of acres held.[73] Unfortunately it is only the Munster model that gives spatial expression to this idea. Four objectives can be plausibly attributed to its designer: to keep each farmhouse within the boundaries of a one-piece farm; to avoid strip holdings and other awkward shapes; to locate each house beside a road; and to minimise the isolation of farmers by grouping their houses into clusters of from two to six, preferably, it seems, with each cluster representing a single socio-economic category. The overall population density envisaged for this rural utopia was about half that actually existing in the midlands of rural England at the same period, a measure of the more generous land allotments thought necessary to entice the English immigrant across the water. Of course no one would expect this rigid if highly ingenious conception to be put into practice, or even to be generally understood. In fact, outside the villages surveyed by Pynner and Raven, the houses of substantial

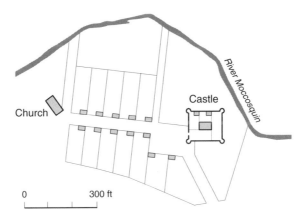

Figure 6.4 Plan of Macosquin, Co. Londonderry, c. 1615

Source: Redrawn by permission from J.S. Curl, *The Londonderry Plantation, 1609–1914* (Chichester, 1986).

planters seem seldom to have been grouped together. The non-manorial cluster was for social inferiors (with or without a single superior), who were unfortunately ignored in most contemporary discussion of the rural settlement problem.

A scattered distribution of planter farming families, though often condemned as dangerous, seems implicit in the wide spacing of the nucleated villages postulated by plantation theory and was certainly a fact of early seventeenth-century Irish life. To establish this point more firmly, three kinds of evidence may be noted. First, planters were often said to have jeopardised their own safety by living too far apart. This accusation was made in Munster by Lord Mountjoy, who found it:

> strange that in the last plot for the plantation of Munster there were limitations how much in demesne and how much in farm and tenancy, how many buildings should be erected [in fact no published plot includes such a stipulation], how many Irish should be admitted, but not restraint that they mought build sparsim at their pleasure, much less any condition that they should make places fortified and defensible.[74]

Despite Mountjoy's desire to learn from experience, his successor as lord deputy was to make a very similar comment on the emerging rural settlement pattern of plantation Ulster.[75] The same point was put in more general terms by the pamphleteer Richard Lawrence as late as 1655.[76] Next there is the evidence of the early surveyors. The ten large houses on the lands of the Grocers' Company in 1617 were divided among six townlands,[77] and in Co. Londonderry as a whole, in 1624, there were only fourteen English villages but 312 townlands planted with English settlers, presumably not in villages.[78] This mention of townlands in an early seventeenth-century context points to a third source of testimony, which is Ireland's modern territorial network. The townland, with its average size of 326 statute acres, is intrinsically unsuited to most kinds of plantation theory, being too large for the perceived optimum size of tenant farm and too small to accommodate a respectable village. Yet it survives as well in the planted districts as anywhere else, usually with a name of Gaelic origin, and in the early landlord era proved a favourite receptacle for the single leasehold, functionally independent of its neighbours and morphologically distinct from them. In Irish settlement history the townland's success was the plantation's failure.

The centrifugal behaviour of the British tenant is thus easily demonstrated. It is also easily explained. The larger the farm, the greater the convenience of living in the centre of it rather than on the edge or outside; and, thanks to defective surveying, most plantation farms were much larger than any advocate of village settlement imagined.[79] Another stimulus to settlement dispersal, seldom mentioned then or now, may well have been the high density of Ireland's early seventeenth-century road network. In the absence of contemporary road maps this suggestion is dangerously dependent on the idea of period-form, but if the roads and lanes of mid-Ulster and north Wexford, for example, are as old as they look there was no shortage of roadside plantation sites remote from both towns and villages.

It remains to consider the history of native Irish rural settlement during the period covered by this chapter. Although theoretically excluded from most plantation projects by a policy of apartheid, Irishmen were still seen as a threat or at least an affront. The defended farmstead or rath, it is true, could now be dismissed as an irrelevance or at best an antiquarian curiosity, even in such deeply Gaelic areas as south Armagh in 1600.[80] But undefended Irish houses were too scattered and too flimsy, and therefore too locationally unstable, to suit an Englishman's ideas about tranquillity and 'decency'. Chichester, planning for Ulster, wanted the Irish to be 'drawn from their course of running up and down the country with their cattle and settled in towns and villages'.[81] He evidently valued English villages for their defensibility and Irish villages for their vulnerability. Given the balance of military power after the flight of the earls, this argument was less illogical than it looks: a cluster of native houses would have been easier for soldiers to burn than the same number of houses evenly dispersed.

Whether 'running up and down' was an endemic fact of native Irish rural life or a form of wartime evasive action appears to be still uncertain. Both interpretations are compatible with the existence of small settlement clusters – small enough to be seen by some observers as instances of 'scattering' – long known in Irish historical geography as 'clachans'. There is considerable evidence for this kind of settlement in the building symbols shown on contemporary maps of pre-plantation Ireland, especially if a cluster is defined following modern geographical precedent as any group of three or more dwellings. (The number of specimens can be enormously increased if we assume that clusters are also denoted by the single conventional circles used for undifferentiated rural settlements on small-scale regional and national maps of Ireland like those of Robert Lythe (1571) – an assumption often made in interpreting the same kind of abstract symbol in Timothy Pont's sixteenth-century maps of Scotland.)[82]

On pre-plantation maps the easiest way of classifying cabin clusters is by their spatial relationship to other settlement-features. A cluster next to a large and durable building may well be durable itself. Clusters formed entirely of small houses or cabins are harder to defend against Chichester's charge of running up and down. One problem here is that pre-plantation maps of Ireland are not usually accurate enough for otherwise unidentifiable settlements on them to be located on the ground or transferred to a modern base map. This criticism does not apply to the kind of large-scale estate cartography that began to flourish in the 1620s, though since an estate map must be later than the corresponding plantation the ethnic and historical status of its settlement-content can only be a matter of opinion. The most promising examples found so far are Thomas Raven's maps of the barony of Farney, Co. Monaghan, in 1634, which include numerous presumably native cabin-clusters of from two to six houses.[83] These and other seventeenth-century estate maps might well assist the archaeologist in choosing clachan sites for detailed investigation.[84] In the past such links between library work and fieldwork have been disappointingly rare, but they are just the kind of interdisciplinary endeavour that the Group for the Study of Irish Historic Settlement was established to promote.

Acknowledgements

Thanks are due to Dr Brian Lacey for advice about the early history of Londonderry, to Dr Howard Clarke, Dr Raymond Gillespie and Dr Rolf Loeber for kindly giving access to their unpublished work, and to Sheila McMurrow for drawing my maps.

Notes

1 L.M. Cullen, *Irish Towns and Villages* (Dublin, 1979), reviewed by T. Jones Hughes in *Irish Geography*, xiv (1981), 101; L.M. Cullen, *The Emergence of Modern Ireland, 1600–1900* (London, 1981), 63–66.

2 J.H. Andrews, 'The making of Irish geography, 1: William Petty', in *Irish Geography*, ix (1976), 100–103; Marquess of Lansdowne, *The Petty Papers*, ii (London, 1927), 112.

3 D.B. Quinn, 'A discourse on Ireland (circa 1599): a sidelight on English colonial policy', in *Proceedings of the Royal Irish Academy*, xlvii C (1942), 151–156; D.B. Quinn, 'Sir Thomas Smith (1513–77) and the beginnings of English colonial theory', in *Proceedings of the American Philosophical Society*, lxxix (1945), 543–560; D.B. Quinn, 'Edward Walshe's "Conjectures" concerning the state of Ireland, 1552', in *Irish Historical Studies*, v (1947), 303–322; D.B. Quinn, 'Ireland and sixteenth-century European expansion', in *Historical Studies*, i (1958), 20–32; D.B. Quinn, 'Renaissance influences in English colonisation', in *Transactions of the Royal Historical Society*, 5th series, xxvi (1976), 73–93; D.G. White, 'The Tudor plantations in Ireland before 1571', unpublished PhD thesis, Trinity College, Dublin (1968).

4 A. Simms, 'The influence of the classical precedent on English plantation theories in Ireland', in *Convegnio Internazionale, 1 Paesaggi Rurali Europei*, (1975), 483–491.

5 *Ancient Irish Histories: The Works of Spencer, Campion, Hanmer and Marleburrough*, 2 vols (Dublin, 1809); C. Lennon, *Richard Stanihurst the Dubliner, 1547–1618* (Dublin, 1981); M.R. James, 'The Carew MSS', in *English Historical Review*, xliii (1927), 261–267; R.B. Gottfried, 'The early development of the section on Ireland in Camden's *Britannia*', in *English Literary History*, x (1943), 117–130; E. Spenser, *A View of the State of Ireland* (ed. W. Renwick, Oxford, 1970); John Davies, *A discoverie of the true causes why Ireland was never entirely subdued, nor brought under obedience of the crowne of England, until the beginning of his majesties happie reigne* (ed. J. Barry, Shannon, 1969); T.W. Moody, F.X. Martin and F.J. Byrne (eds), *A New History of Ireland*, iii (Oxford, 1976).

6 Spenser, *View of the State of Ireland*, 14.

7 *Calendar of State Papers, Ireland, 1611–14*, 495.

8 G. Hill, *An Historical Account of the Plantation in Ulster, at the Commencement of the Seventeenth Century, 1608–1620* (Belfast, 1877), 125.

9 PRO, London, *S.P. 63/121/41, 54, 56*; PRO, London, *M.P.F. 305*; J.H. Andrews, 'Geography and government in Elizabethan Ireland', in N. Stephens and R.E. Glasscock (eds), *Irish Geographical Studies in Honour of E. Estyn Evans* (Belfast, 1970), 187.

10 R.A. Butlin, 'Urban genesis in Ireland, 1556–1641', in R.W. Steel and R. Lawton (eds), *Liverpool Essays in Geography* (London, 1967); R.A. Butlin, 'Irish towns in the sixteenth and seventeenth centuries', in R.A. Butlin (ed.), *The Development of the Irish Town* (London and Toronto, 1977), 61–100.

11 R.J. Hunter, 'Towns in the Ulster plantation', in *Studia Hibernica*, xi (1971), 40–79.

12 PRO, London, *M.P.F. 312 (2)*.

13 *Calendar of State Papers, Ireland, 1606–8*, 405.

14 *Calendar of State Papers, Ireland, 1603–6*, 319–320.

15 D.A. Chart (ed.), *Londonderry and the London Companies, 1609–1629* (Belfast, 1928), 33, 38–39.

16 Fynes Moryson, *Itinerary* (London, 1617).

17 R.J. Hunter, 'Ulster plantation towns, 1609–41', in D. Harkness and M. O'Dowd (eds), *The Town in Ireland* (Belfast, 1981), 55–80; M. McCarthy-Morrogh, *The Munster Plantation; English Migration to Southern Ireland, 1583–1641* (Oxford, 1986).

18 *State Papers Henry VIII*, 3, ii, 326–327.

19 Hunter, 'Towns in the Ulster plantation', 42, 47.

20 Royal Irish Academy, *Transcripts of Irish Municipal Charters, Derry*.

21 Spenser, *View of the State of Ireland*, 128.

22 *Calendar of State Papers, Ireland, 1647–60*, 151.

23 *Calendar of State Papers, Ireland, 1666–69*, 220–222.

24 *Municipal Corporations, Ireland: First Report of Commissioners of Inquiry*, H.C. (1835), 1055, 1063, 1099; R.J. Hunter, 'Sir William Cole and plantation Enniskillen, 1607–41', in *Clogher Record*, ix (1978), 336–350.

25 PRO, London, *M.P.F. 81*.

26 Trinity College, Dublin, *MS 1209*, 67.

27 *Municipal Corporations, Ireland*, 1055.

28 *A New English Dictionary on Historical Principles* (Oxford, 1888–1928).

29 *Municipal Corporations, Ireland*, 1055, 1063, 1099.

30 Simms, 'Classical precedent', 488; D. McCourt, 'County Londonderry: the geographical setting', in *County Londonderry Handbook* (Belfast, n.d.), 39; J.W. Reps, *The Making of Urban America* (Princeton, 1965), 11.

31 *Municipal Corporations, Ireland*, 1063.

32 PRO, London, *M.P.F. 95*.

33 Trinity College, Dublin, *MS 1209*, 14; [T.F. Colby], *Memoir of the City and North Western Liberties of Londonderry, Parish of Templemore* (Dublin, 1837), 98.

34 Trinity College, Dublin, *MS 1209*, 24; Moody, *The Londonderry Plantation, 1609–41* (Belfast, 1939), plate iv.

35 Trinity College, Dublin, *MS 1209*, 41, 42; P. O'Flanagan, 'Bandon', in J.H. Andrews and A. Simms (eds), *Irish Historic Towns Atlas* (Royal Irish Academy, Dublin, 1988).

36 Trinity College, Dublin, *MS 1209*, 24*; Moody, *Londonderry Plantation*, plate iii.

37 R. Loeber, 'A gate to Connacht: the building of the fortified town of Jamestown, County Leitrim, in the era of plantation', in *Irish Sword*, xv (1982–3), 149–162.

38 National Library of Ireland, *21.F.55*; J. Feehan, *Laoise: An Environmental History* (Stradbally, 1983), 393.

39 Reps, *Making of Urban America*, 6.

40 *Municipal Corporations, Ireland*, 1285; J.G. Simms, 'Donegal in the Ulster plantation', in *Irish Geography*, vi (1972), 391.

41 Chart, *Londonderry*, plate 3.

42 C. Bell and R. Bell, *City Fathers: The Early History of Town Planning in Britain* (London, 1969), 49.

43 P. Robinson, 'Some later survivals of box-framed "plantation" houses in Coleraine, County Londonderry', in *Ulster Journal of Archaeology*, xlvi (1983), 129–36.

44 *Municipal Corporations, Ireland*, 1063, 1099.

45 P. Clark and P. Stack, *English Towns in Transition, 1500–1700* (Oxford, 1976), 4–6, 8–10.

46 R. Gillespie, *Colonial Ulster: The Settlement of East Ulster, 1600–1641* (Cork, 1985), 176.

47 PRO, London, M.P.F. 99; P. Ó Conluáin, 'Some O'Neill country maps, 1575–1602', in *Duiche Neill*, i (1987), 21–22.

48 Trinity College, Dublin, MS 1209, 14.

49 B. Adams, 'The diamonds of Ulster and Pennsylvania', in *Ulster Folk and Transport Museum Handbook* (1975–6), 18–20.

50 R.J. Hunter, 'An Ulster plantation town – Virginia', in *Breifne*, iv (1970), 47–48.

51 A.R. Orme, 'Segregation as a feature of urban development in medieval and plantation Ireland', in *Geographical Viewpoint*, ii (1971), 193–206.

52 PRO, M.P.F. 82; G. Camblin, *The Town in Ulster* (Belfast, 1951), plate 2.

53 J.H. Andrews, 'The struggle for Ireland's public commons', in P. O'Flanagan, P. Ferguson and K. Whelan (eds), *Rural Ireland, 1600–1900: Modernisation and Change* (Cork, 1987), 3–4; *Calendar of State Papers, Ireland, 1608–10*, 488.

54 PRO, London, M.P.F. 99; Ó Conluáin, 'Some O'Neill country maps', 21–22.

55 John Speed, *The Theatre of the Empire of Great Britaine* (London, 1612).

56 National Library of Ireland, MS 3137.

57 R. Gillespie, 'Thomas Raven and the mapping of the Claneboy estates', in *Bangor Historical Journal*, i (1981), 6–9.

58 PRO, London, S.P. 62/1/19.

59 PRO, London, S.P. 63/23/24.

60 T.W. Moody, 'The revised articles of the Ulster plantation, 1610', in *Bulletin of the Institute of Historical Research*, xi (1935), 178–183.

61 *Calendar of State Papers, Ireland, 1611–14*, 493.

62 *Calendar of State Papers, Ireland, 1615–25*, 231.

63 J.T. Curl, *The Londonderry Plantation, 1609–1914* (Chichester, 1986), 354.

64 Chart, *Londonderry*; Curl, *Londonderry Plantation*, 354.

65 Hill, *Plantation in Ulster*, 445–590.

66 *Calendar of State Papers, Ireland, 1601–3*, 252.

67 P.S. Robinson, *The Plantation of Ulster: British Settlement in an Irish Landscape, 1600–1670* (Dublin, 1984), 150.

68 Chart, *Londonderry*, 59–60.

69 *Calendar of Patent Rolls, Elizabeth*, 201, 223, 266; P. O'Connor, *Exploring Limerick's Past: An Historical Geography of Urban Development in County and City* (Limerick, 1987).

70 National Library of Ireland., MS 22028; J.H. Andrews, *Irish Maps* (Dublin, 1977).

71 *Calendar of State Papers, Ireland, 1625–32*, 515–516.

72 Curl, *Londonderry Plantation*, plate ccxxviii.

73 PRO, London, S.P. 63/122/56.

74 Historical MSS Commission, *Salisbury MSS*, xiv, 241.

75 R.D. Edwards, 'Letter book of Sir Arthur Chichester', in *Analecta Hibernica*, viii (1938), 75.

76 Richard Lawrence, *The Interest of England in the Irish Transplantation* (Dublin, 1655), 14–18.

77 Curl, *Londonderry Plantation*, 156–157.

78 *Calendar of State Papers, Ireland, 1625–32*, 471.

79 J.H. Andrews, 'The maps of the escheated counties of Ulster, 1609–10', in *Proceedings of the Royal Irish Academy*, lxxiv C (1974), 165–166.

80 *Calendar of State Papers, Ireland, 1600–1*, 21.

81 *Calendar of State Papers, Ireland, 1625–32*, 186; Chart, *Londonderry*, 59.

82 J.C. Stone, *The Pont Manuscript Maps of Scotland: Sixteenth Century Origins of a Blaeu Atlas* (Tring, 1989), 10.

83 P.J. Duffy, 'Farney in 1634: an examination of Thomas Raven's survey of the Essex estate', in *Clogher Record*, xi (1983), 250–252.

84 J.H. Andrews, 'Henry Pratt, surveyor of Kerry estates', in *Journal of the Kerry Archaeological and Historical Society*, xiii (1980), 35; F.H.A. Aalen, 'Perspectives on the Irish landscape in prehistory and history', in T. Reeves-Smith and F. Hamond, *Landscape Archaeology in Ireland* (Oxford, 1983), 367.

7

IRELAND A COLONY

Settlement implications of the revolution in
military-administrative, urban and ecclesiastical
structures, *c*. 1550 to *c*.1730

William J. Smyth

Introduction

After Columbus, the struggle by European powers to control the Atlantic and
the New World brought Ireland's geopolitical location into sharp focus. Ireland,
after about 1530, is progressively redefined as a crucial and strategic springboard
for colonisation and provisioning of, migration to and trade with the New
World.[1] The island also becomes one of the epic battlegrounds in the struggle
between Reformation and Counter-Reformation Europe and is transformed
from a 'kingdom' to a fully-fledged colony by Britain through these processes.[2]
A social revolution also takes place in Ireland which seeks to replace the variety
of social, economic and political structures of late medieval sixteenth-century
Ireland with a single territorial and social system modelled on early modern
England.[3] Thus, Ireland, in the period under review, deepens its European
engagement, becomes an integral part of the European controlled Atlantic
world yet – uniquely amongst Western European countries – becomes a
colonised rather than a colonising country.

From the beginning, it is important to emphasise that the English (and
Scottish) colonial settlement in Ireland was structurally uneven and varied
regionally in its impact.[4] The whole process involved a series of complex social
and cultural changes at all scales which are still only partly understood. For
example, what is still not clear is what interests in the local societies were best
served by the new colonial order, how such external pressures were mediated in
the localities, and what kinds of class changes resulted from the encounters. As
always, we need to be sensitive to the law of unintended effects – and so keep a
necessary distinction between the intent of certain strategies of colonisation
and the rather different effects of such strategies. And there remains one major
imponderable – how would Irish society and settlement have evolved if a political and economic conquest had not taken place? How different would Ireland
then have been to what it eventually became under the new order of things?

In this chapter, the notion of 'settlement' is not confined to the structure and morphology of settlements *per se* but addresses the wider questions of the remaking and settling of early modern Ireland and its regions from the mid-sixteenth century onwards. The main focus will be on the radical changes in political, economic and social structures that followed from military conquest and how settlement transformations are woven into this complex story. The period is of enormous importance and is full of discontinuities, dislocations and trauma. Geographers have as yet not carried out sufficient research on a whole series of issues so the picture is still very unclear.[5] Likewise, the speed, scale and depth of a whole range of regional transformations make it even more difficult to bring order to the story. The strategy adopted here is to look at the critical parameters of territorial organisation – the 'enclosures' for living at a variety of scales – and to seek to understand social and settlement changes within these territorial frames of reference and transformation.

The impact of the 'new state'

In this era of the centralising absolutist state, Ireland's political status and its systems of territorial organisation, both by land and by sea, are radically reformed to serve new ends. Loeber has carefully documented the march of the English military and settlement frontier in sixteenth- and early seventeenth-century Ireland.[6] Figure 7.1 summarises these processes, pinpoints both the extension of the old Pale step-by-step westwards in the 1550s and 1560s and the parallel foundation of strategic military fortifications southwards along the Barrow and northwards to face the still hidden world of Gaelic Ulster. The vulnerability of the capital, Dublin, is reduced with both the consolidation of the series of fortified settlements across north Wicklow and the River Barrow and the solidification of a north–south shield against the resilient Gaelic heartlands of Laois-Offaly to the west. Bridgeheads are built northwards as far as Newry, westwards as far as Athlone and southwards to Waterford city. In the process, areas of Irish resistance and of strong Irish septs are systematically isolated and cut off from one another as were, for example, the O'Tooles and O'Byrnes of Wicklow from the O'Connors and the O'Moores of the midlands. This process of strategic fragmentation was to be further intensified in the conquest and subsequent plantation of Ulster.

A central feature of this early extension of the Pale is the utilisation made of the now dissolved monasteries as key strong points in the reconquest as well as the use made of their extensive Church lands to reward some of the old English lords but more particularly the new English officials and soldiers who are pushed out to colonise the edges of this centralising state's expanding world.[7] These early thrusts (1550–1570) should not be underestimated in settlement terms for these confiscated Church lands became the first anchors of new English settlement and colonisation on the island.

The 1570s and 1580s see the completion of this strategic absorption of the

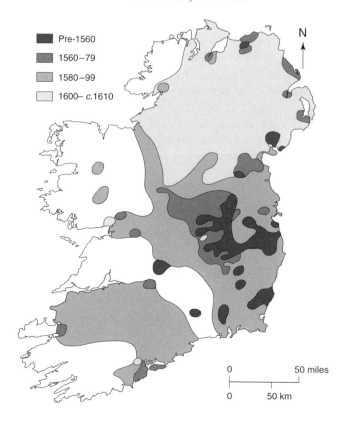

Figure 7.1   The expansion of the English military and settlement frontier, *c.* 1550 to *c.* 1610

Source: After R. Loeber, *The Geography and Practice of English Colonisation in Ireland, 1534 to 1609* (Belfast, 1991).

former Church lands. The crushing of the Desmond rebellion opens up much of the lordships of south Munster to formal state plantation. For the first time, the old English – even if 'degenerate' – see themselves treated no differently than the 'old' Irish. Their estates too are now open to confiscation. The balance of power in this Dublin administration is likewise shifting, and, as Nicholas Canny has noted, English colonial policy – for some time oscillating between strategies of assimilation and coercion – now hardens in favour of the latter approach.[8] McCarthy Morrogh has detailed the fretted, piecemeal character of the areas eventually planted in south Munster.[9] He has also shown that this important south Munster expansion of the gentry from the West Country and further afield in England was not such a radical change for these settlers as, perhaps, later planters were to experience elsewhere. Munster was already a deeply humanised world of towns, markets, road networks and castles. The immigrants

160

here were to decisively accelerate rather than initiate the processes of economic development, new house-building and the ornamentation of the landscapes in this region.

Munster, at least at the elite level, was also a bilingual world, although one suspects the linguistic/cultural frontier is still an important variable here in terms of the content and meaning of social interactions and transactions. However, the key differences between old and new landowners were increasingly of a political and religious nature. In the new colonial and European order, religious affiliation was to be the essential 'ethnic' marker, thus sharply distinguishing in Ireland the more privileged new English Protestant elites from their long or not-so-long established Catholic neighbours whose powers were on the wane. These ethno-political and status distinctions were to explode at a whole series of social levels in 1641.

Elsewhere, English military expansion had extended salients of control to the west and north – westwards towards Galway city and northwards along the old Normanised coastlands of east Ulster to reach Derry and further west along another old medieval corridor that ran from Roscommon into Sligo (see Figure 7.1). The creation of the provincial presidencies of Munster and Connaught in the 1580s also represented a stepping stone on the way to full administrative integration of these regions into the wider state polity. In the process, the O'Briens of Thomond and the Clanrickarde Burkes of Galway steered their respective regions away from the path of confrontation to one of strategic accommodation. In the long term, these decisions and the kinds of administration that followed from them were to help conserve much of the settlement structure and culture of both these regions.[10]

By the 1590s the platforms by sea and by land for the final assault on Gaelic Ireland – on Ulster – had been put in place. Bartlett's maps and sketches help us to understand from an English point of view the literal opening up of the O'Neill countryside.[11] His eye and pen tracks outwards from the Pale through the Gap of the North to reveal the Blackwater River and Charlemont Fort. Finally, the penetration to the O'Neill capital at Dungannon is depicted, its old castle now capped by the flag of St George. And Bartlett is not only recording the military victories and the march of the frontier – he is also very aware of the symbolic inversions as he sketches the deliberately broken inauguration stone of the O'Neills at Tullyoge. The power and ritual of the last regional lordship had finally yielded to the hammer of the centralising state.

Bartlett's maps also underwrite the procession of the governors, commanders, lesser officers and officials of the now coercive colonial power as it penetrates and dominates a world that had defeated the Normans. He notes the positions of the military forts at strategic points within the areas to be controlled. These garrisons were almost invariably to be key settlement foci in the future. Documented too are the evolving networks of roads linking these embryonic nuclei back through the Pale to Dublin and onwards to the core of metropolitan power at London. And underneath the text of the map is the hidden yet routine movement of personnel, goods, information and directives which moved up and down the newly constituted state network. By 1603, Ireland as a whole had been welded to the larger island to constitute a shaky, yet nonetheless single territorial system.

Crucially, this single geographical system involved a relatively new player, that of Scotland, now part of the Union and also part of this process of aggressive colonisation. By 1606, James I of England (James VI of Scotland) had come round to the view that the most effective and cheapest way to control Ireland, and in particular Ulster, was to plant it with loyal Protestant settlers and tenants who could act as a garrison in times of crisis.[12] Clearly, the Ulster plantation and the more informal processes of colonisation and settlement put in place both before and after the formal plantation were to have momentous consequences for the settlement history of Ireland.

Informal Scottish settlement had accelerated from the mid-sixteenth century onwards. Much of this was concentrated in the expanding MacDonnell domain of 'the Route' (between Coleraine and Ballycastle) and the Glens of Antrim where highland and island soldiers eventually put down roots. Further south, County Down saw significant infiltration from the mid-century by lowland Scots. There were also a number of abortive attempts to formally plant these north-eastern coastal peninsulas.[13] However, by 1603, the notion of a seemingly underpopulated land had caught the imagination of people in Scotland and England and Ulster became part of a wider Atlantic frontier which stretched from Newfoundland to Virginia and on to Bermuda and Guiana.[14] The propaganda in relation to the fruitfulness of Ulster land was complemented by the vacuum that followed the Nine Years War. All of Ireland had suffered under the Elizabethan Irish wars but Ulster suffered the most. The exact scale and extent of the depopulation in Ulster by 1607 is now impossible to measure – some estimates suggest that its population may have been halved in this devastating period.[15] And unlike Munster, Ulster was to be planted and settled in an era of rising tensions between the established Anglican Church, the embryonic Presbyterian Church and a Catholic Church in the process of reconstruction.

The earliest Scottish settlements were dictated by two main forces – geographical proximity and state strategy. Under the patronage of James I, Montgomery and Hamilton became key figures in laying down the anchors for settlement in east Down, Phillips was important at Coleraine and early infiltration also occurred around Derry.[16] These coastal areas nearest to Scotland were earliest and most intensively settled. This was also crucial from a strategic point of view for these early Scottish footholds acted both as a defence for the ever expanding state world of the King and also as a series of funnelling points for later inland colonisation. This came with the plantation proper of the six escheated counties as O'Neill, O'Donnell and others finally yielded to the incessant campaign of nibbling at, and quarrelling about, their local privileges and residual estates which was carried on by the always capable, determined and aggressive incomers.

The centralising metropolitan state now moved to formally and literally put in place a more carefully planned and mature plantation which would see the full panoply of settlers – from lords to artisans – brought in to run and build the towns, seignories, bawns, mills and ironworks. Attempts at village concentration of farmers and artisans yielded to both existing territorial arrangements and a pastoral economy.[17] Thus the rural immigrant settlement pattern became embedded in ancient townlands. A very complicated amalgam of both old and new worlds was thus grafted onto one of the oldest corners of Europe.

New colonists moved in from both Scotland and England and, as Philip Robinson has noted, a significant sorting out process ensued which saw a consolidation of settlement in the coastal lands to the east and north and substantial and permanent penetration in along the richest river valleys nearest these key coastlands.[18] As Hunter points out, the residual Irish lands were strategically fragmented one by one and closely supervised by the servitor estates.[19] Segregation on planter estates intensified and, as Robinson has highlighted for County Tyrone, this process was legalised after 1628 with the Irish tenants confined to one-quarter of the area of such estates.[20] Such 'Irish' lands were almost invariably in the upland and poorest townlands. As early as 1660, levels of segregation, as measured by the number of rural townlands without any 'Irish', ranged between 5 to 10 per cent of all townlands in the Ulster borderlands to a peak of over 20 per cent in the core area of planter settlement in north Armagh, south Antrim and east Londonderry.

Percival Maxwell carefully summarises the consequences of this pattern of settlement, displacement and subordination: 'Deprived of the land they loved and defended for so long, often uprooted from their homes and always under pressure to change their customs and way of life, the Irish deeply resented the intrusion of the newcomers.'[21] He also rightly notes that since the Ulster Irish had become a subject people between 1610 and 1641, 'their voice has almost entirely perished with the passage of time' and 'we are forced to use the barest scraps of evidence that have survived'.[22] Petty's barony maps of the early 1650s confirm the equally scrappy and fragmented character of the Irish estates and their associated settlements.

The 1641 rebellion in Ulster was prompted by a range of issues, relating to lordly status, Church revenues, problems of landed indebtedness, the battle between the King and Parliament in England and the clearly uneven consequences of a rapid agrarian and market revolution,[23] but the scale and power of the immigrant thrusts into the region must have been a central factor in itself. It may well be that the levels of immigration in the 1630s were also rising above the already very high levels in the early years of plantation. The marginalisation of both the Irish elites and the country people generally had probably reached a critical new threshold in the late 1630s. The dynamism of the settler frontier at this time is also suggested by immigrant expansion in the borders of Longford, north Sligo and Mayo where two Scottish-born bishops were established in the 1630s.[24] Immigrant settlement in Ulster and its borderlands was also being consolidated at a time when religious conflict raged across Europe and when identities locally were being forged around either a Protestant colonial or a Counter-Reformation Catholic Irish ethos. The bitterness of 1641 and its aftermath arose, in part at least, from these deep, structural tensions.

Yet the effective conquest of Ireland followed on from rather than was achieved by the military and plantation processes *per se*. This conquest was also profoundly administrative, legal and economic in character and took root in the years between 1603 and 1641. Hans Pawlisch in his work on Sir John Davies has itemised the judge-made laws which transformed definitions of property and territory in Ireland. As he shrewdly notes, in previous centuries it was the 'old' Irish population which was put outside the law; now it was Irish notions of territory and systems of property which were outlawed.[25] The extension of the common law system of property rights turned land into a marketable commodity, powerfully standardised land-measures and landholding arrangements island-wide and made central the concept of private property. As an integral part of the new estate system, the leasing contract became a powerful instrument for regularising and reordering life and land use in the townlands. A whole series of key legal decisions were made, not least with regard to the re-appropriation of the Bann fisheries, in favour of the new government and its agents.[26] New law had thus become a central instrument of colonisation and state expansion just as undermining the legal titles to land held by the old elites saw new estates vastly augmented by enterprising and ruthless colonists such as Boyle and St Leger in Munster, the Hamiltons, Chichesters and Montgomerys in Ulster, and Parsons in Dublin and the midlands, to name but a few of the freebooters.[27]

It is also clear that the final clearance of many woodlands and scrublands for strategic, industrial and settlement purposes was one of the most significant environmental changes wrought in late sixteenth- and early seventeenth-century Ireland. Woodlands were seen as the last bastions of resistance and were, therefore, military targets. The woods also fuelled the wide distribution of forges, tanneries and in some cases glassworks. Their disappearance also opened up about a further one-eighth of the land of Ireland for primary colonisation and the construction of new farmlands. The settlement of the former woodlands has not yet received a proper assessment by historical geographers. This clearance and settlement of the woodland also highlighted the frontier characteristics of the Irish experience – the wolf retreated in the face of this onslaught as did the woodkern. Both were treated similarly. Later on, the felling of the trees was to become a central metaphor for the destruction of the old aristocracy.

One of the most enduring administrative achievements with the most significant settlement consequences was the solidification of the county shiring system. The administrative experiences of the southern and eastern counties were older and more enduring – witness the social depth and routine character of this type of administrative structure as revealed in the sheriff's returns for

County Kilkenny in 1637.[28] The real revolution in county administration was taking place in the midlands, in the west and in the north with the mountainous lands of Wicklow becoming the final county area to be carved out by 1605.

A whole series of consequences flowed from the completion of this shiring process. First, units of local government and administration were now firmly bounded and focused on a specific central place – the county town. Many of the new county towns were built on the foundation of the focal points of the old lordships – that of Monaghan and the MacMahons, Tyrone and O'Neill's Dungannon, Fermanagh and Maguire's Enniskillen and Cavan around O'Reilly's earlier urban foundation. But there was a further crucial difference in administrative terms. 'Lordship' largely pivoted around strong individual personalities and shifting kin and family alliances. County administration was now in the hands of a *routine*, uniform group of state officials, i.e. bureaucrats who answered to Dublin and ultimately to London. The county towns became the centres of the garrison, assize courts and local administration generally, their status boosted by the acquisition of gaol houses, session houses, schools and churches and most particularly by grants for fairs and markets.

Beneath the county, the barony structures came to gradually displace the rule of the sub-chiefs. It is significant that the barony remains a central territorial entity in Petty's comprehensive mapping of the counties in the early 1650s. Beneath the barony, a rudimentary system of parish administration was slowly being reconstituted. We are still not clear of the extent and effectiveness of old and new manor courts but these were likely to have been more influential at the critical local level than has hitherto been allowed for in the literature. Certainly the figure of the parish constable gains in stature and functions as the seventeenth century progresses.

The transformation of the cities and towns

Equally fundamental to Irish society and settlement was the transformation in the distribution, status and functions of its cities and towns. As late as the 1570s, the well-being of what Sidney called 'the commonwealth' in Ireland was seen to depend on the old towns.[29] Municipal privileges were then further augmented. Thus, by the late sixteenth century, the Irish port towns were largely self-sufficient. Each commanded its own limited hinterland and conducted its own foreign trade. Each of the towns and especially the ports looked to different parts of the continental mainland or to England rather than to one another for trade. It was, therefore, far from being an integrated urban system. The merchants of the old towns went out into the countryside negotiating their rights from local lords so as to buy and sell amongst the local population.[30] Almost all the towns were walled, chartered institutions, striking in their separateness from a profoundly rural culture. Butlin's description is apt:

Irish towns … were generally peripherally distributed, with the port towns [as along the Boyne and the three 'sister' rivers of the southeast] being related to groups of satellite towns in the interior. The port towns were the largest towns, and were part of a Western European trading system, but they also maintained a high degree of autonomy notwithstanding the necessity for trading with the Irish inhabitants in their immediate hinterlands.[31]

The towns' walled exteriors were matched by the relatively closed nature of municipal life; each, like the merchant tribes of Galway city and the Tirrys, Galweys and Roches in Cork city, was characterised by a closed circuit of powerful elite families. As Sheehan and Cullen have pointed out,[32] Dublin's pre-eminence was then only marginally ahead of that of Galway. Linked with Bristol and facing west to the great opportunities of the Iberian Peninsula and the Atlantic, the latter city contained a population of c. 4,000 in 1600, perhaps only 1,000 fewer than the capital. As I have noted elsewhere, there is still in 1570 a striking correspondence between the hinterlands of the great ports and the distribution of the great lordships – a forging of a necessary alliance between the lordship as a political-administrative system and that of the port city and its hinterland as a commercial trading system.[33]

All of this was to change after 1580 with new political conditions laid down for urban office-holders. Both the emerging requirement of the taking of the Oath of Supremacy by government officials and the growth of Counter-Reformation culture in urban life drove a wedge between the new and old English urban elites. Change was also coming in the whole area of state revenues, where only the duty from wine imports (established in 1569) provided any income for the state from the towns. The notion of reformation was not only religious but was also now vigorously applied to towns, trade, customs, revenue, manners and language. Late sixteenth- and early seventeenth-century regional conflicts further suggested to the English their need to regulate and control the towns. Not surprisingly then, the old urban edges were to be surrounded by great Elizabethan forts, symbolising England's intention to regain control not only in the lordships but crucially in the towns themselves.

As Sheehan has demonstrated, urban recusant protests in the early 1600s, although primarily religious in character, were also concerned with the defence of charter liberties. Mountjoy's response to Waterford Corporation when they claimed certain rights by charter was chilling in its impact; he told the city fathers that 'he would cut King John's charter in pieces with King James's sword' if he was not admitted to the city.[34] Old corporate privileges were thus disposed of. A new absolutist order was being written into the urban fabric. Likewise, the garrisoning of the old towns continued apace until the mid-seventeenth century.

Further centralisation of control came in 1611 when all grants of tolls and customs were removed from the cities to the Crown. In 1607–8 customs dues yielded only *c.* 1.2 per cent of the total Irish revenue. By 1623, it comprised about a quarter of state income and by 1637–8 custom receipts were at least six times those of 1623, a measure both of further state control and a buoyant economic order.[35] The new Jacobin state, therefore, proceeded in systematic fashion to break the grip of the towns on trade and customs. As Treadwell notes:

> From being cosseted, quasi-autonomous allies of the Crown, Anglo-Irish merchant communities found themselves reduced to the unfamiliar and unpalatable role of regular taxpayers, their cosy municipal monopolies constantly challenged by the customs farmers' interest in expanding the volume of taxable trade of all merchants.[36]

A profound geographical transformation was therefore in process – instead of relatively clearly defined and isolated port cities, characterised by autonomous circuits of trade and local control of surpluses, a national state system in the management of an integrated urban hierarchy was being put in place. The towns were made subject to the state's coffers and in the process linked together in a loose but still single unit. This pattern was further accentuated and extended geographically with the great rush of urban foundations between 1600 and 1641, especially those in Ulster. These new urban foundations and the creation of a large number of parliamentary boroughs culminated in the engineering of a Protestant majority in the Irish Parliament. This was achieved as early as 1613, and apart from very short periods, was never to be interrupted until the Act of Union abolished that Irish Parliament.

However, Irish cities and towns still retained some privileges up until the 1641 'rebellion'. The Cromwellian conquest and settlement was to see a radical revolution in the character of the larger towns. As Barnard has brilliantly outlined,[37] Cromwellian policy with regard to Irish urban centres during the Commonwealth had three objectives: strategic, political and economic. Cromwellian strategy was not only to debar Catholics from membership of civil government and from juries but also set about expelling the old merchant families from within the walls. The Cromwellians, therefore, set about reconstructing both the social and political components of port-city and county towns rather than creating new corporations. In the political arena, these processes were to be geared to encouraging the election of safe mayors and aldermen. Finally, and equally important, towns were seen as the key hinges in Ireland's economic development for government revenues depended on urban prosperity. Yet outside Dublin, the expulsion of Catholic merchants was to temporarily retard economic recovery, for the loss of the old Catholic families meant a reduction in key shipping and infrastructural wealth and above all in the overseas contacts for trade.

As Barnard correctly notes, the removal of Catholic property owners from the towns was of equal importance to the uprooting of Catholic landed proprietors[38] yet this process has received little attention in the literature. This policy was pursued vigorously in Dublin and as early as 1643 the towns of Limerick, Waterford and Wexford were offered for sale at £30,000, £25,000 and £7,500 respectively. No sales resulted but this was the start of the policy to take these key towns out from under Catholic control. Indeed in 1653 half the houses in the cities of Limerick, Waterford and Cork were reserved for sale. Still in the mid-1650s much property stood empty, especially in Cork, Galway, Limerick and Waterford, a symbol of the traumas and dislocation of the previous decade, as well as the utterly transformed character of Irish urban life after the Cromwellians.

Dublin was the single greatest gainer from all these transformations (Figure 7.2). In the first half of the seventeenth century, Dublin was the centre of Parliament, of the law courts, of the university and had two cathedral chapters. As Petty documented, it suffered much depopulation during the plague of the early 1650s, yet the Cromwellian policy of expulsion of Catholic merchants was still vigorously pursued in the city. By 1660, English settlers outnumbered the Irish by three to one in the city core with the Irish marginalised to the suburbs. But, unlike other cities, these expulsions did not have a dramatic effect on Dublin's trade. From the first decades of the seventeenth century Protestant merchants were gaining a stranglehold on Dublin's growing trade and during the Commonwealth this hold was to become a monopoly. They were the great beneficiaries of Dublin's increasingly pivotal role as Ireland's nerve-centre of administration and trade in the 1650s. As Barnard has pointed out, the most critical effects of Cromwellian rule in Dublin were religious and economic.[39] The Protestant community in Dublin was consolidated into a very powerful body, including many influential people of a non-conformist persuasion. Second, Dublin was to be the great beneficiary of economic centralisation under Cromwell's rule. It benefited too from the enormous centralisation of administration and law and its established role as an educational, medical and social focus of immigrant life also expanded. According to Petty, over one-fifth of all the big houses in Ireland were located in Dublin in 1672, as well as 85 per cent of all houses with more than ten chimneys. Overall, the city had grown dramatically, from c. 5,000 in 1600 to 30,000 in 1660, c. 50,000 in 1685 to reach close on 100,000 in 1730 when it became one of the largest cities in Europe.

By the early 1660s the fruits of Cromwellian expulsion policies were also clear in other cities. The old city of Waterford had been stripped of its Catholic majority – within its three central wards Protestants now formed a majority. Cork city exhibited a similar pattern as did old inland cities like Clonmel and Kilkenny.[40] Galway, given its strategic importance in the west and its strong continental links was given special treatment. In 1655, its long-established Catholic merchant families were expelled from the city. The Protestant inhabitants who settled there were much poorer and had little experience of trade. The wars, plagues and these expulsions had long-lasting effects on the status of

Galway. Its long-term decline began in the 1650s. The old ties with the Continent were severed and the new settlers did not have the skills and resources to create a new trading network.[41] This gaining of urban control and the demographic transformation achieved in key ports and county towns was to be one of the most powerful and permanent contributions of Cromwellian rule to Ireland.

Figure 7.2 seeks to summarise the size, distribution and ethnic structure of towns and cities in 1660. Three types of regions with rather different urban structures and lifestyles are revealed. An elaborate urban hierarchy characterises the east, south-east and increasingly the north-east of Ireland. The midlands and the border areas of the old feudalised world generally are characterised by a still developing urban hierarchy. In the remoter, mainly western regions, urban settlement hierarchies and ways of living were still only in their infancy. A striking feature of the map is the almost exclusive dominance of the settler population in the often newly planted towns of Ulster. Beyond this region, the towns with a 20–40 per cent planter population highlight a significant buffer zone stretching from Sligo through Roscommon into south Down. A more hidden urban Ireland is also revealed in the south and east 'where the often walled, sometimes small but often socially and morphologically complex borough towns'[42] are still overwhelmingly dominated by Irish and old English town dwellers. It is clear that it was these old, enduring and adaptive urban societies which underpinned the higher population densities and complex rural settlement hierarchies of late medieval Ireland. Figure 7.2 thus provides a graphic illustration of the coexistence on this small island of very different urban cultures in the mid-seventeenth century.

Twelve revenue precincts were also established during the Cromwellian period. By 1700, the number had increased to thirty (see also Figure 7.2, Box B). These urban-centred functional regions represented a new ordering of space in the service of the state and the economy. As Gillespie has outlined, 'trade was, of course, regulated by law, whether grants of market rights, control of customs or regulation of property rights'.[43] Gradually also, the standardisation of weights and measures spread as did uniform mechanisms of exchange generally. The distribution of the permanent barracks of horse and foot soldiers also symbolised the consolidation of other spatial orders – significantly the greatest density of such garrisons ran through the middle of the country from Derry to Cork. Overall, the contrasts with the 1570s could not have been greater. Instead of semi-autonomous and independent trading regions controlling most of their own surpluses, we now have an integrated system of functional urban regions, acting as the collectors of revenue which is funnelled through to Dublin and London. And instead of small or large local lordships with their own militia, we have a network of colonial garrisons under a single command and a county system of government which is powerfully anchored on Dublin.

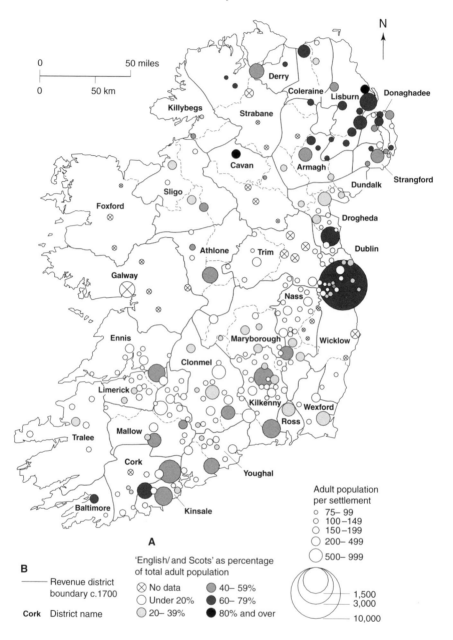

0   50 miles

0   50 km

Derry

Coleraine   Lisburn   Donaghadee

Killybegs   Strabane

Cavan   Armagh

Strangford

Dundalk

Sligo

Foxford

Drogheda

Athlone   Trim   Dublin

Galway

Nass

Ennis   Maryborough   Wicklow

Clonmel

Limerick

Kilkenny   Wexford

Ross

Mallow

Tralee

Cork

Youghal

Baltimore   Kinsale

A

Adult population
per settlement

○   75– 99
○   100 –149
○   150 –199
○   200– 499
○   500– 999

B

Revenue district
boundary c.1700

Cork   District name

'English/ and Scots' as percentage
of total adult population

⊗ No data   ◔ 40– 59%
○ Under 20%   ● 60– 79%
◑ 20– 39%   ● 80% and over

1,500
3,000

10,000

Figure 7.2   Distribution and ethnic composition of urban places *c.* 1660 and Revenue
District boundaries and centres by 1700

Ecclesiastical 'reformations'

The story of the townland, and especially that of the parish, in seventeenth century Ireland is not just at the heart of understanding the settlement history of the period but profoundly underpins later settlement and social history as well. Running parallel to this secular territorial and settlement reorganisation by the state, Ireland saw the radical transformation of its ecclesiastical functions, their territorial structures and settlements. As Stein Rokkan has pointed out, the creation of a state church such as that of the English Anglican Church involved the use of the vernacular language (English) in its ritual and administration.[44] Such processes led to the creation of new linguistic/religious spaces across Western Europe which were characterised by sharp confessional boundaries. The centralising nation-state, if Protestant, operated a closed style of recruitment and control of its clergy within its own linguistic space. In contrast, the Counter-Reformation Catholic countries still operated a supranational multi-lingual network of religious personnel and exchanges. In Ireland, these two competing ecclesiastical systems clashed head on. And unique in Western Europe, two parallel and competing church systems became deeply embedded in the landscape, in systems of parochial administration and in people's minds.

As we have seen, the expansion of the early English military frontier was often literally built on the ruined foundations of the dissolved monasteries. Likewise, there is an interlocking geographical and temporal synthesis between the (re)establishment of this country system and effective transfer of diocesan and parochial facilities – including the crucial question of tithe-collection – from the old Church to the colonial state Church which inherited these long-established territorial structures and functions. As Alan Ford has documented, the sixteenth-century Reformation Church, while not without its successes in the towns, amongst a minority of the old English elite and in parts of the Gaelic world, was, on the whole, bedevilled by poorly trained clergy, low incomes, absenteeism and rampant pluralism in the management of parishes.[45]

The great failure of the Reformation/Anglican Church in Ireland was the failure to assimilate and control the population of the Pale region and the older towns. The progressive alienation and growing self-consciousness of the old English from the 1570s onwards, and their eventual exclusion from office and political influence was one key factor here. A second key factor was the long-standing importance of extra-territorial links between both strands of the Irish Catholic tradition – Gaelic and Old English – and the continent and especially Spain and France. The critical decade of decision may have been the 1580s, the critical reorientation developed in the 1590s as Irish seminaries were established in Spain and the then Spanish Netherlands. Already by 1607, as many as one-third of all Irish Colleges abroad were established and as many as 73 per cent of all the continental seminaries were founded before 1630.[46] A confident European-centred Counter-Reformation culture was thus being put in place, however slowly and fitfully and however regionally and ethnically differentiated.

Between the 1580s and the 1620s, then, the battle lines were drawn as two parallel and bitterly opposed systems of Church administration and ritual were crystallised. And critical to the geography of religion and settlement was the fact that the core region of the country centred on the Pale and the wealthier towns of the south-east – key old English cities of power, status and information networks – had now become emphatically Catholic in ethos and the centres of what came to be termed the recusant Church. If the Anglican Church had been successful in this core area at this early crucial stage, the cultural and settlement geography of Ireland would have been very different indeed.

In consequence, by the first decades of the seventeenth century, the Anglican Church in Ireland had become an establishment Church of officers and administrators, manned by English-born bishops and catering essentially for a new English and sometimes Scottish (as in Fermanagh) immigrant population. It was generally but not invariably imbued with an elitist exclusive ideology with its roots in both a colonial status and a specific theology.[47] The settlement and cultural consequences of these mutations were immense. Because of the weaknesses of the Anglican Church in so many regions, many of the old parish churches – ancient foci of settlement – ended up in ruins. For example, in the diocese of Dublin, there is a striking regional gradation in the ruination of old parish churches. In the city of Dublin and the deanery of Taney (Dundrum) the great majority of the old parish churches were in good repair in 1615. However, in the deaneries of Bray, Ballymore Eustace and Leixlip, just over half of the parish churches were in repair at this time following a massive decline in the quality of their church buildings between 1531 and 1615. On the fringes of the diocese in Kildare and parts of Wicklow, the decline in the status of parish churches is devastating, with 82 per cent of churches in the deanery of Castledermot already beyond repair in 1615.[48] While the 1615 report may have been a little over-critical of the state of church buildings generally, it is still striking to note that a further seventy-nine parish churches in the diocese are classified as 'being in ruins' by 1630. Whatever the specific merits of the evidence, there is no doubt that a radical transformation of the ecclesiastical landscape of the diocese of Dublin had already taken place by 1630.

This pattern was replicated across most of this island. In 1615, dioceses with above average scores relating to the condition of parish churches were all located in Leinster with Ferns boasting the highest percentage (78 per cent) of churches in good repair. Only Ross/West Cork and Lismore/Waterford displayed an above average level of church maintenance in Munster, a pattern partially coincident with significant immigrant settlement. In contrast, a key axis of church decline and dereliction stretched from Waterford city via Cashel and Limerick to Killaloe. This area of Anglican weaknesses, as evidenced by the woeful condition of its churches, reached its peak in Kilfenora where no church was in good repair and in Ardfert where only three of the parish churches were still viable. On the other hand, above average maintenance of church buildings characterised west and north Connaught. The dioceses of Kilmacduagh, Killala,

Achonry and Elphin all show above 50 per cent maintenance of parish churches, a pattern more characteristic one assumes (given the absence of survey data) of the northern dioceses.

The situation in the southern half of the country reveals further Anglican decline between 1615 and 1622. While recognising that the 1622 figures are likely to be more accurate, the comparative materials show for Kildare and Meath a drastic deterioration (-50 per cent) in the condition of church buildings in this short seven-year period, thus confirming 'other accounts of the appalling state of church fabric in the Pale area'.[49] In contrast, and possibly due to the Earl of Ormond's patronage, the diocese of Ossory shows a slight improvement ($+17$ per cent) in the number of churches deemed to be in repair by 1622. Yet overall, as Alan Ford emphasises, the Catholic Church went unchallenged in many of the parishes of the Pale and in Munster by 1622.[50]

The decay of so many churches in so many places was a symbol of the particular failure of the Anglican Church in Ireland by the early seventeenth century. The Catholic population's resistance is, perhaps, best explained not only by the failure to support the local church but also in the deliberate strategies taken to ruin these churches and their livings once they had been appropriated to what was perceived as 'the heretic church'. This resistance pivoted around the power bases of the old resident gentry families and likewise on the survival of a significant number of Catholic tithe farmers who withheld this source of material support from the local vicars.

Ulster dioceses were relatively free from the often crippling effects of impropriate rectories. Indeed following on from the plantation, Anglican bishops in Ulster carefully ensured that their church would be generously endowed with both land and incomes.[51] Not surprisingly, therefore, the density of clergy was greatest in the richer northern dioceses, particularly in the lowland areas dominated by the settlers. The upland and marginal areas, mainly inhabited by the Irish, were more likely to be manned in a pluralist and absentee fashion.

Outside of Ulster, the number of impropriate rectories continued to rise between 1615 and 1634. Already in 1615, about 60 per cent of the recorded parishes for non-Ulster dioceses were impropriate – the proportion reached close to 70 per cent by 1622 and was well over this percentage by 1634.[52] Here again regional variations are significant and have long-term settlement implications. The Pale region had a higher than average level of impropriate parishes and this proportion was still rising in dioceses like Kildare between 1615 and 1634. On the other hand, the dioceses of south Leinster exhibited levels of impropriation 10 per cent below the norm. Munster exhibits a highly varied pattern with Ardfert, Emly, Cashel and Cloyne similar to the Pale region. Indeed the level of impropriation rose by a further 33 per cent in the diocese of Emly between 1615 and 1634. On the other hand, Thomond's Killaloe and the relatively well-planted dioceses of Cork and Ross had under 50 per cent of their parishes in an impropriate condition. With the notable exception of Tuam, in all of the Connaught dioceses at least 85 per cent of rectories were impropriate, a product of long-established gentry encroachment on Church revenues, a process accentuated by the vacuum after the Reformation. This was the region where 'respect for the Church of Ireland' was clearly at its lowest. The Catholic Church clearly would not have to face a difficult path of reconstruction in that province.[53]

The zones of weaknesses for the Anglican Church, whether described in terms of decayed church fabric, absentee clergy and/or high levels of impropriate rectories were conversely the regions of greatest Counter-Reformation resistance and Catholic reconstruction. And it was this resistance – domestic and episcopal, and complex and multi-layered in its territorial expressions – which made Ireland an exceptional place on the seventeenth-century West European stage. It was the only country where the Counter-Reformation succeeded against the will of the head of the state and the instruments of government.[54]

As Patrick Corish has documented, post-Reformation Ireland inherited an untidy medieval parish system.[55] The Normanised areas were characterised by small, sometimes compact parishes where lay lords had rights of clerical nomination. In the Gaelic areas, powerful local kin groups controlled the coarbial and erenagh rights to church land and wealth in regions where the observant friars played key ritual and circulation functions. In addition, the diocesan parochial system had been seriously compromised in non-Gaelic areas by the former widespread appropriation of parishes by the now 'dissolved' religious orders. Such parishes had already suffered from problems of absenteeism and amalgamation before the Reformation era. However, underneath the complex mosaic of official Church territories, the Counter-Reformation Church had other strengths to build on and other difficulties to overcome. The localised nature of religious traditions primarily centred around domestic rituals of birth, marriage and death. The great importance of patron-days, holy wells and pilgrimage-going all gave a specific kind of richness and vitality to religious life. However, from the Tridentine Church's point of view, the failure of the medieval Church to fully Christianise a number of these rituals – and particularly those relating to the wake and the funeral – was to remain a long-standing problem as was the need to re-educate much of the population in the basic tenets of Christianity. Powerful kin groups involved in ecclesiastical affairs also remained an enduring problematic feature, while also giving their own distinctive strength to the local church.

It is possible to argue that between the 1580s and the 1620s, the Counter-Reformation Church succeeded in building up a sufficient cadre of newly trained priests to lay the foundations for a resurgent Church. In 1622–3, it is estimated that the Catholic Church was being served by c. 1,100 priests, which represented a ratio of priests to parishioners of c. 1:1,360.[56] By the early 1630s, in dioceses as diverse as Elphin, Fermoy, Waterford, Tuam, Kerry, Killaloe and Kildare, the number of parish priests comes close to matching the total number of reconstituted Catholic parishes that we know of by the early eighteenth century. Of these dioceses, Ferns seems less well favoured than those of the western dioceses that stretched from Kerry through Tuam to Elphin. Overall, as Corish has demonstrated, a genuine *public* Catholic Church had emerged by the 1630s – 'fitting awkwardly into the Commonwealth' – yet tolerated.[57] And communal attendance at Sunday Mass became a central symbol of this reinvigorated Church.

Figure 7.3 attempts to summarise the long-term amalgamation of medieval parishes into new parochial units by the resurgent Catholic Church. The greatest rationalisation of old medieval parishes was to occur in this well-developed region of the Pale, along the Barrow Valley and on into the core axis of late medieval power that stretched from Wexford through Kilkenny, Waterford and south Tipperary on to Limerick and north Kerry with a salient southwards into east and coastal Cork and northwards through the great middle heartland of County Clare. The old north–south corridor of east Connaught also saw a significant restructuring of parish boundaries as did the long-settled region of

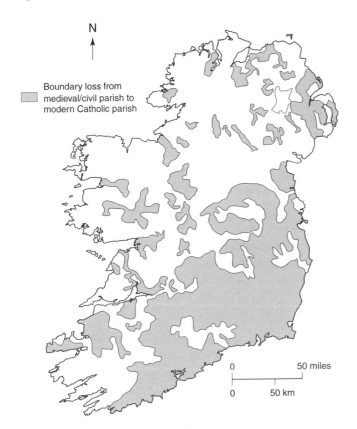

N

Boundary loss from medieval/civil parish to modern Catholic parish

0   50 miles

0   50 km

Figure 7.3   Continuities (unshaded) and losses (shaded) in the distribution of modern Catholic parish boundaries, as compared with the medieval parish network

east Down and south Antrim. In the remainder of the country, the older, coarser network of medieval parishes still constituted, for the most part, suitable 'enclosures' to meet the demands of a Church rebuilding along Tridentine lines.

Over the whole period under review, however, the resurgent Catholic Church underwent periods of massive trauma before the rudimentary framework of new parishes would begin to solidify by the early eighteenth century. During the Commonwealth period, Catholicism was deemed not to exist, intensive religious persecution followed and a majority of priests were either executed or transported out of the country. Nuns too were victims of Cromwellian persecution. Dublin was hardest hit by these legislative measures set up for 'discovering and repressing of Popish recusants'[58] while, on the other hand, the diocese of Meath in the rich lands of the Boyne appears to have sustained its parish structure almost intact.

By c. 1660 there were only 500 to 550 priests in place to begin the process of reconstruction once again. This represented about one priest per 2,300–500 Catholic parishioners, half the equivalent ratio reported on in 1622.[59] The parish system had again fallen into disarray, with, in this case, a greater tendency for survival shown in Connaught, a poorer situation in Ulster, poorer again in Munster, with the Catholic Church under greatest pressure in Leinster. The immediate post-Cromwellian period saw a greater fragmentation not only in religious practice but also in class structures. The old gentry patronage of the Church was often destroyed or displaced. Irish society generally became fragmented even further, pulled in different directions by old and new landlords, by priest and parson and a schizophrenic parish system. It was out of this period that the mythology of the 'heroic' phase of the Catholic Church's history was forged – culminating in the memory of the implementation of the Penal Laws which reached a climax in the first two decades of the eighteenth century. Yet in the same period and especially from the 1670s onwards key ecclesiastical structures and religious practice were reconstituted along Tridentine lines. Parochial and diocesan organisations were revitalised to begin again the ongoing challenge to a decentralised, kin-based and increasingly vital folk-culture. By 1704/5, c. 1,100 priests gave a reasonably satisfactory ratio of one priest to every 1,600 parishoners, given that as many as 424 regulars (4 out of 10 from the Galway port-region) were shipped to 'foreign parts' in 1698.[60]

The towns were to remain the core anchors of the Counter-Reformation Church, characterised by a greater concentration of religious, both secular and regular, the greater role played by women members and, overall, more diverse sources of material support both for a still rich liturgical tradition and for the sustenance of religious personnel. The religious gradations then worked outwards from the cities and towns in a series of circles to the still quasi-Christian communities in the most rural areas. Patrick Corish's regionalisation of post-Tridentine religious patterns of vitality by the 1670s is suggestive: in the first rank comes Dublin, second come the other towns, third rural Munster and Leinster, followed by Connaught and finally Ulster.[61]

This picture is confirmed in 1731. In that year the House of Lords compiled a Report on 'the state of popery' from returns made by magistrates and Anglican clergy. This report suggests that c. 1,445 secular priests and 254 regulars functioned in the country. This is certainly an underestimate – there are no returns for the diocese of Kerry or for a number of parishes in some other dioceses. As Connolly notes, the returns for secular priests represent a minimum estimate while those for the regulars were clearly incomplete.[62] Their numbers were certainly double and more likely to be closer to three times the official figure, i.e. about 760. Overall, one may safely suggest a total number of priests of c. 2,360. Assuming the population of Ireland to be c. 2.5 million in 1732 and that, at most, 1.875 million or c. 75 per cent were Catholic, this suggests a ratio of priest to parishioner of 1:800. This is an impressive ratio in the context of both earlier and later patterns of priest/people relationships.

However, the actual material conditions under which the Catholic religion was practised – especially the condition of its churches – varied dramatically across the island. The 1731 report provides descriptions of the conditions under which the population heard Mass in most dioceses. The great dichotomy is between those parishes and regions with established Mass-houses and those dioceses and parishes where Mass was said in the open air, on the mountain, 'or under some sort of shed, built up occasionally to shelter the priest from the weather'.[63] Figure 7.4 attempts to summarise this evidence, concentrating on the relative significance of such open air Mass sites vis-à-vis formal Mass-houses and chapels.

Across an extensive region over the middle half of the island, from Meath and Dublin diocese in the east to Ossory, Waterford and Limerick in the south and across to Tuam in the west, Mass-houses were essentially dominant. However rudimentary some of these buildings were, they point to the already solid position of the Church in these dioceses. Ferns, Leighlin, Cloyne, Cork and Ross (and possibly Kerry) were also characterised by a clear majority of Mass-houses, but still retained a number of 'movable altars in the fields'.[64] In the north Midlands, Elphin and Clonmacnoise appear to be similar in the character of Mass provision. The beginnings of a belt of weakness emerges in the northern part of the diocese of Armagh and stretches north of a line that goes westwards to embrace the dioceses of Achonry and Killala in north Connaught. Here a significant number of the centres of Catholic worship were open-air sites. In Ulster, the situation deteriorates even further in Raphoe, Clogher, Derry and the northern half of Armagh, where, in contrast to the southern dioceses, a significant majority of places for Sunday Mass were mobile in character and unprotected. Down and Conor and Dromore return the poorest conditions for the Catholic Church, and are also – because of this weakness – the regions most likely to have seen the greatest assimilation of older populations to the new church denominations. In Down and Conor, it was nine times as likely that a Catholic would attend Mass in the open air rather than in a proper chapel in 1731, and this ratio was 6 to 1 in Dromore. Corish's model of

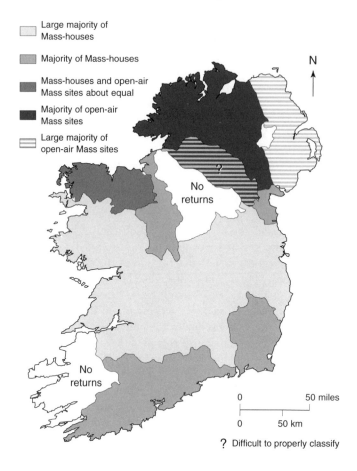

Figure 7.4 Relative distribution of Mass-houses as compared with open-air Mass sites c. 1731

the geographical distribution of Church vitality in 1670 is strongly supported, if with minor modifications, by the evidence of the 1731 report. Likewise, Connolly's survey of the whole report is very succinct and apt:

> Two things are immediately evident from the resulting reports. The first is the scale and level of Catholic ecclesiastical organisation; a generous ratio of clergy to people; an uneven but still extensive, provision of places of worship; a network of both elementary and more advanced schools; and large numbers of regular clergy some of them living in settled communities. The second is the general absence of concealment. The Anglican clergy and lay officials charged with making the returns were all clearly informed as to the location of mass-houses, schools, and communities of religious as well as the identity

not just of parish clergy but of bishops, vicars-general and other digni-
taries.[65]

The Catholic Church was still technically an illegal and proscribed Church;
it would still be subject to periodic repression, consequent on the political mood
of the day, but it is also clear by 1731 that a moral community of enormous
power and durability had emerged from the traumas of the later sixteenth and
the seventeenth centuries.

Alan Gailey's work on the Scots element in north Irish popular culture is
very helpful in seeking to elucidate a third critical geography of religious institutions and settlements in seventeenth-century Ireland – that of the Presbyterian
Church.[66] Figure 7.5 seeks to summarise his detailed work on the establishment
of Presbyterian congregations in the north. It is difficult to pinpoint the very
earliest congregations 'for they depend on recognition of presbyterial forms of
church government and worship within an essentially episcopalian setting'.[67]
Gailey has identified 148 foundations between 1613 and 1720 (a further six
were added before 1735). In the first originating phase in the dissemination of
Presbyterianism between 1613 and 1640, early foci emerge in East Tyrone, in
two parts of Co. Antrim – in the east between Larne and Islandmagee and to
the west around Lough Neagh – and in north-east Down and Strangford Lough.
At least thirteen such congregations were established by 1641, representing c. 9
per cent of all those established up to 1720.

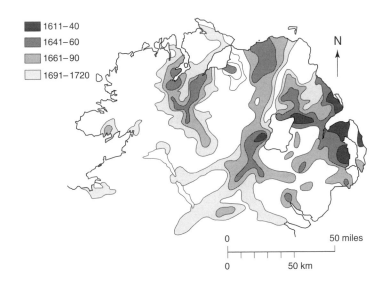

Figure 7.5 Geographical spread of Presbyterian congregations from c. 1611 to 1720

Source: After R.A. Gailey, 'The Scots element in north Irish popular culture: some problems in
the interpretation of historical acculturation', *Ethnologia Europea*, 8 (1975).

The second key diffusion stage in the spread of Presbyterianism occurred in the critical two decades from 1641 to 1660. As Gailey notes, 'equivocation between Presbyterian and Protestant episcopal forms of government continued until c. 1638'.[68] However, formal presbyterial ecclesiastical structures in the north of Ireland originated with the army Presbyteries formed by chaplains who accompanied the Scots army which crossed over to Ulster to help defeat the Irish 'rebellion' of 1641. Close on 40 per cent of the fifty-seven new Presbyterian congregations established between 1641 and 1660, were actually established in the traumatic 1640s. In this context, consolidation of the early Scots areas of settlement in east Down and south Antrim appears most pronounced during these difficult years. Dundonald was one such place 'where a whole society transplanted itself and brought to Dundonald the speech and manners of the Scottish lowlands'.[69] Likewise, in the early 1650s key new areas of development of Presbyterian congregations took place in the Lower Bann Valley, down the Foyle basin and along Lough Swilly in north-east Donegal. More than 60 per cent of the congregations established in these two decades began after 1651, reflecting, in part, the massive influx of new Scots over this period as a whole.

The period 1641–60 was therefore crucial for both the consolidation of original foci and the development of a number of new core areas. Of all congregations established up until 1720, at least 39 per cent were constituted in this brief critical period. Over the next three decades – between 1661 and 1690 – a further thirty-four congregations (23 per cent of total) were established especially in north-west Antrim, east Co. Londonderry and east Tyrone. Equally important, former nuclei are now being linked together as along the Bann Valley into east Tyrone and from mid-Armagh into mid- and south Down. In the fourth phase, between 1691 and 1715, a further forty-four congregations (29 per cent) were added. This is also a critical consolidation phase with both an intensification and consolidated expansion of key areas of Scots Presbyterian settlement between the Swilly and Lough Foyle basins, a merging of Bann Valley and south Antrim cores to extend deep inland into Fermanagh and more particularly mid-Monaghan and Cavan. The powerful vector of English Anglican settlement extending south from Belfast Lough along the Lagan Valley into north Armagh still remains on the map while strong links have been forged between Presbyterian communities in mid-Armagh with those in much of north and east Down. New outlying foci were also emerging in south Donegal and Sligo. These latter areas, as well as west Down, much of south Armagh, Cavan, Monaghan and Louth were to see continued Presbyterian expansion well into the mid-eighteenth century.

The apparent rapid decline in the vitality and expansiveness of the Presbyterian Church as evidenced in the few foundations after c. 1715 is, however, somewhat misleading. From 1672, with modifications in 1689 and 1719, the ministers of what was technically an illegal Church received a fixed royal grant – the *regium donum*. Ministers, therefore, after 1715 sensibly resisted the setting up of new congregations, which would have diminished their share of the grant.[70] Outside of Dublin, however, and the small yet vital Quaker establishments also in the midlands and the south, it was Ulster-Scots Presbyterians who constituted the core body of the dissenting Church in Ireland. For complex political and religious reasons, Presbyterianism remained subject to harassment in certain religious matters such as those relating to marriages solemnised in Presbyterian meeting houses, as well as to a number of civil disabilities. Their members, therefore, occupied a middle position between the favoured established Church and that of the Catholic Church in terms of their status and disabilities.

As Louis Cullen has pointed out, and unlike the often sponsored English settlers in Ulster who came to occupy mainly positions of economic dependence, Scots Presbyterians – 'lusty, able-bodied, hardy and stout' – were much more likely to be independent migrants with capital reserves of their own.[71] They thus fostered a dynamic, youthful frontier of expansion not only in the more sparsely populated borderlands of Ulster but also by competing vigorously and displacing both Irish Catholics and English Anglican settlers in the rich lowlands of the Foyle, east Donegal and of Tyrone. This dynamism was also, in part, a product of the highly disciplined and cohesive structure of Presbyterian ecclesiastical congregations. As Connolly has noted, after the creation of the Synod of Ulster in 1691, Presbyterianism 'was an autonomous and highly organised ecclesiastical polity. The discipline which the kirk session exercised over its members was both strict and broadly defined.'[72] Presbyterian members and lay elders exercised social control not only in matters broadly religious and moral but also in relation to a whole series of economic transactions, including land-lord–tenant relationships. A description of 1716 graphically identifies the specific ethos and strengths of Irish/Ulster Presbyterianism:

> They are a people embodied under their own lay elders, presbyteries and synods and come to their sacraments in crowds of three or four thousand from 20 to 40 miles about, and they make laws for themselves and allow not that the civil magistrate has any right to control them and will be just so far the King's subjects as their lay elders and Presbyters will allow them.[73]

They also retained echoes of a radical civic – not to say republican – tradition. A further strength, and a worry for the Anglican Church, was their constant interaction with Scotland proper. However, as Gailey has argued, their long settlement in Ireland was to gradually lead to greater cultural assimilation along quite a number of fronts with the other peoples of the north of Ireland.[74]

Apart from the general and regional dimensions of the settlement implications of the above ecclesiastical transformations, there were also profoundly important *specific* settlement consequences as well. First, Ireland developed a dual diocesan system which – with the amalgamation of Anglican dioceses on the one hand and displacement of the Catholic bishops from old diocesan foci on the other – led to the fossilisation of a large number of ancient centres of ecclesiastical power. Killaloe, Ferns, Elphin, Cashel and Clogher spring immediately to mind. Equally important, new centres of Catholic diocesan power were to emerge at, for example, Enniscorthy, Thurles, Ennis, Sligo and Monaghan. Finally, the importance of most of the old monasteries and nunneries vanished forever – never to be restored as focal points either of settlement or of formal ritual.[75]

Even more crucial transformations took place at the parochial scale. We have already delineated the geography of the transformation of parish size and boundary structures. Within the older medieval parishes, therefore, many ancient parish foci were deserted. Since these centres ceased to have any meaning for the great majority of the local population, so their small parish hamlets and villages also died. I have dealt at length with dimensions of this question elsewhere.[76] Equally important, the now footloose Catholic Church was establishing new centres of community worship and power scattered throughout a newly reconstructed countryside. Embryonic chapel villages were already beginning to emerge by 1731. Presbyterian communities were likewise building a new settlement structure across the northern half of the country. Where the Anglican Church remained strong as in midland, east and south-east Leinster and in Ulster, it either helped to sustain older village life or became a central element in the newly established estate villages which Louis Cullen has documented.[77] In summary, the geography of ecclesiastical settlement had been turned upside down with displacement, innovation and reconstruction the central themes.

Notes and references

1 K.R. Andrews, N.P Canny and P.E.H. Hair (eds), *The Westward Enterprise*, (Liverpool, 1978); R. Gillespie, 'Explorers, exploiters and entrepreneurs, 1500–1700', in B.J. Graham and L.J. Proudfoot (eds), *A Historical Geography of Ireland* (London, 1993), pp. 123–57; W.J. Smyth, 'The western isle of Ireland and the eastern seaboard of America: England's first frontiers', in *Irish Geography*, XI (1978), pp. 1–22.

2 C. Brady and R. Gillespie (eds), *Natives and Newcomers* (Dublin, 1986); N.P. Canny, *Kingdom and Colony: Ireland in the Atlantic World 1560–1800* (Baltimore, 1988).

3 R. Gillespie, *The Transformation of the Irish Economy 1550 – 1700* (Studies in Irish Economic and Social History 6, Dundalk, 1991).

4 J. Ruane, 'Colonialism and the interpretation of Irish historical development', in M. Silverman and P.H. Gulliver (eds), *Approaching the Past – Historical Anthropology through Irish Case Studies* (Columbia University Press, 1992), pp. 293–323.

5 The study of the historical geography of sixteenth- and seventeenth-century Ireland is still only in its infancy – the work of historian Kenneth Nicholls on the sixteenth century highlights the possibilities here for geographers. The seventeenth century is currently receiving more attention from a handful of geographers and a growing

cadre of historians (referenced throughout this work) who are bringing new life and insights to this crucial period.

6 R. Loeber, *The Geography and Practice of English Colonisation in Ireland 1534 to 1609* (Group for the Study of Irish Historic Settlement, 3, Athlone, 1991).

7 Ibid., pp. 11–22; B. Bradshaw, *The Dissolution of the Religious Orders in Ireland under Henry VIII* (Cambridge, 1974).

8 N.P. Canny, 'Early modern Ireland, *c.* 1500–1700', in R. Foster (ed.), *The Oxford Illustrated History of Ireland* (Oxford University Press, 1989), pp. 104–60.

9 M. McCarthy-Morrogh, *The Munster Plantation: English Migration to Southern Ireland 1583–1641* (Oxford, 1986); see also his excellent chapter in Brady and Gillespie (eds) *Natives and Newcomers*, pp. 171–90.

10 B. Cunningham, 'Native culture and political culture, 1580–1640', in Brady and Gillespie (eds) *Natives and Newcomers*, pp.148–70 and also her work on 'The composition of Connaught in the lordships of Clanricard and Thomond 1577–1642', in *Irish Historical Studies*, Vol. 24 (1984), pp. 1–14.

11 G.A. Hayes McCoy (ed.), *Ulster and other Irish Maps, c. 1600* (Dublin, 1964).

12 M. Perceval-Maxwell, *The Scottish Migration to Ulster in the Reign of James I* (1973), pp. 5–14, 73–5.

13 P.S. Robinson, *The Plantation of Ulster: British Settlement in an Irish Landscape, 1600–1670* (Dublin, 1984), pp. 43–53; see also M. Perceval-Maxwell, *Scottish Migration*, pp. 10–14.

14 Smyth, 'England's first frontiers'; N. Canny, *Kingdom and Colony*; D.B. Quinn, ' The Munster plantation: Problems and opportunities', *Journal of the Cork Historical and Archaeological Society*, 71 (1966), pp. 19–40; Perceval-Maxwell, *Scottish Migration*, pp. 12–15.

15 Ibid., p. 17.

16 Robinson, *The Plantation of Ulster*, especially Chapters 1 and 2; see also Perceval-Maxwell, *Scottish Migration*, pp. 52–3.

17 Robinson, *The Plantation of Ulster*, pp. 91–108.

18 Ibid., pp. 109–29; Perceval-Maxwell, *Scottish Migration*, pp. 52–60.

19 R.J. Hunter, 'Towns in the Ulster plantation', in *Studia Hibernica*, 11 (1971), pp. 40–79.

20 Robinson, *The Plantation of Ulster*, pp. 103–4.

21 Percival-Maxwell, *Scottish Migration*, p. 152.

22 Ibid., p. 152.

23 R. Gillespie, 'The end of an era – Ulster and the outbreak of the 1641 Rising', in Brady and Gillespie (eds) *Natives and Newcomers*, pp. 191–214; B. MacCuarta (ed.), *Ulster 1641: Aspects of the Rising* (Belfast, 1993).

24 A. Ford, *The Protestant Reformation in Ireland 1590–1641* (Frankfurt, 1985); see also his excellent summary 'The Protestant Reformation in Ireland', in Brady and Gillespie (eds) *Natives and Newcomers*, pp. 50–74.

25 H. Pawlisch, *Sir John Davies and the Conquest of Ireland: A Study in Legal Imperialism* (Cambridge, 1983).

26 Ibid., p. 96.

27 W.J. Smyth, 'Exploring the social and cultural topographies of sixteenth- and seventeenth-century County Dublin', in F.H.A. Aalen and K. Whelan (eds), *Dublin, City and County: From Prehistory to Present* (Dublin, 1992), pp. 135–8; see also D. Jackson,

Intermarriage in Ireland 1530–1650 (Montreal, 1975) and L.M. Cullen, chapter on 'Social and cultural frontiers', in *The Emergence of Modern Ireland* (London, 1981), pp. 109–39.

28 W.J. Smyth, 'Territorial, social and settlement hierarchies in seventeenth century Kilkenny' in W. Nolan (ed.) *Kilkenny: History and Society* (Dublin, 1990), pp. 125–58.

29 A. Sheehan, 'Irish towns in a period of change 1558–1641', in Brady and Gillespie (eds) *Natives and Newcomers*, pp. 93–119.

30 N.P. Canny, *The Elizabethan Conquest of Ireland* (Sussex, 1976), pp. 4–10.

31 R.A. Butlin, 'Irish towns in the sixteenth and seventeenth centuries', in R.A. Butlin (ed.), *The Development of the Irish Town* (London, 1977), p. 7; see also his 'Land and people *c.* 1600', in T.W. Moody *et al.* (eds), *History of Ireland*, III (Oxford, 1976), pp. 142–67.

32 L.M. Cullen, 'The growth of Dublin 1600–1900: Character and heritage', in Aalen and Whelan (eds) *Dublin City and County*, p. 251; see also Sheehan, 'Irish towns'.

33 W.J. Smyth, 'Society and settlement in seventeenth-century Ireland – the evidence of the "1659" census', in W.J. Smyth and K. Whelan (eds), *Common Ground: Essays on the Historical Geography of Ireland* (Cork University Press, 1988), pp. 58–60.

34 Sheehan, 'Irish towns', p. 110.

35 Gillespie, *Irish Economy 1550–1700*, p. 62.

36 V.W. Treadwell, 'The establishment of the farm in the Irish customs, 1603–10', in *English Historical Review*, XCIII (1978), p. 602.

37 T.C. Barnard, *Cromwellian Ireland: English Government and Reform in Ireland 1649–60* (Oxford, 1975); see also his 'Planters and policies in Cromwellian Ireland', in *Past and Present*, 61 (1973), pp. 31–69.

38 Barnard, *Cromwellian Ireland*, pp. 50–3.

39 Ibid., pp. 77–89.

40 Smyth, 'The evidence of the 1659 Census' in Smyth and Whelan (eds), *Common Ground*, pp. 76–9.

41 L.M. Cullen, *The Emergence of Modern Ireland 1600–1900* (London, 1981), pp. 26–7; Barnard, *Cromwellian Ireland*, pp. 55–8.

42 Smyth, 'The evidence of the 1659 Census', in Smyth and Whelan (eds), *Common Ground*, p. 79.

43 Gillespie, *Irish Economy 1550–1700*, p. 25.

44 S. Rokkan, 'Territories, centres and peoples in Europe', in J. Gottman (ed.), *Centre and Periphery* (London, 1980), pp. 161–80.

45 Ford, *Protestant Reformation*, especially pp. 1–18, 98–122 and 243–92. See also N. Canny, 'Protestants, planters and apartheid in early modern Ireland', in *Irish Historical Studies* XXV (98) (1986), pp. 105–15.

46 B. Millet, 'Irish literature in Latin, 1550–1700', in Moody *et al.* (eds) (1976), *New History of Ireland*, III, pp. 564–7.

47 Ford, *Protestant Reformation*, pp. 70–4; N. Canny, 'Why the Reformation failed in Ireland: Une question mal posée', in *Journal of Ecclesiastical History*, 30 (4) (1979), pp. 423–41.

48 Smyth, 'Sixteenth- and seventeenth-century County Dublin', in Aalen and Whelan (eds), *Dublin, City and County*, pp. 157–9.

49 Ford, *Protestant Reformation*, pp. 111–12.

50 Ibid., pp. 98–100.

51 Robinson, *Ulster Plantation*, pp. 69–72.

52 This part of the analysis is based on the appendiced tables in Ford's *Protestant Reformation*, pp. 81–9 and 113–15.

53 Ibid., pp. 137–42.

54 K. Bottingheimer, 'The failure of the Reformation in Ireland: Une question bien posée', in *Journal of Ecclesiastical History*, 6 (2) (1985), pp. 196–207.

55 P. Corish, *The Catholic Community in the Seventeenth and Eighteenth Centuries* (Dublin, 1981), pp. 21–2.

56 Ibid., p. 26.

57 Ibid., pp. 33–4.

58 Many repressive legislative measures against the practice of Catholicism were then introduced, i.e. 'an Act for convicting, discovery and repressing of Popish recusants', 'an Act for the better observation of the Lord's Day', etc.

59 Corish, *Catholic Community*, p. 49.

60 'An account of the Roman clergy according to a return made April 1698', Mss. Letter in the Royal Society Library, London.

61 Corish, *Catholic Community*, pp. 43–72.

62 S.J. Connolly, *Religion, Law and Power: The Making of Protestant Ireland 1660–1770* (Oxford, 1992).

63 'Report on the state of popery in Ireland', in *Archivium Hibernicam*, Vol I (1912) pp. 10–27; Vol. II (1913) 108–56; Vol. III (1914) 124–58; Vol. IV (1914) 131–77.

64 Ibid.

65 Connolly, *Religion, Law and Power*, pp. 149–52.

66 R.A. Gailey, 'The Scots element in north Irish popular culture: some problems in the interpretation of historical acculturation', *Ethnologia Europea*, 8 (1975), pp. 2–21.

67 Ibid., pp. 3–4.

68 Ibid., p. 4 ; see also Connolly, *Religion, Law and Power*, pp. 167–8.

69 P. Carr, *The Most Unpretending of Places – A History of Dundonald County Down* (Belfast, 1987), p. 69.

70 Gailey, 'Scots element', pp. 6–9.

71 L.M. Cullen, 'Ireland and France 1600–1900', in L.M. Cullen and F. Furet (eds), *Ireland and France: 17th–20th Centuries – Towards a Comparative Study of Rural History* (Paris, 1980), pp. 1–20 ; see also his *Emergence of Modern Ireland*, pp. 109–10.

72 Connolly, *Religion, Law and Power*, pp. 167–8.

73 Ibid., p. 168.

74 Gailey, 'Scots element', pp. 16–21.

75 T. Jones Hughes, 'Village and towns in nineteenth-century Ireland', in *Irish Geography*, 14 (1981), pp. 99–106. See also his 'Administrative divisions and the development of settlement in 19th-century Ireland', in *University Review*, 3 (6) (1964), pp. 8–15.

76 W.J. Smyth, 'Property, patronage and population; reconstructing the human geography of mid-seventeenth-century Tipperary', in W. Nolan (ed.), *Tipperary: History and Society* (Dublin, 1985), pp. 104–38 and 'Territorial, social and settlement

hierarchies in seventeenth-century Kilkenny', in W. Nolan and K. Whelan (eds), *Kilkenny: History and Society* (Dublin, 1990), pp. 125–58.

77 L.M. Cullen, *Irish Towns and Villages* (Irish Heritage Series, No. 25, Dublin, 1980).

8

SETTLEMENT AND SOCIETY IN EIGHTEENTH-CENTURY IRELAND

Kevin Whelan

'Is ar scáth a cheile a mhaireann na daoine.'

Despite its undoubted significance, the eighteenth century has long been neglected by historical geographers.[1] No doubt this is largely due to the fact that it is a century which lacks major benchmark surveys, comparable to the Civil or Down Surveys for the seventeenth, and the Griffiths and Ordnance Survey maps for the nineteenth. Accordingly, although detailed analyses now exist for these two centuries, the eighteenth century is still a silent one in historical geographical discourse. Yet, its significance is undeniable: Cullen observes that 'The Irish man-made landscape is essentially one of the eighteenth century.'[2] This chapter then is a preliminary attempt to bridge the hiatus and special attention is paid to linking up the seventeenth- and nineteenth-century work; in so doing, a strong diachronic dimension can be added to literature which is heavily synchronic in orientation. Thus, the chapter looks at a 'long' eighteenth century, with frequent regressions to the seventeenth-century context, and extrapolations into the first half of the nineteenth. The focus is sharply on the interrelationship between society and settlement, especially as this is revealed in the landscape. However, settlement is treated here in a broad sense as a text, a multi-layered document, full of human intentionality, a culture code which embodies different levels of meaning. Couched in these terms, the study of settlement can move away from 'the cold facts of land and landscape' and engage with a much warmer and broader spectrum of meanings. In this view settlement is both medium and message, site and symbol, terrain and text.[3]

To penetrate the eighteenth century, we must begin by discarding some of the most venerable concepts in Irish historical geography more particularly those associated with Estyn Evans.[4] He cast Irish society in the eighteenth and nineteenth centuries into a monolithic 'peasant' framework. Inevitably, this formulation biased work on Ireland towards the small-farm world of the Atlantic fringe and west Ulster, which best approximated this 'peasant' model.

A second formulation was that this 'peasant' world was fundamentally a time-less one, a little tradition which endured through the centuries, and with underlying continuities with remote prehistory. Thus, by intensive fieldwork in modern western (especially north-western) areas, one could recover intact an immemorial, aboriginal settlement pattern. Prolific, persuasive and accessible, Evans's work popularised this conceptualisation of Irish society as an ancient peasant survival, especially in the west, a great European refuge area on the rim of the continent, preserving forms which had long disappeared at the centre. By studying these timeless survivals in the modern world, one could trace the whole sweep of Irish settlement history from its genetic origins in prehistory. Because they were timeless, these settlements could be largely studied by patient fieldwork, supplemented if necessary by archaeological excavations: it was unnecessary to adopt the methods of the historian and a document-free methodology was endorsed. Evans also believed that ethnic groups had their distinctive (and enduring) settlement forms and that ethnic origins were a powerful explanatory force in the quest for the origins of settlement.

All those postulations by Evans and his followers have been undermined by more recent work. In two devastating critiques (no less seminal in their influ-ence for being circulated in samizdat form), Andrews challenged the anthropogeographic methodology because of its fundamentally ahistoric chronological approach, its ethnic stereotyping and its unwarranted assumption (rather than demonstration) of millennial continuities.[5] Simultaneously, a series of papers by Jones Hughes quietly killed the 'peasant' model of pre-Famine Ireland.[6] He showed that the peasant scenario elided class differences by ignoring the intense social stratification of pre-Famine Irish life. Jones Hughes substituted an approach which highlighted the regional dynamics and settle-ment effects of this social stratigraphy. In so doing, he established (long before it became fashionable among historians) that pre-Famine Ireland was not an undifferentiated mass of unrelieved poverty and that class, itself determined by broader economic forces, was the key to understanding Irish settlement history in the post-seventeenth-century period. In one of the most incisive paragraphs ever published in Irish historical geography, Jones Hughes commented on Evans' favoured far-west fringe:

> Yet we must not overemphasise the significance of these places as the ultimate conservatories of Gaelic culture at least as far as the material aspects of that culture are concerned. Collectively they represented some of the poorest and most inaccessible parts of western Europe and it is certain that most of them only experienced close and permanent settlement by farming people at a very late date and that these late colonisers were probably refugees evicted from adjoining more desir-able regions. Consequently during the eighteenth and nineteenth centuries, these barren lands were savagely carved up into diminutive lots to satisfy the most primitive needs of despairing communities, so

that we must look in vain here for any surviving traces of the genetic element of the modern Irish rural landscape.[7]

Contrast this with Evans' formulation: 'Conventional history is at a loss where, as in the west of Ireland, history and prehistory seem to co-exist and all time is foreshortened into a living present.'[8] Or:

> For many years, I have studied archaeological and ethnographic evidence for the early diffusion and secular persistence of a cultural pattern which had its origins in pre-Celtic antiquity and which proved capable of absorbing and assimilating new elements brought in by successive intrusions, whether Celtic warrior, Christian missionary or Anglo-Norman knight.[9]

From the ruins of these earlier conceptualisations, it is imperative to build a new model of the nature of the historical geography of eighteenth-century Ireland. The framework of such a model can be built from an interlocking series of regional archetypes, based on economic, social and settlement criteria. These archetypes – recurring themes in the text of landscape – allow a more nuanced approach to the study of the period. Four archetypes emerge: pastoral (with cattle fattening and dairying components), tillage, small-farm and proto-industrial.

Archetype 1: pastoralism

The pastoral tradition in Ireland has been primarily oriented towards cattle, although sheep have been locally and periodically important. Given the edaphic and climatic regime, Ireland has a comparative European advantage in fat cattle production. Accordingly, once the focus of sea-borne trade moved decisively towards the Atlantic in the seventeenth century, Ireland's role in the provisions trade blossomed. Ireland was simultaneously integrated into the expanding English mercantilist economy, and the rapid articulation of the north Atlantic commercial world opened voracious markets for livestock products. These twin markets generated an export-oriented agricultural sector. The English market was catered for by the export of live cattle, and created few forward or backward linkages. The Atlantic market was for beef and butter, products which sustained economic diversification.[10]

Cattle fattening

The zone of permanent pasture in Ireland, closely tied to a limestone base, had twin cores in north-east Leinster and in inner Connaught (mid-Roscommon on the celebrated plains of Boyle, east Mayo and east Galway). In between these two areas, there was an aureole, waxing and waning in response to commodity price dynamics and located in the confused interdigitations of the midland counties, where good and bad land mingled promiscuously in the alternating bogs and meadows of Offaly, Longford and Westmeath. This fattening area pulsed and subsided from its heartlands, allowing the identification of aggressive and recessive phases in the history of Irish pastoralism.

Before the destruction of the Irish woollen industry by English mercantilist acts in the late seventeenth century, sheep were expanding on the dry pastures of counties Tipperary, Roscommon, east Galway and Carlow; by the 1760s, the surge in tillage was pushing the ewes and the bullocks back into more restricted areas. In the post-Napoleonic period, the bullock again reasserted itself. In settlement terms, the seventeenth–early eighteenth-century pastoral expansion had erosive effects on old village structures in the areas which it was colonising. The concentration of deserted villages in the pastoral transition zone hints that the desertion phase was in this period (not the late medieval as has been frequently suggested). Glasscock's map of deserted sites shows a concentration precisely in this pastoral expansion zone – a triangle linking counties Limerick, Carlow and Roscommon.[11]

As London's hinterland swept ever outwards, it overrode Dublin's own Von Thunen rings. Up to the later seventeenth century, Dublin had its tillage zone in close proximity. The River Boyne is described c. 1690 as 'the old Rubicon of the Pale and the frontier of the corn country'.[12] Given London's appetite for cattle, the old granary of Dublin inside the Pale was displaced to the south-east, with fat cattle (being finished for the Smithfield market) colonising the old tillage fields. Today in winter light, in south Meath and north Kildare, one can still discern the broad corn ridges of the tillage phase under the modern pastures.

The transition from an intensive tillage to an extensive pastoral economy may have dissolved old villages. Displacement of village-based tillage farmers (scullogues, or gneevers in seventeenth-century parlance) was achieved via the leasing mechanism; if cattle prices were sufficiently high, grazing could simply outbid tillage. From as far away as County Sligo, Charles O'Hara provides a clinical dissection of this process in the 1720s.

> By the year 1720, the demands for store cattle for the south had reached us, and the breeding business grew more profitable. Many villages were turned off and the lands which they had occupy'd stocked with cattle. Some of these village tenants took mountain farms but many more went off and I shall fix 1726 for the period of this change for it was in that year that graziers encouraged by the markets first raised the price of land in order to cant the cottagers out of their farms.[13]

Nicholas Taaffe, writing in 1766 (and primed by Charles O'Conor of Belanagare in the middle of the grazing county of Roscommon) also lamented the decline of the 'scullogs':

communities of industrious housekeepers who in my own time herded together in large villages and cultivated the lands everywhere, till as leases expired, some rich grazier, negotiating privately with a sum of ready money, took the lands over their heads. This is a fact well known. The sculoag race, that great nursery of labourers and manufacturers, has been broken and dispersed in every quarter and we have nothing in lieu but those most miserable wretches on earth, the cottagers [cottiers].[14]

From County Mayo at the end of the eighteenth century, McParland observed that 'grazing drives the natives away from the fertile fields into the swamps and mountains'.[15] In the cattle fattening areas, the grazier holding became the cornerstone of leasing policy and therefore of the settlement pattern. A grazier (frequently an absentee) held a very large grassland farm, poorly enclosed, devoted solely to cattle fattening. A resident herdsman (herd) looked after the cattle. As leases were assigned by the townland, graziers usually held a townland, or series of townlands, in this manner. At the apogee of their success, Tipperary graziers like the McCarthys in the Glen of Aherlow held almost 14,000 acres and the Scullys of the Golden area held twenty townlands in this fashion.[16] Given its extensive mode of land use, the grazier economy created a desolate landscape with an attenuated social structure and only rudimentary settlement forms, where the lonely box-Georgian grazier houses were shadowed by the crude cabins of the herds. These grazier's holdings developed on the better limestone soils and were frequently juxtaposed with small farm, cluster-based settlements on adjacent marginal, hilly or boggy ground. This pattern, evident in the 1749 census of the diocese of Elphin, was driven by the ruthless efficiency of the leasing mechanism.[17] In this manner, the Irish paradox of an inverse relationship between population pressure and good land was established. The close juxtaposition of the two systems also helps explain why houghing (the maiming of cattle) became so prevalent as a form of social protest – a moral economy pitting itself against a commercial one. The first agrarian secret society in Ireland, the Houghers, evolved precisely in this fashion, in the east Connaught area undergoing the transition from plough to cow in the early eighteenth century.[18] The silent, empty world of grazing bullocks was one of the most striking regional variants in eighteenth-century Ireland, elsewhere so often a noisy, crowded, complex society.

The dairying/beef system

The areas of fat cattle production in Connaught and Leinster were predominantly geared to supplying live cattle to the English market. By contrast, Atlantic markets swallowed Irish beef and butter. There were two components in Irish-American trade, one directed to the West Indies, the other to the north American mainland.[19] Once the Caribbean islands moved to a widespread sugar monoculture in the mid-1660s, provisions had to be imported to feed the planters. The Munster provisions trade between 1670 and1720 was the main source of food. The Barbados governor in 1675 observed re Ireland that 'from thence we feed so many mouths as must be used in the management of the sugaries'.[20] In the Caribbean trade, Ireland's comparative advantage lay in her ability to organise her agricultural resources into sophisticated food producing and packaging industries that effectively complemented the West Indian sugar industry, itself the most aggressively expanding sector of the colonial economy. This was augmented by the growth of the victualling trades and the shipment of beef and butter, both to the Continent and to the Atlantic economies. All these developments exerted a positive influence on dairying and cattle rearing and the export trade fostered the rise of an indigenous mercantile class, and intensified local multiplier effects. These flows reinforced the major ports of the east and south, especially Cork and Waterford, which commanded rich, wide hinterlands, accessible by navigable river systems.[21] Both ports were at the cutting edge of the Atlantic economy, which allowed them to achieve a deep market penetration across all the strata of rural society in their riverine hinterland. These hinterlands became the most prosperous agricultural regions in eighteenth- and early nineteenth-century Ireland, accompanied by the six-fold growth of rents between 1700 and 1800, the commercialisation of dairying and cattle rearing, and by the sharpening and deepening of the social stratigraphy.[22]

The dairyman system was the distinctive feature of the rural economy of mid-Munster, especially in the Lee and Blackwater valleys, and was developed around the Cork butter market, one of the largest in contemporary Europe.[23] Commercialised dairying in this region can be traced from the 1660s, although it is still unclear whether the dairyman system itself is of Gaelic or West Country origin. The system involved the unusual (for Ireland) practice of leasing 20–40 cows to dairymen, in return for a butter rent. The dairyman disposed of calves and had some other perquisites, to make the venture profitable for him. Like the graziers, the dairyowner was a head tenant, and at the apex of the system could be a *fear mile bó* (a man of 1,000 cows). The celebrated Art O'Laoghaire is a good example of the social and cultural milieu of this social layer.[24] By the end of the century, the butter rent was giving way to a cash equivalent, and small independent cow owners (generally mixed farmers) were emerging. Pig keeping was invariably integrated with dairying, because the skim milk was an excellent feeding stuff. In its phase of aggressive expansion in the mid-eighteenth century, dairying displaced the joint tenancy small tillage (barley, oats, potatoes) farmers (or 'gneevers' in Munster terminology). Rev. James Mockler, a Protestant clergyman, described the process in 1775:

> The country about Mallow and I believe all over Munster is of late years much thinned and stripped of its inhabitants to make room for bullocks, sheep and dairy cows. Rich folks were never half so fond as they have been within these 10 or 12 years past, of taking farms and

increasing their stocks of cattle; dairy cows mostly all over the counties of Cork, Kerry and Waterford, bullocks and dairy cows in counties Limerick and Clare, sheep, bullocks and dairy cows in County Tipperary. The writer hereof knew about a dozen villages in the parish of Mallow inhabited about 15 years ago by six or eight snug warm cottiers [gneevers] and at present, there is but one dairyman in each of these villages, and in some few of them, one or two labourers.[25]

From south County Kilkenny, where dairying was diffusing in the 1760s from Munster, Tighe's *Statistical Observations* notes exactly the same process: 'In the Welsh mountains, tillage occupied 40–50 years ago large tracts now given up to the dairy; and the ruins of some villages may be seen in the middle of those unimproved pastures.'[26]

The influence of dairying peaked between 1750 and 1770, literally losing ground thereafter to a resurgent commercialised tillage farming. Dairying enjoyed a second efflorescence in the late nineteenth century in the same area based on the spread of co-operative dairying. In general, the mid-Munster dairying zone from the seventeenth to the twentieth centuries has been a resilient and innovative area, a backbone of radical conservatism which underpinned the emerging nation-forming class.[27] Andrews offers an incisive summary. 'As the most fertile part of Ireland in which the British failed to make a lasting impact, the lowlands of the south-west offered the best prospects for a modernised version of the indigenous pastoral economy.'[28]

However, it is important with both the fattening and dairying components of commercialised pastoralism not to reify these archetypes, nor to privilege their autonomy. Both zones had numerous and essential linkages to the small-farm world which lay beyond or above them. Calves were the currency of exchange; they were gradually filtered east and south as they grew older. The intense commercialisation of these transactions is manifested in the prevalence of cattle fairs, which functioned as interchange points between the rearing and the fattening/dairy areas.[29] The largest fairs – Ballinasloe (one of the three largest in Europe), Banagher, Athlone, Mullingar, Knockcroghery – were those best positioned to act as hinges: numerous (1,500 fair sites were operational at some stage between 1600 and 1800) minor ones lubricated the west–east movement. As commercialisation intensified under the hothouse effect of the Atlantic provisions trade, fair sites proliferated; in County Cork, the figure soared from 12 to 145 between 1735 and 1795.[30] Fairs were crucial in articulating a nation-wide economy. The essential symbiotic linkage between small farm and large farm also effectively demolishes the old 'two Ireland' concept, based with mistaken clarity on the differentiation between a commercialised 'east' and a subsistence 'west' in the pre-Famine Irish economy.[31] If such an idea had any conceptual validity, it was in a vertical (social) not horizontal (spatial) stratification.

At a micro-level, the close spatial juxtaposition of good and bad land in

Ireland lent an environmental symmetry to the interdependence of breeding and finishing areas. Looking west from a dairying valley around Mallow in 1775, Mockler commented: 'the county of Kerry, mostly mountainous, is only noted for rearing young stock of all sorts.'[32] Breeding grounds tended to be coarse, moory pastures in hilly or boggy areas; fattening grounds were the limestone-floored lowlands. Thus local contrasts between farming systems could be intense especially in mid-Munster where sandstone anticlines and limestone synclines formed the substrate. The presence cheek by jowl of two radically different farming systems was an inevitable source of friction in times of economic transition, especially when dairying or cattle fattening entered an expansive phase. In such situations (as in the 1760s or mid-1780s) cattle spread aggressively into the surrounding upland areas. Their expansion was halted by the pre-emptive violence of the agrarian secret societies – the Whiteboys and Rightboys.[33] The mid-Munster base of these movements is explicable in terms of that region's distinctive economy and environment. It is still unclear to what extent the moral economy of these societies was effective in stabilising existing distributions of farm systems and in preventing the emergence of a full blooded capitalist agriculture of the Scottish type.

Archetype 2: tillage

The second great archetype is tillage – essentially mixed farming, but with a specialisation in intensive commercial tillage. Built out of the environmentally favoured Anglo-Norman coastlands, the tillage zone waxed strongly in the second half of the eighteenth century, kick-started by bounties on the transport of flour to Dublin (from 1758) and then accelerating as European demand soared in the Napoleonic period. Between 1815 and the Famine, tillage began to retract painfully to its earlier cores. By the late eighteenth century, the tillage zone was concentrated in the south-east of the country, encompassed within a triangle linking Cork, Dundalk and Wexford.[34] In the pre-mechanised era, tillage farms, as a labour intensive mode of production, were much smaller than their pastoral counterparts. Tillage areas therefore had a tighter settlement framework, with a fine mesh of farms, fields, fences, villages and towns. In old tillage areas, this settlement infrastructure pre-dated the eighteenth century. As early as 1683, an observer described the Barony of Forth in south County Wexford. 'The whole Barony at a distance viewed in times of harvest represents a well cultivated garden, with diversified plots.'[35] Given more complex economic functions, tillage areas had a more developed social structure than their skeletal pastoral equivalents, with artisans especially evident. Landlordism was also considerably more muted in the tillage farm system which was much more difficult to regulate than the grazier system. Accordingly, estate owners in tillage areas tended to be marginalised into a rent-collecting, intermarrying superstructure. As a result, settlement in tillage areas exhibited more continuity than in pastoral areas. Tillage towns were busy, bustling places, unlike pastoral ones, where the intermittent cattle fair was the prime lifeline.

However, the most salient point about the commercialisation of the tillage economy was the spectacular increase in the number of agricultural labourers. Many of these were accommodated as cottiers, labourers who were given a cabin and a potato garden (up to 1 acre) in return for their labour. The farmer supplied dung for the garden, and the potato crop was an ideal precursor to the subsequent cereal crop. Expansion in the tilled area was achieved by expanding the number of cottiers. This created a cottier necklace around the perimeter of the tillage farms, the social dichotomy mirrored in the micro-segregation. Bell describes the process in 1804:

> The master never fed a labourer of this description [cottier]. It was on the contrary a chief object with him to keep such a person as far away from his dwelling as possible. He therefore allowed him to occupy, at some remote corner of his farm, a miserable hut, a mere shell, formed of mud or sods, without loft, apartment or partition and sometimes without any other covering than that of straw or with any other chimney than the door. In one corner of this hovel was lodged his cow, while in the opposite corner were his wife and children and himself.[37]

On large (30 hectares plus) farms, the dependent cottier houses could run to double figures. The cottier necklace was the main form of settlement for agriculture labourers, but one could also find straggles of cabins along roads or lanes (equidistant between two farms), in dishevelled cross-roads clusters, in shanties on the edge of towns and villages, or piling up in the back lanes.

Irish society therefore evolved from a seventeenth-century status where social differences among native occupiers was limited to a situation where the farmer/labourer split became decisive in the more developed regions. The tillage parishes of County Louth were dominated by labourers in 1831 (Tables 8.1, 8.2), the product of a more complex farming structure which sharpened the social divide between farmer and labourer. The hiving off of farmers and labourers into discrete settlement forms may be a late seventeenth-, early eighteenth-century phenomenon. On the mid-seventeenth-century Down Survey maps, the cabin cluster around the tower house is the settlement expression of a society where the classes shared a site. Capitalist penetration prised these elements apart, and the labourers were dispersed to the edge of the farms, which performed a fly-catcher function. Occasionally, one can catch a glimpse of this fission, as in the creation of a new settlement away from the farm village of Luffany in south Kilkenny to house the labourers.[38] Andrews supplied the best summation:

> Hastily dismissed by many travel writers, ignored altogether by many map makers, the crude thatched cabins of the very poor had begun to

gather more thickly around the margins of farms and demesnes, along the verges of public highways and outside the respectable quarters of the towns, as if seeping through the cracks of an otherwise well-ordered geographical system.[39]

As well as great poverty, tillage areas also sustained agribusinesses, which invigorated the towns in the later eighteenth century – mills, breweries, malthouses, distilleries. After the bounties for transport of flour to the Dublin market were instituted in 1758, large-scale flour milling expanded in the 1760s and 1770s with mid and south Kilkenny (the valleys of the Kings River and the Nore) acting as an innovative area in technology and intensification.[40] As a result, Dublin's grain hinterland shifted south, allowing south Meath and north Kildare to revert to pastoralism. There were 100 mills listed in the incomplete Civil Survey for County Meath, and 91 in County Kildare, reflecting the earlier granary function.[41] Breweries, distilleries and malthouses also sprang up in response to a vibrant local agricultural economy. By 1796, Wexford town alone had 210 malthouses and in 1797 the town employed 100 small ships in carrying malt to Dublin.[42]

The post-Napoleonic retrenchment of tillage had two major effects. In the zone of retreat, disturbances followed in the wake of the demise of the employment opportunities afforded by commercial tillage farming. In the three decades

Table 8.1   Percentage of population who were agricultural labourers, 1831, Ardee Barony, Co. Louth (by Civil Parish)

	%		%
STICKILLIN	78	DROMIN	63
SMARMORE	72	TALLONSTOWN	54
KILDEMOCK	68	STABANNON	54
SHANLIS	62	CLONKEEN	50
RICHARDSTOWN	58	MAPASTOWN	54
MOSSTOWN	58	CHARLESTOWN	59

Table 8.2   1850 – Labourer/Big Farm Relationship

No. of townlands with 100+ acre farms	No. of townlands with > 50% agricultural labourer	No. of co-extensive townlands	BARONY
83	109	55	ARDEE
9	9	7	LOUTH
40	50	34	FERRARD
68	90	43	DUNDALK UPPER

after 1815, tensions simmered in the volatile transitional tillage borderlands, stretching along a Tipperary–Roscommon axis. Barracks were disproportionately located in this zone.[43] Indeed, agrarian violence was found invariably at the peripheries, not the cores of these great zones. Second, many labourers were dislocated in the transition and gave rise to a great shifting underclass in Irish society in the immediate pre-Famine period. In Ballina in 1835, a commentator noted 'if you were going among them for twenty years you would not know their faces, they come and go so fast'.[44] Their existential marginality was mirrored in their settlement marginality. This period witnessed the explosive expansion of shanties on the edge of towns, bogside squatter colonies like the Erris 'Troglodytes' or the wretched settlers of the wet desert of the Bog of Allen, despairing assaults on commonages, or on the limits of cultivation, which were pushing up to over 1,000 feet. There was a long-run social cost to the rapid commercialisation of Irish agriculture in the eighteenth century. The old partnership (village) and small-farm (gneever) communities were squeezed out and the proliferation of agricultural labourers was accompanied by a narrowing of their diet towards a monotonous and dangerous dependence on the potato.

Taken together, the tillage, dairying and fattening zones comprised the large-farm world of eighteenth- and early nineteenth-century Ireland. Jones Hughes has plotted 7,200 farms of £100 plus rating in the Griffiths Valuation and their distribution pattern shows the crucial components in the emergence of modern Ireland.[45] In the post-Famine period, selective emigration bled the agricultural labourer class dry and tenant proprietorship led to the legislative euthanasia of the landlord class; only the big farmer endured.[46] One should therefore stress the stability and continuity represented by these large farmers; there are very suggestive parallels between their 1850 distribution and that of the late medieval tower houses. There may also be much stronger familial and therefore cultural, social and political continuity than has hitherto been suspected.[47] An urgent agenda for the next decade of work is to make explicit the linkages between the substantive bodies of work on the mid-seventeenth (spearheaded by Smyth) and mid-nineteenth (spearheaded by Jones Hughes) centuries.[48]

However, the social cleavages of Ireland were immersed in a deceptively homogeneous landscape, due to the lack of conspicuous consumption. Patrick Knight describes this milieu well from Ballycroy in County Mayo:

In 1813, I slept at a man's house who had 100 head of black cattle and 200 sheep, and there was not a single chair or stool in his house, but one three legged one, no bed but rushes, no vessel for boiling their meals but one, nor any for drinking milk out of but one, the madder which was handed around indiscriminately to all who sat around the potato basket (myself among the rest) placed upon the pot for a table; yet this man was said to be very rich, besides the stock named above.[49]

The same understatement could be seen in the vernacular farmhouses even in the tillage areas. The hurrying traveller, passing rapidly through the roadside raggle-taggle of miserable cabins, was overwhelmed by images of poverty; he failed to notice the discreet, but comfortable world of the strong farmer, embedded in the centre of their farms and insulated from the perimeter of poverty around them. The seat behind the coachman was therefore a biased one in pre-Famine Ireland. It is in this broad sense, perhaps that one should inter-pret the concept of the 'Hidden Ireland'. Corkery's twin insistence of approaching it only from the evidence of Gaelic poetry and of locating it largely in west Munster is misleading.[50] The real 'Hidden Ireland' of the eighteenth century was incarnated not in the *cos-mhuintir*, the proliferating poverty-stricken base of the social pyramid, nor in the flamboyant but restricted world of the Munster middlemen; the real custodians of tradition were the comfortable, Catholic, strong farm class (a Norman-Gaelic hybrid) of south Leinster and east Munster, who provided stability and continuity.[51]

Archetype 3: small farming

The large-farm world can be contrasted with that dominated by small scale family farms – the area that best approximates the 'peasant' model promulgated by Evans. This small-farm zone had two main components – the drumlin belt and the ragged fringe stretching from west Donegal to west Cork along the peninsular reaches of Atlantic Ireland. It is imperative to note that this small-farm world was a spatially restricted one: it was never the dominant archetype, even at the height of its extent on the eve of the Famine. Contrary to Evans' postulated continuities, large swathes of this small-farm world were essentially new phenomena, a response to the surging demographic profile of Ireland between 1600 and 1840, which saw its population soar from 1 million to 8.5 million. This explosion necessitated massive reclamation, intense subdivision and expansion into previously unsettled area, aided by the potato's propensity to flourish even in wet, thin, nutrient-poor soils. Much of the drumlin and Atlantic regions were only heavily settled as an outreach product of unre-strained population growth. Some of the most classic small-farm communities can trace their origins to the eighteenth century. Rann na Feirste, in Evans' favoured Rosses, was first permanently settled *c.* 1750. Only the rundale village and hand tool cultivation allowed these areas to be won for farming peoples. In County Mayo at the end of the century, McParland noted: 'The villages are almost as numerous as the tenanted farms, because till very lately numbers of the common people used to take farms in conjunction and build their houses in clusters.'[52]

In a settlement sense, much of the west of Ireland was but newly settled, an adventitious and desperate veneer born out of unprecedented demographic circumstances. While much of the settlement in these marginal west coast lands is late, pockets of older settlement existed there. A useful distinction can be drawn between the 'old' and the 'new' west. The 'old' west consisted of those parts of the Atlantic seaboard which had known continuous intensive settlement prior to the eighteenth century – areas like Corca Dhuibhne, the head of Galway Bay, and the Burren in County Clare. The Burren itself deserves careful consideration in settlement terms; in 1732 at the height of the colonial period, it was the single most undisturbed barony in the whole island.[53] Some of the key elements in the understanding of Irish settlement history may lie hidden in that craggy kingdom, where lithic building techniques provide a superb archaeological record. Finally, the west of Ireland had undoubtedly known previous settlement spasms but these had been short-lived, as they had breached environmental equilibria, initiated ecological regression and had eventually been abandoned. One such surge was in the Neolithic (best known from the Céide Fields project); another was in the Early Christian period. The potato and rundale village phase of settlement eventually fell victim to the fragile ecological base, with its limited recuperative potential. The new 'west' did not have in any meaningful terms a continuous settlement history from the prehistoric period onwards.

Archetype 4: proto-industrialisation

Beef and butter were two of the great Irish exports of the eighteenth century. Linen was the third.[54] The growth of the Ulster linen industry to be among the world's leading half dozen industries by 1800 was based on a number of factors.

1   Ulster landlords in the later seventeenth century became aware that their agricultural production suffered edaphic, climatic and locational disadvantages; they were therefore keen to encourage their tenants to diversify their production so as to keep rentals buoyant.
2   Ulster (unlike Scotland, for example) could grow its own flax and thereby integrate linen production in a controlled fashion.
3   Landlords and central government encouraged the rapid development of an efficient marketing system, which allowed independent farmer-weavers to flourish. This lent flexibility and resilience to Irish production methods as opposed to the more urban-based, putting-out system prevalent elsewhere.
4   Irish linens were cheaper to produce in a low labour cost environment and the link to Dublin–London financial services plus their custom-free status in Britain gave them a competitive advantage.

Linen production soared in these favourable circumstances, sustained by technological, infrastructural and organisational innovation.

The end product was an immense proto-industrial system. As elsewhere in Europe, this was accommodated by subdivision of leaseholdings, intense population growth and the incorporation of women and children into the workforce.[55] The Ulster countryside was festooned with a myriad of small weaver-farming holdings, especially in the linen triangle between Belfast, Dungannon and

Newry. In turn, this area created a prosperous aureole of agricultural production (oats, cattle, potatoes and turf) which also supplied yarn to the spinning zones. This aureole arcs from north Connaught to north Leinster and fell within the broad Belfast hinterland. A 1740 account from County Monaghan illustrates well the push given by northern demands to these supply areas.

> This county, which was naturally rough and barren, is greatly reclaimed by the labour of the husbandman. The hills that were then (c.1700) deemed barren are now under proper husbandry being cleared of brushwood and heath. This county formerly bred good horses but the tillage with the inhabitants is so increased that the farms are so little ... being generally from 10 to 30 acres – that there is no pasture for studs or breeding of cattle or any sort more than what is necessary for the immediate service of the farm.[56]

Intensification of agricultural production via small, diligently laboured family farms triggered massive demographic growth. By 1770, there were 42,000 weavers in Ulster; by 1820 at the height of the proto-industrial phase, this had reached 70,000. In 1821, Ulster's population of 2 million was greater than the total population of Scotland. Population densities were very heavy – County Armagh had over 500 per square mile by 1841. Linen production was especially suited to inferior land such as the difficult drumlin country of south Ulster. This adaptation to poor land (again a European wide predilection of proto-industrialisation) is illustrated by the inability of the linen industry to make any impression on the fertile fattening lands of north Leinster.[57] The spread of the weaver/farmer had one other often disregarded side effect; it obliterated the large farmer in Ulster.[58] By 1841 the average farm size in County Armagh was 5 acres and by 1850 only 10 per cent of the total number of large farms in Ireland were in that province. Yet Ulster remained a province where the landlord influence was strong, especially in the east. Thus, nineteenth-century Ulster ended up in the anomalous position of being a province of great estates but small farms. The success of the linen industry promoted commercialisation. A 1792 pamphleteer observed: 'we may justly say that the County of Armagh is a hotbed of cash for the industrious farmer and weaver'.[59] The industry therefore ensured the continued vitality of its towns, to which the brown linen markets were a major fillip.[60] By 1800, Belfast's future industrial glory was not yet adumbrated; only with the industrialisation of linen, and with the rise of cotton production, did Belfast centralise the Ulster economy around itself, and push back Dublin's hinterland.

Crawford's investigations have elucidated the complex internal geography of this proto-industrial macro-region.[61] In the period from 1780 to 1820 four distinct sub-regions can be identified: (1) the linen triangle, (2) south Armagh, Monaghan and east Cavan, (3) north Antrim and (4) west Ulster (Tyrone, east Donegal, west Cavan and Fermanagh). The quality of linen produced in these four regions varied widely. Only the fine product of the linen triangle was capable of adapting easily to factory production (and in particular to mill spun yarn). The coarser linens of the other regions were rendered technologically obsolescent and were killed off by the influx of cheap industrial textiles from Belfast and the British cotton manufacturers. Only this microcosmic approach can satisfactorily explain how the Ulster linen industry in the 1780–1820 period could simultaneously industrialise and de-industrialise. The impact of de-industrialisation on the outer zone can be clearly seen in the rise of seasonal migration there, a functional substitute for off-farm income. In 1834, the heaviest seasonal migration was located precisely in the area from which weavers had been displaced, stretching from north Louth to Sligo.[62]

Crawford's recent work had also demolished the influential thesis of Conrad Gill's *The Rise of the Irish Linen Industry*, that in the 1760s the Ulster industry moved from a primitive cottage (proto-industrial) phase to a modern capitalist factory-based phase, and that the transition was signalled by the advent of the putting-out system.[63] In fact, the independent farmer-weaver, working through the vibrant brown linen markets, flourished right through the whole span of the century; no extensive putting-out system ever developed, except in highly specialised sectors like damask production. Crawford's work explains why such a dense pattern of small farms persisted in south Ulster and especially in County Armagh. It also has devastating implications for some of the most quoted 'explanations' of the nature of political and social change in later eighteenth-century Ulster and especially on the origins of the Orange Order and Defenders.[64] Like the Burren, County Armagh is an area whose settlement history is likely to carry nation-wide significance and which badly requires systematic research by historical geographers.[65]

We have now identified four leading regional archetypes in Ireland in a 'long' eighteenth century, albeit in a simplistic fashion and focusing primarily on the settlement/society dialectic. These regional archetypes are merely conceptual scaffolding and should not be mistaken for the building itself; they should not be treated as reified abstractions and their intellectual shelf life should be short, as they are inevitably replaced by better products. However, even this limited survey establishes a number of conclusions.

1   The older notion of a 'peasant' Ireland should be discarded as simplistic and deterministic. It should be replaced by a more sophisticated understanding of the intense social stratification of Irish life in this period and the associated regional dynamics which underpin this pronounced stratigraphy.

2   The concept of the 'two Irelands' should be decisively rejected. Irish society as a whole was decisively, indeed precociously, commercialised, as illustrated by the complex integration of the different economic regions.

3   It may be possible in the future to pinpoint dates which mark major transition phases in settlement transformation. Some like 1815 are well known;

others (1695?, 1720?, 1740?, 1770?), remain to be clarified and their regional relevance explored.

4   More detailed work like Crawford's on Ulster and Dickson's on the Cork region is required to provide precise spatial and temporal specifications of those regions. In particular, we need to understand more fully the under-researched zone from north Kerry to Mayo, and to fill the gaping research hole in the midlands, especially in the transitional counties of Offaly, Longford and Westmeath.

5   Nation-wide generalisations should be assessed for their validity in each of these contrasting regions.

Notes

1 Major surveys now exist for the seventeenth and nineteenth centuries. W. Smyth, 'Society and settlement in seventeenth-century Ireland: the evidence of the "1659 census"', in W. Smyth and K. Whelan (eds), *Common Ground: Essays on the Historical Geography of Ireland* (Cork, 1988), pp. 55–83. T. Jones Hughes, 'Society and settlement in nineteenth-century Ireland', in *Irish Geography*, V (1965), pp. 79–96, and 'Historical geography of Ireland from circa 1700', in G. Davies (ed.), *Irish Geography 1934–1984* (Dublin, 1984) pp. 149–166. The major article on eighteenth-century Ireland is J. Andrews' chapter (widely accepted as the best in the volume) 'Land and people *c*. 1780' in T. Moody and W. Vaughan (eds), *New History of Ireland*, IV (Oxford, 1986), pp. 236–64.

2 L. Cullen, 'Man, landscape and roads; the changing eighteenth century', in W. Nolan (ed.), *The Shaping of Ireland* (Cork, 1986), p. 124.

3 D. Cosgrove and P. Jackson, 'New directions in cultural geography', in *Area*, XIX (1987), pp. 85–101. See also E. Said, 'Representing the colonised: anthropological interlocutors', in *Critical Inquiry*, XV (1989), pp. 205–25.

4 A bibliography of the work of Estyn Evans can be found in R. Buchanan, E. Jones and D. McCourt (eds), *Man and his Habitat: Essays Presented to Emyr Estyn Evans* (London, 1971), pp. 264–76. His most influential books were *Irish Heritage: The Landscape, the People and their Work* (Dundalk, 1942); *Mourne Country: Landscape and Life in South Down* (Dundalk, 1951); *Irish Folkways* (London, 1957); *The Personality of Ireland: Habitat, Heritage and History* (Cambridge, 1973); *Ireland and the Atlantic Heritage: Selected writings* (Dublin, 1996).

5 Both these papers were presented to the annual conference of Irish geographers. 'The ethnic factor in Irish historical geography' (1974); 'The geographical study of the Irish past' (1977).

6 A bibliography can be found in A. Horner, 'The published writing of T. Jones Hughes', in Smyth and Whelan (eds), *Common Ground*, pp. 320–23.

7 Jones Hughes, 'Society and settlement', pp. 93–4.

8 Evans, *Personality of Ireland*, p. 87.

9 Ibid., p. 27.

10 There is a fuller development of these arguments in K. Whelan, 'Ireland in the Atlantic world 1600–1800', in H. Nitz (ed.), *The Early Modern World System in Geographical Perspective* (Stuttgart, 1993), pp. 204–18.

11 The map is at p. 169 in R. Glasscock, 'Moated sites and deserted boroughs and villages: Two neglected aspects of Anglo-Norman settlement in Ireland', in N. Stephens and R. Glasscock (eds), *Irish Geographical Studies in Honour of E. Estyn Evans* (Belfast, 1970), pp 162–77. For a broader survey of London's expanding

hinterland, see E. Wrigley, 'A simple model of London's importance in changing English society and economy', in *Past and Present*, XXXVII (1967), pp. 44–70.

12 J. Gilbert (ed.), *A Jacobite Narrative of the War in Ireland 1689–91* (Dublin, 1892), p. 12.

13 C. O'Hara, An Account of County Sligo in the Eighteenth century, National Library of Ireland, Ms 20, 397.

14 N. Taaffe, *Observations on Affairs in Ireland from the Settlement in 1691 to the Present Time* (Dublin, 2nd edn, 1766), p. 13.

15 E. MacParland, *A Statistical Survey of County Mayo* (Dublin, 1802), p. 122.

16 For the McCarthys, see A. Young, *A Tour in Ireland in 1776 and 1779* (Dublin, repr., 1970), ii, p. 391. For the Scullys, see J. O'Donoghue, 'The Scullys of Kilfeakle – Catholic middlemen of the 1770s', in *Tipperary Historical Journal*, ii (1989), pp. 38–51.

17 A Census of the Diocese of Elphin in 1749, Nat. Archives, Ms 2466.

18 S. Connolly, 'The Houghers – agrarian protest in early eighteenth-century Ireland', in C. Philpin (ed.), *Nationalism and Popular Protest in Ireland* (Cambridge, 1987) pp. 139–62.

19 T. Truxes, *Irish–American Trade 1660–1783* (Cambridge, 1988).

20 Ibid., p. 86.

21 For Waterford, see J. Mannion, 'The maritime trade of Waterford in the eighteenth century', in Smyth and Whelan (eds), *Common Ground*, pp. 208–25. For Cork, see A. Fahy, 'The spatial differentiation of commercial and residential functions in Cork city 1787–1863', in *Irish Geography*, XVII (1984), pp. 205–25 and 'Residence, workplace and patterns of change: Cork 1787–1863', in P. Butel and L. Cullen (eds), *Cities and Merchants* (Dublin, 1986), pp. 41–52.

22 D. Dickson, 'An economic history of the Cork region in the eighteenth century', unpublished PhD thesis, Dublin University, 1977. The map of Bianconi coach services in the period 1815–40 also vividly illustrates this. See T. Freeman, *Pre-Famine Ireland* (Manchester, 1957), p. 115.

23 Dickson, 'An economic history of the Cork region'. See also D. Dickson, 'Middlemen', in T. Bartlett and D. Hayton (eds), *Penal Era to Golden Age* (Belfast, 1979), pp. 162–87, and 'Property and social structure in eighteenth-century south Munster', in L. Cullen, and F. Furet (eds), *Ireland and France. Towards a Comparative Study of Rural History* (Paris, 1980), pp. 129–38. L. Cullen, 'Catholic social classes under the penal laws', in T. Power and K. Whelan (eds), *Endurance and Emergence: Catholics in Ireland in the Eighteenth Century* (Dublin, 1990), pp. 57–84.

24 On Art O'Laoghaire, see L. Cullen, *The Emergence of Modern Ireland* (London, 1981), pp. 28–89. For an edition of Caoineadh Airt O'Laoghaire, see S. O'Tuama (ed.), *Caoineadh Airt Ui Laoghaire* (Dublin, 1963).

25 J. Mockler, 'A report of the district around Mallow in 1775', in *Cork Historical and Archaeological Society Journal* (1915), p. 23.

26 W. Tighe, *Statistical Observations Relative to the County of Kilkenny made in 1800 and 1801* (Dublin, 1802), p. 261.

27 For radical conservatism, see W. Smyth, 'Continuity and change in the territorial organisation of Irish rural communities, part 1', in *Maynooth Review*, XIX (1975), pp. 51–73. For the concept of the nation-forming class, see E. Larkin, *The Historical Dimensions of Irish Catholicism* (Washington, 1984).

28 J. Andrews, 'The geographical element in Irish History', in *New History of Ireland, I* (forthcoming).

29 P. O. Flanagan, 'Markets and fairs in Ireland 1600–1800', in *Journal of Historical Geography*, XI (4) (1985), pp. 364–78, and 'Settlement development and trading in Ireland 1600–1800', in T. Devine and D. Dickson, (eds), *Ireland and Scotland*

1600–1850 (Edinburgh, 1983), pp. 146–50; T. Jones Hughes, 'Village and town in Ireland', in *Irish Geography*, XIV (1981), pp. 96–106.

30 Dickson, 'Economic history of the Cork region', Chapter IV.

31 J. Johnston, 'The "Two Irelands" at the beginning of the nineteenth century', in Stephens and Glasscock (eds), *Irish Geographical Studies*, pp. 224–43.

32 Mockler, 'The district around Mallow', p. 26. For an excellent local study vividly illustrating the hill–plain dialectic, see W. Smyth, 'Landholding changes, kinship networks and class transformations in rural Ireland: a case-study from County Tipperary', in *Irish Geography*, XVI (1983), pp. 16–35.

33 There is now a truly voluminous literature on secret societies. This is well reviewed in two major collections of articles; S. Clark and J. Donnelly (eds), *Irish Peasants: Violence and Political Unrest 1780–1914* (Manchester, 1983) and Philpin, *Nationalism and Popular Protest*. There is a significant revision of the Whiteboy debate in T. Power, *Land, politics and society in eighteenth-century Tipperary*, (Oxford: Clarendon Press, 1993).

34 See the map of the corn trade in 1780 in Andrews (1986), p. 246.

35 H. Hore (ed.), 'An account of the barony of Forth in the county of Wexford written at the close of the seventeenth century', in *Journal of the Royal Society of Antiquaries of Ireland*, VIII (1862–3), pp. 53–83. The quotation is at p. 60.

36 K. Whelan, 'Town and village in Ireland 1600–1900', in A. P. Vervloot and A. Verhoeve (eds), *The Transformation of the European Rural Landscape, 1770–1914* (Brussels, 1992), pp. 298–306.

37 R. Bell, *A Description of the Conditions and Manners of the Peasantry of Ireland such as they were between the years 1789 and 1790* (London, 1804), pp. 8–9.

38 O. O'Kelly, *The Placenames of County Kilkenny* (Kilkenny, repr., 1985), p. 136.

39 Andrews (1986), p. 264.

40 L. Cullen 'The social and economic evolution of county Kilkenny in the seventeenth and eighteenth centuries', in W. Nolan and K. Whelan (eds), *Kilkenny. History and Society* (Dublin, 1990), p. 277.

41 L. Cullen, 'Eighteenth-century flour-milling in Ireland', in *Irish Economic and Social History*, IV (1977), pp. 5–25.

42 K. Whelan, 'The Catholic community in eighteenth-century county Wexford', in Power and Whelan (eds), *Endurance and Emergence*, pp. 129–70.

43 Jones Hughes, 'Village and town in Ireland', p. 102.

44 *Poor Law Inquiry, Ireland* (1836), British Parliamentary Paper p. 368.

45 T. Jones Hughes, 'The large farm in nineteenth-century Ireland', in A. Gailey and D. Ó'hOgáin (eds), *Gold under the Furze* (Dublin, 1982), pp. 93–100.

46 S. Clark, *Social Origins of the Irish Land War* (Princeton, 1979).

47 See K. Whelan, 'The Catholic Church in county Tipperary 1700–1900', in W. Nolan (ed.), *Tipperary. History and Society* (Dublin, 1985), pp. 215–55.

48 Cullen, *Emergence of Modern Ireland*.

49 P. Knight, *Erris in the Irish Highlands* (Dublin, 1836), p. 104.

50 D. Corkery, *The Hidden Ireland – A Study of Gaelic Munster in the Eighteenth Century* (Dublin 1924); L. Cullen, *The Hidden Ireland: Reassessment of a concept* (Gigginstown, 1988).

51 K. Whelan, 'The regional impact of Irish Catholicism 1700–1850', in Smyth and Whelan (eds), *Common Ground*, pp. 253–77; K. Whelan, 'Gaelic Survivals', in *Irish Review*, VII (1989), pp. 139–42.

52 MacParland, *Mayo*, p. 80.

53 The figures of the numbers of Catholics and Protestants at a baronial level are available in Lambeth Palace Library. 'An abstract of the number of Protestant and Papist families as returned to the Hearth Money, anno 1732', ff. 43–8.

54 The following section is largely based on the work of W. Crawford. W. Crawford, 'The political economy of linen: Ulster in the eighteenth century', in C. Brady, M. O'Dowd and B. Walker (eds), *Ulster: An Illustrated History* (London, 1989) pp. 134–57; 'The evolution of the linen trade in Ulster before industrialisation', in *Irish Economic and Social History*, XV (1988), pp. 32–53; 'Draper and bleacher in the early Ulster linen industry', in L. Cullen and P. Butel, (eds), *Négoce et industrie en France et en Irelande aux XVIIIᵉ et aux XIXᵉ siècle* (Paris, 1986), pp. 113–20; 'The social structure of Ulster in the eighteenth century', in Cullen and Furet (eds), *Ireland and France*, pp. 117–28; 'Economy and society in south Ulster in the eighteenth century', in *Clogher Record* (1975), pp. 245–58; 'The origins of the linen industry in north Armagh and the Lagan Valley', in *Ulster Folklife*, XVII (1971), pp. 42–71; 'Ulster landowners and the linen industry', in T. Ward and R. Wilson (eds), *Land and Industry* (Newtown Abbot, 1971), pp. 134–8.

55 P. Kriedte, *Peasants, Landlords and Merchant Capitalists* (Leamington Spa, 1983). P. Kriedte et al., *Industrialisation before Industrialisation: Rural Industry in the Genesis of Capitalism* (Cambridge, 1981); L. Clarkson, *Proto-Industrialisation* (London, 1985); C. Vandenbroeke, 'Mutations économiques et sociales en Flandres au cours de la phase proto-industrielle 1650–1850', in *Révue du Nord*, LXIII (1981), pp. 73–94.

56 W. Crawford, 'The re-shaping of the borderlands *c.* 1700–1840', in R. Gillespie and H. O'Sullivan (eds), *The Borderlands* (Belfast, 1989), pp. 93–106. The quotation is at p. 95.

57 Smyth, 'Settlement and society', pp. 76–79. The map on p. 78 is especially revealing.

58 Jones Hughes, 'Large farm'. See also W. Crawford. 'The Ulster Irish in the eighteenth century', in *Ulster Folklife*, XXVIII (1982), pp. 24–32.

59 Cited in D. Miller, *Peep-o-day Boys and Defenders: Selected Documents on the County Armagh Disturbances 1784–96* (Belfast, 1990), p. 46.

60 See the map in Andrews, 'Land and people', p. 250 and the comments re Lisburn in J. Kelly (ed.), *The Letters of Lord Chief Baron Edward Willes 1757–62* (Aberystwyth, 1990), p. 33.

61 Crawford, 'Evolution of the linen trade'.

62 Johnston, 'The "Two Irelands"', in Stephens and Glasscock (eds) *Irish Geographical Studies*, map, p. 237.

63 C. Gill, *The Rise of the Irish Linen Industry* (Oxford, 1925).

64 K. Whelan, *The Tree of Liberty: Radicalism, Catholicism and the Construction of Irish Identity 1760–1830* (Cork: Cork University Press, 1996).

65 The earlier literature on the Armagh disturbances is reviewed in D. Miller 'The Armagh troubles 1784–95', in Clark and Donnelly (eds), *Irish Peasants*, pp. 155–91, an article praiseworthy for its expert use of maps. Cullen's *Emergence of Modern Ireland* is also essential for an understanding of eighteenth-century County Armagh.

9

TRENDS IN NINETEENTH- AND TWENTIETH-CENTURY SETTLEMENT

Patrick J. Duffy

Present settlement landscapes ... come from a past about which
we understand something, through a present that is bewildering
in its diversity and complexity, and will pass to a future which is
thankfully hidden.[1]

Introduction

At any time the settlement landscape which envelops people is a legacy of relict
and evolving features. While newly developing landscapes can never escape the
restraining impact of past legacies, an appreciation of the significance in themselves of present and more recent trends is important. Attitudes by the current
generation to their settlement inheritance, for example, have a significant
impact on the shape and fate of this heritage. Modifications to the landscape –
incrementally adding to the legacy or in part replacing it – occur within these
parameters of awareness. Thus the general rise in environmental or landscape
consciousness has had profound implications for the most recent phase of settlement history-in-the-making.

In terms of time, the present and its works become part of the past soon
enough! If settlement change is a measure of society's ongoing modification of
the landscape, then settlement patterns are in process all round us and it is
incumbent on us to take some account of what is happening. Popular and
indeed 'official' conceptions of settlement in Ireland have generally tended to
focus on the oldest parts of the legacy – medieval buildings and the built environment of the post-medieval period, especially the seventeenth and eighteenth
centuries. The Office of Public Works' (OPWs') *Sites and Monuments Record*
and its *Archaeological Surveys* have concentrated on documenting buildings and
features up to 1700, which seems to reflect an official reluctance to attribute
significance to more recent 'modern' accretions. Work by An Taisce, the Irish
Georgian Society and the Ulster Architectural Heritage Society, and the
Penguin series on *The Buildings of Ireland* contain more up-to-date reflections on
the Irish built environment.[2]

In the following discussion, which focuses on settlements in the modern period, we will look at the most significant contributions to our settlement landscape from the post-Famine period onwards. But it will also be important to realise the significance of the last fifty or one hundred years in terms of how our awareness of historic settlements changed our approach to the making of the settlement landscape. It was really only during this period that settlement *per se*, as an important cultural/material legacy worthy of special treatment, emerged. Indeed, apart from archaeological and antiquarian interests, professional engagement with, as well as popular interest in, settlement studies was a late development. The Group for the Study of Irish Historic Settlement was founded only thirty years ago. An Taisce (the National Trust for Ireland) was founded in 1948 and membership remained at a couple of hundred until the late 1960s when it rose to 2,500.[3] The Irish Georgian Society, with a specific focus on the preservation of Ireland's Georgian architecture, was established in 1958 and by 1969 its membership was 5,000. Undoubtedly Ireland's break with the UK in 1921 insulated it from the earlier British initiatives in protection and conservation of the built environment with probable adverse consequences for the Irish settlement landscape. The other chapters in this volume on the histories of earlier settlements in Ireland might ultimately be seen as products of fundamental and comparatively recent shifts in intellectual attitudes to 'settlement'. The publication and sell-out in 1997 of the *Atlas of the Irish Rural Landscape*[4] is a measure of how widespread and popular is this awareness at the present time. As a result, the past thirty years in Ireland has seen a comprehensive acknowledgement of the cultural and economic importance of landscapes and settlement, leading to an increasing amount of potentially useful political intervention.

It might be said that it is the living, evolving landscape, laid down over the past century or so, which has the greatest potential impact on all earlier legacies and which will influence future directions in settlement. In order to properly understand the holistic context of our settlement heritage, it is important to be aware of the nature of the most recent layers which have been added to what has sometimes been suggestively referred to as the palimpsest of landscape (Figure 9.1).

Main parameters in Irish settlement development up to the present

In looking at the developing character of Irish settlement since the mid-nineteenth century, the following broad themes provide a social, economic and environmental context.

- Emigration and rural depopulation
- Internal migration from west to east
- Low urban growth before the 1960s
- Underdevelopment in the more 'rural' and marginal land areas

- Public authority intervention in housing and settlement provision
- Farm abandonment and consolidation
- Road network contraction and abandonment
- Field enlargement
- Afforestation of marginal landscapes
- Limited maintenance of older settlement heritage
- Rejection of vernacular settlement legacies
- Popular interest in 'modern' settlement
- Inappropriate developments in many districts before 1963

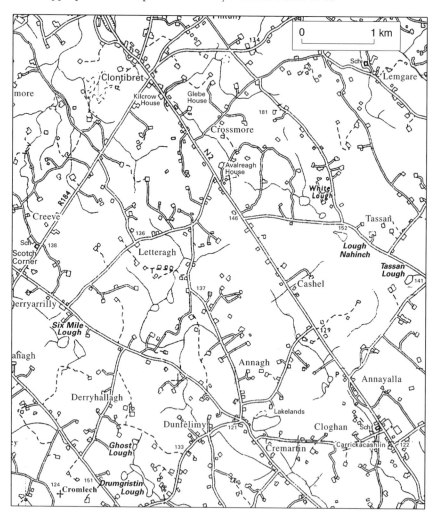

Figure 9.1   Dispersed rural settlement pattern, south Ulster, 1970s
Source: From OSNI, 1:50,000.

- Settlement planning following the 1963 planning legislation, compromised by concessions to agricultural lobby, developer interests and local politics
- Planning policies resulted in standardisation in the shaping of settlement landscapes
- Bottom-up pressure for persisting one-off housing in rural areas
- 'Bungalisation' and 'ribbonisation' of the Irish landscape
- CAP-induced alterations to landscape as agriculture became more industrialised from the 1970s.
- EU-directed and tourism-driven conservation of landscape diversity since the 1980s.
- Residual elements of dereliction and decay persist side by side with modernisation of the landscape

Post-Famine adjustments in settlement

The hundred years after the Famine saw particular changes and contributions to the shape of Irish settlement patterns. 'Life in so tranquil a country as Ireland does not alter rapidly', as Sean O Faoláin said in the 1940s.[5] An Ordnance Survey official commented ten years ago in relation to the slowness of revisions of large-scale maps in this century, that nothing much had happened in most of the Irish landscape for over one hundred years. This is a fair assessment of how the settlement landscape fared after the Famine as the country embarked on a long period of demographic contraction and decline. In the decade of the Famine, Ireland lost 282,000 houses, and in the fifty years from 1851, a further 200,000, in both cases mostly cabins of the poorest class. Apart from the dominant demographic impact of the Famine, which had obvious settlement repercussions, there were other fundamental transitions in economy which instigated changes in settlement and population. Emigration and rural depopulation was associated with a century-long shift to a low-labour cattle economy. Decline in tillage and rural textiles, and industrial consolidation in east Ulster led to decline in many industrial and estate villages dependent on a vibrant tillage economy. And country towns in general experienced a slow stagnation from the 1840s: indeed Ireland's 'urban' revolution had to wait until the 1960s. Therefore, even general trends indicate that settlement landscapes in the nineteenth century were principally characterised by processes of contraction and withdrawal which are still manifest in the withered scars of potato gardens 'quilted under heather and bracken' at the very margins of existence high up on mountainsides in the west.[6]

To appreciate the attrition which took place in settlement and associated landscape components in the decades after the Famine, one has got to comprehend the enormity of the decline in the rural population especially. Huge swathes of countryside lost well in excess of half their population. In many parts of western and north-western counties like Clare, Mayo, Galway and Monaghan the population fell by 50 per cent in the 1840s alone. In the mid-

nineteenth century, the significance of the link between population and settlement patterns is clearly captured in the census figures for townlands. A modern
audience can best appreciate this by comparing the population sizes in their
local areas then and now. Townlands which today accommodate populations of
a couple of dozen people contained a couple of hundred over a century ago. For
instance, a selection of townlands in rural south Monaghan shows great
contrasts in population between 1841 and 1985 (see Table 9.1). Even allowing
for substantial changes in family sizes in the meantime, the repercussions for the
making of the settlement landscape are obvious. Changes in house numbers
have an equally dramatic effect. In the remote parish of Pettigo in Donegal for
example, the 1841 population was 4,800 and in 1990 it was 770 approximately.[7]
House numbers in parts of the parish in the mid-nineteenth century and the
1990s are shown in Table 9.2. In Cúl Máine in west Fermanagh, a small selection of townlands shows great changes in house numbers between 1841 and
1990. These huge numbers of people in familiar local landscapes lived in cabins
clustered or dispersed through the fields, many of which melted back into the
landscape in post-Famine decades. These people were also responsible for the
lattice of fields and lanes, the outline shapes of which still represent familiar
lines in the landscape.

In many of the overcrowded landscapes of the mid-nineteenth century,
landowners actively encouraged a thinning out of population and settlement to
clear their estates of the most destitute and to re-establish an economic balance
between population and land on their properties. Comprehensive examples of
geometrically arranged ladder farms and linear dispersal of farmhouses may be

Table 9.1   Population of townlands in rural south Monaghan, 1841 and 1985

Townland	1841 pop.	(1985 pop.) *
Aghinillard	199	(16)
Alts	92	(11)
Ardragh	309	(33)
Barndonagh	106	(11)
Carrickadooey	207	(7)
Corcuilloge	296	(56)
Corlea	167	(10)
Drumbo	162	(19)
Drumbracken	216	(44)
Drumgoosat	177	(31)
Kilmactrasna	170	(20)

* Clogher diocesan census.

Table 9.2   House numbers in Pettigo parish, Co. Donegal, 1841 and 1990

Townland	1841	1990
Aghnahoo glebe	19	3
Ballymacavany	20	5
Belalt north	31	3
Loughfad	10	-
Loughultan	9	-
Meensheefin	11	1

Table 9.3   House numbers in Cúl Máine in west Fermanagh, 1841 and 1990

	1841	1990
Drumoyagh	19	3
Glenarm	47	12
Largy	43	7
Meenmore	19	4
Sheemuldoon	24	9

found in parts of the congested areas of Donegal, Sligo, Mayo and Galway, often in the midst of older haphazardly arranged field plans. During the last half of the nineteenth century indeed, assisted emigration by landowners and other agencies, often with state encouragement, might be said to represent the principal policy in rural settlement rationalisation in Ireland. Clearances, evictions and assisted emigration represented the dark side of the landlord world and reaped a harvest of hostility among the descendants of those who emigrated.

Whatever the ultimate good sense of encouraging people to seek a new life overseas and of securing the livelihood of those tenants left behind, the interest of many of the landowners and their agents in reorganising their estates was often expressed in aesthetic terms not calculated to appease an oppressed tenantry. As indicators of landscape and settlement development, however, these sentiments are of interest to us. Landlord correspondence in the decades after the Famine repeats the themes of improvement characteristic since the eighteenth century. In many of the most overcrowded regions in the 1850s and 1860s 'improvement' undoubtedly meant a substantial redesign of landscape, break-up of rundale house clusters, rearrangement of fields and roads, building bridges, digging drains and planting hedges. E.P. Shirley, in an address to his

Plate 9.1 One of hundreds of disused Church of Ireland churches, reflecting severe decline in rural congregations

tenantry in Monaghan in the 1840s, mentioned all the qualities which improving landlords aspired to but which may not have matched his tenants' priorities. His concerns were for 'improvement, comfort and respectability … order, tidiness and cleanliness', 'to encourage the growth of ornamental and useful timber' and the removal of the very small tenants through emigration.[8] William Steuart Trench, the agent, at the same time, recommended new houses, extensions, rearranged farmyards and the relocation of many houses. One tenant who looked for assistance in 1845, for example, was described: 'house very bad nearly falling, it is on the side of the coach road and looks very bad … '; another house was a 'miserable dirty hovel and a shame to see on the roadside'.[9]

In the parish of Drumkeeran in Fermanagh in 1834:

> the generality of the cottages of the poor are of a miserable description, evincing neither comfort nor cleanliness. Unless in the bogs, few are built of sods, stone being the general material, and in as many cases clay as cement instead of mortar is used.[10]

In Clogher parish in Co. Tyrone:

> there is very little order, cleanliness or neatness in general to be found either in the houses of the more wealthy farmers or in the cottages of the poor. The turf stack often approaches within a few yards of the door and thus intersects the view and stops the currency of the air. The

yard in front of the house is full of the odour of the cow house and stable....The lanes and approaches to the house are narrow, rough and filthy in the extreme ...[11]

One of the Shirley tenants in 1845, according to the agent 'was so careful of his dung heap that he keeps it at the foot of his bed'. After the Famine, many more landowners tried to tidy up the settlement legacy, by encouraging improvements. One among many, the Shirley estate belatedly invested in drainage and enclosure, as well as improvements in housing conditions such as second storeys, slates and roof timbers, gates, extensions and out-offices.

Improving moral values like order, tidiness, cleanliness informed the landowners' attitudes to landscape: their priority was a sort of morality of landscape which highlights a continuing theme throughout the following century in both private and public environmental and landscape initiatives. Today's landscape might be interpreted as the attempted imposition of many of these qualities, and the frequently adverted to disorder and anarchy in many aspects of Ireland's settlement patterns probably embodies spatial paradoxes resulting from basic conflicts in popular cultural attitudes to landscape and settlement organisation.

Agents of change in settlement

There were two main influences on the settlement fabric represented, for example, in buildings, roads and fields. In the first place, what might be broadly termed private enterprise was always the most important agent of change, whether this was the individual enterprise of farmers and ordinary inhabitants, or more institutional activities of landlordism or industrial or philanthropic agencies involved in planned urban settlement.

In the second place, changes brought about by public intervention, whether by the state or local authorities, while not as universal in terms of settlement landscapes, certainly increased in significance throughout the whole period. Drummond's 1837 admonition that 'property has its duties as well as its rights' signals the beginning of state intervention to correct the inadequacies of private enterprise (in environmental as well as social contexts) which accelerated in the following decades. In Ireland the ultimate expression of state intervention in settlement terms was the 1963, and subsequent, planning acts. In reviewing the modern period, therefore, public intervention was to become most important in contributing to today's settlement legacy, in terms not only of building and landscape but even more in terms of legislation and policy directives which shaped the context of settlement change.

In the eighteenth century and earlier, public intervention was limited – though Ireland with its colonial history and seventeenth-century plantations had more of it than most. The nineteenth century, however, witnessed a fairly rapid escalation in state involvement in all aspects of social and economic life in Ireland, paralleled in most cases by a huge amount of data collection through censuses and government commisssions of enquiry. The Board of Works, the Ordnance Survey, the Griffiths Valuation, the Congested Districts Board and the Land Commission were all representative of an increasingly proactive state role. Many of these undertakings had clear implications for landscape and settlement, either in terms of assembling important informational data bases or in remodelling farmscapes and settlements.

A great many aspects of rural and regional development were deficient under private enterprise. Before the twentieth century, the most all-embracing expression of privately sponsored changes in the landscape was the estate system, through whose structures from the eighteenth century most of the lineaments of the landscape were laid down by tenants and townspeople. Many areas and estates participated in a Europe-wide trend which has been designated as the 'age of improvement', encapsulating what might broadly be termed the modernisation of the landscape.[12] In much of the east of the country, for instance, the estate owners encouraged and facilitated improvements which still distinguish its settlement legacy, notably in terms of mansions, demesnes, parklands, estate and industrial villages, as well as agricultural improvements such as drainage, field enclosures, woodland plantations, farmhouses, cottages and other buildings.

Of greater significance, perhaps, were the more negative consequences of the estate system, especially in large parts of the west and more marginal landscapes generally. The Famine calamity was presaged in much of the west in a landscape crisis of inferior wasteland reclamation, gross fragmentation of fields, and mushrooming of squalid and unhygienic cabin clusters – uncontrolled and underfunded by estate owners. Both the population and the settlement landscape it created were in a precarious situation. Much of this apparent settlement chaos in extensively overcrowded regions was attributable to mismanagement in the estate system, little or no controlling intervention by often non-resident estate owners and limited investment in Irish estates by their owners. Interestingly, in these areas where there was little landlord intervention or control, where settlement development was essentially a product of endogenous forces fine-tuned to local conditions by local communities, folklore in one area has attributed the chaotic nature of the rundale villages to the work of 'Lord Rundale' who wanted to ensure that the Irish would 'be always fighting among themselves'![13]

Railway stations and the infrastructural buildings which accompanied the railways represent some of the most important additions to the modern settlement landscape since the mid-nineteenth century, at a time when settlement was mainly characterised by decline and contraction. Indeed the railway engineering of the landscape was comparable in its impact and importance to the current phase of highway construction. The railway buildings, erected in the main by railway companies, often in collaboration with landlords through whose estates they passed, and in the later years of the century in the remoter western districts by the state through the Light Railways Commission, were built to very high standards and continue to make memorable 'architectural statements'.[14] Creameries, primary schoolhouses and Roman Catholic chapels might also be selected to represent another series of important local community contributions to settlement in this non-dynamic period.[15] Their importance to settlement was in their addition of notable architectural features to many land-scapes singularly deficient in these, as well as providing a focus in many dispersed countrysides for shops, public houses and other services.

Depopulation and demographic resurgence

The long period of demographic decline which continued into the twentieth century had a profound impact on settlement across the country. Withdrawal, contraction, retreat, reorganisation, rationalisation, stagnation, decay, are terms which best describe the consequences for fields and houses, lanes and roads in a great many areas. Towns and villages also reflected a climate of depression. In the 1940s and 1950s, T.W. Freeman thought Irish towns ugly, Frank O'Connor thought them boringly indistinguishable – a sameness born of a dormant stag-nating greyness which was a product of continuous decline with little or no renewal of fabric or morphology.[16] Such characterisations of the landscape would have been especially appropriate in parts of Mayo, Roscommon and Leitrim up until the 1970s. Indeed, in north Leitrim, restrictive development control by local planners in the early 1980s was frequently resisted by local lobbies claiming in repeated instances that 'the first house since the Famine' was being stopped by the planners!

Depopulating districts experienced a time lag between demographic decline and settlement response which, for the residual population, added social to landscape malaise. Essentially, a model of such contracting landscapes, common through the north-west and west, would have seen a gradual running down of the main components of the landscape: lanes (boreens form the Irish *bóithrín*) and roads, the marks of a long-lived-in busy landscape originally servicing scores of houses, came to connect up a random pattern of a few residual households. The abandonment of this recent legacy of lanes and trackways contrasts signifi-cantly with the rediscovery and restoration, for heritage tourism purposes, of many older medieval trackways, such as Tóchar Phádraig in west Mayo.[17]

Fields and farms also reflected this decline: in a great many places up to the 1950s and 1960s extensive tracts of land were abandoned to a limbo of rushes and weeds but continued in the ownership of migrated family members – an ironic mirror-image of the negative settlement repercussions of the absentee landlord of a century earlier. 'Landscapes of ruins' would not be an inappro-priate appellation for the nature of much rural settlement in many parts of the countryside up to the 1950s. There was net emigration of 700,000 from the Twenty-Six Counties between 1926 and 1956 which emptied much of the Irish rural landscape. The resultant decay is still reflected in half-roofed outbuildings, rusting corrugated roofs and derelict ruins, often huddling amid significant national monuments from the Middle Ages or alongside lavish modern bungalows. Region-specific, especially in the west and north-west, it leaves a negative impression of precipitate abandonment of stranded landscapes, without the positive attraction of mystery which endows the more ancient ruins for the tourism industry.

The past thirty years has witnessed a demographic recovery in Ireland which has had significant repercussions on rural and urban landscapes. Populations in town and countryside have grown steadily from the 1960s for the first time since the middle of the nineteenth century. The accompanying rural and urban renewal, while it has reached into a great many parts of the country, has shown distinctive regional and local spatial preferences. In general, population recovery beginning in the 1960s has percolated down the urban hierarchy and has diffused from east to west.[18] The result is that the most urbanised regions have shown the most consistent and comprehensive patterns of population growth. While many parts of the west of Ireland, especially more scenic holiday regions, have also participated in this change in fortune, a great many areas in the rural west and north-west still show unmistakeable signs of decline.

For the first time in more than a century, Irish towns have played a critical role in population increase, both as magnets for population growth and as stabilising influences on rural hinterlands. Consequently the most urbanised regions in the east and south have had the most significant recovery and the countrysides in the Dublin metropolitan region and in the rural regions of most large towns in the country have had population growth. Close examination of this change at rural level also reflects the urban orientation of the revival: growth is reflected in new settlements which show a definite orientation towards the main roads connecting towns (Figure 9.2a). The consequence has been the renewal of many rural landscapes and communities in areas that demonstrate high degrees of accessibility to urban centres. Many of these new houses, located in suburban-type settings, are a sort of shop window on newly emerging settlement landscapes which hides the scars of decline and dereliction in the more remote by-ways and backwaters.

Public interventions in settlement patterns

In the climate of decline caused by the poverty and underdevelopment of many regions, the principal agencies which could stabilise the situation were various manifestations of the state. Rural poverty and population decline were for long diagnosed as being caused by poor living conditions and so a variety of authorities embarked on programmes to improve housing conditions.

The Poor Law introduced in 1840s represented the first tentative steps by the state to attempt to ameliorate local conditions. Occasionally in post-Famine years this involved some house building to rectify severe problems of deprivation among the poorer classes. But it was the Congested Districts Board (CDB) which made the most impact on settlement and landscape in the later nine-teenth century, leaving a pattern of houses and fields which is still in evidence over extensive parts of the west of Ireland. Established to relieve congestion and poverty in the small-holdings of the western counties, the Board was responsible for breaking up and re-ordering thousands of rundale house clusters and intri-cately meshed fields and gardens. Clusters were broken up and houses located in general close to their own farms and fields. Housing conditions in many of these areas were particularly bad and a number of models of improved houses often echoing local building styles, were developed.[19] In many cases distinctive 'striped' fields running from new-built roads with road-side houses were built

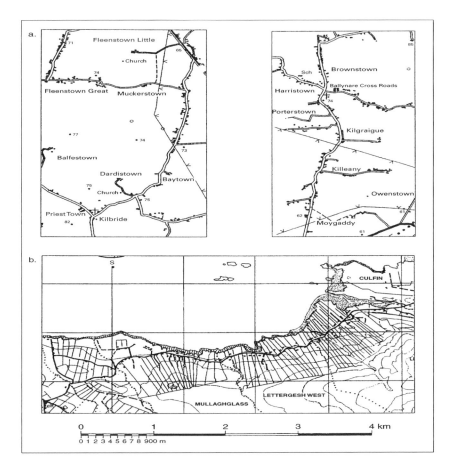

Figure 9.2   (a) New ribbon development in Co. Meath, 1990s; (b) Reorganised late nineteenth-century ladder farms

Source: (a) From OSI 1:50,000; (b) From *The Mountains of Connemara* (Roundstone, Co. Galway: Folding Landscapes), 1988.

(Figure 9.2b). The pattern of ribbon-like settlement has been replicated in the modern bungalow settlements of many parts of the western countrysides.

Following political independence in 1922, rural land reform was allocated to the Land Commission which continued many of the policies of the CDB. In a period of continuing rural decline, the Land Commission was responsible for a significant amount of settlement remodelling in many countrysides. While it continued to work in the small-farm landscapes of the west, its biggest achievement took place in some of the most underpopulated countrysides of Ireland. The empty pasturelands of Roscommon and east Connaught, and especially the mid-Leinster counties of Kildare and Meath, saw extensive results of Land Commission policy which were the converse of the congested areas work. Estates and large farms were broken up in the years from the late 1930s until the 1960s and allocated to selected migrant farmers from the west. Thousands of farmhouses were built for migrants from Mayo, Leitrim, Donegal, Clare and Kerry in distinctive groups and patterns in the deep soils and high hedges of the midlands. Land Commission farmhouses and outbuildings were built to a small number of modest designs which have made a notable contribution to the midland landscapes just as their occupants did to midland society. Often located on newly built Land Commisssion roads, the farmsteads were located close together for company in these empty landscapes, and the farms and new smaller fields were carved out of enormous older pastures. With new hedges, or more often wire-fencing, these Land Commission settlements make a distinctive contribution to the settlement landscape which has been largely unexamined (see Figure 9.3).[20]

The contribution of local authorities to emerging settlement patterns has been significant also. The housing conditions of the poorer classes had clearly been a problem legacy from well back into the nineteenth century. The severe reduction in the numbers of poor during and after the Famine, and the emigration of large numbers of rural labourers in the agricultural changes after the Famine, reduced the housing crisis somewhat, but, following the creation of county councils as an effective local government in 1898, public attempts at local housing reform began. Irish county councils were pioneers in the area of labourers' housing in Ireland, due mainly to the poor quality of the thatched houses which they occupied and the inability of landlords or farmers to provide adequate replacements.[21] Up to 1921 approximately 50,000 labourers' cottages were constructed singly or in small groups along the country roads convenient to the large farms on which they might seek employment. Just as the CDB was catering for the needs of the small-holders in the west, the council cottages were principally constructed in Leinster and Munster where most of the labourers lived. However, constantly declining opportunities on farms and a search for social and economic efficiencies in housing location meant that short terraces of cottages and small housing estates were frequently erected on the edges of towns and villages as the twentieth century progressed. Other public-type initiatives in housing and settlement which were to have a more localised

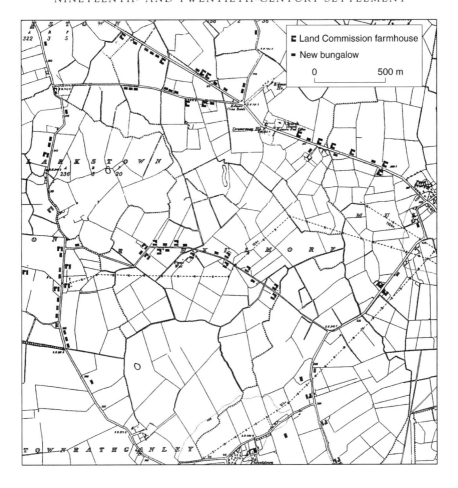

Figure 9.3   Land Commission farms in south Meath

impact were those of Bord na Móna (the Irish Turf Board) and the Electricity Board.

The biggest contribution made by the state to settlement changes in this century followed the introduction for the first time of comprehensive planning legislation in 1963.[22] Accompanying a radical programme of economic revitalisation, the 1963 Local Government (Planning and Development) Act compelled local authorities to produce five-yearly development plans. With some exceptions, most notably in agriculture, all development had to go through the planning process. From this time onwards, therefore, all new settlement and housing in town and country reflects the imposition of a standard set of rules about siting and location relative to a variety of other landscape elements. In practice, environmental and physical planning, while rigidly centralised under the Minister from the outset, was on a learning curve from 1963. A great many mistakes were made, a great deal of laxity existed in relation to development control in many rural areas and a considerable amount of interference by local politicians with professional plans was par for the course. The result was that the great surge in population and settlement which followed economic growth through the 1960s to the 1990s was less strictly controlled than might have been the case, with unfortunate landscape consequences in many instances (Figure 9.4).

Since the 1980s, there has been a discernible rise in popular interest in many aspects of settlement heritage in Ireland. This has resulted in a growth in legislation on heritage conservation and a greater involvement by planning authorities in maintenance and management of elements of landscape heritage in Ireland. However, there is some concern about this revival of interest in historic buildings and settlements: tourism-driven, Euro-funded and commodified strategies have resulted in shallowly based developments which might frequently be attributed to a lack of understanding of the past.[23] Selective appropriation and social constructions of past landscapes raise many questions about the authentic and the phoney which are of immense importance to settlement conservation

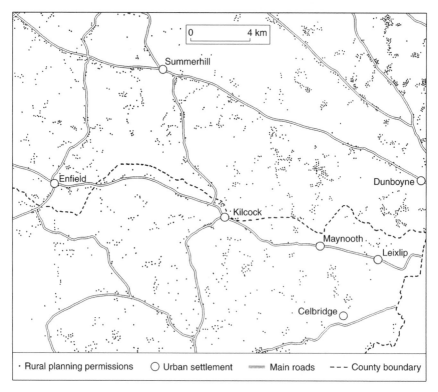

Figure 9.4   Rural planning permissions in the east midlands, 1970s

220

and planning at this time.[24] Public funding for settlement conservation by the state also lacks commitment: the list system and the application of methodologies like Conservation Areas, which have been adopted by planning authorities, lack teeth and many elements of the settlement heritage are in grave danger because of this.[25]

Landscape consequences of changes since the mid-nineteenth century

Looking at the social context and landscape impact of changing settlement we can construct a general summary of trends in the past century and more. The overall *distribution* of settlement has been substantially modified with an ongoing selective transformation of the landscape. There has been a withdrawal from the margins and down the mountainsides. A great many remote and inaccessible areas in the western counties reflect this process of desertion and abandonment in derelict fields, houses and lane networks. There has also been a discernible movement towards the towns and the main roads connecting the towns. In the past thirty years, the rural–urban fringes around the bigger towns and cities represent some of the most notable pressure areas in population, planning and settlement terms. Rural and village landscapes in the Dublin metropolitan region, for example, extending far into counties Meath, Kildare and Wicklow, have been transformed by commuter settlements (Figure 9.5).[26] Holiday and tourism areas exhibit similar pressures to many more urbanised regions. Focused chiefly in the western counties, these are exceptions to the general trend towards stagnation or decline.

The *pattern* of settlement has changed also reflecting new priorities in the twentieth century. Increased urban-based employment, declining agriculture and rising affluence generally have resulted in a huge growth in road-oriented commuter settlements. In extensive holiday tourist regions, gentrification of older buildings and cottages, while preserving many from dereliction, has been paralleled by extensive development of purpose-built holiday bungalows, chalets and apartments, encouraged in recent years by tax-incentive renewal programmes. This has resulted not only in a part-time habitation of the landscape, but also in considerable degradation and overdevelopment of many vulnerable scenic and ecologically sensitive areas.

In reviewing the twentieth century's contribution to Irish settlement history, one would also have to acknowledge the role of destructive changes to the landscape legacy. The claim that the long period of inertia in the Irish landscape has been a force for conservation[27] should not conceal from us the losses which also occurred. Indeed the birth of the state was accompanied by considerable damage to the eighteenth-century Georgian heritage. Upwards of 300 'big houses' were burned in the 1919–23 period[28] and the national rejection of this architectural and landscape inheritance continued until the 1960s. The most destructive consequence of this apathy, complementing greedy property inter-

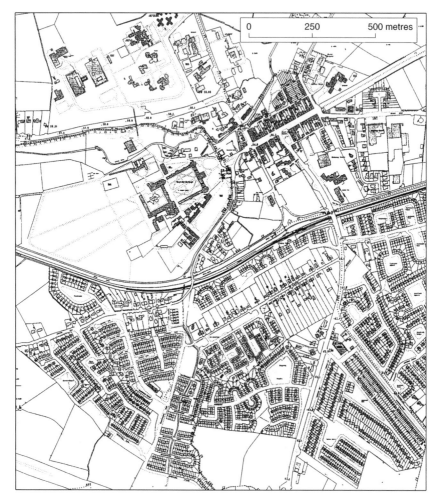

Figure 9.5   Housing estates from the 1970s tacked on to an eighteenth-century village
core, Maynooth, Co. Kildare
Source: From OSI 1:10,000.

ests during the first wave of economic development in the 1960s, was the
extensive demolition of parts of Georgian Dublin.[29] The Minister at the time
probably articulated popular sentiment about the emerging conservation lobby
when he referred to 'belted earls' and 'aesthetic bullies' trying to preserve parts
of the built environment.

Some of the most pervasive destruction occurred in rural landscapes as a
result of agricultural developments and rural settlement renewal. The Common
Agricultural Policy (CAP) has been responsible for a rapid modernisation of
farm structures which has even reached into parts of the most marginal landscapes in the west. For example, the extensive removal of field boundaries on

Slea Head in the Dingle peninsula in Kerry to make the exposed mountainside suitable for ranching epitomises the type of destructive repercussions of the CAP's subsidy schemes. So intricate is the legacy in many parts of the west of Ireland, that the incremental destruction of stone-walling has gone unnoticed for many years: indeed, it is likely that the removal of many surplus walls for road gravelling took place after the Second World War. Hedge and bank removal, however, has been much more characteristic of commercial farming areas in eastern regions and in Northern Ireland.[30]

One of the most visually transforming developments in the settlement landscape has been what has colourfully been called 'bungalow blitz' and 'bungalisation' of the Irish countryside.[31] This settlement response to the demographic recovery since the 1960s is a product of one of the more lax rural planning regimes in Europe and a cultural predisposition among many Irish people to live in the countryside. It also reflects the landscape consequences of a small-farm matrix, a reluctance by planners and politicians to obstruct what has been perceived as the revival of many long dormant communities and a popular apathy about conservation of the countryside. In the past twenty years, as a result of a relaxation of rural planning controls in Northern Ireland, a similar but less intensive pattern of bungalow development has taken place there.[32]

The bungalisation of the Irish countryside is reflected dramatically in housing statistics. Although the bungalow has also been built in urban housing estates, it has been the dominant house type in rural areas since the 1960s. In 1985, 26 per cent of the total of 24,000 new-built houses were detached bungalows. In 1990, 30 per cent of the 19,500 new houses were bungalows. Although the proportions fall to 20 per cent (of 34,000 new houses) in 1996, it is likely that this is due not so much to a decline in rural housing as an increase in large two-storey houses in open countrysides.[33] 'Bungalisation', as a somewhat pejorative term for what some believe to be the negative impact of ribbon development and bad design on the landscape, highlights an important dichotomy in attitudes to settlements in the landscape. A great many people from politicians to rural dwellers see these new settlements as reflecting a dynamic renewal and modernisation of rural Ireland. One civil servant's song of praise for the new settlement landscapes emerging in the 1960s is emblematic of this viewpoint:

> my heart leaps up when I behold a cluster of bright modern bungalows, near a modern school, served by a tarred road, with the majestic curve of pylon-borne power lines sweeping along the mountains and through the brown bogs. And the glitter of the television aerials in the evening light. … And the poetry of the flushing of a wc and the music of a hot bath filling.[34]

Plate 9.2 Ribbon development on leafy rural road in the midlands

Part of the loss to the settlement landscape which is a product of other demo-graphic and economic changes is the loss of a local territorial dimension which was characteristic of settlement and landscapes traditionally. Obviously as settlements declined and the people in them, so also did familiarity with these local places. One of the fundamental aspects of the identity and spirit of settle-ments was the names which went with them. Townland names have survived in tens of thousands because they were recorded by the Ordnance Survey in the nineteenth century; many of the names of farm clusters which no longer have any significance, have also been recorded. Field names were not recorded, except in an unsystematic manner by the Folklore Commission. The 'pyramid of places', supported on a superstructure of detailed and well-known landscapes of field and minor names, and which was an integral part of the settlement pattern, has now been inverted. Today's community and settlement is less local – settlements and landscapes far beyond the locality are as well known and as familiar. This is a fitting testimony to the kind of change which has occurred in this century.

For more than a century we have witnessed an opening up of society, an abandonment of the local landscape and a 'de-localisation' of settlement. The essential local-ness and vernacular texture of local areas has been undervalued in favour of a universal culture of architecture and settlement, reflected in such elements as rectangular house sites along roads containing bungalows, double garages, lawns and *leylandii* hedges. The removal of miles of roadside hedgerows to be replaced with concrete boundary walls, often a mandatory requirement of planning permission, epitomises this standardisation of settlement features.

Settlement landscapes of the future will undoubtedly reflect the application of planning policies which lead to a homogenisation not just in the patterns and processes of landscape evolution, but also in the practice of conservation and management of settlement legacies from earlier periods. In future, there-fore, students of settlements will be looking at landscapes that are a product of deliberate, large-scale planning which is not only a result of global perspectives on landscape management, but is also a reaction to the enormous potential for radical transformation, indeed destruction, of so much of the settlement legacy today.

Notes

1 Roberts (1996: ix).
2 Rowan (1993).
3 Mawhinney (1989: 96).
4 Aalen, Whelan and Stout (1997).
5 O'Faoláin (1947: v).
6 Whelan (1986: 151).
7 Duffy (1993: 27).
8 Public Record Office of Northern Ireland (D3531/C/3/1/7).
9 Public Record Office of Northern Ireland (D3531/M/7/1–5).
10 Day and McWilliams (1992, vol. 14: 66).
11 Day and McWilliams (1990, vol. 5: 59).
12 Graham and Proudfoot (1994).
13 Personal interviews in west Mayo (1997).
14 Killen (1997: 213).
15 Aalen, Whelan and Stout (1997: 177); Gailey (1984); Shaffrey and Shaffrey (1985).
16 P. O'Connor (1995) 77; Frank O'Connor (nd: 268).
17 Corlett (1996).
18 Horner (1986); Horner, Walsh and Harrington (1987).
19 Evans (1957: 27); Aalen (1992: 143).
20 Nolan (1988).
21 Aalen (1992).
22 Bannon (1989).
23 Duffy (1994); Aalen et al. (1997: 236–59).
24 see Brett (1996); Cosgrove (1990: 5).
25 McDonald (1992, 1997).
26 Duffy (1987: 113–23, 1997: 244–5).
27 Royle (1989: 119).
28 Dooley (1997: 648–50).
29 McDonald (1985).
30 Kennedy (1997: 249); Webb (1985).
31 McDonald (1987); Gailey (1977: 187).
32 see Ulster Architectural Heritage Society (1997: xxiv–xxv).
33 Housing Statistics Bulletins.
34 Fitzsimons (1990: 23).

References

Aalen, F.H. (1992) 'Ireland', in C.G. Pooley (ed.) *Housing Strategies in Europe, 1880–1930*, Leicester: Leicester University Press.

Aalen, F.H., Whelan, K. and Stout, M. (eds) (1997) *Atlas of the Irish Rural Landscape*, Cork: Cork University Press.

Bannon, M.J. (ed.) (1989) *Planning: The Irish Experience*, Dublin: Wolfhound.

Brett, D. (1996) *The Construction of Heritage*, Cork: Cork University Press.

Casey, C. and Rowan, A. (1993) *The Buildings of Ireland, North Leinster*, London: Penguin Books.

Clogher Diocesan Census (1985) Unpublished manuscripts, Archive Office, Monaghan.

Corlett, C. (1996) 'Prehistoric pilgrimage to Croagh Patrick', *Cathair na Mart* (Journal of Westport Historical Society) 16.

Cosgrove, D. (1990) 'Landscape studies in geography and cognate fields of the humanities and social sciences', *Landscape Research* 15(3).

Day, A. and McWilliams, P. (1990) *Ordnance Survey Memoirs of Ireland: Parishes of Co. Tyrone*, vol. 5, Belfast: Institute of Irish Studies.

Day, A. and McWilliams, P. (1992) *Ordnance Survey Memoirs of Ireland: Parishes of Co. Fermanagh*, vol. 14, Belfast: Institute of Irish Studies.

Dooley, T. (1997) 'The decline of the big house in Ireland, 1879–1950', unpublished PhD dissertation, National University of Ireland.

Duffy, P.J. (1987) 'The Dublin region: a perspective on the fringe', in A.A. Horner and A.J. Parker (eds) *Geographical Perspectives on the Dublin Region*, Dublin: Geographical Society of Ireland.

Duffy, P.J. (1993) *Landscapes of South Ulster: A Parish Atlas of the Diocese of Clogher*, Belfast: Institute of Irish Studies.

Duffy, P.J. (1994) 'Conflicts in heritage and tourism', in U. Kockel (ed.) *Culture, Tourism and Development: The Case of Ireland*, Liverpool: Liverpool University Press.

Evans, E.E. (1957) *Irish Folk Ways*, London: Routledge.

Fitzsimons, J. (1990) *Bungalow Bashing*, Kells: Kells Publishing Company.

Gailey, A. (1977) 'Vernacular dwellings of Clogher diocese', *Clogher Record* 9(2): 187–231.

Gailey, A. (1984) *Rural Houses of Northern Ireland*, Edinburgh: Donald.

Graham, B.J. and Proudfoot, L.J. (1994) *Urban Improvement in Provincial Ireland, 1700–1840*, Athlone: Group for the Study of Irish Historic Settlement.

Horner, A.A. (1986) 'Rural population change in Ireland', in P. Breathnach and M. Cawley (eds) *Change and Development in Rural Ireland*, Geographical Society of Ireland.

Horner, A.A., Walsh, J. and Harrington, P. (1987) *Population in Ireland: A Census Atlas*, Dublin: University College Dublin.

Kennedy, E. (1997) 'Field boundaries and landscape change', in F.H. Aalen, K. Whelan and M. Stout (eds) *Atlas of the Irish Rural Landscape*, Cork: Cork University Press.

Killen, J. (1997) 'Communications', in F.H. Aalen, K. Whelan and M. Stout (eds) *Atlas of the Irish Rural Landscape*, Cork: Cork University Press.

McDonald, F. (1985) *The Destruction of Dublin*, Dublin: Gill and Macmillan.

McDonald, F. (1987) 'Bungalow blitz' and 'The ribbon that's strangling Ireland', *Irish Times* 12 Sept. and 15 Sept.

McDonald, F. (1992) 'Skin-deep commitment to conservation', *Irish Times* 22 Sept.

McDonald, F. (1997) 'Heritage treasures at risk of going to rot', *Irish Times* 25 Oct.

Mawhinney. K. (1989) 'Environmental conservation, concern and action, 1920–1970', in M.J. Bannon (ed.) *Planning: The Irish Experience, 1920–1988*, Dublin: Wolfhound.

Nolan, W. (1988) 'New farms and fields: migration policies of state land agencies', in W.J. Smyth and K. Whelan (eds) *Common Ground: Essays on the Historical Geography of Ireland*, Cork: Cork University Press.

O'Connor, F. (nd) *Leinster, Munster and Connaught*, London: Robert Hale Ltd.

O'Connor, P. (1995) 'Review of *Irish Country Towns*', *Irish Geography* 28(1).

O'Faoláin, S. (1947) *An Irish Journey*, London: Green and Co.

Roberts, B.K. (1996) *Landscapes of Settlement: Prehistory to the Present*, London: Routledge.

Royle, S.A. (1989) 'The historical legacy in modern Ireland', in R.W.G. Carterand A.J. Parker (eds) *Ireland: A Contemporary Geographical Perspective*, London: Routledge.

Shaffrey, P. and Shaffrey, M. (1985) *Irish Countryside Buildings: everyday architecture in the rural landscape*, Dublin: The O'Brien Press.

Ulster Architectural Heritage Society (1997) *Buildings at Risk*, vol. 4, Belfast: Ulster Architectural Heritage Society.

Webb, R. (1985) 'Farming and the landscape', in F.H. Aalen (ed.) *The Future of the Irish Rural Landscape*, Dublin: Trinity College.

Whelan, K. (1986) 'The Famine and post-Famine adjustment', in W. Nolan (ed.) *The Shaping of Ireland*, Cork and Dublin: Mercier.

10

PERSPECTIVES ON IRISH
SETTLEMENT STUDIES

Anngret Simms

Changing themes in the study of Irish historic settlements

Historic settlement research in Ireland is not only a successful field of study in its own right but it is also a way of life. This is why, almost thirty years after its foundation, the Group for the Study of Irish Historic Settlement is still going strong. I have been asked to set the scene for future research into the settlement history of Ireland, as it was my good fortune to be President of the Group on the occasion of its twentieth birthday. My reflections will be biased towards the contribution of historical geographers, as I am most familiar with their work.[1]

In the tradition of the founding fathers

Before we can talk about the future beyond the research presented in this volume we should briefly acknowledge the work on which our present studies build. Two people, whose names appear frequently in this volume, have actively shaped the foundation years of Irish historic settlement studies. These were E.E. Evans and T. Jones Hughes, who held the first appointments in Geography at Queen's University Belfast (1928–68) and University College Dublin (1950–87), respectively. As the discipline of geography only became established in Irish universities with their generation, it is not surprising that these men came from across the Irish Sea, from Wales.[2] What is more significant for us is that their research focused on rural settlement and society, while T.W. Freeman, the first geographer in Trinity College Dublin (1936–46), was primarily a population geographer, whose work on pre-Famine Ireland is an important contribution to the historical geography of early nineteenth-century Ireland.[3] P. Flatrès's book, *Géographie rurale de quatre contrées celtiques* (Rennes, 1957), looking at Ireland as part of the Atlantic fringe of Europe, had a great influence in his time, because it stressed the European dimension in the interpretation of the Irish landscape.

Evans's work was based on field-work and focused on traditional rural settlement patterns and house-types along the north-western Atlantic fringe of Ireland, while Jones Hughes's research explored nineteenth-century documentary sources and was focused on questions of power in society as mediated through land-holding. In their students we see the emergence of two different strands of settlement studies. One developed at Belfast with scholars like R.H. Buchanan, D. McCourt, B. Proudfoot and younger scholars, whose work on the traditional rural landscape was based primarily on field observations.[4] The other emanated from Dublin with scholars like W.J. Smyth, S. Smith, P. Duffy, W. Nolan, K. Whelan and P. O'Connor, whose research is focused on the importance of institutions and cultural factors for the formation of the Irish landscape.[5]

The earlier impetus for Evans's work had come from archaeology, which might have influenced his fascination with origins and cultural diffusion. The landscape was his main source of evidence. Written documents played little part in his research. The focus of his interest was the small clustered settlements in the north of Donegal, which, following the Scottish example, he called 'clachans'. The 'clachans' were surrounded by arable land, which was periodically redistributed, according to a system called 'run-rig' or 'rundale'.[6]

One of the past problems of Irish settlement studies, which J.H. Andrews had the courage to address, was that E.E. Evans and his students put forward the idea that 'clachans' and their associated field-systems were features which had been part of the Irish landscape since prehistory until they were finally mapped by the Ordnance Survey in the early nineteenth century. But evidence for the existence of 'clachans' and 'rundale' before the eighteenth century is very scarce. Why were the Belfast geographers at the time so determined to go beyond hard evidence? Probably because they believed in the concept of the cultural continuity from Irish prehistory to the present. They also did not hesitate to assume that the settlement patterns which they found in Ulster were also typical for the rest of the country and that land-use systems from the prehistoric period continued more or less unchanged to the present day! Today we have a stronger belief in the independence of the past. As the discussions in the previous chapters show, work based on medieval and early modern documentation favours a model of settlement development which focuses on the dynamic nature of cultural change in the landscape and stresses the importance of differences between regions.

Jones Hughes always deliberately distanced himself from the landscape school. His main interest belonged to the agrarian society of nineteenth-century Ireland and his sources are the nation-wide government surveys of that period. They include the population Census (every ten years after 1800), a statistical survey of landownership called after its director – the Griffith Valuation (1849–65) – and the first 6 inches to 1 mile Ordnance Survey maps (1833–46), which were produced for the whole country in order to provide a basis for taxation.

The regional differentiation of Irish landscapes was of great interest for Jones Hughes, less as expressed in different settlement patterns as in variations of place-names and personal names, which would offer an explanation for the different ethnic origin of population groups who make up the Irish people. Jones

Hughes showed that place-name studies make a real contribution towards a better understanding of the settlement history of Ireland. The most important place-name element in Ireland is the Gaelic 'baile' with the corresponding English 'town'. These two place-name elements, in connection with personal names, are complementary. For example in the north of the province of Leinster, where Anglo-Norman colonisation was very successful, place-names with the suffix 'town' are frequent, while in the province of Connaught in the west of the island the suffix 'baile' is widespread. One of the intriguing questions for which we still have to find an answer is why we find so many Gaelic field-names on nineteenth-century estate-maps in areas which were once under strong Anglo-Norman influence, as for example in County Dublin.

The topic which most fascinated Jones Hughes was the influence of lordship on Irish rural society. The confiscation of land which followed the Cromwellian wars in the seventeenth century allowed the formation of large estates in Protestant hands. The architecture of the elegant estate-houses, in classical style surrounded by demesne land and estate walls, has spread in amazing conformity from the east to the west coast in spite of regions with greatly differing modes of agricultural production. Jones Hughes pointed out that the estate system was much more invasive in the agriculturally poorer regions of the west than in the richer regions of the east. He repeatedly drew attention to the cultural meaning of Irish market-places in the nineteenth century. Near to the market-place stood the court-house, the school and the established church, usually paid for by the Protestant landlord. The Catholic church was located on the periphery of the town not far from the fair-green. The land acts introduced by Gladstone at the end of the nineteenth century allowed the tenants to become the owners of their land. The big estate houses lost their function and many of them fell into ruins. It would be an important task for the future to establish a country-wide survey in how far these houses continue under new guises or have fallen into ruins.[7]

Fortunately for us, Jones Hughes also had a large number of students who continued his work. Their interest is mainly focused on the institutions which were important for the formation of modern Ireland. After the emancipation of the Catholic church at the beginning of the nineteenth century it was this institution which had the greatest impact on the shaping of the landscape. New diocesan centres were established in the large populous county towns rather than in the old medieval diocesan centres. Thus Thurles became the new Catholic diocesan centre in Tipperary instead of Cashel. In many instances the building of new Catholic churches in the nineteenth century led to the establishment of new villages, named 'chapel-villages' by K. Whelan.[8]

A problem of interpretation concerning Jones Hughes's work is whether he is right in describing the landscape change brought about by the landlords in the nineteenth century exclusively as an expression of a colonial society, or whether this change represents, at least in part, a modernisation process. In fact, many changes in the cultural landscape of eighteenth- and nineteenth-century

Ireland are not the result of landlord directives but are due to the initiative of the tenant-farmers. The building of the eighteenth-century Georgian squares in Dublin has been described by Jones Hughes as the strongest expression of British colonialism in Ireland. The elegant Georgian town-houses are indeed built like their English counterparts, but the actual layout of the squares and the architecture of the monumental buildings in Dublin from that period are not particularly English, rather following the mode of other classical buildings in Europe at that time. In the context of Irish history the concept of colonialism can obscure as much as it can enlighten.

History of cartography and settlement studies

Another name which crops up frequently in the preceding chapters of this book is that of J.H. Andrews (formerly of Trinity College Dublin), who bridges the generations.[9] Having an unrivalled expertise in the history of cartography in Ireland he has written a book on the history of the Irish Ordnance Survey with the intriguing title A Paper Landscape (Dublin, 1975) and one on Irish map-makers called Plantation Acres (Belfast, 1985). It is his hypothesis that in countries where dramatic changes in property ownership are imposed from outside the production of maps has a much higher priority than in countries with greater social stability. That, in a nutshell, is the reason why Ireland is better endowed with early Ordnance Survey maps than England.

Andrews set the standard for the rigorous examination of documentary sources in Irish settlement studies, which he himself applied particularly to the plantation period. Those who feel indebted to his research come from a very wide circle of scholars. His recent book on Shapes of Ireland (Dublin, 1997) is a treasure trove for settlement historians, as were his previous books. In some way he has acted as the conscience of Irish settlement studies by asking critical questions about widely held assumptions, which appeared not to have been backed up by sufficient evidence from the sources.[10]

A. Horner, an expert on Irish maps in his own right, has also explored their potential for settlement history, as he did in his paper on two eighteenth-century maps of Carlow town.[11] A. Bonar Law's most recent publication of The Printed Maps of Ireland, 1612–1850 (Dublin, 1998) will make more cartographic source material available for settlement studies.

Reconstructing past settlement patterns

When R. Glasscock, the founder of the Group for the Study of Irish Historic Settlement started his work in Queen's University, Belfast, in the 1960s, he introduced the approach of the British Deserted Medieval Village Research Group (founded in 1952 by M.W. Beresford, J.G. Hurst and others) and of the Moated Sites Research Group (set up in 1971) to Irish settlement studies. Hence the emphasis in his work was on the recording and mapping of relict features of former settlements in the landscape.[12] Many of his students, including B. Graham, G. Barrett and T. Barry, were trained in the method of reconstructing medieval settlement in Ireland with the focus on surviving structures in the field.

The map of medieval settlement in County Meath compiled by B. Graham was, I believe, the first case study of an integrated medieval settlement landscape.[13] His methodological approach was to combine the mapping of medieval relict features in the field with contemporary documentary evidence and to present an interpretation of the settlement pattern by linking it to the feudal system. He also applies this approach to his study of medieval urbanisation in this volume. T. Barry's work, as presented in this book, is largely based on the identification and mapping of medieval settlement structures and their explanation in a historical context.[14] G. Barrett brought the expertise of taking air photographs to her studies and so she succeeded in greatly extending our knowledge of known historic settlement sites.[15]

In the 1970s in Ireland the encouragement to use contemporary documents for the reconstruction of medieval settlement came via H. Jäeger from the University of Würzburg, who worked closely with colleagues in University College Dublin. His work on settlement and environmental history is predominantly based on documentary evidence.[16] In 1975 the Dublin Historic Settlement Group[17] was founded from the Department of Medieval History in University College Dublin, which provided a framework for the interdisciplinary approach to settlement studies in the Dublin area. As honorary secretaries H.B. Clarke and A. Simms, supported by others, have promoted over the last twenty years comparative settlement studies on a European level by inviting continental researchers to lecture on their work.

Important historical work has been done on Viking and Anglo-Norman Dublin by H.B. Clarke as reflected in his map *The Medieval Town in the Modern City* (Dublin, 1978) and in the two companion volumes on *Medieval Dublin* (Dublin, 1990), which he edited. The introduction to the first of these volumes contains a revealing analysis of how the changing political climate in Ireland has influenced research on the early origins of the capital city.[18]

More recently a volume in the comparative studies of viking settlement in Ireland and Scandinavia has been produced jointly by H.B. Clarke, M. Ní Mhaonaigh and R. Ó Floinn, entitled *Ireland and Scandinavia in the Early Viking Age* (Dublin, 1998). Based on the evidence of the written sources F. Kelly has produced a painstaking reconstruction of the early history of Irish agriculture in his recent book *Early Irish Farming* (Dublin, 1997). Familiarity with early medieval Irish documentation made it possible for C. Doherty to reconstruct Gaelic settlement and society in Ireland before the Anglo-Norman invasion and to establish the contemporary European context, as he does in his chapter in this book. M. Herity brought the recording skills of the archaeologist to the study of early medieval settlement in Ireland and contributed to the topic of the layout of early medieval monastic sites.[19] The enigma of the 'rath', the most ubiquitous early medieval Irish settlement form, has been explored by M. Stout, also an author in this book, on the basis of statistical analysis and primary source material. In his book, *The Irish Ringfort* (Dublin, 1997) he provides a model which succeeds in integrating the 'rath' with the other settlement features of the time.

The excavation of Viking sites in the centre of our present-day towns, Dublin and Waterford foremost, facilitated important research which is reflected in a growing body of publications. The Dublin excavations are published jointly by the Royal Irish Academy with the National Museum. The two volumes by P.F. Wallace on *The Viking-Age Buildings of Dublin* (Dublin, 1992) and the volume on *Environment and Economy in Viking Age Dublin* (Dublin, 1993) by S. Geraghty are of special interest for settlement studies. The archaeological excavation reports on Patrick Street, Nicholas Street and Winetavern Street, published in 1997 by C. Walsh, provide an excellent contextual insight into these rescue excavations, as do the volume on *Waterford Excavations* edited by M. Hurley *et al.* in the same year and the four volumes on the archaeological excavations in Temple Bar, Dublin. P.F. Wallace's magisterial article on the archaeological identity of the Hiberno-Norse town in Ireland succeeds in putting the individual reports into an overall context.[20]

Research has been done on medieval manors as reflected in A. Empey's work on medieval settlement in County Tipperary and A. Simms's reconstruction of the former Augustinian grange at Duleek in County Meath, and of the former royal manor of Newcastle Lyons in County Dublin, on the basis of manorial extents whose Latin texts have been published.[21] Also, with emphasis on unpublished contemporary documents as source material for settlement studies M. Hennessy undertook his work on the reconstruction of the geography of the Anglo-Norman colony in Tipperary.[22]

T. McNeill's recent book on *Castles in Ireland: Feudal Power in a Gaelic World* (London, 1997) illustrates how societies with contested space, as in Ireland after the Anglo-Norman invasion of AD 1169 the role of castles is all the more powerful. R. Stalley's volume on *The Cistercian Monasteries of Ireland* (New Haven, 1987) is about the vital parts played by the Cistercians in introducing buildings of a monumental scale and the first gothic architecture to this island. It is an important contribution to the study of medieval ecclesiastical settlement in Ireland.

Historical studies on the Plantation period inevitably focus on the establishment of new settlements. The work by P. Robinson on *The Plantation of Ulster* (Belfast, 1984), by R. Gillespie on *Colonial Ulster. The Settlement of East Ulster, 1600–1641* (Cork, 1985) and by M. McCarthy Morrogh on *The Munster Plantation: English Migration to Southern Ireland, 1583–1641* (Oxford, 1986) contains substantial information on the settlement patterns of the time. The small volume by R. Loeber published in the series of the Group for the Study of Irish Historic Settlement addresses the topic of *The Geography and Practice of English Colonisation in Ireland from 1534 to 1609* (Athlone, 1991). It includes a distribution map of English settlements in seventeenth-century Ireland and their classification.

In spite of the importance of the eighteenth century for the formation of the Irish landscape, most work on this period has been done by architects rather than settlement historians. Therefore, K. Whelan's chapter in this book is of particular importance, focusing as it does on the regional impact of Irish Catholicism in the eighteenth century and on the importance of the social organisation and cultural aspirations of that society on the formation of the landscape. Previously A. Horner gave a good lead with his article on Carton in County Kildare, as a case study of the making of an Irish demesne, as did P.J. Duffy with his reconstruction of the territirial organisation of Gaelic landownership in County Monaghan, and W. Nolan with his exploration of settlement and society on the glens of Wicklow in the eighteenth century.[23] On the basis of a major funded project, B.J. Graham and L.J. Proudfoot have explored the influence of the landlords on planning and urban growth in the eighteenth century and published the preliminary results in the series of the Group for the Study of Irish Historic Settlement under the title *Urban Improvement in Provincial Ireland, 1700–1840* (Athlone, 1994).[24] Proudfoot's monograph on *Urban Patronage and Social Authority. The Management of the Duke of Devonshire's Towns in Ireland, 1764–1891* (Washington, 1995) is an attempt to present the landlord influence in a theoretical framework. L. Cullen has written on the growth of Dublin between 1600 and 1900 and E. Sheridan's work has provided the comparative framework for Dublin as a European capital.[25]

Key texts (1970s to 1990s)

The student of settlement studies in Ireland in the 1970s was fortunate to have as his companion three major textbooks. For many of us T. Orme's *Ireland* (London, 1970), while part of an international series on regional geographies, was the first encounter with settlement history. He succeeded in contextualising the major phases of settlement development in Ireland. F. Mitchell's book *The Irish Landscape* (London, 1976) focused on the environmental history of Ireland based on scientific evidence such as for example pollen analysis. The new edition of this book, prepared jointly with M. Ryan, has the title *The Shell Guide to Reading the Irish Landscape* (Dublin, 1986). F. Aalen's book *Man and the Landscape in Ireland* (London, 1978) was a first statement on the contribution of the historical geographer to the understanding of the making of the Irish cultural landscape through time.

Then there were some important volumes in more specific fields. A. Gailey's *Rural Houses of Northern Ireland* (Edinburgh, 1984) is a good example of work on vernacular housing. H. Glassie's *Passing the Time in Ballymenone: Folklore and History of an Ulster Community* (Dublin, 1986) is probably one of the best books ever written on the rural local geography of Ireland and includes substantial passages on settlement, in particular on the social and cultural significance of house types and land use.

The publication of the volume *An Historical Geography of Ireland* (Dublin, 1993) edited by B. Graham and L. Proudfoot, provides a more recent benchmark for the presentation of historical settlement studies in Ireland. Geographers and historians contributed to the volume, reflecting the interdisciplinary nature of Irish historic settlement studies. T. Barry's book *The Archaeology of Medieval Ireland* (London, 1987) provides a valuable survey of the contribution of archaeology to settlement studies in Ireland.

We must now turn to recent *Festschrifts*. The first two were dedicated to E.E. Evans; one was edited by N. Stephens and R.E. Glasscock with the title *Irish Geographical Studies in Honour of E.E. Evans* (Belfast, 1970) and the other by R.H. Buchanan, E. Jones and D. McCourt with the title *Man and his Habitat: Essays Presented to E.E. Evans* (London, 1971). Almost twenty years later came the volume of essays collected for T. Jones Hughes. This book, edited by W.J. Smyth and K. Whelan and published in 1988 in Cork under the title *Common Ground*, demonstrated a far-ranging use of source material by geographers from the medieval period into the nineteenth century. The next two volumes reflect the interdisciplinary character of settlement research in Ireland as it had become by the 1980s. One entitled *Settlement and Society* (for F.X. Martin, O.S.A.) was edited by J. Bradley and was published in Kilkenny in 1988. The other, entitled *Dublin, City and County: Prehistory to Present* (for J.H. Andrews) was edited by F.H.A. Aalen and K. Whelan and was published in Dublin in 1992. The essays collected and edited by H. Murtagh in commemoration of N.W. English appeared under the title *Irish Midland Studies* (Athlone, 1980). This was a valuable regional study as is the volume edited by E. Rynne on *North Munster Studies* (Limerick, 1967). Another volume to be mentioned is the collection of essays for Kevin Ó Danachair with the delightful title *Gold under the Furze: Studies in Folk Tradition* (Dublin, 1982) edited by A. Gailey and D. Ó hÓgáin, as well as studies in honour of P. Healy, *Dublin and beyond the Pale* (Dublin, 1998), edited by C. Manning.

Particularly enjoyable are the regional monographs. Among those E.E. Evans' *Mourne Country* (Dundalk, 1951) has become a classic in the French mould of writing about regions. W. Nolan's *Fassadinan: Land, Settlement and Society in South-East Ireland, 1600–1850* (Dublin, 1975) is a regional study of a community which was involved in farming as well as in mining. P.J. Duffy's *Landscapes of South Ulster: A Parish Atlas of the Diocese of Clogher* (Belfast, 1993) provides a good example of geography at the parish level. The volume entitled *Cavan: Essays on the History of an Irish County* (Dublin, 1995), edited by R. Gillespie, focuses on the complicated fabric of the past in that county.

The Irish County Histories series, for which W. Nolan acts as general editor, present interdisciplinary essays on the history of Irish counties. They are the Irish equivalent to the English Victoria County History.[26] These volumes contain most valuable contributions to the settlement history of particular regions through time. It would be a challenge to use this material in order to construct major settlement zones over the whole of the country.

Two studies in particular recreate medieval landscapes. One is A.P. Smyth's innovative book on *Celtic Leinster: Towards an Historical Geography of Early Irish Civilisation*, AD 500–1600 (Dublin, 1982) and the other is T.E. McNeill's portrait of *Anglo-Norman Ulster: The History and Archaeology of an Irish Barony*, 1177–1400 (Edinburgh, 1980). And finally we delight in mentioning *The Atlas of the Irish Rural Landscape* (Cork, 1997) edited by F. H. A. Aalen, K. Whelan and M. Stout, which has become a bestseller and succeeded in reaching a large group of people who would otherwise never read about the Irish rural landscape.

Urban settlements in historical perspective

In common with settlement studies in other European countries the emphasis in Ireland was focused, until the 1970s, on rural settlement research. The few exceptions included G. Camblin's work on *The Towns in Ulster* (Belfast, 1951), and the volume which R.A. Butlin edited on *The Development of the Irish Town* (London, 1977).

J. Bradley (Dublin) and B. Graham (Belfast) were perhaps the first to work on the urbanisation of medieval Ireland, producing distribution maps and, in Bradley's case, a long list of valuable individual case studies.[27] The aim of considering medieval urbanisation in Ireland in a European context led to the publication of the two volumes *The Comparative History of Urban Origins in Non-Roman Europe* (Oxford, 1985), edited by H.B. Clarke and A. Simms.

P.J. O'Connor's work *Exploring Limerick's Past: An Historical Geography of Urban Development* (Newcastle West, 1987) provides a good regional case study of urban development. The recent publication of J. Prunty's book *Dublin Slums, 1800–1925* (Dublin, 1997) sets the social problems of the nineteenth century into a spatial context and provides a good counterpart to Mary Daly's previous book on *Dublin: The Deposed Capital* (Cork, 1985).

The study of the historical topography of Irish towns as expressed in town-plans was advanced when, in 1986, the first fascicle of the *Irish Historic Towns Atlas* series, which forms part of a European-wide project of historic towns atlases, was published under the editorship of J.H. Andrews with K.M. Davies as cartographic editor. H.B. Clarke and R. Gillespie joined the editors at later stages. The Irish atlas was set up through the support of the Royal Irish Academy. So far seven fascicles have been published providing a detailed database for future urban research and an interpretation of the history of individual towns. The atlas helps to redress the previous lack of research on Irish towns.[28]

The two volumes on *Irish Country Towns* (Cork, 1994 and 1995), edited by A. Simms and J. Andrews and one on *Irish Cities* (Cork, 1995) edited by H.B. Clarke, were the result of three Thomas Davies lecture series on Irish towns which were broadcast on the radio. They were designed to reach a wider audience. The Local History series emanating from Maynooth since 1996, with R. Gillespie as editor, contributes to our knowledge of individual places.[29] The large number of case studies provided by the historical atlas, the radio-talks and the local history series provides the material for future comparative work.

The promotion of heritage towns by *Bord Failte*, the Government Tourist Board, has given research into the topographical and socio-economic history of Irish towns an immediate importance. And so in co-operation between the Geography Department in University College Dublin and *Bord Failte*, a guide book called *Irish Towns: Guide to Sources* (Dublin, 1998) was produced for anyone who has committed him or herself to explore the rich heritage of Irish towns.[30]

Challenges for the future

A widening of the agenda

We have come to see landscapes as representations of culture. If we learn to read their symbolic meaning, we will better understand the current debate on cultural identities in Ireland. C. Harris encourages us to go in this direction with the following advice: 'The challenge, it seems to me, is to retain our respect for the archives and our steeping in the complexities of particular places, while enlarging our ability to situate these studies in broader contexts of ideas.'[31]

K. Whelan's chapter in this book on the eighteenth century reflects this new discourse. Settlements are no longer looked upon as individual objects of study but 'in a broad sense as a text, a multi-layered document, full of human intentionality, a culture code which embodies different levels of meaning'. The operative word here is meaning. The intention is to understand the iconography of the landscape for what it can tell us about the politically, economically and culturally dominant group in society. In his view settlement is both medium and message, site and symbol, terrain and text.

The study of the meaning of the Irish landscape, both rural and urban, reflects an increasing concern with issues of representation, contested space and identity. N. Johnson has examined how monuments in the Irish countryside reflect nationalism and B. Graham has studied the Protestant representations of Ulster.[32] In a collection of essays *In Search of Ireland* (London, 1997) edited by him, Graham expresses the belief that the political problems in Ireland are created by conflicts and confusions of identity which find expression in the landscape. The younger generation is keen to explore these questions in order to better understand the cultural and political environment in which they live. More work needs to be done in this field.[33]

The concept of continuity and change

A major issue which is related to the question of cultural identity is that of continuity and change in the Irish landscape. There was a period when major changes in the history of Irish settlement were attributed solely to immigrants from abroad from the Neolithic period onwards via the Celts, Vikings, Anglo-Normans to the English. The greatest long-term importance was attached to the Celts, as the cultural identity of the country was linked to their civilisation through language and material culture. In the final chapter of his book, *Pagan Celtic Ireland, the Enigma of the Irish Iron Age* (London 1994), B. Raftery questions how much distinctly Celtic evidence there is in the Irish archaeological material of the Iron Age. Instead of thinking in terms of larger groups of Celtic people immigrating into the country, we should perhaps think of a small elite group who came and influenced artistic style and language.

Similar questions are asked for the period of transition from the Iron Age to the Early Christian period where, rather than focusing on a break in settlement structures, continuities are regarded as an important element. G. Cooney, writing in this book on the continuity from the Iron Age to the Early Christian period says: 'It is perhaps ironic that a time traditionally seen as bringing an end to a major phase of Irish settlement should increasingly be seen to continue trends in settlement form and location.' The evolutionary model, suggesting the re-use of land through different phases of development in the landscape, clearly wins out.

The question of continuity of settlement locations and structures becomes very important in the medieval period in the context of land-holding, the formation of manorial settlement and the process of urbanisation. We are not alone in Ireland in raising the issue of the nature of continuity on settlement sites. C. Dyer wrote in 1990, in an article on the future of medieval rural history studies in England, that archaeologists have come to deny the invasion hypothesis which implied that every change in culture was attributed to the arrival of new waves of immigrants from the Continent.[34] This is a field which needs more attention and it is possible that place-name research might provide some of the answers.

The study of place-names and surnames covers all the diverse aspects of Ireland. The study by S. Ó Catháin and P. O'Flanagan of place-names in a remote townland in County Mayo published in 1975 under the title *The Living Landscape* demonstrates the cultural and socio-economic significance of the place-names and explains the factors involved in their creation.[35] On the basis of place-name analysis W.J. Smyth suggests that the Norse must have had a stronger impact on rural settlement than we believed hitherto. He considers that the seventeenth century is at the heart of understanding modern Ireland and that settlement historians should make more use of the Irish sources for that period. The completed series on Irish place-names published by the Institute of Irish Studies in Belfast is a significant new development in this area.[36]

The landscape of Gaelic Ireland

There is a growing consciousness that our discourse of the medieval settlement history of Ireland is strongly influenced by the availability of Latin sources for those settlements which were established under the Anglo-Normans. In contrast, we are hindered by the scarcity of Gaelic-language sources for settlements in those regions of Ireland which remained under Gaelic control. C. Doherty has used medieval Irish sources in his contribution to this book, as in earlier publications, to explore the socio-economic structure of early Irish history. T. O'Keeffe has recently tried to address the problem of Gaelic settlement in his article on rural settlement and cultural identity in Gaelic Ireland in the medieval period.[37]

In September 1997 R. Loeber (of the University of Pittsburgh), with the support of the Department of Medieval History in Trinity College Dublin, called together a group of people with the aim of discussing how we could increase our knowledge of the landscape of Gaelic Ireland. Loeber's aim was to create a picture of the condition of the country at the eve of the Plantations, yet most of the others in the group were primarily interested in the landscape of Gaelic Ireland in the medieval period.

On this occasion K. Simms (of the Department of Medieval History, Trinity College Dublin) pointed out that the student of Gaelic landscape history was faced with the problem that there were few contemporary physical structures of institutional life. The literary nature of all written sources provided little information on settlements except for land grants and boundaries. Most secular records were kept by members of the Bardic School, who got their elementary training in poetry. Nevertheless the Brehon Law Tracts, published in six volumes, give some information, as do the Bardic poems and hagiographical texts.[38]

On the same occasion L. Fitzpatrick (of the Department of Archaeology, University College Galway) suggested that we should try to construct a territorial map of the Early Christian period, beginning with those areas where we know that the documentation is best. This working group held another meeting in Dublin in 1999 and will continue to do so in the future. The work by A.P. Smyth on Celtic Leinster, which we have already mentioned and the research by C. Doherty, K. Simms and M. Stout have provided fundamental insights, but more research needs to be done into this complex topic.

The long-neglected late medieval period

Curiously we know more about the early origins of Irish towns than their later development. With the exception of some studies, as for example A. O'Brien's work on Dungarvan, we have little information on economic life in medieval towns and the late medieval crisis.[39] The theme was discussed in a European context in 1996 at a conference in Birmingham, where H.B. Clarke spoke on decolonisation and urban decline in late medieval Ireland.[40]

For a long time settlement historians have called for the excavation of a medieval rural settlement in Ireland. At last it looks as if such an undertaking will be possible through the Discovery Programme, a state-sponsored archaeological research institution, which was established in 1991 under the chairmanship of G. Eogan. Its aim is to improve our knowledge of human history in Ireland from its very beginning. The preferred method of surveying for this programme is Geographical Information System, which allows a large amount of data to be measured at speed.[41] This programme is innovative and has already produced several important monographs.

New bodies of source material

The publication of whole archive-depositories as, for example *Guide to Sources for Irish History 1485–1641 in British Archives* by B. Donovan and D. Edwards, published in 1997 by the Irish Manuscript Commission, will open up new sources. Many of the Commission's previously published texts throw light on settlement history and should be explored under that aspect.

Welcome new developments are the publication of the *Ordnance Survey Memoirs for Northern Ireland* by the Institute of Irish Studies in Belfast, as well as the volumes of the Northern Ireland Place-name Project housed in the Department of Celtic in the Queen's University of Belfast. The publication of an archaeological inventory for the country undertaken by the Board of Public Works in Dublin is another important primary source for settlement studies. For eleven counties the work has already been published, and for the others it is in preparation.[42]

The National Monuments Branch has carried out a site and monuments record for the whole of the country. The availability of this record (SMR) on a searchable digital database is a great help in studies of prehistoric and early historic settlement. There is less material available for later settlements and it would be desirable to update the record. J. Bradley was commissioned to carry out the Urban Archaeological Record by the Office of Public Works. It is an important resource for research on medieval towns in Ireland and it is regrettable that the material has not yet been made available in print.

The Buildings of Ireland series provides detailed information on the architectural history of individual buildings in Irish towns. So far two volumes have been published, one on *North-West Ulster* (London, 1979) by A. Rowen and the other on *North-West Leinster* (London, 1993) by C. Casey and A. Rowen.

Comparative studies

The old saying adapted from Kipling, 'What should they know of Ireland who only Ireland know' is still very true. No doubt Irish settlement historians could learn from comparisons with the evolution of settlement in other parts of the Atlantic world, in particular with Scotland and Wales, but also with continental Europe. The comparison of medieval colonisation in Ireland with other colonisation movements in medieval Europe has been attempted.[43]

The two volumes, already mentioned, on *The Comparative History of Urban Origins in Non-Roman Europe* (Oxford, 1985), edited by H.B. Clarke and A. Simms, focus on the origin of towns in early medieval Europe and on urban colonisation in high medieval Europe in that part of Europe which was never occupied by the Romans. The volume with collected essays on *Medieval Frontier Societies* (Oxford, 1989) edited by R. Bartlett and A. Mackay explores culture and politics in its regional dimension in Europe and includes Ireland as one of its case studies. The volumes on *Irland und Europa: Ireland and Europe. The Early Church*,[44] edited by P. Ní Chatháin and M. Richter, link major cultural regions of Europe and contain valuable material on the settlement history of early medieval Ireland. The volume edited by L.M. Cullen and F. Furet on *Ireland and France, 17th–20th Centuries: Towards a Comparative Study of Rural History* (Paris, 1980) focuses on historical aspects of land-holding in these two regions of Europe. Further comparative studies of Irish settlements with similar settlements in other European regions would greatly enhance our understanding of Ireland in a European context.

A practical step in this direction might be to attempt joint meetings between the Group for the Study of Irish Historic Settlement and the Medieval Village Research Group in England and Ireland alternatively, focused on particular topics, as for example: which were the main agents behind the desertion of medieval nucleated settlements in the Later Middle Ages? Equally, some formal contact with the Standing Conference of European Rural Geographers and the Ruralia group, who pursue medieval rural settlement on a European level, could be of benefit for local settlement historians in Ireland. Indeed, such a joint meeting did already happen once, when the Moated Sites Research Group, based in England held a joint meeting with our group in Tipperary in the 1970s. Maybe the time has come to recognise our own questions and answers in the context of the research being carried out by other European settlement historians.

Environmental history

Finally we come to the issue which might very well be the most important one. In the past the focus of research in the medieval and early modern period was very much on land-holding and the spatial organisation of society. The major overall studies written so far on the environment of Ireland in a historic perspective are F. Mitchell's books on the Irish landscape, which we have mentioned already. He was interested in the human situation of early communities in an environmental setting.

In archaeology, environmental studies have become a strong sub-discipline. A good example is B. Raftery's research on wetland sites. He excavated massive oak trackways at Corlea in County Longford.[45] G. Cooney's work on the environment of Neolithic settlements and M. Monk's research on prehistoric vegetation change, dendrochronology and pollen analysis have yielded information on the environmental change in historical periods.[46] It would be desirable, in the future, to co-ordinate these results even more than at present with documentary evidence of environmental conditions.

We should revisit our sources and explore how much they can tell us about the environmental transformation of the Irish landscape through time. F. Kelly's book on *Early Irish Farming* (Dublin, 1993) demonstrates how the Irish law texts of the seventh and eight centuries can yield information on domesticated animals, hunting, flowers, dye-plants, farmhouses, trees and woodland. T. Bolger has recently investigated the *Calendar of Archbishop Alen's Register, c. 1172–1534*, a record of land held by Christ Church Cathedral under this aspect, and found a rewarding amount of information on the management of forest land, the use of turbary and the fertility of the land.[47] The seventeenth-century Down Survey maps give information on environmental conditions with their frequent references to 'red bogs'. I. Leister has given a lead for such studies in her Tipperary book with a map showing the distribution of forest and its degenerate forms based on the Civil Survey.[48]

Real understanding of the processes which brought about environmental change in Ireland can only come from co-operation between the disciplines of archaeology, geography and history with the palynologists and paleo-environmental researchers. Combining these different elements was the strength in the work of the late F. Mitchell and we must continue his tradition.

Conclusion

There are enough challenges to keep the Group for the Study of Irish Historic Settlement busy for a long time to come. Its great strength is its interdisciplinary nature which will facilitate the exploration of the more complex problems of settlement. It appears that the question of the character of the Gaelic landscape and the nature of the transformation from the Gaelic to the Anglo-Norman landscape in Ireland still hold many unanswered questions. For example, in the half century before the Anglo-Normans arrived the term 'castle' (*castle* or *caislen*) appears in Gaelic vocabulary, hinting that the Irish invented the stone castle for themselves before the arrival of the colonisers in 1169.[49] It is not easy to determine how much the Anglo-Normans built on their predecessors' achievements and how much their institutions and settlements were a complete innovation for the country.[50] The other major issue for future research must be environmental change, which would connect with the environmental problems of our own time. And last but not least, there is the wide field of urban studies, where different aspects of the urban society should be studied in their topographical context.

When faced with the list of outstanding problems in Irish settlement history, it might be helpful if the Group for the Study of Irish Historic Settlement chose as the topic for their annual meeting, not only a regional theme, as has happened so far, but also one of the outstanding problems areas which we have identified.[51]

Whatever we decide to do, we will look at settlements as part of the continuous remaking of the Irish landscape. We will approach the different aspects of settlement history in Ireland with an inquisitive mind, informed by ever changing intellectual climates, but always drawn by the spirit which W.B. Yeats evoked:

> And send imagination forth
> Under the day's declining beam, and call
> Images and memories
> From ruin or from ancient trees,
> For I would ask a question of them all.

(W.B. Yeats 1933)

Notes

1 See also R.H. Buchanan, 'Historical geography of Ireland pre-1700', in the Jubilee Volume of *Irish Geography* (1984), pp. 129–148. A. Simms, 'Genetische Siedlungsforschung in Irland mit besonderer Berücksichtigung der Siedlungsgeographie', in K. Fehn *et al.* (eds), *Genetische Siedlungsforschung in Mitteleuropa und seinen Nachbarräumen* (Bonn, 1988), pp. 319–343. A. Buttimer, 'Gatekeeping geography through National Independence: stories from Harvard and Dublin', in *Erdkunde*, 49, 1 (1995), pp. 3–16.

2 Both came from the Institute of Geography and Earth Sciences at the University of Aberystwyth, where they studied anthropogeography under H.J. Fleure. An appreciation of T. Jones Hughes's work can be found in J.H. Andrews, 'Jones Hughes's Ireland: A literary quest', in W.J. Smyth and K. Whelan (eds) *Common Ground* (Cork, 1988) pp.1–21, and in R. Glasscock, 'E.E. Evans: 1905–1989', in *Journal of Historical Geography*, 17, 1 (1991), pp. 87–91.

3 T.W. Freeman, *Pre-Famine Ireland* (London, 1957).

4 R.H. Buchanan, 'Rural settlement in Ireland', in N. Stephens and R.E. Glasscock (eds), *Irish Geographical Studies* (Belfast, 1970), pp. 146–160. D. McCourt, 'The dynamic quality of Irish rural settlement', in R.H. Buchanan, E. Jones and D. McCourt (eds), *Man and His Habitat* (London, 1971). B. Proudfoot, 'The economy of the Irish rath', in *Medieval Archaeology*, 5, pp.94–122.

5 The work of these scholars is listed under the relevant sub-sections.

6 Evans had a strong interest in the prehistoric period and in 1953 he published jointly with M. Gaffikin a paper on: 'Megaliths and raths', in *Irish Naturalists Journal*, 5, pp. 242–252, which was apparently the first study of prehistoric settlement patterns in Ireland. He succeeded in supplying this kind of research with institutional backing when, in 1961, with governmental support, he founded the Ulster Folk-Museum in Belfast, and in 1968 the Institute for Irish Studies at the Queen's University in Belfast. He presented a synthesis of his own work in his books *Irish Folk Ways* (1957) and *Irish Heritage* (1973) and particularly so in his last book *The Personality of Ireland* (Cambridge, 1973).

7 Among the most influential of Jones Hughes's articles were the following: T. Jones Hughes, 'Society and settlement in nineteenth century Ireland', in *Irish Geography*,

5, 2, pp. 79–96. T. Jones Hughes, 'Town and baile in Irish place-names', in N. Stephens and R.E. Glasscock (eds) *Irish Geographical Studies in Honour of E.E. Evans* (Belfast, 1970) pp. 244–258. T. Jones Hughes, 'The large farm in nineteenth century Ireland', in A. Gailey and D. Ó hÓgáin (eds), *Gold under the Furze: Studies in Folk Tradition Presented to Caoimhín Ó Damachair* (Dublin, 1982) pp. 93–100.

8 K. Whelan, 'The Catholic Parish', in *Irish Geography* (1983), pp. 1–15.

9 An appreciation of J.H. Andrews's work is found in K. Whelan: 'Beyond a paper landscape: J.H. Andrews and Irish historical geography', in F.H.A. Aalen and K. Whelan (eds) *Dublin City and County: from Prehistory to Present* (Dublin, 1992), pp. 379–424.

10 His hitherto unpublished critical papers were highly influential. They include: 'The ethnic factor in Irish historical geography' (1974); 'The geographical study of the Irish past' (1977); 'Space, time and subject matter in Irish settlement studies' (1977) and 'Villages in pre-plantation Ireland: the cartographic evidence' (1989).

11 A. Horner, 'Two eighteenth-century maps of Carlow town', in *Proceedings of the Royal Irish Academy*, 78C, 5 (1978), pp. 115–126.

12 R.E. Glasscock, 'The study of deserted medieval settlement in Ireland', in M.W. Beresford and J.W. Hurst (eds), *Deserted Medieval Village Studies* (London, 1971), pp. 279–301.

13 B. Graham, 'Anglo-Norman settlement in County Meath', in *Proceedings of the Royal Irish Academy*, 75C, 11 (1975), pp. 223–248.

14 T. B. Barry, *Medieval Moated Sites of South-East England*, British Archaeological Reports, 35 (Oxford, 1977). His research students continue this tradition, as the following list of publications on medieval settlement structures will show: C.T. Cairns, *Irish Tower Houses: A County Tipperary Case Study* (Athlone 1987); A. Jordan, 'Date, chronology and evolution of the County Wexford Tower House', in *Journal of the Wexford Historical Society*, 13 (1990–1), pp. 30–82; H. Long, 'Three settlements of Gaelic Wicklow: Rathgall, Balinacoar and Glendalough', in K. Hannigan and W. Nolan (eds), *Wicklow, History and Society* (Dublin 1994), pp. 237–265; M. McAuliffe, 'The use of tower houses and fastnesses in the Desmond rebellion 1565–1583', in *Journal of the Kerry Archaeological and Historical Society*, 24 (1991), pp. 105–112.

15 G.F. Barrett, 'Problems of spatial and temporal continuity of rural settlement in Ireland, AD 400–1169', in *Journal of Historical Geography*, 8 (1982), pp. 245–260.

16 H. Jäeger knew C. Darby (London and Cambridge) personally and was well aware of his work on reconstructing the geography of medieval England, based on the great Doomsday book, the popular name of the great survey of England completed in 1086. Jäeger's own approach is well documented in the following article: H. Jäeger, 'Land use in Medieval Ireland', in *Irish Economic and Social History*, x (1983), pp. 51–65.

17 The Dublin Historic Settlement Group was founded on the initiative of D. Bethell and A. Simms under the patronage of F.X. Martin, O.S.A.

18 It is intended to publish H.B. Clarke's medieval section of the Dublin fascicle in the *Irish Historic Towns Atlas* series in 2000.

19 M. Herity, 'The layout of Irish early Christian monasteries', in P. Ní Chatháin and M. Richter (eds), *Ireland and Europe: The Early Church*, (Stuttgart, 1984), pp. 105–116.

20 L. Simpson, Excavating at Isolde's Tower, Dublin, No. 1, Dublin, 1994; L. Simpson, *Excavations at Essex Street West*, Dublin, No. 2, Dublin, 1995; M. Gowan and G. Scally, *Exchange Street Upper/Parliament Street, Dublin*, No. 4, Dublin, 1996; L. Simpson, *Temple Bar West*, No. 5, Dublin, 1999; P.F. Wallace, 'The archaeological identity of the Hiberno-Norse town', *Journal of the Royal Society of Antiquities of Ireland*, 122, pp. 35–66.

21 C.A. Empey, 'Medieval Knocktopher: A study in manorial settlement', in *Old Kilkenny Review*, 2 (1982), pp. 329–342. A. Simms, 'Rural settlement in medieval Ireland: The example of the royal manors of Newcastle-Lyons and Esker in South County Dublin', in B.K. Roberts and R.E. Glasscock (eds), *Villages, Fields and Frontiers*, British Archaeological Reports, No. 185 (Oxford, 1983), pp. 133–152. A. Simms, 'The geography of Irish manors: The example of the Llanthony cells of Duleek and Colp in County Meath', in J. Bradley (ed.), *Settlement and Society in Medieval Ireland* (Kilkenny, 1989), pp. 291–315.

22 M. Hennessy, 'Manorial organisation in early thirteenth-century Tipperary', in *Irish Geography*, 29, 2 (1996), pp. 116–125, and 'The Anglo-Norman colony in County Tipperary, c. 1185–c. 1540', PhD Thesis (University College Dublin, 1998).

23 A. Horner, 'Carton, Co. Kildare: A case-study of the making of an Irish demesne', in *Irish Georgian Society*, 18 (Dublin, 1975), pp. 45–104. See also P.J. Duffy, 'The territorial organisation of Gaelic landownership', in *Irish Geography* (1981), pp. 1–26. W. Nolan, 'Society and settlement in the valley of Glenasmole c. 1750–c. 1900', in Aalen and Whelan (eds), *Dublin: City and County*, pp. 181–228.

24 See also: B.J. Graham and L.J. Proudfoot, 'Landlords, planning and urban growth in eighteenth- and early nineteenth-century Ireland', in *Journal of Urban History*, XVIII, 3 (1992), pp. 308–329.

25 L. Cullen, 'The growth of Dublin 1600–1900: character and heritage', in F.H.A. Aalen and K. Whelan (eds), *Dublin: City and County* (Dublin, 1992), pp. 252–277. E. Sheridan, 'Dublin and Berlin: A comparative geography of two eighteenth-century European capitals', PhD thesis (University College Dublin, 1993).

26 The following volumes of the Irish County History Series have appeared so far: *Tipperary* by W. Nolan and K. Whelan (eds) (Dublin, 1985); *Wexford* by W. Nolan and K. Whelan (eds) (Dublin, 1987); *Kilkenny* by W. Nolan and K. Whelan (eds) (Dublin, 1990); *Dublin* by F.H.A. Aalen and W. Nolan (eds) (Dublin, 1992); *Waterford* by W. Nolan, T. Power and D. Cowman (eds) (Dublin, 1992); *Cork* by P. O'Flanagan and C. Buttimer (eds) (Dublin, 1993), *Wicklow* by K. Hannigan and W. Nolan (eds) (Dublin, 1994); *Donegal* by W. Nolan, L. Ronayne and M. Dunlevy (eds) (Dublin, 1995); *Galway* by G. Moran and R. Gillespie (eds) (Dublin, 1996); *Down* by L. Proudfoot (ed.) (Dublin, 1997); *Offaly*, by W. Nolan and T. O'Neill (eds) (Dublin, 1998).

27 B.J. Graham, 'The evolution of urbanisation in medieval Ireland', in *Journal of Historical Geography*, 5 (1979), pp. 111–125. J. Bradley, 'Planned Anglo-Norman towns in Ireland', in H.B. Clarke and A. Simms (eds), *The Comparative History of Urban Origins in Non-Roman Europe*, Vol. 2 (Oxford, 1985), pp. 411–467.

28 *Irish Historic Towns Atlas* series, edited by A. Simms, H.B. Clarke, R. Gillespie with J.H. Andrews as consultant editor and M. Davies as cartographic editor, published by the Royal Irish Academy. Publications so far include: *No. 1: Kildare* by J. Andrews (Dublin, 1986); *No. 2: Carrickfergus* by P. Robinson (Dublin, 1986); *No. 3: Bandon* by P. O'Flanagan (Dublin, 1988); *No. 4: Kells* by A. Simms with K. Simms (Dublin, 1990); *No. 5: Mullingar* by J. Andrews with M. Davies (Dublin, 1992); *No. 6: Athlone* by H. Murtagh (Dublin, 1994); *No. 7: Maynooth* by A. Horner (Dublin, 1995); *No. 8: Downpatrick* by R. Buchanan with T. Wilson (Dublin, 1997); *No. 9: Bray* by K.M. Davies (Dublin, 1999).

29 Maynooth Local History Studies, publications with an impact on settlement studies: D. Broderick, *The Dublin–Dunleer Turnpike, 1731–1855* (Dublin, 1996); W. Gacquin, *Roscommon before the Famine, 1749–1845* (Dublin, 1996); B.T. King, *Carlow: Manor and Town, 1674–1721* (Dublin, 1997); B. O'Dalaigh, *Ennis in the Eighteenth Century* (Dublin, 1995); C. Smith, *Dalkey: Society and Economy in a Small Medieval Irish Town* (Dublin, 1996); J. Crawford, *St Catherine's Parish, Dublin 1840–1900* (Dublin, 1996); N. McHugh, *Drogheda Before the Famine* (Dublin, 1998); J. Gilligan, *Graziers and*

Grasslands (Dublin, 1998); L. Clare, *Victorian Bray* (Dublin, 1998); M. Lambe, *A Tipparary Landed Estate* (Dublin, 1998).

30 W. Nolan and A. Simms, (eds), in co-operation with R. Ni Neill and Y. Whelan, *Irish Towns: Guide to Sources* (Dublin 1998).

31 C. Harris, 'Power, modernity, and historical geography', in *Annals of the Association of American Geographers* (1991), pp. 671–683.

32 B. Graham, 'No place of the mind: Contested Protestant representations of Ulster', in *Ecumene* 1, 3 (1994), 257–281. N. Johnson, 'Sculpting heroic histories: Celebrating the centenary of the 1798 rebellion in Ireland', in *Transactions of the Institute of British Geographers*, NS 19 (1994), pp. 78–93.

33 See Y. Whelan, 'Turning space into place: the power of street nomenclature', in *Baile* (Dublin, 1997), pp. 70–74. Y. Whelan, 'Reading the city as text: the iconography of independent Dublin', PhD thesis (University College Dublin, forthcoming).

34 C. Dyer, 'The past, the present and the future in medieval rural history', in *Rural History*, 1, 1 (1990), pp. 37–49.

35 S. Ó Catháin and P. O'Flanagan *The Living Landscape, Kilgalligan, Erris, County Mayo* (Dublin 1975).

36 G. Toner and M.B. Ó Mainnín, *Place-names of Northern Ireland Vol. 1; County Down 1: Newry and South-West Down* (Belfast 1992).

37 C. Doherty, 'The monastic town in early medieval Ireland', in H.B. Clarke and A. Simms, (eds), *The Comparative History of Urban Origins* (Oxford, 1985), pp. 45–76. C. Doherty, 'Exchange and trade in early medieval Ireland', in *Journal of the Royal Society of Antiquaries of Ireland*, 110 (1980), pp. 67–89. T. O'Keeffe, 'Rural settlement and cultural identity in Gaelic Ireland, 1000–1500', in *Ruralia* I, Pamatky Archeologicke-Supplementum 5 (Praha, 1996), pp. 142–153.

38 K. Simms, 'Nomadry in medieval Ireland: The origins of the *Oreaght* or *Caoraigheacht*', in *Peritia*, Vol. 5 (1980), pp. 379–391.

39 A. O'Brien, 'Development and evolution of the medieval port and borough of Dungarvan, County Waterford *c*. 1200–*c*. 1530', in *Cork Historical and Archaeological Society Journal*, XCII (1987), pp. 85–94.

40 H.B. Clarke, 'Decolonisation and the dynamics of urban decline in Ireland, 1300–1500', in T.R. Slater, (ed.), *Towns in Decline* (forthcoming).

41 G. Eogan, 'The Discovery Programme: Initiation, consolidation and development', in *Negentiende Kron-Voorrdraacht*, edited by W. H. Metz, Stichting Nederlands Museum voor Anthropologie en Praehistorie (Amsterdam, 1997).

42 The following volumes have been published so far: *Archaeological Inventory of County Monaghan* by A.L. Brindley (Dublin, 1986); *Archaeological Inventory of County Carlow* by A.L. Brindley (Dublin, 1993); *Archaeological Inventory of County Louth* by V.M. Buckley (Dublin, 1986); *Archaeological Survey of County Louth* by V.M. Buckley and P.D. Sweetman (Dublin, 1991); *Archaeological Inventory of County Galway* by P. Gosling (Dublin, 1993); *Archaeological Survey of County Donegal* by B. Lacy (Lifford, 1983); *Archaeological Inventory of County Meath* by M.J. Moore (Dublin, 1987); *Archaeological Inventory of County Wexford* by M.J. Moore (Dublin, 1995); *Archaeological Inventory of County Cavan* by P.O. Donovan (Dublin, 1995); *Archaeological Inventory of County Cork, Vol. 1, West Cork* by D. Power (Dublin, 1992); *Archaeological Inventory of County Cork, Vol. 2, East and South Cork* by D. Power (Dublin, 1994); *Archaeological Inventory of County Laois* by P.D. Sweetman (Dublin, 1995); *Archaeological Survey of the Barony of Ikerrin* by G.T. Stout (Dublin, 1984); *North Kerry Archaeological Survey* by C. Toal (Dingle, 1995).

43 A. Simms, 'Core and periphery in medieval Europe: The Irish experience in a wider context', in S.J. Smyth and K. Whelan, (eds), *Common Ground* (Cork, 1988), pp. 22–40. R. Bartlett, 'The high medieval colonial aristocracies of the medieval

ages', in R. Bartlett and A. Mackay (eds), *Medieval Frontier Societies* (Oxford, 1989), pp. 23–47.

44 P. Ní Chatháin and M. Richter (eds), *Irland und Europa im Früheren Mittelalter/ Ireland and Europe in the early Middle Ages* (Stuttgart, 1996); H. Lowe, *Die Iren und Europa im Früheren Mittelalter* (1982); P. Ní Chatháin and M. Richter, *Irland und Europa / Ireland and Europe* (Stuttgart, 1984); Ní Chatháin, P. and Richter, M., *Irland und die Christenheit / Ireland and Christendom* (Stuttgart, 1987).

45 B. Raftery, *Trackways Through Time* (Rush, Co. Dublin, 1990). B. Raftery (ed.), *Trackway Excavations in the Mountdillon Bogs, Co. Longford, 1985–1991*, Irish Achaeological Wetland Unit Transactions, Vol. 3 (Dublin, 1996).

46 G. Cooney and E. Grogan, *Irish Prehistory: A Social Perspective* (Dublin, 1994). M. Monk, 'Archaeological study of samples from pipeline sites', in J.H. Renfrew (ed.), *New Light on Early Farming: Recent Developments in Palaeoethnobotany* (Edinburgh, 1991), pp. 315–328.

47 T. Bolger, 'The environmental history of County Dublin in the medieval period (based on Archbishop Alen's Register c. 1172–1534, edited by C. McNeill, Dublin, 1950)', M.Phil. thesis (University College Dublin, 1998).

48 I. Leister, *Das Werden der Agrarlandschaft in der Graftchaft Tipperary (Ireland)*, Marburger Geographische Schrifter, 18 (Marburg, 1963), p. 66.

49 Quoted after T. O'Keeffe, 'Rural settlement and cultural identity in Gaelic Ireland, 1000–1500', in *Ruralia I* (Prague, 1996), pp. 142–53.

50 This issue appears like a leitmotif in S. Duffy's book on *Ireland in the Middle Ages* (Dublin, 1994).

51 This is how the working-group for Historic Settlement Studies in Central Europe, co-ordinated since 1976 by Professor K. Fehn in Bonn, works: the group meets annually to discuss a particular theme, which will be explored by invited speakers. Over the last five years these themes have included the topic of 'Settlements in mountain regions'; 'Origin and development of smaller towns'; 'Settlement desertion' and 'Breaks in the development of the cultural landscape'. With regard to these topics the aspect of 'space–time comparison' is important. The lectures represented at these meetings are published in the annual journal *Siedlungsforschung (Archäologie–Geschichte–Geographie)* in Bonn.

BIBLIOGRAPHY

Compiled by Ruth Johnson

Manuscript sources

Calendar of the Patent and Close Rolls of Chancery in Ireland, from the 18th to the 45th of Queen Elizabeth.

Calendar of Justiciary Rolls, Ireland.

Government Publications Office, *Housing Statistics Bulletins.*

Historic Manuscripts Commission, *Salisbury MSS.*

Lambeth Palace Library, London, Ms. 1742, *Incomplete abstract of 1732 census of Ireland Barony by Barony.*

Monaghan Archive Office, *Clogher Diocesan Census* (1985) Unpublished manuscripts.

Municipal Corporations in Ireland, First Report of Commissioners of Inquiry H.C. 1835, xxvii, xxviii, 1836, xxiv.

National Archives Ms. 2466, *A Census of the Diocese of Elphin in 1749.*

National Library of Ireland, 21.F.55, *Maps of Co. Leix.*

National Library of Ireland, MS 3137, *Thomas Phillips Military Survey of Ireland 1685.*

National Library of Ireland, Ms. 20,397, C. O'Hara *An Account of County Sligo in the Eighteenth Century.*

National Library of Ireland, Uncatalogued, *Lismore Papers.*

Public Records Office, London, *Calendar of State Papers Ireland, 1596–7.*

Public Records Office, London, *Calendar of State Papers, Ireland* HMSO, London.

Public Records Office, London, S.P. 62, 63., *State Papers, Ireland, Philip and Mary to Elizabeth.*

Public Records Office, London, MPF, *Maps and Plans.*

Royal Irish Academy, *Transcripts of Irish Municipal Charters.*

Royal Society Library, London, *An account of the Roman clergy according to a return made April 1698* Mss. Letter.

Statute Rolls Edw. IV (II)

Trinity College Library, Dublin, MS 1209, *Hardiman Atlas.*

Printed and secondary sources

Aalen, F.H.A. (1978) *Man and the Landscape in Ireland* (London: Academic Press).

Aalen, F.H.A. (1983) 'Perspectives on the Irish landscape in prehistory and history', in T. Reeves-Smyth and F. Hamond (eds) *Landscape Archaeology in Ireland* (Oxford B.A.R.) Brit. Ser. 116: 357–377.

248

Aalen, F.H.A. (1992) 'Ireland', in C.G. Pooley (ed.) *Housing Strategies in Europe 1880–1930* (Leicester: Leicester University Press).

Aalen, F.H.A. (ed.) (1985) *The Future of the Irish Rural Landscape* (Dublin: Trinity College).

Aalen, F.H.A. and Whelan, K. (eds) (1992) *Dublin City and County from Prehistory to Present: Studies in Honour of J.H. Andrews* (Dublin: Geography Publications).

Aalen, F.H.A. and Whelan, K. (eds) (1992) *Irish County History Series: Dublin* (Dublin).

Aalen, F.H.A., Whelan, K. and Stout, M. (eds) (1997) *Atlas of the Irish Rural Landscape* (Cork: University Press).

Adams, B. (1975–6) 'The diamonds of Ulster and Pennsylvania', in *Ulster Folk and Transport Yearbook* 18–20.

Addleshaw, G.W.O. (1953) *The Beginnings of the Parochial System* (York: University of York, Borthwick Institute of Historical Research, St Anthony's Hall Publications No. 3).

Addleshaw, G.W.O. (1954) *The Development of the Parochial System from Charlemagne (768–814) to Urban II (1088–1099)* (York: University of York, Borthwick Institute of Historical Research, St Anthony's Hall Publications No. 6).

Addleshaw, G.W.O. (1963) *The Pastoral Organisation of the Modern Dioceses of Durham and Newcastle in the Time of Bede* (Jarrow Lecture, Jarrow on Tyne).

Andrews, J.H. (1970) 'Geography and government in Elizabethan Ireland', in N. Stephens and R.E. Glasscock (eds) *Irish Geographical Studies in Honour of E. Estyn Evans* (Belfast: Department of Geography, Queen's University).

Andrews, J.H. (1974) 'The ethnic factor in Irish historical geography', unpublished paper presented to the Annual Conference of Irish Geographers.

Andrews, J.H. (1974) 'The maps of escheated counties of Ulster 1609–10', *Proceedings of the Royal Irish Academy* 74C: 133–170.

Andrews, J.H. (1975) *A Paper Landscape* (Oxford: Clarendon Press).

Andrews, J.H. (1976) 'The making of Irish geography, I: William Petty', *Irish Geography* 9: 100–103.

Andrews, J.H. (1977) 'Space, time and subject matter in Irish settlement studies', unpublished lecture.

Andrews, J.H. (1977) 'The geographical study of the Irish past', unpublished paper presented to the Annual Conference of Irish Geographers.

Andrews, J.H. (1977) *Irish Maps* (Dublin: Eason and Son Ltd).

Andrews, J.H. (1980) 'Science and cartography in Ireland. William and Samuel Molyneux', *Proceedings of the Royal Irish Academy* 80C: 231–250.

Andrews, J.H. (1980) 'Henry Pratt, surveyor of Kerry estates', *Journal of the Kerry Archaeological and Historical Society* 13: 5–38.

Andrews, J.H. (1985) *Plantation Acres* (Belfast: Ulster Historical Foundation).

Andrews, J.H. (1986) 'Land and people c. 1780', in T.W. Moody and W.E. Vaughan (eds), *New History of Ireland, IV* (Oxford: Clarendon Press for the Royal Irish Academy), 236–264.

Andrews, J.H. (1986) *Kildare* (Dublin: Irish Historic Towns Atlas).

Andrews, J.H. (1987) 'The struggle for Ireland's public commons', in P. O'Flanagan, P. Ferguson and K. Whelan (eds) *Rural Ireland 1600–1900: Modernisation and Change* (Cork: Cork University Press), 1–23.

Andrews, J.H. (1988) 'Jones Hughes's Ireland: a literary quest', in W.J. Smyth and K. Whelan (eds) *Common Ground* (Cork).

Andrews, J.H. (1997) *Shapes of Ireland* (Dublin: Geography Publications).

Andrews, J.H. (1998) *Interpreting the Irish Landscape: Explorations in Settlement History* (Irish Settlement Studies, No. 6, forthcoming).

Andrews, J.H. (forthcoming) 'The geographical element in Irish history', in *New History of Ireland, I.*

Andrews, J.H. with Davies, M. (1992) *Irish Historic Towns Atlas: Mullingar* (Dublin).

Andrews, K.R., Canny, N.P. and Hair, P.E.H. (eds) (1978) *The Westward Enterprise: English Activities in Ireland, the Atlantic and America, 1480–1650* (Liverpool: Liverpool University Press).

Anon (1912–14) 'Report on the state of popery in Ireland', in *Archivium Hibernicum* Vol. I (1912), 10–27; Vol. II (1913), 108–156; Vol. III (1914), 124–158; Vol. IV (1914), 131–177.

Applebaum, S. (1972) 'Roman Britain', in H.P.R. Finberg, *The Agrarian History of England and Wales, Vol. II* (Cambridge: Cambridge University Press), 264–265.

ApSimon, A.M. (1969) 'The earlier Bronze Age in the north of Ireland', *Ulster Journal of Archaeology* 3rd Ser. 32: 28–72.

ApSimon, A.M. (1976) 'Ballynagilly and the beginning and end of the Irish Neolithic', in S.J. de Laet (ed.) *Acculturation and Continuity in Atlantic Europe* (Bruges, Dissertationes Archaeologicae Gandenses) 16: 15–30.

Baillie, M.G.L. (1979) 'An interim statement on dendrochronology at Belfast', *Ulster Journal of Archaeology* 42: 72–84.

Baillie, M.G.L. (1986) 'The central post from Navan Fort', *Emania* 1: 20–21.

Baillie, M.G.L. (1988) 'Marker dates – turning prehistory into history', *Archaeology Ireland* 2: 154–155.

Baillie, M.G.L. (1991) 'Dating the past', in M. Ryan (ed.) *The Illustrated Archaeology of Ireland* (Dublin: Country House), 15–19.

Baillie, M.G.L. and Munro, M.A.R. (1988) 'Irish tree rings, Santorini and volcanic dust veils', *Nature* 332: 1–3.

Bange, F. (1984) 'L'ager et la villa: structures du paysage et du peuplement dans la région mâcconaise à la fin du Haut Moyen Âge (ixe–xie siècles)', *Annales, Économies, Sociétés, Civilisations* 39, 3: 529–569.

Bannon, M.J. (ed.) (1989) *Planning: The Irish Experience* (Dublin: Wolfhound).

Barker, G. (1985) *Prehistoric Farming in Europe* (Cambridge: Cambridge University Press).

Barnard, T.C. (1973) 'Planters and policies in Cromwellian Ireland', in *Past and Present* 61: 31–69.

Barnard, T.C. (1975) *Cromwellian Ireland: English Government and Reform in Ireland 1649–1660* (Oxford: Oxford University Press).

Barrett, G. (1972) 'The ring-fort: a study in settlement geography with special reference to southern County Donegal and the Dingle area, County Kerry', unpublished PhD thesis (Queen's University of Belfast).

Barrett, G. (1982) 'Problems of spatial and temporal continuity of rural settlement in Ireland, AD 400 to 1169', *Journal of Historical Geography* 8, 3: 245–260.

Barrett, G. (1982) 'Ring-fort settlement in County Louth: sources, patterns and landscapes', *Journal of the County Louth Archaeological and Historical Society* 20, 2: 77–95.

Barrett, G. (1983). 'The reconstruction of proto-historic landscapes using aerial photographs: case studies in County Louth', *Journal of the County Louth Archaeological and Historical Society* 20, 3: 215–236.

Barrett, G. and Graham, B. (1975) 'Some considerations concerning the dating and distribution of ringforts in Ireland', *Ulster Journal of Archaeology* 39: 33–45.

Barry, J.V.L. (ed.) (1969) *A discourse of the true causes why Ireland was never entirely subdued, nor brought under obedience of the crowne of England until the beginnings of his majesties happie reigne* by J. Davies (Shannon: Irish University Press).

Barry, T. (1987) *The Archaeology of Medieval Ireland* (London, reprinted 1994).

Barry, T.B. (1993) 'Late medieval Ireland: the debate on social and economic transformation, 1350–1550', in B.J. Graham and L.J. Proudfoot (eds) *An Historical Geography of Ireland* (London: Academic Press), 108.

Bartlett, R. (1989) 'The high medieval colonial aristocracies of the medieval ages', in R. Bartlett and A. Mackay (eds) *Medieval Frontier Societies* (Oxford), 23–47.

Bartlett, R. and Mackay, A. (1989) *Medieval Frontier Societies* (Oxford).

Bartlett, T. and Hayton, D. (eds) (1979) *Penal Era and Golden Age: Essays in Irish History 1690–1900* (Belfast: W. and G. Baird, for Ulster Historical Foundation).

Bateson, J.D. (1973) 'Roman material from Ireland: a reconsideration', *Proceedings of the Royal Irish Academy* 73C: 21–97.

Bell, C. and Bell, R. (1969) *City Fathers: The Early History of Town Planning in Britain* (London: Barrie and Rockliffe, the Cressett Press).

Bell, R. (1804) *A Description of the Conditions and Manners of the Peasantry of Ireland such as they were Between the Years 1789–1790* (London), 43.

Bennett, I. (1989) 'The settlement pattern of ringforts in County Wexford', in *Journal of the Royal Society of Antiquaries of Ireland* 119: 50–61.

Beresford, M.W. (1967) *New Towns of the Middle Ages* (London).

Beresford, M.W. and Hurst, J.G. (eds) (1971) *Deserted Medieval Villages* (London: Lutterworth Press).

Bergin, O. (1925) 'The passing of the old order', *Studies* 14: 403–407.

Berry, H.F. (1915) *A History of the Royal Dublin Society* (London: Longmans, Green and Co).

Bieler, L. (ed.) (1963) *The Irish Penitentials*, Scriptores Latini Hiberniae 5: 54, 56 (Dublin: Institute for Advanced Studies).

Bieler, L. (1979) *Patrician texts in the Book of Armagh*, Scriptores Latini Hiberniae 10 (Dublin: Institute for Advanced Studies).

Binchy, D.A. (ed.) (1941) *Crith Gablach* (Dublin: Institute for Advanced Studies, reprinted 1970).

Binchy, D.A. (1954) 'Secular institutions', in M. Dillon (ed.) *Early Irish Society* (Dublin: Thomas Davies Lecture Series), 52–65.

Binchy, D.A. (1962). 'The passing of the old order', in B. Ó Cuív (ed.) *Proceedings of the International Congress of Celtic Studies Held in Dublin, 6–10 July 1959* (Dublin), 119–132.

Binchy, D.A. (1975) 'Irish history and Irish law', *Studia Hibernica* 15: 7–36.

Binchy, D.A. (1978) *Corpus Iuris Hibernici ad fidem manuscriptorum i–iv* (Dublin: Institiuid Ard-Leinn).

Binford, L.R. (1980) 'Willow smoke and dogs' tails: hunter-gatherer settlement system and archaeological site form', *American Antiquity* 45: 4–20.

Binford, L.R. (1983) *In Pursuit of the Past* (London: Thames and Hudson).

Bitel, L. (1990) *Isle of the Saints: Monastic Settlement and Christian Community in Early Ireland*, 2nd edn (London: Cornell University Press).

Blair, J. (1988) 'Minster churches in the landscape', in D. Hooke (ed.) *Anglo-Saxon Settlements* (Oxford: Basil Blackwell), 35–58.

Bliss, A. (1976) 'The development of the English language in early modern Ireland', in T.W. Moody, F.X. Martin and F.J. Byrne (eds) *A New History of Ireland, III* (Oxford: University Press), 554–558.

Bonar Law, A. (1998) *The Printed Maps of Ireland, 1612–1850* (Dublin).

Bonsall, C. (ed.) (1989) *The Mesolithic in Europe* (Edinburgh: John Donald).

Boserup. E. (1965) *The Conditions of Agricultural Growth* (London: Allen and Unwin).

Bottingheimer, K. (1985) 'The failure of the Reformation in Ireland: une question bien posée', *Journal of Ecclesiastical History* 6, 2: 196–207.

Bourke, E. (1989) 'Stoneyford: a first-century Roman burial from Ireland', *Archaeology Ireland* 3, 2: 56–57.

Bradley, J. (1985) 'Planned Anglo-Norman towns in Ireland', in H.B. Clarke and A. Simms (eds) *The Comparative History of Urban Origins in Non-Roman Europe* (Oxford), 411–467.

Bradley, J. (1985) 'The medieval towns of Tipperary', in W. Nolan (ed.) *Tipperary: History and Society* (Dublin), 34–59.

Bradley, J. (1988) 'The interpretation of Scandinavian settlement in Ireland', in J. Bradley (ed.) *Settlement and Society in Medieval Ireland: Studies Presented to F. X. Martin, o.s.a.* (Kilkenny), 49–78.

Bradley, J. (ed.) (1988) *Settlement and Society in Medieval Ireland: Studies Presented to F.X. Martin, o.s.a.* (Kilkenny: Boethius).

Bradley, J. (1990) 'The early development of the town of Kilkenny', in W. Nolan and K. Whelan (eds) *Kilkenny: History and Society* (Dublin), 63–73.

Bradley, J. (1990) 'The role of town-plan analysis in the study of the medieval Irish town', in T.R. Slater (ed.) *The Built Form of Western Cities* (Leicester) 39–59.

Bradley, J. and Halpin, A. (1994) 'The topographical development of Scandinavian and Anglo-Norman Cork', in P. O'Flanagan and C.G. Buttimer (eds) *Cork: History and Society* (Dublin), 15–44.

Bradley, R.J. (1984) *The Social Foundations of Prehistoric Britain* (London: Longman).

Bradley, R.J. and Chapman, R.W. (1984) 'Passage graves in the European Neolithic: a theory of converging evolution', in G. Burenhult, *The Archaeology of Carrowmore: Environmental Archaeology and the Mesolithic Tradition at Carrowmore, Co. Sligo, Ireland* (Stockholm: Institute of Archaeology, University of Stockholm, Theses and Papers in North-European Archaeology 14), 348–356.

Bradshaw, B. (1974) *The Dissolution of the Religious Orders in Ireland under Henry VIII* (Cambridge: Cambridge University Press).

Brady, C. and Gillespie, R. (eds) (1986) *Natives and Newcomers: Essays on the Making of Irish Colonial Society, 1534–1641* (Dublin: Irish Academic Press).

Brady, C., O'Dowd, M. and Walker, B. (eds) (1989) *Ulster: An Illustrated History* (London: Batsford).

Breathnach, P. and Cawley, M. (eds) (1986) *Change and Development in Rural Ireland* (Maynooth: Geographical Society of Ireland).

Brett, D. (1996) *The Construction of Heritage* (Cork: University Press).

Brindley, A.L. (1986) *Archaeological Inventory of County Monaghan* (Dublin).

Brindley, A.L. and Kilfeather, A. (comp.) (1993) *Archaeological Inventory of County Carlow* (Dublin: Stationery Office).

Broderick, D. (1996) *The Dublin–Dunleer Turnpike, 1731–1855* (Dublin: Maynooth Local History Studies).

Buchanan, R.H. (1970) 'Rural settlement in Ireland', in N. Stephens and R.E. Glasscock (eds) *Irish Geographical Studies in honour of E. Estyn Evans* (Belfast: Queen's University).

Buchanan, R.H. (1984) 'Historical geography of Ireland pre-1700', *Irish Geography* Jubilee Volume: 129–148.

Buchanan, R.H. and Wilson, T. (1997) *Irish Historic Towns Atlas: Downpatrick* (Dublin: Royal Irish Academy).

Buchanan, R.H., Jones, E. and McCourt, D. (eds) (1971) *Man and his Habitat: Essays Presented to Emyr Estyn Evans* (London: Routledge and Kegan Paul).

Buckley, V. (1986) 'Ulster and Oriel souterrains – an indicator of tribal areas?', *Ulster Journal of Archaeology* 49: 108–110.

Buckley, V. (1986) *Archaeological Inventory of County Louth* (Dublin: Stationery Office).

Buckley, V. (1990) *Burnt Offerings* (Dublin: Wordwell).

Buckley, V. and Sweetman, P. (1991) *Archaeological Survey of County Louth* (Dublin: Stationery Office).

Burenhult. G. (1980) *The Archaeological Excavation at Carrowmore, Co. Sligo, Ireland: Excavation Seasons 1977–1979* (Stockholm: Institute of Archaeology, University of Stockholm, Theses and Papers in North European Archaeology 14).

Burenhult, G. (1984) *The Archaeology of Carrowmore: Environmental Archaeology and the Mesolithic Tradition at Carrowmore, Co. Sligo, Ireland* (Stockholm: Institute of Archaeology, University of Stockholm, Theses and Papers in North-European Archaeology 14).

Burgess, C.B. and Shennan, S. (1976) 'The Beaker phenomenon: some suggestions', in C.B. Burgess and R. Miket (eds) *Settlement and Economy in the Third and Second Millennia BC* (Oxford, B.A.R. Brit. Ser. 33), 309–331.

Butel, P. and Cullen, L.M. (eds) (1986) *Cities and Merchants: French and Irish Perspectives on Urban Development, 1500–1900* (Dublin: Trinity College).

Butler, L.A.S. (1979) 'The "monastic city" in Wales: myth or reality?', *Bulletin of the Board of Celtic Studies* 28: 458–467.

Butlin, R.A. (1967) 'Urban genesis in Ireland, 1556–1641', in R.W. Steel and R. Lawton (eds) *Liverpool Essays in Geography: A Jubilee Collection* (London: Longmans, Green and Co. Ltd).

Butlin, R.A. (1976) 'Land and people c. 1600', in T.W. Moody, F.X. Martin and F.J. Byrne (eds) *History of Ireland, III* (Oxford: Clarendon Press), 142–167.

Butlin, R.A. (1977) 'Irish towns in the sixteenth and seventeenth centuries', in R.A. Butlin (ed.) *The Development of the Irish Town* (London: Croom Helm), 76.

Butlin, R.A. (ed.) (1977) *The Development of the Irish Town* (London: Croom Helm and Totowa, NJ: Rowman and Littlefield).

Buttimer, A. (1995) 'Gatekeeping geography through National Independence: stories from Harvard and Dublin', *Erdkunde* 49, 1: 3–16.

Byrne, F. (1967) 'Early Irish society (1st–9th century)', in T.W. Moody and F.X. Martin (eds) *The Course of Irish History* (Cork: Mercier Press), 43–60.

Byrne, F.J. (1971) 'Tribes and tribalism in early Ireland', *Ériu* 22: 128–166.

Cairns, C.T. (1987) *Irish Tower Houses* (Belfast: Group for the Study of Irish Historical Settlement).

Cairns, C.T. (1987) *Irish Tower Houses: A County Tipperary Case Study* (Athlone).

Camblin, G. (1951) *The Town in Ulster* (Belfast: Wm Morris and Son).

Campbell, J. (1979) 'Bede's words for places', in P.H. Sawyer (ed.) *Names, Words and Graves: Early Medieval Settlement* (School of History, University of Leeds), 34–54.

Canny, N. (1973) 'The ideology of colonisation in England and America', *William and Mary Quarterly* 30: 573–598.

Canny, N. (1976) *The Elizabethan Conquest of Ireland: A Pattern Established* (Hassocks: Harvester Press).

Canny, N. (1979) 'Why the reformation failed in Ireland: une question mal posée', *Journal of Ecclesiastical History* 30, 4: 423–441.

Canny, N.P. (1986) 'Protestants, planters and apartheid in early modern Ireland', *Irish Historical Studies* 25, 98: 105–115.

Canny, N.P. (1988) *Kingdom and Colony: Ireland in the Atlantic World 1560–1800* (Baltimore: Johns Hopkins University Press).

Canny, N. (1989) 'Early modern Ireland, c. 1500–1700', in R. Foster (ed.) *The Oxford Illustrated History of Ireland* (Oxford: University Press), 104–160.

Carleton, S.T. (1991) *Heads and Hearths: The Hearth-Money Rolls and Poll-Tax returns for County Antrim 1660–1669* (Belfast: Public Record Office for Northern Ireland).

Carr, P. (1987) *The Most Unpretending of Places – A History of Dundonald County Down* (Belfast: White Row Press).

Carter, R.W.G. and Parker, A.J. (eds) (1989) *Ireland: a Contemporary Geographical Perspective* (London: Routledge).

Case, H.J. (1969) 'Settlement patterns in the north Irish Neolithic', *Ulster Journal of Archaeology* 3rd Ser. 32: 3–27.

Casey, C. and Rowan, A. (1993) *The Building of Ireland: North Leinster* (London: Penguin Books).

Caulfield, S. (1977) 'The beehive quern in Ireland', *Journal of the Royal Society of Antiquaries of Ireland* 107: 3–27.

Caulfield, S. (1978) 'Neolithic fields: the Irish evidence', in H.C. Bowen and P.J. Fowler (eds) *Early Land Allotment* (Oxford, B.A.R. Brit. Ser. 48), 137–144.

Caulfield, S. (1981) 'Some Celtic problems in the Irish Iron Age', in D. Ó Corráin (ed.) *Irish Antiquity* (Blackrock, Co. Dublin: Four Courts Press), 205–215.

Caulfield, S. (1983) 'The Neolithic settlement of North Connaught', in T. Reeves-Smyth and F. Hamond (eds) *Landscape Archaeology in Ireland* (Oxford, B.A.R. Brit. Ser. 116), 195–215.

Charles-Edwards, T. (1984) 'The church and settlement', in P. Ní Chatháin and M. Richter (eds) *Ireland and Europe: The Early Church* (Stuttgart: Klett-Cotta), 160–175.

Charles-Edwards, T. (1993) *Early Irish and Welsh Kinship* (Oxford: Clarendon Press).

Chart, D.A. (ed.) (1928) *Londonderry and the London Companies 1609–1629* (Belfast: HMSO).

Clark, P. and Slack, P. (1976) *English Towns in Transition, 1500–1700* (Oxford: Oxford University Press).

Clark, S. (1979) *Social Origins of the Irish Land War* (Princeton: Princeton University Press).

Clark, S. and Donnelly, J. (eds) (1983) *Irish Peasants: Violence and Political Unrest 1780–1914* (Manchester: Manchester University Press).

Clarke, D.L. (1976) 'Mesolithic Europe: the economic basis', in G. de Sieveking, I.H. Longworth and K.E. Wilson (eds) *Problems in Economic and Social Archaeology* (London: Duckworth), 449–482.

Clarke, D.V., Cowie, T.G. and Foxon, A. (1985) *Symbols of Power* (Edinburgh: HMSO).

Clarke, H.B. (1978) *The Medieval Town in the Modern City* (Dublin).

Clarke, H.B. (1990) *Medieval Dublin* (Dublin).

Clarke, H.B. (ed.) (1995) *Irish Cities* (Cork).

Clarke, H.B. (forthcoming) 'Decolonisation and the dynamics of urban decline in Ireland, 1300–1500', in T.R. Slater (ed.) *Towns in Decline*.

Clarke, H.B. and Simms, A. (1985) 'Towards a comparative history of urban origins', in H.B. Clarke and A. Simms (eds) *The Comparative History of Urban Origins in Non-Roman Europe* (Oxford), 669–714.

Clarke, H.B. and Simms, A. (1985) *The Comparative History of Urban Origins in Non-Roman Europe* (Oxford).

Clarke, H.B., Ní Mhaonaigh, M. and Ó Floinn, R. (1998) *Ireland and Scandinavia in the Early Viking Age* (Dublin).

Clarkson, L. (1985) *Proto-Industrialisation: The First Phase of Industrialisation* (Basingstoke: Macmillan).

Cleary, R.M., (1983) 'Excavations at Lough Gur, Co. Limerick: Part III', *Journal of the Cork Historical and Archaeological Society* 88: 51–80.

Cleary, R.M., Hurley, M.F. and Twohig, E.A. (eds) (1987) *Archaeological Excavations on the Cork-Dublin Gas Pipeline 1981–1982* (Cork: Archaeological Studies No. 1).

Colby, T. (1837) *Memoir of the City and North Western Liberties of Londonderry, Parish of Templemore* (Limavady: North West).

Comyn, D. and Dineen, P. (eds) (1901–8) *Foras Feasa ar Éirinn*, 4 vols, by S. Céitinn (London: Nutt, for Irish Texts Society).

Condit, T. (1996) 'Rings of truth at Trim Castle, Co. Meath', *Archaeology Ireland* 10, 3: 30–33.

Connolly, S.J. (1985) 'Law, order and popular protest in early 18th-century Ireland: the case of the Houghers', in P.J. Corish (ed.) *Radicals, Rebels and Establishments* (Belfast: Appletree Press), 51–68.

Connolly, S.J. (1987) 'The Houghers – agrarian protest in early eighteenth-century Ireland', in C. Philpin (ed.) *Nationalism and Popular Protest in Ireland* (Cambridge: Cambridge University Press), 139–162.

Connolly, S.J. (1992) *Religion, Law and Power: The Making of Protestant Ireland 1660–1770* (Oxford: Clarendon Press).

Cooney, G. (1979) 'Some aspects of the siting of megalithic tombs in County Leitrim', *Journal of the Royal Society of Antiquaries of Ireland* 109: 74–91.

Cooney, G. (1983) 'Megalithic tombs in their environmental setting, a settlement perspective', in T. Reeves-Smyth and F. Hamond (eds) *Landscape Archaeology in Ireland* (Oxford B.A.R. Brit. Ser. 116).

Cooney, G. (1987/88) 'Irish Neolithic settlement and its European context', *Journal of Irish Archaeology* 4: 7–11.

Cooney, G. (1990) 'The place of megalithic tomb cemeteries in Ireland', *Antiquity* 64: 741–753.

Cooney, G. (forthcoming) 'Irish Neolithic landscapes and land use systems; the implications of field systems', *Rural History*.

Corish, P. (1981) *The Catholic Community in the Seventeenth and Eighteenth Centuries* (Dublin: Helicon).

Corish, P.J. (ed.) (1985) *Radicals, Rebels and Establishments* (Belfast: Appletree Press).

Corkery, D. (1924) *The Hidden Ireland – A Study of Gaelic Munster in the Eighteenth Century* (Dublin: Gill).

Corlett, C. (1996) 'Prehistoric pilgrimage to Croagh Patrick', *Cathair na Mart* (Journal of the Westport Historical Society) 16.

Cosgrove, D. and Jackson, P. (1987) 'New directions in cultural geography', *Area* 19: 95–101.

Coughlan, P. (1990) 'Cheap and common animals: the English anatomy of Ireland', in T. Healy and J. Sawday (eds) *Literature and the English Civil War* (Cambridge: Cambridge University Press), 205–223.

Crawford, W. (1971) 'The origins of the linen industry in north Armagh and the Lagan Valley', *Ulster Folklife* 17: 42–71.

Crawford, W. (1971) 'Ulster landowners and the linen industry', in T. Ward and R. Wilson (eds) *Land and Industry* (Newton Abbot: David and Charles), 134–138.

Crawford, W. (1972) *Domestic Industry in Ireland* (Dublin: Gill and MacMillan).

Crawford, W. (1975) 'Economy and society in south Ulster in the eighteenth century', *Clogher Record* 1975: 245–258.

Crawford, W. (1980) 'Draper and bleacher in the early Ulster linen industry', in L. Cullen and P. Butel (eds) *Négoce et industrie en France et en Irelande aux XVIIIe et XIXe Siècle* (Paris: Éditions du Centre National de la Recherche Scientifique), 113–120.

Crawford, W. (1980) 'The social structure of Ulster in the eighteenth century', in L. Cullen and F. Furet, *Irelande et France* (Paris: Editions de l'École des Hautes Études en Sciences Sociales), 117–128.

Crawford, W. (1982) 'The Ulster Irish in the eighteenth century', *Ulster Folklife* 28: 24–32.

Crawford, W. (1988) 'The evolution of the linen trade in Ulster before industrialisation', *Irish Economic and Social History* 15: 32–53.

Crawford, W. (1989) 'The political economy of linen: Ulster in the eighteenth century', in C. Brady, M. O'Dowd and B. Walker (eds) *Ulster: An Illustrated History* (London), 134–157.

Crawford, W. (1989) 'The re-shaping of the borderlands c. 1700–1840', in R. Gillespie and H. O'Sullivan (eds) *The Borderlands* (Belfast), 93–106.

Crotty, R. (1986) *Ireland in Crisis: A Study in Capitalist Colonial Underdevelopment* (Dingle: Brandon).

Cuisenier, J. and Guadagnin, R. (eds) (1988) *Un village au temps de Charlemagne: moines et paysans de l'abbaye de Saint-Denis du VIIe siècle à l'an mil* (Paris: Éditions de la Réunion des Musées Nationaux).

Cullen, L.M. (1974–5) 'Population trends in seventeenth-century Ireland', *Economic and Social Review* 6: 149–165.

Cullen, L.M. (1977) 'Eighteenth-century flour milling in Ireland', *Irish Economic and Social History* 4: 5–25.

Cullen, L.M. (1979) *Irish Towns and Villages* (Dublin: Eason and Son Ltd, Irish Heritage Series No. 25).

Cullen, L.M. (1980) 'Ireland and France 1600–1900', in L.M. Cullen and F. Furet (eds) *Ireland and France: 17th–20th Centuries – Towards a Comparative Study of Rural History* (Paris: Éditions de l'École des Hautes Études en Sciences Sociales), 1–20.

Cullen, L.M. (1981) 'Social and cultural frontiers', in L.M. Cullen (ed.) *The Emergence of Modern Ireland* (London: Batsford Academic), 109–139.

Cullen, L.M. (1981) *The Emergence of Modern Ireland, 1600–1900* (London: Gill and MacMillan).

Cullen, L.M. (1986) 'Man, landscape and roads: the changing eighteenth century', in W. Nolan (ed.) *The Shaping of Ireland* (Cork: Mercier Press).

Cullen, L.M. (1988) *The Hidden Ireland – Reassessment of a Concept* (Gigginstown, Mullingar: Lilliput Press).

Cullen, L.M. (1990) 'Catholic social classes under the penal laws', in T. Power and K. Whelan (eds) *Endurance and Emergence: Catholics in Ireland in the Eighteenth Century* (Dublin: Irish Academic Press), 54–84.

Cullen, L.M. (1990) 'The social and economic evolution of county Kilkenny in the seventeenth and eighteenth centuries', in W. Nolan and K. Whelan (eds) *Kilkenny. History and Society: Interdisciplinary Essays on the History of an Irish County* (Dublin: Geography Publications).

Cullen, L.M. (1992) 'The growth of Dublin 1600–1900: character and heritage', in F.H.A. Aalen and K. Whelan (eds) *Dublin. City and County* (Dublin: Geography Publications), 252–277.

Cullen, L.M. and Butel, P. (eds) (1986) *Négoce et industrie en France et en Irelande aux XVIIIe et XIXe Siècle* (Paris: Éditions de l'École des Hautes Études en Sciences Sociales).

Cullen, L.M. and Furet, F. (1980) *Ireland and France, 17th–20th Centuries: Towards a Comparative Study of Rural History* (Paris: Éditions de l'École des Hautes Études en Sciences Sociales).

Culleton, E. and Mitchell, G. (1976) 'Soil erosion following deforestation in the Early Christian period in South Wexford', *Journal of the Royal Society of Antiquaries of Ireland* 106: 120–123.

Cunningham, B. (1984) 'The composition of Connaught in the lordships of Clanricard and Thomond 1577–1642', *Irish Historical Studies* 24: 1–14.

Cunningham, B. (1986) 'Native culture and political culture, 1580–1640', in C. Brady and R. Gillespie (eds) *Natives and Newcomers* (Dublin: Irish Academic Press), 148–170.

Cuppage, J. (1986) *Archaeological Survey of the Dingle Peninsula* (Ballyferriter: Oidreacht Chorcha Dhuibhne).

Curl, J.S. (1986) *The Londonderry Plantation, 1609–1914* (Chichester).

Daly, M. (1985) *Dublin: The Deposed Capital* (Cork).

Daly, M. and Dickson, D. (1990) *The Origins of Popular Literacy in Ireland: Language and Educational Development, 1700–1920* (Dublin: Department of Modern History, Trinity College and University College Dublin).

Darvill, T.C. (1979) 'Court cairns, passage graves and social change in Ireland', *Man* 14: 311–327.

Daultrey, S., Dickson, D. and Ó Gráda, C. (1982) 'Hearthtax, household size and Irish population change 1672–1821', *Proceedings of the Royal Irish Academy* 82C: 125–150.

Davies, G. (ed.) (1984) *Irish Geography 1934–1984* (Dublin).

Davies, M. (1998) *Bray* (Dublin: Irish Historic Towns Atlas).

Davies, O. (1947) 'Types of rath in Southern Ulster', *Ulster Journal of Archaeology* 10: 1–14.

Davies, R.R. (1990) *Domination and Conquest* (Cambridge).

Davies, W. (1982) *Wales in the Early Middle Ages* (Leicester: Leicester University Press).

Day, A. and McWilliams, P. (1990) *Ordnance Survey Memoirs of Ireland. Parishes of Co. Tyrone*, Vol. 5 (Belfast: Institute of Irish Studies).

Day, A. and McWilliams, P. (1992) *Ordnance Survey Memoirs of Ireland. Parishes of Co. Fermanagh*, Vol. 14 (Belfast: Institute of Irish Studies).

de Laet, S. (ed.) (1976) *Acculturation and Continuity in Atlantic Europe* (Bruges: Dissertationes Archaeologicae Gandenses, 16).

de Paor, M. and de Paor, L. (1961) *Early Christian Ireland* (London: Thames and Hudson).

Demolon, P. (1989) 'Villes et villages dans le nord-est de la Neustrie du VIᵉ au XIᵉ siècle', in H. Atsma (ed.) *La Neustrie: les pays au nord de la Loire de 650 à 850*, Vol. 2 (Sigmaringen: J. Thorbecke), 435–437.

Denecke, D. and Shaw, G. (eds) (1988) *Urban Historical Geography* (Cambridge: Cambridge University Press).

Devine, T. and Dickson, D. (eds) (1983) *Ireland and Scotland 1600–1800* (Edinburgh: John Donald).

Dewailly, J.M. and Dion, R. (eds) (1988) *Campagnes et littoraux d'Europe (Mélanges offert à Pierre Flatrès)* (Société Géographe de Lille).

Dickson, D. (1977) 'An economic history of the Cork region in the eighteenth century', unpublished PhD thesis (Trinity College Dublin).

Dickson, D. (1979) 'Middlemen', in T. Bartlett and D. Hayton (eds) *Penal Era and Golden Age: Essays in Irish History 1690–1900* (Belfast: W. and G. Baird, for Ulster Historical Foundation), 162–185.

Dickson, D. (1980) 'Property and social structure in eighteenth-century south Munster', in L. Cullen and F. Furet (eds) *Ireland and France, 17th–20th Century: Towards a Comparative Study of Rural History* (Paris: Éditions de l'École des Hautes Études en Sciences Sociales).

Dickson, D. (1987) *New Foundations – Ireland 1660–1800* (Dublin: Helicon Press).

Dobbs, A. (1731) *An Essay on the Trade of Ireland* (Dublin: Brown and Rogers).

Dodgshon, R.A. (1987) *The European Past: Social Evolution and Spatial Order* (London).

Doherty, C. (1982) 'Some aspects of hagiography as a source for Irish economic history', *Peritia* 1: 300–328.

Doherty, C. (1985) 'The monastic town in early medieval Ireland', in H.B. Clarke and A. Simms (eds) *The Comparative History of Urban Origins in Non-Roman Europe: Ireland, Wales, Denmark, Germany, Poland and Russia from the Ninth to the Thirteenth Century* (Oxford B.A.R. Int. Ser. 255, vol. 1), 45–75.

Doherty, C. (1991) 'The cult of St Patrick and the politics of Armagh in the seventh century', in J.M. Picard (ed.) *Ireland and Northern France, AD 600–850* (Dublin: Four Courts Press), 61–65.

Donovan, B. and Edwards, D. (1997) *Guide to Sources for Irish History 1485–1641 in British Archives* (Irish Manuscript Commission).

Donovan, P.O. (1995) *Archaeological Inventory of County Cavan* (Dublin).

Doody, M.G. (1987) 'Ballyveelish, Co. Tipperary', in R.M. Cleary, M.F. Hurley and E.A. Twohig (eds) *Archaeological Excavations on the Cork–Dublin Gas Pipeline (1981–1982)* (Cork: Archaeological Studies No.1), 9–35.

Doody, M.G. (1987) 'Late Bronze Age huts at Curraghatoor, Co. Tipperary', in R.M. Cleary, M.F. Hurley and E.A. Twohig (eds) *Archaeological Excavations on the Cork–Dublin Gas Pipeline (1981–1982)* (Cork: Archaeological Studies No.1), 36–42.

Dooley, T. (1997) 'The Decline of the Big House in Ireland 1879–1950', unpublished PhD thesis (National University of Ireland).

Driscoll, S. and Nieke, M. (eds) (1988) *Power and Politics in Early Medieval Britain and Ireland* (Edinburgh: Edinburgh University Press).

Duby, G. (1974) *The Early Growth of the European Economy* (London).

Duffy, P.J. (1971) 'The evolution of estate properties in South Ulster 1600–1900', in M.W. Beresford and J.W. Hurst (eds) *Deserted Medieval Village Studies* (London), 84–109.

Duffy, P.J. (1981) 'The territorial organisation of Gaelic landownership and its transformation in County Monaghan 1591–1640', *Irish Geography* 14: 1–26.

Duffy, P.J. (1983) 'Farney in 1634: an examination of Thomas Raven's survey of the Essex estate', *Clogher Record* 11: 248–251.

Duffy, P.J. (1987) 'The Dublin region: a perspective on the fringe', in A.A. Horner and A.J. Parker (eds) *Geographical Perspectives on the Dublin Region* (Dublin: Geographical Society of Ireland).

Duffy, P.J. (1988) 'The evolution of estate properties in South Ulster 1600–1900', in W.J. Smyth and K. Whelan (eds) *Common Ground: Essays on the Historical geography of Ireland* (Cork: University Press), 84–109.

Duffy, P.J. (1993) *Landscapes of South Ulster: A Parish Atlas of the Diocese of Clogher* (Belfast: Institute of Irish Studies).

Duffy, P.J. (1994) 'Conflicts in heritage and tourism', in U. Kockel (ed.) *Culture, Tourism and Development: The Case of Ireland* (Liverpool: University Press).

Duffy, P.J. (1997) 'The nuts and bolts in making the Irish landscape', in *Group for the Study of Irish Historical Settlement Journal* 7.

Duignan, M. (1944) 'Irish agriculture in early historic times', *Journal of the Royal Society of Antiquaries of Ireland* 74: 127–128.

Dyer, C. (1990) 'The past, the present and the future in medieval rural history', *Rural History* 1, 1: 37–49.

Edwards, K.J. (1979) 'Palynological and temporal inference in the context of prehistory, with special reference to the evidence from lake and peat deposits', *Journal of Archaeological Science* 6: 255–270.

Edwards, K.J. (1985) 'The anthropogenic factor in vegetational history', in K.J. Edwards and W.P. Warren (eds) *The Quaternary History of Ireland* (London: Academic Press), 187–220.

Edwards, K.J. and Hirons, K.R. (1984) 'Cereal pollen grains in pre-elm decline deposits: implications for the earliest agriculture in Britain and Ireland', *Journal of Archaeological Science* 11: 71–80.

Edwards, K.J. and Warren, W.P. (eds) (1985) *The Quaternary History of Ireland* (London: Academic Press).

Edwards, K.J., Hamond, F.W. and Simms, A. (1983) 'The medieval settlement of Newcastle Lyons, Co. Dublin: an interdisciplinary approach', *Proceedings of the Royal Irish Academy* 83C, 351–376.

Edwards, N. (1990) *The Archaeology of Early Medieval Ireland* (London: Batsford).

Edwards, R.D. (1938) 'Letter book of Sir Arthur Chichester', *Analecta Hibernica* 8: 5–177.

Empey, C.A. (1982) 'Medieval Knocktopher: a study in manorial settlement', in *Old Kilkenny Review* 2: 329–342.

Empey, C.A. (1986) 'Conquest and settlement patterns of Anglo-Norman settlement in North Munster and South Leinster', *Irish Economic and Social History* 13: 5–31.

Empey, C.A. (1988) 'The Anglo-Norman settlement in the cantred of Eliogarty', in John Bradley (ed.) *Settlement and Society in Medieval Ireland: Studies Presented to F. X. Martin, o.s.a.* (Kilkenny), 207–228.

Eogan, G. (1974) 'Regionale gruppierungen in der Spatbronzezeit Irlands', *Archaologisches Korrespondenzblatt* 4: 319–327.

Eogan, G. (1983) *Hoards of the Irish Later Bronze Age* (Dublin: University College Dublin).

Eogan, G. (1984) *Excavations at Knowth 1* (Dublin: Royal Irish Academy Monographs in Archaeology 1).

Eogan, G. (1986) *Knowth and the Passage Tombs of Ireland* (London: Thames and Hudson).

Eogan, G. (1991) 'Prehistoric and early historic culture change at Brugh na Bóine', *Proceedings of the Royal Irish Academy* 91C: 105–132.

Eogan, G. (1997) 'The Discovery Programme: initiation, consolidation and development', in W. H. Metz (ed.) *Negentiende Kron-Voorrdraacht* (Amsterdam: Stichting Nederlands Museum voor Anthropologie en Praehistorie).

Etchingham, C. (1991) 'The early Irish church: some observations on pastoral cares and dues', *Ériu* 42: 99–118.

Evans, E.E. (1939) 'Some survivals of the Irish open field system', *Geography* 24: 24–28.

Evans, E.E. (1942) *Irish Heritage: The Landscape, the People and their Work* (Dundalk: Dundalgan Press).

Evans, E.E. (1951) *Mourne Country* (Dundalk).

Evans, E.E. (1951) *Mourne Country: Landscape and Life in South Down* (Dundalk: Dundalgan Press).

Evans, E.E. (1957) *Irish Folkways* (London: Routledge).

Evans, E.E. (1965) 'The Scotch Irish in the New World', *Journal of the Royal Society of Antiquaries of Ireland* 95: 39–49.

Evans, E.E. (1973) *The Personality of Ireland. Habitat, Heritage and History* (London: Cambridge Univerity Press). Revised edition, Belfast: Blackstaff Press, 1981.

Evans, E.E. and Gaffikin, M. (1935) 'Belfast Naturalist's Field Club survey of antiquities: megaliths and raths', *Irish Naturalist's Journal* 5: 242–252.

Evans, J.G., Limbrey, S. and Cleere, H. (eds) (1975) *The Effects of Man on the Landscape: the Highland Zone* (London: C.B.A. Res. Report 11).

Fahy, A. (1984) 'The spatial differentiation of commercial and residential functions in Cork City 1787–1863', *Irish Geography* 17: 205–225.

Fahy, A. (1986) 'Residence, workplace and patterns of change: Cork 1787–1863', in P. Butel and L.M. Cullen (eds) *Cities and Merchants* (Dublin: Trinity College), 41–52.

Fahy, E. (1969) 'Early settlement in the Skibbereen area', *Journal of the Cork Archaeological and Historical Society* 74: 147–156.

Fanning, T. (1981) 'Excavation of an Early Christian cemetery and settlement at Reask, County Kerry', *Proceedings of the Royal Irish Academy* 81C: 3–172.

Faris, M.J. (ed.) (1976) *The Bishop's Synod ('The first Synod of St Patrick')* A Symposium with Text Translation and Commentary (Francis Cairns, School of Classics, University of Liverpool).

Farrelly, J. (1989) 'A sample study of ringforts in County Leitrim', unpublished MA thesis (University College, Dublin).

Feehan, J. (1983) *Laoise, an Environmental History* (Stradbally: Ballykilcavan Press).

Finberg, H.P.R. (1972) *The Agrarian History of England and Wales* (London: Cambridge University Press).

Finberg, H.P.R. (1976) *The Formation of England 550–1042* (St Albans: Paladin).

Fitzpatrick, E. and O'Brien, C. (1998) *The Medieval Churches of County Offaly* (Dublin).

Fitzpatrick, R. (1989) *God's Frontiersmen – the Scots-Irish Epic* (London: Weidenfeld and Nicholson in association with Channel 4 and Ulster TV/Chatswood, New South Wales: Peribo).

Fitzsimons, J. (1990) *Bungalow Bashing* (Kells: Kells Publishing Company).

Flanagan, D. and Flanagan, L. (1994) *Irish Place Names* (Dublin: Gill and MacMillan).

Flatrès, P. (1957) *Géographie rurale de quatre contrées celtique* (Rennes).

Ford, A. (1986) 'The Protestant Reformation in Ireland', in C. Brady and R. Gillespie (eds) *Natives and Newcomers* (Dublin), 50–74.

Ford, A. (1987) *The Protestant Reformation in Ireland 1590–1641* (Frankfurt am Main: Verlag Peter Man).

Foster, R. (ed.) (1989) *The Oxford Illustrated History of Ireland* (Oxford: University Press).

Frame, R. (1977) 'Power and society in the Lordship of Ireland, 1272–1377', *Past and Present* 76: 3–33.

Freeman, M.A. (ed.) (1944) *The Annals of Connacht (AD 1224–1544)* (Dublin: Institute for Advanced Studies).

Freeman, T.W. (1957) *Pre-Famine Ireland* (Manchester: Manchester University Press).

Gacquin, W. (1996) *Roscommon before the Famine, 1749–1845* (Dublin: Maynooth Local History Studies).

Gailey, R.A. (1975) 'The Scots element in north Irish popular culture: some problems in the interpretation of historical acculturation', *Ethnologia Europea* 8: 2–21.

Gailey, R.A. (1977) 'Vernacular dwellings of Clogher diocese', *Clogher Record* 9, 2: 187–231.

Gailey, R.A. (1984) *Rural Houses of Northern Ireland* (Edinburgh).

Gailey, R.A. and Ó hÓgáin, D. (eds) (1982) *Gold under the Furze: Studies in Folk Tradition* (Dublin: Glendale Press).

Geraghty, S. (1993) *Environment and Economy in Viking Age Dublin: Botanical Remains from Fishamble Street, Dublin* (Dublin).

Gibson, A.M. and Simpson D.D.A. (1987) 'Lyles Hill, Co. Antrim', *Archaeology Ireland* 1: 72–75.

Gilbert, J. (1892) *A Jacobite Narrative of the War in Ireland 1689–1691* (Shannon: Irish University Press).

Gill, C. (1925) *The Rise of the Irish Linen Industry* (Oxford).

Gillespie, R. (1981) 'Thomas Raven and the mapping of the Clandeboy estates', *Bangor Historical Journal* 1: 6–9.

Gillespie, R. (1985) *Colonial Ulster: The Settlement of East Ulster, 1600–1641* (Cork: University Press).

Gillespie, R. (1986) 'The end of an era – Ulster and the outbreak of the 1641 Rising', in C. Brady and R. Gillespie (eds) *Natives and Newcomers* (Dublin: Irish Academic Press), 191–214.

Gillespie, R. (1991) *The Transformation of the Irish Economy 1550–1700*, Studies in Irish Economic and Social History 6 (Dundalk: Dundalgan Press).

Gillespie, R. (1993) 'Explorers, exploiters and entrepreneurs, 1500–1700', in B.J. Graham and L.J. Proudfoot (eds) *A Historical Geography of Ireland* (London: Academic Press), 123–157.

Gillespie, R. and O'Sullivan, H. (eds) (1989) *The Borderlands: Essays on the History of the Ulster-Leinster Border* (Belfast: Queen's University).

Glanville Jones, R.J. (1961) 'The tribal system in Wales: a re-assessment in the light of settlement studies', *Welsh History Review* 1: 111–114.

Glanville Jones, R.J. (1962) 'Die Entwicklung die ländlichen Beseidlung in Wales', *Zeitschrift für Agrareschichte und Agrarsoziologie* 10: 174–176.

Glanville Jones, R.J. (1972) 'Post-Roman Wales', in H.P.R. Finberg, *The Agrarian History of England and Wales*, Vol. I: ii (London: Cambridge University Press), 281–282.

Glanville Jones, R.J. (1989) 'The Dark Ages', in D. Huw Owen (ed.) *Settlement and Society in Wales* (Cardiff: University of Wales Press), 177–197.

Glasscock, R.E. (1970) 'Moated sites and deserted boroughs and villages: two neglected aspects of Anglo-Norman settlement in Ireland', in N. Stephens and R.E. Glasscock (eds) *Irish Geographical Studies in Honour of E. Estyn Evans* (Belfast: Queen's University), 162–177.

Glasscock, R.E. (1971) 'The study of deserted medieval settlements in Ireland', in M.W. Beresford and J.G. Hurst (eds) *Deserted Medieval Villages* (London: Lutterworth Press), 279–301.

Glasscock, R.E. (1987) 'Land and people, *c.* 1300', in A. Cosgrove (ed.) *A New History of Ireland: II: Medieval Ireland, 1169–1534* (Oxford), 205–239.

Glasscock, R.E. (1991) 'E.E. Evans: 1905–1989', *Journal of Historical Geography* 17, 1: 87–91.

Glassie, H. (1986) *Passing the Time in Ballymenone: Folkore and History of an Ulster Community* (Dublin).

Gleeson, D. (1947) *Roscrea: Town and Parish* (Dublin).

Gosling, P. (1993) *Archaeological Inventory of County Galway, 1 (West Galway)* (Dublin: Stationary Office).

Gottfried, R.B. (1943) 'The early development of the section on Ireland in Camden's Britannia', *English Literary History* 10: 117–130.

Gottman, J. (ed.) (1980) *Centre and Periphery: Spatial Variation in Politics* (London: Sage Publications).

Gowan, M. (1992) 'Excavations of two souterrain complexes at Marshes Upper, Dundalk, County Louth', *Proceedings of the Royal Irish Academy* 92C: 55–121.

Gowen, M. (1988) *Three Irish Gas Pipelines: New Archaeological Evidence in Munster* (Dublin: Wordwell).

Gowen, M. and Tarbett, C. (1988) 'A third season at Tankardstown', *Archaeology Ireland* 2, 4: 156.

Graham, B.J. (1975) 'Anglo-Norman settlement in County Meath', *Proceedings of the Royal Irish Academy* 75C, 11: 223–248.

Graham, B.J. (1977) 'The towns of medieval Ireland', in R. A. Butlin (ed.) *The Development of the Irish Town* (London), 28–60.

Graham, B.J. (1979) 'The evolution of urbanisation in medieval Ireland', *Journal of Historical Geography* 5: 111–125.

Graham, B.J. (1987) 'Urban genesis in early medieval Ireland', *Journal of Historical Geography* 13: 3–16.

Graham, B.J. (1988) 'Medieval settlement in County Roscommon', *Proceedings of the Royal Irish Academy* 88C: 30–31.

Graham, B.J. (1988) 'Economy and town in Anglo-Norman Ireland', in John Bradley (ed.) *Settlement and Society in Medieval Ireland: Studies Presented to F. X. Martin, o.s.a.* (Kilkenny), 241–260.

Graham, B.J. (1988) 'The definition and classification of medieval Irish towns', *Irish Geography* 21: 20–32.

Graham, B.J. (1988) 'The town in the Norman colonisations of the British Isles', in D. Denecke and G. Shaw (eds) *Urban Historical Geography: Recent Progress in Britain and Germany* (Cambridge), 37–52.

Graham, B.J. (1993) 'Early medieval Ireland: settlement as an indicator of economic and social transformation, c. 500–1100', in B.J. Graham and L.J. Proudfoot (eds) *An Historical Geography of Ireland* (London), 19–57.

Graham, B.J. (1993) 'The high middle ages: c. 1100 to c. 1350', in B. J. Graham and L. J. Proudfoot (eds) *An Historical Geography of Ireland* (London), 58–98.

Graham, B.J. (1994) 'The search for common ground: Estyn Evans's Ireland', *Transactions of the Institute of British Geographers* NS 19: 183–201.

Graham, B.J. (1994) 'No place of the mind: contested Protestant representations of Ulster', *Ecumene* 1, 3: 257–281.

Graham, B.J. (1997) *In Search of Ireland* (London).

Graham, B.J. and Proudfoot, L.J. (1992) 'Landlords, planning and urban growth in eighteenth- and early nineteenth-century Ireland', *Journal of Urban History* 18, 3: 308–329.

Graham, B.J. and Proudfoot, L.J. (eds) (1993) *An Historical Geography of Ireland* (London: Academic Press).

Graham, B.J. and Proudfoot, L.J. (eds) (1994) *Urban Improvement in Provincial Ireland, 1700–1840* (Athlone).

Graham, J.M. (1953) 'Transhumance in Ireland', *The Advancement of Science* 10, 37: 75.

Greene, D. and Kelly, F. (eds) (1970) *Irish Bardic Poetry: Texts and Translations together with an Introductory Lecture by Osborn Bergin, with a Foreword by D.A. Binchy* (Dublin: Institute of Advanced Studies).

Groenman van Waateringe, W. (1983) 'The early agricultural utilisation of the Irish landscape: the last word on the Elm decline', in T. Reeves-Smyth and F. Hamond (eds) *Landscape Archaeology in Ireland* (Oxford, B.A.R. Brit. Ser. 116), 217–232.

Grogan, E. (1988) 'The pipeline sites and the prehistory of the Limerick area', in M. Gowen (ed.) *Three Irish Gas Pipelines: New Archaeological Evidence in Munster* (Dublin: Wordwell), 148–157.

Grogan, E. and Eogan, G. (1987) 'Lough Gur excavations by Sean P. Ó Ríordáin: further Neolithic and Beaker habitations on Knockadoon', *Proceedings of the Royal Irish Academy* 87C: 299–506.

Guadagnin, R. (1988) 'Archéologie de l'habitat rural du haut Moyen Âge', in J. Cuisenier and R. Guadagnin (eds) *Un village au temps de Charlemagne: moines et paysans de l'abbaye de Saint-Denis du VIIe siècle à l'an mil* (Paris: Éditions de la Réunion des Musées Nationaux), 142–144.

Gwynn, E.J. and Purton, W.J. (eds) (1911) 'The monastery of Tallaght', *Proceedings of the Royal Irish Academy* 29C: 115–179.

Hamlin, A. (1992) 'The early Irish church: problems of identification', in N. Edwards and A. Lane (eds) *The Early Church in Wales and the West: Recent Work in Early Christian Archaeology, History and Place-Names* (Oxford: Oxbow Monograph 16), 138–144.

Hancock, W. *et al.* (eds and trans.) (1865–1901) *Ancient Laws of Ireland*, 5 vols, Commissioners for Publishing the Ancient Laws and Institutes of Ireland (London: Longman).

Hannigan, K. and Nolan, W. (eds) (1994) *Irish County History Series: Wicklow* (Dublin).

Harbison, P. (1973) 'The earlier Bronze Age in Ireland', *Journal of the Royal Society of Antiquaries of Ireland* 103: 93–153.

Harbison, P. (1988) *Pre-Christian Ireland* (London: Thames and Hudson).

Harding, D.W. (ed.) (1976) *Hillforts, Later Prehistoric Earthworks in Britain and Ireland* (London: Academic Press).

Harkness, D. and O'Dowd, M. (eds) (1981) *The Town in Ireland* (Belfast: Appletree Press).

Harris, C. (1991) 'Power, modernity and historical geography', *Annals of the Association of American Geographers* 81, 4: 671–683.

Harrison, R. (1980) *The Beaker Folk* (London: Thames and Hudson).

Hayes McCoy, G.A. (ed.) (1964) *Ulster and other Irish Maps, c. 1600* (Dublin: Stationery Office for the Irish Manuscripts Commission).

Healy T. and Sawday, J. (eds) (1990) *Literature and the English Civil War* (Cambridge: Cambridge University Press).

Henderson, J. and Ivens, R. (1992) 'Dunmisk and glass making in Early Christian Ireland', *Antiquity* 66: 52–64.

Hennessy, M. (1998) 'The Anglo-Norman colony in County Tipperary, c. 1185–c. 1540', PhD thesis (University College Dublin).

Herity, M. (1974) *Irish Passage Graves* (Dublin: Irish University Press).

Herity, M. (1981) 'A Bronze Age farmstead at Glenree, Co. Mayo', *Popular Archaeology* 2, 9: 36–37.

Herity, M. (1983) 'A survey of the royal site of Cruacain in Connacht I: introduction, the monuments and topography', *Journal of the Royal Society of Antiquaries of Ireland* 113: 121–142.

Herity, M. (1987) 'A survey of the royal site of Cruachain in Connacht III: ringforts and ecclesiastical sites', *Journal of the Royal Society of Antiquaries of Ireland* 17: 125–141.

Herity, M. and Eogan, G. (1977) *Ireland in Prehistory* (London: Routledge and Kegan Paul).

Herries Davies, G.L. (ed.) (1984) *Irish Geography: The Geography Society of Ireland Golden Jubilee, 1934–1984* (Dublin: Geography Publications).

Hill, G. (1877) *An Historical Account of the Plantation in Ulster at the Commencement of the Seventeenth Century, 1608–1620* (Belfast: M'caw, Stevenson and Orr).

Hilton, R.H. (1979) 'Towns in English feudal society', *Review* 3: 3–20.

Hilton, R.H. (1984) 'Small town society in England before the Black Death', *Past and Present* 105 (Nov.): 53–78.

Hilton, R.H. (1985) 'Medieval market towns and simple commodity production', *Past and Present* 109 (Nov.): 3–23.

Hilton, R.H. (1992) *English and French Towns in Feudal Society: A Comparative Study* (Cambridge).

Hodder, I. (1987) *Reading the Past* (Cambridge: Cambridge University Press).

Hodder, I., Isaac, G. and Hammond, N. (eds) (1981) *Patterns of the Past* (Cambridge: Cambridge University Press).

Hore, H. (ed.) (1862–3) 'An account of the barony of Forth in the county of Wexford written at the close of the seventeenth century', *Journal of the Royal Society of Antiquaries of Ireland* 8: 53–83.

Horner, A.A. (1975) 'Carton, Co. Kildare: a case-study of the making of an Irish demesne', *Irish Georgian Society* 18 (Dublin): 45–104.

Horner, A.A. (1978) 'Two eighteenth-century maps of Carlow town', *Proceedings of the Royal Irish Academy* 78C, 5: 115–126.

Horner, A.A. (1986) 'Rural population change in Ireland', in P. Breathnach and M. Cawley (eds) *Change and Development in Rural Ireland* (Maynooth: Geographical Society of Ireland).

Horner, A.A. (1988) 'The published writings of T. Jones Hughes', in W.J. Smyth and K. Whelan (eds) *Common Ground: Essays on the Historical Geography of Ireland* (Cork: University Press), 320–323.

Horner, A.A. (1995) *Irish Historic Towns Atlas: Maynooth* (Dublin).

Horner, A.A. and Parker A.J. (eds) (1987) *Geographical Perspectives on the Dublin Region* (Dublin: Geographical Society of Ireland).

Horner, A.A., Walsh, J. and Harrington, P. (1987) *Population in Ireland: a Census Atlas* (Dublin: University College Dublin).

Hughes, T.J. (1981) 'Review of Irish towns and villages by L.M. Cullen, 1979', *Irish Geography* 14: 101.

Hunter, R.J. (1970) 'An Ulster plantation town – Virginia', *Breifne* 4: 43–51.

Hunter, R.J. (1971) 'Towns in the Ulster plantation', *Studia Hibernica* 11: 40–79.

Hunter, R.J. (1978) 'Sir William Cole and plantation Enniskillen, 1607–1641', *Clogher Record* 9: 336–350.

Hunter, R.J. (1981) 'Ulster plantation towns, 1609–1641', in D. Harkness and M. O'Dowd (eds) *The Town in Ireland* (Belfast: Appletree Press), 55–80.

Hurley, M., Scully, O.M.B., McCutcheon, S.W.J. (eds) (1997) *Late Viking Age and Medieval Waterford: Excavations 1986–1992* (Waterford: Waterford Corporation).

Ivens, R. (1987) 'The Early Christian monastic enclosure at Tullylish, County Down', *Ulster Journal of Archaeology* 50: 55–121.

Ivens, R. (1988) 'Secrets of a hilltop: Dunmisk, Co. Tyrone', in A. Hamlin and C. Lynn (eds) *Pieces of the Past* (Belfast: HMSO), 27–29.

Ivens, R. (1989) 'Excavations at Dunmisk Fort, Co. Tyrone, 1984–1986', *Ulster Journal of Archaeology* 52, 17–110.

Jackson, D. (1975) *Intermarriage in Ireland 1530–1650* (Montreal and Minneapolis: Cultural and Educational Productions).

Jackson, K. (1972) *The Gaelic Notes in the Book of Deer* (London: Cambridge University Press).

Jaeger, H. (1983) 'Land use in Medieval Ireland', *Irish Economic and Social History* 10: 51–65.

James, M.R. (1927) 'The Carew MSS', *English Historical Review* 43: 261–267.

James, T.A. (1992) 'Air photography of ecclesiastical sites in south Wales', in N. Edwards and A. Lane (eds) *The Early Church in Wales and the West: Recent Work in Early Christian Archaeology, History and Place-Names* (Oxford: Oxbow Monograph 16), 62–76.

Jelicic, L. and O'Connell, M. (1992) 'History of vegetation and land use from 3200 B.P. to the present in the north-west Burren, a karstic region of western Ireland', *Vegetation History and Archaeobotany* 1, 1: 19–140.

Jochim, M.A. (1976) *Hunter Gatherer Subsistence and Settlement: A Prehistoric Model* (London: Academic Press).

Johnson, N. (1994) 'Cast in stone: monuments, geography and nationalism', *Environment and Planning: Society and Space* 13: 51–65.

Johnson, N. (1994) 'Sculpting heroic histories: celebrating the centenary of the 1798 rebellion in Ireland', *Transactions of the Institute of British Geographers* NS 19: 78–93.

Johnston, J. (1970) 'The "Two Irelands" at the beginning of the nineteenth century', in N. Stephens and R.E. Glasscock (eds) *Irish Geographical Studies* (Belfast: Appletree Press), 224–243.

Jones Hughes, T. (1964) 'Administrative divisions and the development of settlement in 19th-century Ireland', *University Review* 3, 6: 8–15.

Jones Hughes, T. (1965) 'Society and settlement in nineteenth-century Ireland', *Irish Geography* 5: 79–96.

Jones Hughes, T. (1970) 'Town and baile in Irish place-names', in N. Stephens and R.E. Glasscock (eds) *Irish Geographical Studies in Honour of E.E. Evans* (Belfast), 244–258.

Jones Hughes, T. (1981) 'Villages and towns in nineteenth-century Ireland', *Irish Geography* 14: 96–106.

Jones Hughes, T. (1982) 'The large farm in nineteenth-century Ireland', in A. Gailey and D. Ó hÓgáin (eds) *Gold under the Furze: Studies in Folk Tradition Presented to Caoimhín Ó Damachair* (Dublin), 93–100.

Jones Hughes, T. (1984) 'Historical geography of Ireland from circa 1700', in G. Davies (ed.) *Irish Geography 1934–1984* (Dublin), 149–166.

Jope, E. (ed.) (1966) *An Archaeological Survey of County Down* (Belfast).

Jordan, A. (1990–1) 'Date, chronology and evolution of the County Wexford Tower House', *Journal of the Wexford Historical Society* 13: 30–82.

Kavanagh, R.M. (1973) 'The encrusted urn in Ireland', *Proceedings of the Royal Irish Academy* 73C: 507–617.

Kavanagh, R.M. (1976) 'Collared and cordoned urns in Ireland', *Proceedings of the Royal Irish Academy* 76C: 293–493.

Kelly, F. (1988) *A Guide to Early Irish Law* (Dublin: Institute for Advanced Studies).

Kelly, J. (ed.) (1990) *The Letters of Lord Chief Baron Edward Willes 1757–1762* (Aberystwyth: Boethius Press).

Kennedy, E. (1997) 'Field boundaries and landscape change', in F.H.A. Aalen, K. Whelan and G. Stout (eds) *Atlas of the Irish Rural Landscape* (Cork: University Press).

Killen, J. (1997) 'Communications', in F.H.A. Aalen, K. Whelan and G. Stout (eds) *Atlas of the Irish Rural Landscape* (Cork: University Press).

King, B.T. (1997) *Carlow: Manor and Town, 1674–1721* (Dublin: Maynooth Local History Studies).

Knight, P. (1836) *Erris in the Irish Highlands* (Dublin).

Kockel, U. (ed.) (1994) *Culture, Tourism and Development: The Case of Ireland* (Liverpool: Liverpool University Press).

Kuchenbuch, L. (1978) *Bäuerliche Gesellschaft und Klosterrschaft im 9. Jahrhundert. Studien zur Sozialstruktur der Familia der Abtei Prüm* (Wiesbaden).

Lacy, B. (1983) *Archaeological Inventory of County Donegal* (Lifford: Donegal County Council).

Larkin, E. (1984) *The Historical Dimensions of Irish Catholicism* (New York: P. Arno).

Lawrence, R. (1655) *The Interest of England in the Irish Transplantation* (London: Henry Hills).

Le Goff, J. (1980) *Time, Work and Culture in the Middle Ages*, translated by Arthur Goldhammer (Chicago: University of Chicago Press).

Lecky, W.E.H. (1892) *A History of Ireland in the Eighteenth Century* (London: Longmans and Green).

Leister, I. (1963) *Das Werden der Agrarslandschaft in der Grafschaft Tipperary (Irland)* (Marburg: Geographisches Institute der Universität Marburg).

Leister, I. (1976) *Peasant Open-field Farming and Territorial Organisation in County Tipperary* (Marburg: Geographisches Institute der Universität Marburg).

Lennon, C. (1981) *Richard Stanihurst the Dubliner, 1547–1618* (Dublin: Irish Academic Press).

Lewis, C., Mitchell-Fox, P. and Dyer, C. (1997) *Village, Hamlet and Field* (Manchester: Manchester University Press).

Loeber, R. (1980) 'Civilisation through plantation: the projects of Mathew De Renzi', in H. Murtagh (ed.) *Irish Midland Studies in Commemoration of N.W. English* (Athlone: Old Athlone Society), 121–135.

Loeber, R. (1982–3) 'A gate to Connacht: the building of the fortified town of Jamestown, County Leitrim, in the era of the plantation', *Irish Sword* 15: 149–152.

Loeber, R. (1988/9) 'New light on Co. Wexford architecture and estates in the 17th century', *Journal of the Wexford Historical Society* 12: 66–71.

Loeber, R. (1991) *The Geography and Practice of English Colonisation in Ireland, 1534 to 1609* (Belfast: The Group for the Study of Irish Historic Settlement, 3).

Long, H. (1994) 'Three settlements of Gaelic Wicklow: Rathgall, Balinacoar and Glendalough', in K. Hannigan and W. Nolan (eds) *Wicklow, History and Society* (Dublin) 237–265.

Lorren, C. (1989) 'Le village de Saint-Martin de Trainecourt à Mondeville (Calvados), de l'antiquité au Haut Moyen Âge', in H. Atsma (ed.) *La Neustrie: les pays au nord de la Loire de 650 à 850*, Vol. 2 (Sigmaringen: J. Thorbecke), 439–465.

Lucas, A. (1989) *Cattle in Ancient Ireland* (Kilkenny: Boethius).

Lydon, J.F. (1972) *The Lordship of Ireland in the Middle Ages* (Dublin: Gill and MacMillan).

Lynch, A. (1981) *Man and the Environment in South-West Ireland, 4000 BC – AD 800: A Study of Man's Impact on the Development of Soil and Vegetation* (Oxford: B.A.R. Brit. Ser. 85).

Lynn, C.J. (1977) 'Trial excavations at the Kings' Stables, Tray Townland, County Armagh', *Ulster Journal of Archaeology* 40: 42–62.

Lynn, C.J. (1980) 'The Dorsey and other linear earthworks', in B.G. Scott (ed.) *Studies on Early Ireland: Essays in Honour of M.V. Duignan* (Belfast: AYIA), 121–128.

Lynn, C.J. (1981–2) 'The excavation of Rathmullan, a raised rath and motte in County Down', *Ulster Journal of Archaeology* 44–45: 65–171.

Lynn, C.J. (1983) 'Some "early" ring-forts and crannogs', *Journal of Irish Archaeology* 1: 47–58.

Lynn, C.J. (1986) 'Navan Fort – a draft summary account of D.M. Waterman's excavations', *Emania* 1: 11–19.

Lynn, C.J. (1987) 'Deer Park Farms, Glenarm, County Antrim', *Archaeology Ireland* 1: 11–15.

McAuliffe, M. (1991) 'The use of tower houses and fastnesses in the Desmond rebellion 1565–1583', *Journal of the Kerry Archaeological and Historical Society* 24: 105–112.

MacCarthy-Morrogh, M. (1986) 'The English presence in early seventeenth-century Munster', in C. Brady and R. Gillespie (eds) *Natives and Newcomers* (Dublin: Irish Academic Press), 171–190.

MacCarthy-Morrogh, M. (1986) *The Munster Plantation: English Migration to Southern Ireland, 1583–1641* (Oxford: Clarendon Press).

McCone, K. (1990) *Pagan Past and Christian Present* (Maynooth Monographs 3).

McCormick, F. (1983) 'Dairying and beef production in Early Christian Ireland, the faunal evidence', in T. Reeves-Smyth and F. Hamond (eds) *Landscape Archaeology in Ireland* (Oxford B.A.R. Brit. Ser. 116), 253–267.

McCormick, F. (1988) 'Animal bones from Haughey's Fort', *Emania* 4: 24–27.

McCormick, F. (1992) 'Early faunal evidence for dairying', *Oxford Journal of Archaeology* 11: 201–209.

McCormick, F. (1995) 'Cows, ringforts and the origins of Early Christian Ireland', *Emania* 13: 33–37.

McCourt, D. (1964) 'County Londonderry: the geographical setting', in *County Londonderry Handbook* (Belfast: Nicholson and Bass).

MacCuarta, B. (ed.) (1993) *Ulster 1641: Aspects of the Rising* (Belfast: Queen's University, Institute of Irish Studies).

McDonald, F. (1985) *The Destruction of Dublin* (Dublin: Gill and MacMillan).

McDonald, F. (1987) 'Bungalow blitz', *Irish Times* 15 Sept.

McDonald, F. (1992) 'Skin-deep commitment to conservation', *Irish Times* 22 Sept.

McDonald, F. (1997) 'Heritage treasures at risk of going to rot', *Irish Times* 25 October.

McErlearn, T. (1983) 'The Irish townland scheme of landscape organisation', in T. Reeves-Smyth and F. Hamond (eds) *Landscape Archaeology in Ireland* (Oxford B.A.R. Brit. Ser. 116), 315–339.

McLeod, N. (1986) 'Interpreting early Irish laws: status and currency (part 1)', *Zeitschrift für Celtische Philologie* 41: 46–65.

McLeod, N. (1987) 'Interpreting early Irish laws: status and currency (part 2)', *Zeitschrift für Celtische Philologie* 42: 41–115.

McMinn, J. (1994) *Jonathan's Travels: Swift and Ireland* (Belfast: Appletree Press).

McNeill, C. (1950) *Calendar of Archbishop Alen's Register, c. 1172–1534* (Dublin).

MacNeill, E. (1923) 'Ancient Irish law: law of status and franchise', *Proceedings of the Royal Irish Academy* 36: 265–316.

McNeill, T.E. (1980) *Anglo-Norman Ulster: The History and Archaeology of an Irish Barony, 1177–1400* (Edinburgh).

McNeill, T.E. (1997) *Castles in Ireland: Feudal Power in a Gaelic World* (London: Routledge).

MacNiochaill, G. (1964) *Na Buirgeisi XII–XV Aois*, 2 vols (Dublin: Clo Morainn).

MacNiochaill, G. (1981) *The Red Book of the Earls of Kildare* (Dublin: Stationery Office).

MacNiochaill, G. (1985) *Irish Population before Petty: Problems and Possibilities* (Dublin: National University of Ireland).

MacParland, E. (1802) *A Statistical Survey of County Mayo* (Dublin).

Mallory, J.P. (1988) 'Trial excavations at Haughey's fort', *Emania* 4: 5–20.

Mallory, J.P. and Hartwell, B. (1984) 'Donegore Hill', *Current Archaeology* 8: 271–275.

Mallory, J.P. and McNeill, T.E. (1991) *The Archaeology of Ulster: From Colonization to Plantation* (Belfast: Queen's University, Institute for Advanced Studies).

Manning, C. (1984) 'The excavation of the Early Christian enclosure of Killederdadrum in Lackenavorna, County Tipperary', *Proceedings of the Royal Irish Academy* 84C: 135–181.

Manning, C. (1985) 'A Neolithic burial mound at Ashleypark, Co. Tipperary', *Proceedings of the Royal Irish Academy* 85C: 61–100.

Manning, C. (1986) 'Archaeological excavation of a succession of enclosures at Millockstown, Co. Louth', *Proceedings of the Royal Irish Academy* 86C: 134–181.

Manning, C. (ed.)(1998) *Dublin and beyond the Pale* (Bray: Wordwell).

Mannion, J. (1988) 'The maritime trade of Waterford in the eighteenth century', in W.J. Smyth and K. Whelan (eds) *Common Ground: Essays on the Historical Geography of Ireland* (Cork: University Press).

Marquess of Lansdowne (ed.) (1927) *The Petty Papers*, 2 vols (London: Constable and Co. Ltd).

Mawhinney, K. (1989) 'Environmental conservation concern and action 1920–1970', in M.J. Bannon (ed.) *Planning: The Irish Experience, 1920–1970* (Dublin: Wolfhound Press).

Meenan, R. (1985) 'Deserted medieval villages of Co. Westmeath', unpublished M.Litt. thesis (Trinity College Dublin).

Mercer, R. (ed.) (1981) *Farming Practice in British Prehistory* (Edinburgh: Edinburgh University Press).

Meyer, K. (ed. and trans.) (1892) *Aislinge Meic Conglinne. The Vision of Mac Conglinne* (London: David Nutt).

Miller, D. (1983) 'The Armagh troubles 1784–1795', in S. Clark and J. Donnelly (eds) *Irish Peasants. Violence and Political Unrest 1780–1914* (Manchester: University Press), 155–191.

Miller, D. (1990) *Peep-o-day Boys and Defenders. Selected Documents on the Disturbances in County Armagh, 1784–1796* (Belfast: Public Records Office for Northern Ireland).

Miller, E. and Hatcher, J. (1978) *Medieval England: Rural Society and Economic Change 1086–1348* (London: Longman).

Millet, B. (1976) 'Irish literature in Latin, 1550–1700', in T.W. Moody et al. (eds) *New History of Ireland III* (Oxford: Oxford University Press).

Mitchell, G.F. (1956) 'Post-boreal pollen-diagrams from Irish raised-bogs', *Proceedings of the Royal Irish Academy* 57B: 14–251.

Mitchell, G.F. (1965) 'Littleton Bog, Tipperary: an Irish agricultural record', *Journal of the Royal Society of Antiquaries of Ireland* 95: 121–132.

Mitchell, G.F. (1970) 'Some chronological implications of the Irish Mesolithic', *Ulster Journal of Archaeology* 3rd Ser., 33: 3–14.

Mitchell, G.F. (1972) 'Some Ultimate Larnian sites at Lake Deravaragh, Co. Westmeath', *Journal of the Royal Society of Antiquaries of Ireland* 102: 160–173.

Mitchell, G.F. (1976) *The Irish Landscape* (London).

Mitchell, G.F. (1989) *Man and the Environment in Valencia Island* (Dublin: Royal Irish Academy).

Mitchell, G.F. and Ryan, M. (1986) *The Shell Guide to Reading the Irish Landscape* (Dublin: Country House).

Mitchell, G.F. and Ryan, M. (1997) *Reading the Irish Landscape* (Dublin).

Mockler, J. (1915) 'A report of the district around Mallow in 1775', *Cork Historical and Archaeological Society Journal* 1915: 23.

Molloy, K. and O'Connell, M. (1987) 'The nature of the vegetational changes at about 5000 B.P. with particular reference to the elm decline: fresh evidence from Connemara, western Ireland', *New Phytologist* 107: 203–220.

Monk, M. (1988) 'Excavations at Lisleagh ringfort, north County Cork', *Archaeology Ireland* 2: 57–60.

Monk, M.A. (1985/6) 'Evidence from macroscopic plant remains for crop husbandry in prehistoric and early historic Ireland: a review', *Journal of Irish Archaeology* 3: 31–36.

Monk, M. and Sheehan, J. (eds) *Early Medieval Munster: Archaeology, History and Society* (Cork).

Moody, T.W. (1935) 'The revised articles of the Ulster plantation, 1610', *Bulletin of the Institute of Historical Research* 11: 178–183.

Moody, T.W. (1939) *The Londonderry Plantation 1609–1641* (Belfast: Wm Mullan and Son).

Moody, T.W. (1976) 'Introduction', in T.W. Moody et al. (eds) *History of Ireland, III* (Oxford: Clarendon Press), 1.

Moody, T.W. and Martin, F.X. (eds) (1967) *The Course of Irish History* (Cork: Mercier).

Moody, T.W., Martin, F.X. and Byrne, F.J. (eds) (1976) *A New History of Ireland, III* (Oxford: Clarendon Press).

Moore, M.J. (1987) *Archaeological Inventory of County Meath* (Dublin: Stationery Office).

Moore, M.J. (1996) *Archaeological Inventory of County Wexford* (Dublin: Stationery Office).

Moran, G. and Gillespie, R. (eds) (1996) *Irish County History Series: Galway* (Dublin).

Moryson, F. (1617) *Itinerary* (London).

Movius, H.L. (1942) *The Irish Stone Age: Its Chronology, Development and Relationships* (Cambridge: Cambridge University Press).

Müller-Wille, M., Dörfler, W., Meier, D. and Kroll, H. (1988) 'The transformation of rural society, economy and landscape during the first millennium AD: archaeological and palaeobotanical contributions from Northern Germany and Southern Scandinavia', *Geografiska Annaler* 70B: 53–68.

Murphy, G. (1956) *Early Irish Lyrics: Eighth to Twelfth Century* (Oxford: Clarendon Press).

Murtagh, H. (1980) *Irish Midland Studies* (Athlone).

Murtagh, H. (1994) *Irish Historic Towns Atlas: Athlone* (Dublin).

Musset, L. (1966) 'Peuplement en bourgage et bourgs ruraux en Normandie', in *Cahiers de Civilisation Medievale* 9: 177–208.

Mytum, H. (1992) *The Origins of Early Christian Ireland* (London: Routledge).

Näsman, U. (1989) 'The Germanic Iron Age and Viking Age in Danish archaeology: a survey of the literature 1976–1986', *Journal of Danish Archaeology* 8: 159–187.

Newman, C. and Fenwick, J. (1997) *Tara: An Archaeological Survey* (Dublin: Royal Irish Academy for the Discovery Programme).

Ní Chatháin, P. and Richter, M. (eds) (1984) *Ireland and Europe: The Early Church* (Stuttgart: Klett-Cotta).

Ní Chatháin, P. and Richter, M. (1987) *Irland und die Christenhiet: Bibelstudien und Mission (Ireland and Christendom: The Bible and the Missions* (Stuttgart: Klett-Cotta).

Nicholls, K.W. (1972) *Gaelic and Gaelicised Ireland in the Middle Ages* (Dublin).

Nicholls, K.W. (1976) *Land, Law and Society in Sixteenth-Century Ireland* (Cork: National University of Ireland, O'Donnell Lecture).

Nicholls, K.W. (1984) 'The land of the Leinstermen', *Peritia* 3: 535–538.

Nicholls, K.W. (1987) 'Gaelic society and economy in the high middle ages', in A. Cosgrove (ed.) *A New History of Ireland: II: Medieval Ireland, 1169–1534* (Oxford), 397–438.

Nitz, H. (ed.) (1993) 'The Early Modern World System' *Geographical Perspective* (Gottingen).

Nolan, W. (1975) *Fassadinan, Land, Settlement and Society in South-East Ireland 1600–1850* (Dublin).

Nolan, W. (ed.) (1985) *Tipperary, History and Society* (Dublin: Geography Publications).

Nolan W. (ed.) (1986) *The Shaping of Ireland* (Cork and Dublin: Mercier Press).

Nolan, W. (1988) 'New farms and fields: migration policies of state land agencies', in W.J. Smith and K. Whelan (eds) *Common Ground. Essays on the Historical Geography of Ireland* (Cork: University Press).

Nolan, W. (ed.) (1990) *Kilkenny: History and Society* (Cork: Mercier).

Nolan, W. (1992) 'Society and settlement in the valley of Glenasmole c. 1750–c. 1900', in F.H.A. Aalen and K. Whelan (eds) *Dublin. City and County* (Dublin), 181–228.

Nolan, W. and O'Neill, T. (eds) (1998) *Offaly: History and Society* (Dublin).

Nolan, W. and Simms, A. (eds) (1998) *Irish Towns: Guide to Sources* (Dublin).

Nolan, W. and Whelan, K. (eds) (1985) *Irish County History Series: Tipperary* (Dublin).

Nolan, W. and Whelan, K. (eds) (1987) *Irish County History Series: Wexford* (Dublin).

Nolan, W. and Whelan, K. (eds) (1990) *Irish County History Series: Kilkenny* (Dublin).

Nolan, W., Ronayne L. and M. Dunlevy (eds) (1995) *Irish County History Series: Donegal* (Dublin).

Nolan, W., Power T. and D. Cowman (eds) (1992) *Irish County History Series: Waterford* (Dublin).

O'Brien, A.F. (1986) 'Medieval Youghal: the development of an Irish seaport trading town, *c.*1200 to *c.*1500', *Peritia* 5: 346–78.

O'Brien, A.F. (1987) 'Development and evolution of the medieval port and borough of Dungarvan, County Waterford *c.* 1200–*c.* 1530', *Cork Historical and Archaeological Society Journal* 92: 85–94.

O'Brien, E. (1990) 'Iron Age burial practices in Leinster: continuity and change', *Emania* 7: 37–42.

Ó Catháin, S. and O'Flanagan, P. (1975) *The Living Landscape, Kilgalligan, Erris, County Mayo* (Dublin).

Ó Conluain, P. (1987) 'Some O'Neill country maps 1575–1602', *Dúiche Néill* 1: 13–24.

O'Connell, M. (1987) 'Early cereal-type pollen records from Connemara, western Ireland and their possible significance', *Pollen and Spores* 29: 207–224.

O'Connell, M. (1991) 'Vegetational and environmental changes in Ireland during the Later Holocene', in M. O'Connell (comp.) *The Post-Glacial Period (10,000–0 B.P.): Fresh Perspectives*, extended summaries of lectures (Galway), 21–25.

O'Connor, F. (1950) *Leinster, Munster and Connaught* (London: Robert Hale).

O'Connor, F. (1995) 'Review of Irish Country Towns', *Irish Geography*, 28, 1.

O'Connor, P. (1987) *Exploring Limerick's Past: An Historical Geography of Urban Development in County and City* (Limerick, Newcastle West: Oireacht na Mumhar Books).

O'Conor, K. (1991) 'The later construction and use of motte and bailey castles in Ireland: new evidence from Leinster', *Journal of the Kildare Archaeological Society* 17: 13–29.

O'Conor, K. (1998) *The Archaeology of Medieval Rural Settlement in Ireland* (Dublin: Discovery Programme Monographs 3).

O'Conor, K. (1998) 'The moated site on Inishatirra Island, Drumharlow Lough, Co. Roscommon', *County Roscommon Historical and Archaeological Journal* 7.

Ó Corráin, D. (1978) 'Nationality and kingship in pre-Norman Ireland', in T.W. Moody (ed.) *Nationality and the Pursuit of National Independence* (Belfast: Appletree Press), 1–35.

Ó Corráin, D. (1981) 'Early Irish churches: some aspects of organisation', in D. Ó Corráin (ed.) *Irish Antiquity: Essays and Studies Presented to Professor M.J. O'Kelly* (Cork: Tower Books), 327–341.

Ó Corráin, D. (ed.) (1981) *Irish Antiquity: Essays and Studies Presented to Professor M.J. O'Kelly* (Cork: Tower Books)

Ó Corráin, D. (1983) 'Some legal references to fences and fencing in early historic Ireland', in T. Reeves-Smyth and F. Hamond (eds) *Landscape Archaeology in Ireland* (Oxford B.A.R. Brit. Ser. 116), 247–252.

Ó Corráin, D. (1994) 'Early Ireland: direction and re-direction', *Bullán* 1: 1–15.

Ó Cuív, B. (1976) 'The Irish language in the early modern period', in T.W. Moody, F.X. Martin and F.J. Byrne (eds) *A New History of Ireland, III* (Oxford: Oxford University Press), 526–530.

O'Dalaigh, B. (1995) *Ennis in the Eighteenth Century* (Dublin: Maynooth Local History Studies).

O'Donoghue, J. (1989) 'The Scullys of Kilfeakle – Catholic middlemen of the 1770s', *Tipperary Historical Journal* 2: 38–51.

O'Donovan, P. (comp.) (1995) *Archaeological Inventory of County Cavan* (Dublin: Stationery Office).

O'Faoláin, S. (1947) *An Irish Journey* (London: Green & Co.)

Ó Fiaich, T. (1971–2) 'Filíocht Uladh mar fhoinse don stair shóisialta san 18ú hAois', *Studia Hibernica* 11–12: 80–129.

O'Flaherty, B. (1982) 'A locational analysis of the ringfort settlement of North County Kerry', unpublished MA thesis (University College Cork).

O'Flanagan, P. (1983) 'Settlement development and trading in Ireland 1600–1800', in T. Devine and D. Dickson (eds) *Ireland and Scotland 1600–1800* (Edinburgh: John Donald), 146–150.

O'Flanagan, P. (1985) 'Markets and fairs in Ireland 1600–1800: index of economic development and regional growth', *Journal of Historical Geography* 11, 4: 364–378.

O'Flanagan, P. (1988) *Irish Historic Towns Atlas: Bandon* (Dublin: Royal Irish Academy).

O'Flanagan, P. and Buttimer, C.G. (eds) (1993) *Cork: History and Society* (Dublin: Geography Publications).

O'Flanagan, P., Ferguson, P. and Whelan, K. (eds) (1987) *Rural Ireland 1600–1900: Modernisation and Change* (Cork: University Press).

O'Grady, S. (ed. and trans.) (1892) *Silva Gadelica (i–xxxi): A Collection of Tales in Irish with Extracts Illustrating Persons and Places* (London/Edinburgh: Williams and Norgate).

Ó hEochaidh, S. (1944) 'Buailteachas i dTír Chonaill', *Béaloideas* 13: 130–158.

O'Keefe, T. (1996) 'Rural settlement and cultural identity in Gaelic Ireland, 1000–1500', *Ruralia* I, Paratky archeologicke-Supplementum 5 (Prague), 142–153.

O'Kelly, M.J. (1982) *Newgrange: Archaeology, Art and Legend* (London: Thames and Hudson).

O'Kelly, M.J. (1989) *Early Ireland* (Cambridge: Cambridge University Press).

O'Kelly, M.J., Cleary, R.M. and Lehane, D. (1983) *Newgrange, Co. Meath, Ireland: The Late Neolithic/Beaker Period Settlement* (Oxford, B.A.R., Int. Ser. 190).

O'Kelly, O.W.A. (1985) *The Placenames of County Kilkenny* (Kilkenny: Archaeological Society).

Ó Murchú, C. (1982) 'Land and society in 17th-century County Clare', unpublished PhD thesis (National University of Ireland).

O'Nuallain, S. (1972) 'A Neolithic house at Ballyglass, near Ballycastle, Co. Mayo', *Journal of the Royal Society of Antiquaries of Ireland* 102: 49–56.

O'Nuallain, S. (1983) 'Irish portal tombs: topography, siting and distribution', *Journal of the Royal Society of Antiquaries of Ireland* 113: 75–105.

O'Nuallain, S. (1984) 'A survey of stone circles in Cork and Kerry', in *Proceedings of the Royal Irish Academy* 84C: 1–77.

O'Nuallain, S. (1989) *Survey of the Megalithic Tombs of Ireland* 5 (Dublin: Stationery Office).

O'Rahilly, C. (1952) *Five Seventeenth-Century Political Poems* (Dublin: Institute for Advanced Studies).

Ó Ríordáin, S. (1940) 'Excavations at Cush, County Limerick', *Proceedings of the Royal Irish Academy* 45C: 83–181.

Ó Ríordáin, S.P. and Hunt, J. (1942) 'Medieval dwellings at Caherguillamore, County Limerick', *Journal of the Royal Society of Antiquaries of Ireland* 72: 37–63.

O'Sullivan, A. and Sheehan, J. (1996) *The Iveragh Peninsula: An Archaeological Survey of South Kerry* (Cork).

O'Sullivan, J. (1990) 'The Lisnagun project', *Archaeology Ireland* 4: 23–25.

Ó Tuama, S. (ed.) (1963) *Caoineadh Airt Ui Laoghaire* (Dublin).

Ó Tuama, S. (1978) *Filí Faoi Scéimhle: Sean Ó Ríordain agus Aogan O Rathaille* (Dublin: Stationery Office).

Ó Tuama, S. and Kinsella, T. (eds) (1981) *An Duanaire 1600–1900: Poems of the Dispossessed* (Mountrath: Dolmen Press).

Orme, A.R. (1971) 'Segregation as a feature of urban development in medieval and plantation Ireland', *Geographical Viewpoint* 2: 193–206.

Orme, T. (1970) *Ireland* (London).

Orpen, G.H. (ed. and trans.) (1892) *The Song of Dermot and the Earl* (Oxford: Clarendon Press).

Otway-Ruthven, A.J. (1965) 'The character of Norman settlement in Ireland', in *Historical Studies* 5: 75–84.

Oxford English Dictionary (1888–1928) *A New English Dictionary on Historical Principles* (OED) (Oxford: Oxford University Press).

Patterson, N. (1991) 'Archaeology and the historical sociology of Gaelic Ireland', *Antiquity* 65: 734–738.

Patterson, N. (1994) *Cattle Lords and Clansmen: The Social Structures of Early Ireland*, 2nd edn (London/Notre Dame: University of Notre Dame Press).

Pawlisch, H. (1985) *Sir John Davies and the Conquest of Ireland: A Study in Legal Imperialism* (Cambridge: Cambridge University Press).

Perceval-Maxwell, M. (1973) *The Scottish Migration to Ulster in the Reign of James I* (London: Routledge and Kegan Paul).

Petty, W. (1691) (repr. 1970) *Political Anatomy of Ireland* (London: Brown and Rogers).

Philpin, C. (ed.) (1987) *Nationalism and Popular Protest in Ireland* (Cambridge: Cambridge University Press).

Pilcher, J.R., Smith, A.G., Pearson, G.W. and Crowder, A. (1971) 'Land clearance in the Irish Neolithic: new evidence and interpretation', *Science* 172: 560–562.

Plummer, C. (1910) *Vitae Sanctorum Hiberniae* (Oxford: Oxonii, E. Tyopgrapheo Clarendoniano).

Power, D. (comp.) (1992) *Archaeological Inventory of County Cork, 1 (West Cork)* (Dublin: Stationery Office).

Power, D. (comp.) (1994) *Archaeological Inventory of County Cork, 2 (East and South Cork)* (Dublin: Stationery Office).

Power, T. and Whelan, K. (eds) (1990) *Endurance and Emergence. Catholics in Ireland in the Eighteenth Century* (Dublin: Irish Academic Press).

Preece, R.C., Coxon, P. and Robinson, J.E. (1986) 'New biostratigraphic evidence of the post-glacial colonisation of Ireland and for the Mesolithic forest disturbance', in *Journal of Biogeography* 13, 487–509.

Preston-Jones, A. (1992) 'Decoding Cornish churchyards', in N. Edwards and A. Lane (eds) *The Early Church in Wales and the West: Recent Work in Early Christian Archaeology, History and Place-Names* (Oxford: Oxbow Monograph 16), 105–124,

Price, T.D. (1987) 'The Mesolithic of Western Europe', *Journal of World Prehistory* 1: 225–305.

Price, T.D. and Brown, J.A. (eds) (1985) *Prehistoric Hunter-Gatherers: The Emergence of a Cultural Complexity* (London: Academic Press).

Proudfoot, L.J. (1995) *Urban Patronage and Social Authority: The Management of the Duke of Devonshire's Towns in Ireland, 1764–1891* (Washington).

Proudfoot, L.J. (ed.) (1997) *Irish County History Series: Down* (Dublin).

Proudfoot, V.B. (1961) 'The economy of the Irish rath', *Medieval Archaeology* 5: 94–122.

Prunty, J. (1997) *Dublin Slums, 1800–1925* (Dublin).

Pryce, H. (1992) 'Ecclesiastical wealth in early medieval Wales', in N. Edwards and A. Lane (eds) *The Early Church in Wales and the West: Recent Work in Early Christian Archaeology, History and Place-Names* (Oxford: Oxbow Monograph 16), 22–32.

Quinn, D.B. (1942) 'A discourse on Ireland (circa 1599): a sidelight on English colonial policy', *Proceedings of the Royal Irish Academy* 47C: 151–166.

Quinn, D.B. (1945) 'Sir Thomas Smith (1513–1577) and the beginnings of English colonial theory', *Amateur Philological Society Proceedings* 89: 543–560.

Quinn, D.B. (1947) 'Edward Walshe's "conjectures" concerning the State of Ireland, 1552', *Irish Historical Studies* 5: 303–322.

Quinn, D.B. (1958) 'Ireland and sixteenth-century European expansion', in *Historical Studies* 1: 20–32.

Quinn, D.B. (1966) 'The Munster plantation: problems and opportunities', *Journal of the Cork Historical and Archaeological Society* 71: 19–40.

Quinn, D.B. (1976) 'Renaissance influences in English colonisation', *Transactions of the Royal History Society* 5th Ser., 26: 73–93.

Raftery, B. (1974) 'A prehistoric burial mound at Baunogenasraid, Co. Carlow', *Proceedings of the Royal Irish Academy* 74C: 277–312.

Raftery, B. (1976) 'Rathgall and Irish hillfort problems', in D.W. Harding (ed.) *Hillforts, Later Prehistoric Earthworks in Britain and Ireland* (London: Academic Press), 339–357.

Raftery, B. (1976) 'Dowris, Halstatt and La Tène in Ireland: problems of the transition from bronze to iron', in S. de Laet (ed.) *Acculturation and Continuity in Atlantic Europe* (Bruges: Dissertationes Archaeologicae Gandenses 16), 189–197.

Raftery, B. (1981) 'Iron Age burials in Ireland', in D. Ó Corrain (ed.) *Irish Antiquity* (Cork: Tower Books), 173–204.

Raftery, B. (1983) *A Catalogue of Irish Iron Age Antiquities*, 2 vols (Marburg: Marburger Studien zur Vor- und Frugeschichte).

Raftery, B. (1984) *La Tène in Ireland* (Marburg: Veroffentlichung des Vorgeschichtlichen Seminars Marburg).

Raftery, B. (1986) 'A wooden trackway of Iron Age date in Ireland', *Antiquity* 60: 50–53.

Raftery, B. (1990) *Trackways through Time* (Dublin: Headline).

Raftery, B. (1994) *Pagan Celtic Ireland: The Enigma of the Irish Iron Age* (London).

Reeves-Smyth, T. and Hamond, F. (eds) (1983) *Landscape Archaeology in Ireland* (Oxford B.A.R. Brit. Ser. 116).

Renwick, W.I. (ed.) (1970) *A View of the Present State of Ireland* by E. Spenser (Oxford: Clarendon Press).

Reps, J.W. (1965) *The Making of Urban America* (Princeton: Princeton University Press).

Reynolds, S. (1977) *An Introduction to the History of English Medieval Towns* (London).

Reynolds, S. (1994) *Fiefs and Vassals: The Medieval Evidence Reinterpreted* (Oxford).

Riddersporre, M. (1988) 'Settlement site – village site: analysis of the toft structure in some Medieval villages and its relation to Late Iron Age settlements. A preliminary report and some tentative ideas based on Scanian examples', *Geografiska Annaler*, 70B: 75–85.

Roberts, B.K. (1987) *The Making of the English Village* (Harlow: Longman Scientific and Technical).

Roberts, B.K. (1996) *Landscapes of Settlement: Prehistory to the Present* (London: Routledge).

Robinson, P.S. (1983) 'Some late survivals of box-framed "plantation" houses in Coleraine, County Londonderry', *Ulster Journal of Archaeology* 46: 129–136.

Robinson, P.S. (1984) *The Plantation of Ulster: A British Settlement in an Irish Landscape, 1600–1670* (Dublin: Gill and MacMillan).

Robinson, P. (ed.) (1986) *Irish Historic Towns Atlas: Carrickfergus* (Dublin).

Roeck Hansen, B. (1988) 'Settlement change and agricultural structure in the Late Iron Age and Medieval Årland', in *Geografiska Annaler* 70B, 87–93.

Rokkan, S. (1980) 'Territories, centres and peoples in Europe', in J. Gottman (ed.) *Centre and Periphery* (London: Sage Publications), 161–180.

Rowen, A. (1979) *North-west Ulster* (Harmondsworth).

Rowley-Conwy, P. (1981) 'Slash and burn in the temperate European Neolithic', in R. Mercer (ed.) *Farming Practice in British Prehistory* (Edinburgh: Edinburgh University Press), 85–96.

Rowley-Conwy, P., Zvelebil, M. and Blankholm, H.P. (eds) (1987) *Mesolithic Northwest Europe: Recent Trends* (Sheffield: University of Sheffield Department of Archaeology and Prehistory).

Royle, S.A. (1989) 'The historical legacy in modern Ireland', in R.W.G. Carter and A.J. Parker (eds) *Ireland: A Contemporary Geographical Perspective* (London: Routledge).

Ruane, J. (1992) 'Colonialism and the interpretation of Irish historical development', in M. Silverman and P.H. Gulliver (eds) *Approaching the Past – Historical Anthropology through Irish Case Studies* (New York: Columbia University Press), 293–323.

Ryan, M. (1973) 'Native pottery in early historic Ireland', *Proceedings of the Royal Irish Academy* 73C: 619–645.

Ryan, M. (1980) 'An early Mesolithic site in the Irish midlands', *Antiquity* 54: 46–47.

Ryan, M. (1981) 'Poulawack, Co. Clare: the affinities of the central burial structure', in D. Ó Corrain (ed.) *Irish Antiquity* (Cork: Tower Books), 135–146.

Ryan, M. (ed.) (1991) *The Illustrated Archaeology of Ireland* (Dublin: Town House and Country House).

Rynne, C. (1989) 'Archaeology and the early Irish watermill', *Archaeology Ireland* 3: 110–114.

Rynne, E. (1964) 'Some destroyed sites at Shannon Airport, County Clare', *Proceedings of the Royal Irish Academy* 63C, 247–277.

Rynne, E. (1967) *North Munster Studies* (Limerick).

Said, E. (1989) 'Representing the colonised: anthropological interlocutors', *Critical Inquiry* 15: 205–225.

Sawyer, P.H. (1978) *From Roman Britain to Norman England* (London: Methuen).

Scott, B.G. (ed.) (1982) *Studies on Early Ireland* (Belfast: AYIA).

Scrase, A.J. (1989) 'Development and change in burgage plots: the example of Wells', *Journal of Historical Geography* 15: 349–365.

Shaffrey, P. and Shaffrey, M. (1985) *Irish Countryside Buildings: everyday architecture in the rural landscape* (Dublin: The O'Brien Press).

Shanks, M. and Tilley, C. (1987) *Re-constructing Archaeology* (Cambridge: Cambridge University Press).

Shanks, M. and Tilley, C. (1987) *Social Theory and Archaeology* (Oxford: Oxford University Press).

Sharpe, R. (1991) *Medieval Irish Saints' Lives* (Oxford: Clarendon Press).

Sheehan, A. (1986) 'Irish towns in a period of change 1558–1641', in C. Brady and R. Gillespie (eds) *Natives and Newcomers* (Dublin: Irish Academic Press), 93–199.

Sheridan, A. (1985/6) 'Megaliths and megalomania: an account and interpretation of the development of passage tombs in Ireland', *Journal of Irish Archaeology* 3: 17–30.

Sheridan, A. (1986) 'Porcellanite artefacts: a new survey', *Ulster Journal of Archaeology* 49: 19–32.

Sheridan, E. (1993) 'Dublin and Berlin: a comparative geography of two eighteenth-century European capitals', PhD thesis (University College Dublin).

Sherratt, A. (1981) 'Plough and pastoralism: aspects of the secondary products revolution', in I. Hodder, G. Isaac and N. Hammond (eds) *Patterns of the Past* (Cambridge: Cambridge University Press).

Silverman, M. and Gulliver, P.H. (eds) (1992) *Approaching the Past – Historical Anthropology through Irish Case Studies* (New York: Columbia University Press).

Simmons, I.G. and Tooley, M. (eds) (1981) *The Environment in British Prehistory* (London: Duckworth).

Simms, A. (1975) 'The influence of the classical precedent on English plantation theories in Ireland', *Convegno Internazionale 'I Paesagg, Rurali Europei'* 483–491.

Simms, A. (1986) 'Continuity and change: settlement and society in medieval Ireland *c.* 500–1500', in W. Nolan (ed.) *The Shaping of Ireland: The Geographical Perspective* (Cork: Mercier Press), 44–65.

Simms, A. (1988) 'Core and periphery in medieval Europe: the Irish experience in a wider context', in W.J. Smyth and K. Whelan (eds) *Common Ground: Essays on the Historical Geography of Ireland* (Cork), 22–40.

Simms, A. (1988) 'Genetische Siedlungsforschung in Irland mit besonderer Berücksichtigung der Siedlungsgeographie', in K. Fehn, H. Bender, K. Brandt, D. Denecke, F. Irslinger, W. Krings, W. Janssen, H.-J. Nitz, M. Müller-Wille, G. Oberbeck and W. Schick (eds) *Genetische Siedlungsforschung in Mitteleuropa und seinen Nachbarräumen* (Bonn).

Simms, A. and Andrews, J.H. (eds) (1994) *Irish Country Towns* (Cork).

Simms, A. and Andrews, J.H. (eds) (1995) *More Irish Country Towns* (Cork).

Simms, A. and Simms, K. (1990) *Irish Historic Towns Atlas: Kells* (Dublin).

Simms, J.G. (1956) *The Williamite Confiscations in Ireland 1690–1703* (London: Faber and Faber).

Simms, J.G. (1972) 'Donegal in the Ulster plantation', *Irish Geography* 6: 386–393.

Slater, T.R. (1988) 'English medieval town planning', in D. Denecke and G. Shaw (eds) *Urban Historical Geography: Recent Progress in Britain and Germany* (Cambridge), 93–108.

Smith, A.G. (1975) 'Neolithic and Bronze Age landscape changes in Northern Ireland', in J.G. Evans, S. Limbrey and H. Cleere (eds) *The Effects of Man on the Landscape: The Highland Zone* (London: C.B.A. Res. Report 11), 64–74.

Smith, A.G. (1981) 'The Neolithic', in I.G. Simmons and M. Tooley (eds) *The Environment in British Prehistory* (London: Duckworth), 125–209.

Smith, C. (1996) *Dalkey: Society and Economy in a Small Medieval Irish Town* (Dublin: Maynooth Local History Studies).

Smyth, A.P. (1972) 'The earliest Irish annals: their first contemporary entries, and the earliest centres of recording', *Proceedings of the Royal Irish Academy* 72C: 1–48.

Smyth, A.P. (1982) *Celtic Leinster: Towards an Historical Geography of Early Irish Civilisation AD 500–1600* (Dublin: Blackrock).

Smyth, W.J. (1975) 'Continuity and change in the territorial organisation of Irish rural communities, Part I', *Maynooth Review* 89: 51–73.

Smyth, W.J. (1978) 'The western isle of Ireland and the eastern seaboard of America: England's first frontiers', *Irish Geography* 11: 1–22.

Smyth, W.J. (1983) 'Landholding changes, kinship networks and class transformations in rural Ireland: a case study from County Tipperary', *Irish Geography* 16: 16–35.

Smyth, W.J. (1985) 'Property, patronage and population: reconstructing the human geography of mid-seventeenth-century Tipperary', in W. Nolan (ed.) *Tipperary, History and Society* (Dublin: Geography Publications), 104–138.

Smyth, W.J. (1988) 'England's first frontiers', in N. Canny (ed.) *Kingdom and Colony: Ireland in the Atlantic World 1560–1800* (Baltimore).

Smyth, W.J. (1988) 'Society and settlement in seventeenth-century Ireland – the evidence of the "1659" census', in W.J. Smyth and K. Whelan (eds) *Common Ground: Essays on the Historical Geography of Ireland* (Cork: University Press), 58–60.

Smyth, W.J. (1988) 'The dynamic quality of Irish village settlements', in J.M. Dewailly and R. Dion (eds) *Campagnes et littoraux d'Europe (Mélanges offert à Pierre Flatrès)* (Lille), 109–113.

Smyth, W.J. (1990) 'Territorial, social and settlement hierarchies in seventeenth century Kilkenny', in W. Nolan and K. Whelan (eds) *Kilkenny History and Society* (Dublin: Geography Publications), 125–158.

Smyth, W.J. (1992) 'Exploring the social and cultural topographies of 16th- and 17th-century County Dublin', in F.H.A. Aalen and K. Whelan (eds) *Dublin City and County: From Prehistory to Present* (Dublin: Geography Publications), 135–138.

Smyth, W.J. (1992) 'Making the documents of conquest speak: the transformation of property, society and settlement in seventeenth-century Counties Kilkenny and Tipperary', in M. Silverman, and P.H. Gulliver (eds) *Approaching the Past – Historical Anthropology through Irish Case Studies* (New York: Columbia University Press), 276–278.

Smyth, W.J. (1993) 'Review of S.T. Carleton's *Heads and Hearths*', in *Irish Economic Social History* 20: 111–113.

Smyth, W.J. (1993) 'Social, economic and landscape transformations in County Cork from the mid-eighteenth to the mid-nineteenth century', in P. O'Flanagan and C.G. Buttimer (eds) *Cork: History and Society* (Dublin), 655–698.

Smyth, W.J. and Whelan, K. (eds) (1988) *Common Ground. Essays on the Historical Geography of Ireland* (Cork: University Press).

Soulsby, I. (1983) *The Towns of Medieval Wales: A Study of their History, Archaeology and Early Topography* (Drayton Manor).

Speed, J. (1612) *The Theatre of the Empire of Great Britaine* (London: John Snabury and George Humble).

Stafford, T. (1810) *Pacta Hibernia*, new edn of orig. by George Carew, Earl of Talbot (1633), (London).

Stalley, R. (1987) *The Cistercian Monasteries of Ireland* (New Haven).

Steel, R.W. and Lawton, R. (eds) (1967) *Liverpool Essays in Geography: A Jubilee Collection* (London: Longmans, Green and Co. Ltd).

Stephens, N. and Glasscock, R.E. (eds) (1970) *Irish Geographical Studies in Honour of E. Estyn Evans* (Belfast: Department of Geography, Queen's University).

Stokes, W. (ed. and trans.) (1890) *Lives of the Saints from the Book of Lismore* (Oxford).

Stone, J.C. (1989) *The Pont Manuscript Maps of Ireland: Sixteenth-Century Origins of a Blaeu Atlas* (Tring: Map Collector Publications Ltd).

Stout, G. (1984) *Archaeological Survey of the Barony of Ikerrin* (Roscrea: Heritage Society).

Stout, G. and Stout, M. (1992) 'Patterns in the past: County Dublin 5000 BC – 1000 AD', in F.H.A. Aalen and K. Whelan (eds) *Dublin from Prehistory to Present: Studies in Honour of J.H. Andrews* (Dublin), 5–25.

Stout, G. *et al.* (1986–7) 'The Sites and Monuments Record for County Wexford; and introduction', *Journal of the Wexford Historical Society* 11: 4–13.

Stout, M. (1991) 'Ringforts in the South-West Midlands of Ireland', *Proceedings of the Royal Irish Academy* 91C: 201–243.

Stout, M. (1997) *The Irish Ringfort* (Dublin: Four Courts Press).

Swan, L. (1976) 'Excavations at Kilpatrick churchyard, Killucan, County Westmeath: July–August 1973 and 1975', *Riocht na Midhe* 6: 89–96.

Swan, L. (1983) 'Enclosed ecclesiastical sites and their relevance to settlement patterns of the first millennium AD', in T. Reeves-Smyth and F. Hamond (eds) *Landscape Archaeology in Ireland* (Oxford B.A.R. Brit. Ser. 116), 269–294.

Swan, L. (1988) 'The Early Christian sites of County Westmeath', in J. Bradley (ed.) *Settlement and Society in Medieval Ireland: Studies Presented to F.X. Martin, o.s.a.* (Kilkenny: Boethius), 3–32.

Sweetman, P.D. (1985) 'A Late Neolithic/Early Bronze Age pit circle at Newgrange, Co. Meath', *Proceedings of the Royal Irish Academy* 85C: 195–221.

Sweetman, P.D. (1987) 'Excavation of a Late Neolithic/Early Bronze Age site at Newgrange, Co. Meath', *Proceedings of the Royal Irish Academy* 87C: 283–298.

Sweetman, P.D. (1995) *Archaeological Inventory of County Laois* (Dublin).

Taaffe, N. (1766) *Observations on Affairs in Ireland from the Settlement in 1691 to the Present Time*, 2nd edn (Dublin).

Taylor, C.C. (1972) 'The study of settlement patterns in pre-Saxon Britain', in P. Ucko, R. Tringham and G. Dimbleby (eds) *Man, Settlement and Urbanism* (London: Duckworth), 109–113.

Temple, J. (1679) *The Irish Rebellion* (London: A.M. and R.R.).

Thomas, A. (1992) *The Walled Towns of Ireland*, 2 vols (Dublin).

Thomas, C. (1959) 'Imported pottery in Dark-Age western Britain', *Medieval Archaeology* 3: 89–111.

Tighe, W. (1802) *Statistical Observations Relative to the County of Kilkenny made in 1800 and 1801* (Dublin).

Toal, C. (1995) *North Kerry Archaeological Survey* (Dingle).

Toner, G. and Ó Mainnín, M.B. (1992) *Place-names of Northern Ireland, Vol. 1; County Down 1: Newry and South-West Down* (Belfast).

Toumey, C. (1980) 'Raths and clachans: the homogeneity of early Irish society', in *Éire-Ireland* Winter: 86–105.

Treadwell, V.W. (1978) 'The establishment of the farm in the Irish customs, 1603–1610', *English Historical Review* 93: 602.

Truxes, T. (1988) *Irish–American Trade, 1660–1783* (Cambridge: Cambridge University Press).

Ucko, P., Tringham, R. and Dimbleby, G. (ed.) (1972) *Man, Settlement and Urbanism* (London: Duckworth).

University College Dublin Geography Department and Bord Failte (1998) *Irish Towns: Guide to Sources* (Dublin).

Unwin, T. (1988) 'Towards a model of Anglo-Scandinavian rural settlement in England', in D. Hooke (ed.) *Anglo-Saxon Settlements* (Oxford: Basil Blackwell), 77–98.

van Wijngaarden-Bakker, L.H. (1974) 'The animal remains from the Beaker settlement at Newgrange, Co. Meath: first report', *Proceedings of the Royal Irish Academy* 74C: 313–383.

van Wijngaarden-Bakker, L.H. (1986) 'The animal remains from the Beaker settlement at Newgrange, Co. Meath: final report', *Proceedings of the Royal Irish Academy* 86C: 17–111.

van Wijngaarden-Bakker, L.H. (1989) 'Faunal remains and the Irish Mesolithic', in C. Bonsall (ed.) *The Mesolithic in Europe* (Edinburgh: John Donald), 125–133.

VerVloot, P. and Verhoeve, A. (eds) (1992) *The Transformation of the European Rural Landscape, 1770–1914* (Brussels).

Wachtel, N. (1977) *The Vision of the Vanquished: The Spanish Conquest of Peru Through Indian Eyes 1530–1570* (Hassocks, Brighton: Harvester Press).

Waddell, J. (1970) 'Irish Bronze Age cists: a survey', *Journal of the Royal Society of Antiquaries of Ireland* 100: 91–139.

Waddell, J. (1978) 'The invasion hypothesis in Irish prehistory', *Antiquity* 52: 121–128.

Waddell, J. (1990) 'Past imperfect: women in ancient Europe', *Archaeology Ireland* 4, 3: 12–14.

Waddell, J. (1998) *The Archaeology of Prehistoric Ireland* (Galway: Galway University Press).

Wailes, B. (1976) 'Dun Ailinne: an interim report', in D.W. Harding (ed.) *Hillforts: Later Prehistoric Earthworks in Britain and Ireland* (London: Academic Press), 319–338.

Wailes, B. (1990) 'Dun Ailinne: a summary excavation report', *Emania* 7: 10–21.

Wallace, P.F. (1992) *The Viking Age Buildings of Dublin*, 2 vols (Dublin).

Walsh, A. (1987) 'Excavating the Black Pig's Dyke,' in *Emania* 3: 5–11.

Walsh C. (ed.) (1997) *Archaeological Excavations at Patrick, Nicholas and Wine Tavern Streets, Dublin* (Dingle: Brandon Books).

Ware, Sir Thomas (1809) *Ancient Irish Histories: The Works of Spencer, Campion, Hanmer and Marleburrough* 2 vols (Dublin: Hibernica Press).

Warner, R. (1986) 'Comments on "Ulster and Oriel souterrains"', *Ulster Journal of Archaeology* 49: 111–112.

Warner, R. (1988) 'The archaeology of early historic kingship', in S. Driscoll and M. Nieke (eds) *Power and Politics in Early Medieval Britain and Ireland* (Edinburgh: Edinburgh University Press), 47–68.

Warner, R. (1990) 'The "prehistoric" Irish annals: fable or history?', *Archaeology Ireland* 4: 30–33.

Warner, R. (1995) 'Tuathal Techtmar: a myth or ancient literary evidence for a Roman invasion?', *Emania* 13: 23–32.

Watkins, C. (1963) 'Indo-European metrics and archaic Irish verse', *Celtica* 6: 194–249.

Watt, J.A. (1972) *The Church in Medieval Ireland* (Dublin: Gill and MacMillan).

Webb, R. (1985) 'Farming and the landscape', in F.H.A. Aalen (ed.) *The Future of the Irish Rural Landscape* (Dublin: Trinity College).

Whelan, K. (1983) 'The Catholic parish', *Irish Geography* 16:1–15.

Whelan, K. (1985) 'The Catholic Church in County Tipperary 1700–1900', in W. Nolan (ed.) *Tipperary. History and Society* (Dublin: Geography Publications), 215–255.

Whelan, K. (1986) 'The Famine and post-Famine adjustment', in W. Nolan (ed.) *The Shaping of Ireland* (Cork and Dublin: Mercier).

Whelan, K. (1989) 'Gaelic Survivals', in *Irish Review* 7: 139–142.

Whelan, K. (1989) 'The regional impact of Irish Catholicism 1700–1850', in W.J. Smyth and K. Whelan (eds) *Common Ground: Essays on the Historical Geography of Ireland* (Cork: University Press), 253–277.

Whelan, K. (1990) 'The Catholic community in eighteenth-century county Wexford', in T. Power and K. Whelan (eds) (1990) *Endurance and Emergence. Catholics in Ireland in the Eighteenth Century* (Dublin).

Whelan, K. (1991) 'Ireland in the world system, 1600–1800', in H. Nitz (ed.) *The Early Modern World System in Comparative Geographical Perspective* (Stuttgart), 129–170.

Whelan, K. (1991) 'Settlement and society in eighteenth-century Ireland', in G. Dawe and J. W. Foster (eds) *The Poet's Place* (Belfast: Institute of Irish Studies), 45–62.

Whelan, K. (1992) 'Beyond a paper landscape – J.H. Andrews and Irish historical geography', in F.H.A. Aalen and K. Whelan (eds) *Dublin City and County: From Prehistory to Present* (Dublin), 379–424.

Whelan, K. (1992) 'Town and village in Ireland 1600–1900', in P. VerVloot and A. Verhoeve (eds) *The Transformation of the European Rural Irish Landscape* (Brussels), 298–306.

Whelan, K. (1995) 'An underground gentry: Catholic middlemen in the 18th century', in J. Donnelly (ed.) *Irish Popular Culture, 1650–1850* (Dublin: Irish Academic Press).

Whelan, Y. (1997) 'Turning space into place: the power of street nomenclature', in *Baile* (Dublin), 70–74.

Whelan, Y. (n.d.) 'Reading the city as text: the iconography of independent Dublin', PhD thesis (University College Dublin, forthcoming).

White, D.G. (1968) 'The Tudor plantations in Ireland before 1571', unpublished PhD thesis (Trinity College Dublin).

Whittle, A.W.R. (1988) *Problems in Neolithic Archaeology* (Cambridge: Cambridge University Press).

Williams, B. (1976) 'Early Christian landscapes in County Antrim', in T. Reeves-Smyth and F. Hamond (eds) *Landscape Archaeology in Ireland* (Oxford B.A.R. Brit. Ser. 116), 233–246.

Williams, B. and Yates, M. (1984) 'Excavations at Killylane, County Antrim', *Ulster Journal of Archaeology* 97: 63–70.

Williams, E. (1989) 'Dating the introduction of food production into Britain and Ireland', *Antiquity* 63: 510–512.

Williams, N.J.A. (ed.) (1981) *Pairlement Chloinne Tomáis* (Dublin: Institute for Advanced Studies).

Wood, T. (1821) *An Inquiry Concerning the Primitive Inhabitants of Ireland* (Cork).

Woodman, P.C. (1973/4) 'Settlement patterns in the Irish Mesolithic', *Ulster Journal of Archaeology* 3rd Ser., 36–7: 1–16.

Woodman, P.C. (1974) 'The chronological position of the latest phases of the Larnian', *Proceedings of the Royal Irish Academy* 74C: 237–258.

Woodman, P.C. (1977) 'Recent excavations at Newferry, Co. Antrim', in *Proceedings of the Prehistoric Society* 43: 155–200.

Woodman, P.C. (1978) *The Mesolithic In Ireland* (Oxford: B.A.R. Brit. Ser.), 58.

Woodman, P.C. (1983) 'The Glencloy project in perspective', in T. Reeves-Smyth and F. Hamond (eds) *Landscape Archaeology in Ireland* (Oxford B.A.R. Brit. Ser. 116), 25–34.

Woodman, P.C. (1984) 'The early prehistory of Munster', *Journal of the Cork Historical and Archaeological Society* 89: 1–11.

Woodman, P.C. (1985) 'Prehistoric Settlement and Environment', in K.J. Edwards and W.P. Warren (eds) *The Quaternary History of Ireland* (London: Academic Press), 251–278.

Woodman, P.C. (1985) *Excavations at Mount Sandel 1973–1977* (Belfast: HMSO).

Woodman, P.C. (1985) 'Mobility in the Mesolithic of northwestern Europe: an alternative explanation', in T.D. Price and J.A. Brown (eds) *Prehistoric Hunter-Gatherers: The Emergence of a Cultural Complexity* (London), 325–339.

Woodman, P.C. (1986) 'Problems in the colonisation of Ireland', *Ulster Journal of Archaeology* 49: 7–17.

Woodman, P.C. (1989) 'The Mesolithic of Munster: a preliminary assessment', in C. Bonsall (ed.) *The Mesolithic in Europe* (Edinburgh: John Donald), 116–124.

Worlidge, J. (1675) *Systema Agriculturale, being the Mystery of Husbandry Discovered and Laid Open by J.W.* (London: J.C. for Thomas Dring).

Wrigley, E. (1967) 'A simple model of London's importance in changing English society and economy', *Past and Present* 37: 44–70.

Young, A. (1970) *A Tour in Ireland, 1776–1779*, 2 vols (Dublin: Irish Academic Press).

Zvelebil, M., Moore, J.A., Green, S.W. and Hensen, D. (1987) 'Regional survey and analysis: a case study from south east Ireland', in P. Rowley-Conwy, M. Zvelebil and H.P. Blankholm (eds) *Mesolithic Northwest Europe: Recent Trends* (Sheffield: University of Sheffield Department of Archaeology and Prehistory), 9–32.

INDEX

Aalen, F.: settlement studies, contribution to the study of 234

Achonry: mass houses of 176; parish churches, condition of 173

aerial photography 2, 18, 27, 232

Andrews, J.H.: career of 231; *clachans*, research into 229; settlement studies, contribution to 231, 236

Anglo-Norman settlement: boroughs, economic functions of 130–131; boroughs, foundation of 112, 113, 128, 129, 130; castles 112, 113, 129, 133, 233, 242; central authority, weakness of 127, 135; craftsmen, their place in towns 134–135; dispersed settlement forms 116–118; ecclesiastical sites, decline of 125, 127; economic organisation 127–128; *enceintes* 125, **5.1**; feudalism 127–129, 130; Irish society, its effect on 124; lordship 129; markets 131, 133, 134; mercantile towns 135; moated sites 116–118; mottes 112, 113, 114; nucleated settlements, extent of 114; property patterns 133; raths, reuse of 118; ringwork castles 112, 113; rural boroughs 113, 130–131; segregation in the towns of 135; settlement archaeology of 112–118; settlement forms, its effect on 61, 66–67, 112–118; settlement hierarchy, creation of 113, 124–125, 129, 130, 133–134; social organisation 127–129, 130; taxes, collection of 135; town plans 133, **5.3**; town walls 133; towns, foundation of 113, 125, 128, 129, 130, 143–144; towns, morphology of 133; towns, population of 136; towns, social

geography of 135; Ulster, settlement forms of 113–114; urbanisation, process of 129–131; villages, foundation of 113; *see also* castles, English Pale, Gaelic Ireland, Plantation period

Archaeological Survey of Ireland: county inventories, production of 1–2, 87

archaeology: aerial photography 2, 18, 27, 232; county inventories, production of 1–2, 87; dendrochronology, impact of 2, 9; descriptive focus of 3; Discovery Programme 2, 17, 111, 118, 121, 122, 240; low-visibility sites, recognition of 2; New Archaeology 3; radiocarbon dating, impact of 2, 4–5, 10–11; rescue archaeology, impact of 2; social process, its neglect of 2–3; systematic data collection, development of 1–2; theory, its neglect of 3

Ardee, Co. Louth: segregation at 135

Ardfert: impropriate rectories of 173; parish churches, condition of 172

Armagh: ecclesiastical centre 125, 136

Askeaton, Co. Limerick: castle, its relationship to the plantation 150; Franciscan friary, foundation of 119

Athlone, Co. Westmeath 159; cattle fair of 193; segregation at 135

Atlas of the Irish Rural Landscape 207, 236

Augustinians: rural settlement, their effect on 119; *see also* Duleek

axe trade: 16

baile: characteristics of 60, 61, 68; concept of 60, 61; English *town*, its relationship to 61, 66–67; organisation of 70; place